Imagined Democracies
Necessary Political Fictions

This book proposes a revisionist approach to democratic politics. Yaron Ezrahi focuses on the creative unconscious collective imagination that generates ever-changing visions of legitimate power and authority, which compete for enactment and institutionalization in the political arena. If, in the past, political authority was grounded in fictions such as the divine right of kings, the laws of nature, historical determinism, and scientism, today the space of democratic politics is filled with multiple alternative social imaginaries of the desirable political order. Exposure to electronic mass media has made contemporary democratic publics more aware that credible popular fictions have greater impact on shaping our political realities than do rational social choices or moral arguments. The pressing political question in contemporary democracy is, therefore, how to select and enact political fictions that promote peace, not violence, and how to found the political order on checks and balances between alternative political imaginaries of freedom and justice.

Yaron Ezrahi studied political science and philosophy at the Hebrew University of Jerusalem and holds a PhD from Harvard University. He has served as an adviser on science policy to the White House, the U.S. National Academy of Science, the OECD (1969–70), the Israeli Academy of Science and Humanities (1973–83), and the Carnegie Commission on Science (1992). He is the recipient of a National Jewish Book Award and of the Israeli Political Science Association's Lifetime Achievement Award (2009). He has been a member of the Hebrew University faculty since 1972. Other appointments include a fellowship at the Center of Advanced Studies in the Behavioral Sciences at Stanford University and visiting professorships at the University of Pennsylvania, Duke University, Harvard, Princeton, ETH Zurich, Brown University, and The Rockefeller Foundation Bellagio Center. His works include *The Descent of Icarus: Science and the Transformation of Contemporary Democracy*; *Technology, Pessimism, and Postmodernism* (edited with Everett Mendelsohn and Howard Segal); *Rubber Bullets: Power and Conscience in Modern Israel*; and *Israel towards a Constitutional Democracy* (with M. Kremnitzer). He is a cofounder and board member of *The Seventh Eye*, Israel's leading journal of press criticism in Hebrew. His work has also appeared in *Minerva, Science Studies, Social Research, Inquiry, Foreign Affairs, Transactions of the New York Academy of Sciences*, and *The New York Times Magazine*.

Imagined Democracies

Necessary Political Fictions

YARON EZRAHI

The Hebrew University of Jerusalem

CAMBRIDGE
UNIVERSITY PRESS

CAMBRIDGE
UNIVERSITY PRESS

32 Avenue of the Americas, New York NY 10013-2473, USA

Cambridge University Press is part of the University of Cambridge.

It furthers the University's mission by disseminating knowledge in the pursuit of education, learning and research at the highest international levels of excellence.

www.cambridge.org
Information on this title: www.cambridge.org/9781107529922

First published 2012
First paperback edition 2015

A catalogue record for this publication is available from the British Library

Library of Congress Cataloguing in Publication data
Ezrahi, Yaron.
    Imagined democracies : necessary political fictions / Yaron Ezrahi,
    Hebrew University, Jerusalem.
      pages cm
    Includes bibliographical references and index.
    ISBN 978-1-107-02575-2
    1. Democracy.   2. Democracy in literature.   3. Politics in literature.
    4. Political fiction – History and criticism.   5. Mass media – Political aspects.
    I. Title.
    JC423.E968   2012
    321.8–dc23   2012013643

ISBN 978-1-107-02575-2 Hardback
ISBN 978-1-107-52992-2 Paperback

For Ruth –
The Music of My Life
And the Muse of This Book

Contents

Preface

Contemporary democracy is not the deliberative self-governing polity of informed free citizens envisioned by modern Enlightenment thinkers. It is a system of government in which public policy consists of an eclectic patchwork of half-baked programs, where politicians tend to posture rather than act, where the public sphere is more a site of shifting amorphous moods than a clash of ideas. The question guiding this book is how we got here: How did the influential ideas of Locke, Rousseau, Condorcet, Paine, Jefferson, Kant, Mill, and Dewey about rational politics informed by public knowledge and participatory citizenship devolve into democracies where expertise is a diminishing source of authority, where politics mediated by mass media is shaped more by the suasive emotional and cognitive powers of pictures and images than by well-constructed arguments, driven by marketing culture rather than civic ethos, determined by individuals behaving like consumers, not like citizens? It is ironic that the vision of western democratic ideologues like Thomas Paine, who criticized the monarchy as but a "puppet show of state and aristocracy" and idealized politics based on plain arguments and simple public facts inspired by science, ultimately generated democratic political forms that exemplify a close deliberate collaboration between statecraft and stagecraft. Why has our age of documentary photography and electronic public sphere failed to curb political theatricality and restrain the power of political gestures to eclipse or substitute for public policy?

The political metaphor for the modern democratic state was the machine with its self-regulation, its checks and balances, while the emerging family of political metaphors for democratic politics after modernity is associated with the theater. The quality of the political performance of leaders as actors on the public stage is more commonly invoked than any measurable contribution to definable public goals in explicating the conduct of political agents in our time.

In this book I explore processes driving the contemporary shift from modern to postmodern democracies, considering ways that the historical shift between political universes based on faith in the divine right of kings to political worlds legitimated by imagining the state as the embodiment of popular sovereignty can instruct us. Such cases and, more generally, the historical fluctuations between political worlds (grounded alternately or concomitantly in God, nature, scientific utopias, myths of origins, tribal or family genealogies, monumental battles, historical or social laws, etc.) reveal a pressing human urge for safe-seeming, involuntary, and transpolitical anchorage of power veiled by rich sources of signification. In modern democratic states, government by fear and meaningless naked force has been generally delegitimated, although institutionalizing the vision of popular sovereignty or "government by the consent of the people" has been only partial and deeply flawed in many democracies.

In the following I approach the issue of democracy after modernity by examining the problems facing the contemporary collective political imagination in coping with the necessity of replacing or supplementing the anachronistic myths and narratives that have grounded the political order of modern democracies. What could substitute for "natural law," the "autonomous rational individual," "progress," faith in the possibility of rational consensus based on certainties of "scientific truths," and a self-evident "general good" in concealing the unsettling empty dark space at the foundation of the political order? What could replace those modern myths in covering up the meaninglessness and arbitrariness that always lurk at the base of any power structure and threaten to erupt and destroy the existing political universe? I suggest that political history is largely a record of deliberate and intuited efforts to gloss over the secret of this bottomlessness in order to avoid both anarchy and tyranny. In modern democracy, such efforts were concentrated on relating autonomous agency to transparent realities of political power and authority, while contemporary democracy deeply problematizes both. I therefore try at the end of this book to explore some of the ways current democracies can engage this vacuum at the bottom anew.

My own sense of the precariousness of the political order might have started to develop on May 14, 1948, early during Israel's war of independence. Eight years old, I stood in a corridor of the Tel-Aviv Museum and witnessed the creation of a new state as David Ben Gurion read Israel's declaration of independence. In the decades since that day, my awareness of the dilemma of states' foundations has been accentuated by relentless domestic and external challenges to the legitimacy of my state. In the case of Israel, the continual problem of legitimacy is closely related to its conflict with the Palestinians and the particular dilemma of combining the secular and religious Jewish components of Israeli collective identity. In this book, rather than discussing the special Israeli case, I adopt a wider perspective on democracy after modernity, from which I consider the problems shared by contemporary states like America, England, France, and Israel in imagining and practicing democracy.

There is evidence of a growing apprehension of glaring gaps between the experience of contemporary democracies and the vision of popular sovereignty and self-government. These gaps raise the question of whether we are witnessing a crisis of the democratic state or a transition to novel modes of practicing political freedom and equality in our time. In order to understand the nature and dimensions of the shifts in the cultural fabrics and practices of contemporary democracies, I shall pay special attention to the formation of the very modern imaginaries of reality and agency undergoing the most radical changes in our time.

This book's sequence of thirteen chapters grouped in four parts is designed to gradually unfold its theses. My purpose is to show that in the transition from modernity to postmodernity, contemporary democracy must reinvent the cultural and political grounds of governmental power and authority; that the shifting collective political imagination is the principal agent of this process; and that, as in other moments of transition between political worlds, now too the legitimation of the new order requires redrawing the boundaries between facts and fictions, reality and theatricality in politics. Hans Christian Andersen's *The Emperor's New Clothes* has captured the shift of sensibilities that marks such a paradigmatic moment of transition when an innocent eye untutored by celebratory monarchic political aesthetics can resist the spell of majesty and see that the king is just a naked man. At the book's end, I examine the possibility that the future of democracy depends on the ability of contemporary citizens to again shift their gaze and appropriate the new electronic media as a tool for generating novel modes of political participation, seeing, criticizing, and legitimating political power and authority.

Acknowledgments

I first want to thank professors Tamar Peretz-Yablonski, Bruce Chabner, Amiel Segal, Ronald Bann, Shalom Strano, and Shalom Kalnicki for helping me to cope with a medical crisis during the writing of this book. I owe a special debt to Seyla Benhabib whose faith in a work that is somewhat subversive to the current mainstream of our discipline facilitated its publication. I would like to extend my deep thanks to a few scholars who read the entire manuscript or parts of earlier versions and whose comments were very valuable to this work. In addition to years of intellectual dialogue and collaboration that substantially influenced my work, Sheila Jasanoff did not spare her time and efforts to make brilliant suggestions to conceptually clarify my argument and make the text more accessible to students. My thoughts about the political imagination were shaped and tested in the course of endless conversations and joint teaching with my close friends Don Handelman and David Shulman. Don contributed invaluable insights and opened up new intriguing conceptual avenues from his characteristically radical perspective combining theoretical and ethnographic anthropology. David inspired me by his unique ability to combine the scholarly and the poetic and with his encompassing book on the history of the imagination in South India. An early critical reader of the first version of the theoretical chapter, David Nierenberg left a lasting mark on the direction of this work. Gabriel Motzkin has been a constant stimulating intellectual presence throughout and a most original source of scholarly insights into theories of art and the philosophy of time. Ruth Katz donated her rare analytical powers to my constant reassessment of my steps. Ariel Ezrahi read an earlier version of the work with great devotion and did not spare his father some very valuable criticism. Shaul Shenhav and Jonathan Garb read the entire manuscript and enriched it from their unique perspectives. I am deeply indebted to Joachim Nettelbeck for his ongoing intellectual engagement with this project and for generously facilitating my research during my stay in Berlin. Yehuda Elkana, a close friend for nearly half a century, has inspired me by his pioneering work on images of knowledge since we met at Stephen Toulmin's seminar at the Hebrew University in 1965. W. J. T. Mitchell's work on iconology and our ongoing discussions of images in politics were very valuable to my work on "political imaginology."

I owe special gratitude for memorable ongoing conversations with Eyal Chowers, Josef David, Michael Heyd, Gerald Holton, Eva Illouz, Menachem Lorberbaum, Everett Mendelsohn, Ilana Silver, Michael Steinberg, Zeev Sternhell, and Helga Nowotny. My work has been enriched by unforgettable joint teaching and conversations with the late Judith Shklar and Shmuel Eisenstadt. The remarkable discussions at the faculty seminar on contemporary democratic and constitutional theories that Mordechai Kremnitzer and I recently co-directed at the Israel Democracy Institute were a very significant source of new ideas. The interrogating minds of my daughters Talya and Tehila and their ironic response to my work on necessary political fictions were a constant source of delight during this long odyssey. While my debt to all the above people is unlimited, I must carry full responsibility for the content of this book and its flaws.

The production of this book involved several very special persons. I owe special gratitude to Nita Schechet for voluntarily contributing to this book the gift of her talents and insights as an in-house editor. Her works on the poetics of peace and on narratives of revenge and reconciliation in the Israeli conflict have converged with important parts of my work. Talia Trainin contributed very valuable work on the language of earlier versions of this book as well as some literary suggestions. Barbara Schmutzler was indispensable for preparing the manuscript for publication. I thank Kathrin Theurillat for preparing the index.

At Cambridge University Press, senior editor Lewis Bateman was encouraging from the very beginning and guided with an especially caring hand the conversion of the manuscript into a book. His senior editorial assistant, Anne Lovering Rounds, provided exquisitely good professional judgment along the way.

Finally and most importantly, I would like to thank my life partner, Ruth HaCohen, to whom this book is dedicated. Ruth's wisdom, brilliant ideas, cultural scope, and invaluable criticism greatly contributed to this book. Her work on the cultural analysis of music has added a crucial dimension to my work on the cultural analysis of politics and on the role of the performative political imagination in modern and postmodern democracies. Showing how, as political agencies, individuals and collectives are animated and reified by the powers of music, Ruth's work has reinforced my sense of the deep affinities between the logic and dynamics of the flow and transformation of music and politics in time. I am infinitely indebted to her for golden years of close collaboration of minds and hearts.

Introduction

[Men] are enclined [*sic*] to suppose, and feign unto themselves, several kinds of Powers Invisible; and to stand in awe of their own imaginations, and in time of distress to invoke them; as also in time of an expected good success to give them thanks; making the creatures of their own fancy their Gods.

— Hobbes, *Leviathan*

A democratic society cannot fully or at every moment be a democracy. Its precarious existence depends upon mutually reinforcing democratic ideas, political culture, political imaginaries, institutions, and practices. These very elements, which make a system of government democratic, almost never fully coexist in any society. *A democracy, like any other political regime, must be imagined and performed by multiple agencies in order to exist.* Like a symphony, democracy has to be performed reasonably well in order to be realized as a political world. Beethoven's Fifth Symphony cannot be properly rendered in a performance of missing instruments, where the string section lacks leadership, the conductor is tired and not properly focused, the music accompanied by a winter ensemble of coughing listeners in the back rows and by a mobile phone on the left ringing a countermelody.

The performance of democracy usually falls short of its original score. Expected and unexpected interruptions and constraints always ensure a gap between the ideals of a government by, of, and for the people and the ability and desire of the numerous individuals and groups on whom it depends to actually fully enact and institutionalize a democratic political vision. Like the interpretation of a musical work, the interpretation of a written democratic constitution is often contested, and its performance is often dominated by practices that carry it far beyond (or below) the initial vision. The history of modern politics is full of examples of great yet unperformed written democratic constitutions used as a cover for authoritarian politics. Democracy is a particular kind of political order that requires the invention and embodiment of correspondingly particular types of agents (such as citizens and public opinion), procedures, and institutions (such as elections, judicial processes, parliamentary debates, and a free press). Moreover, these agents, institutions, and procedures must be reasonably co-performed in order for a regime to exist as a democracy.

Similarly, a monarchy cannot fully or always be a monarchy. Like a democracy, it requires numerous individuals and groups to institutionalize and enact its basic political imaginary, to perform monarchic politics, monarchic law, monarchic aesthetics and discourse. In western societies, monarchy depended on rituals such as the anointment of a new king (by dabbing consecrated oil on his head) at the coronation ceremony; on verbal and figurative representations of the image of the king as a human god, often modeled on Christ, a figure linking heaven and earth; on the unique splendor of the monarch's garments and residence; and on nonmaterial elements such as the rationalization of the monarchy by court intellectuals and legal experts. All these factored in the performance of the monarchy as a regime. In contrast to the "reality effects" temporarily produced in the theater to capture audience attention and assist in its suspension of disbelief, in any political order, I argue here, what is perceived by the lay public as political reality is actually created by the largely unconscious public's own recursive performative political imagination.

For many centuries in the West and in other parts of the world, monarchies were maintained by a widely believed imaginary, the collective fiction of the divine right of kings. Monarchies were founded on an imaginary enacted in a host of versions by specific rituals, tropes, and institutions. The divine right of kings was a particularly effective collective imaginary in its combination of the already tested and familiar powers of the religious imagination with the earthly political necessities of government.

In the course of time, the sustainability of the political imaginary of the monarchy and the conditions for its effective performance in Western societies have eroded. The rituals, institutions, and intellectual arguments that sustained it have lost much of their power, while another imaginary – the right of popular sovereignty and its supporting practices – has permeated the minds and attitudes of modern publics. Against the pressure of this anti-hierarchical political imaginary, a few clever monarchs initially attempted adjustments in order to survive, incorporating some democratic melodies within the symphony of the monarchy.

Political actors are constantly anxious to reinforce their audience's willing suspension of disbelief. Frederick the Great, for instance, noting new winds blowing, made rhetorical and symbolic gestures recognizing the value of equality and the public good and, like some other European kings, seemed to accommodate the idea that he had been, at least symbolically, elected by his people. But as the imaginary of popular sovereignty was increasingly performed by social and political groups, legal and political theorists, parliamentary institutions, and other democratic cultural and political agencies, the new show turned the surviving kings into mere anachronistic remnants, symbolic or aesthetic, of a past historical performance.

Like all forms of government, monarchic and democratic regimes must be extensively performed in self-sustenance, while the conditions of their respective performances have always been unstable and only partially favorable. Moreover, a regime that is for the most part democratic may, at moments such as wartime, be performed as an authoritarian regime, and an authoritarian regime may have its democratic moments. Awareness of the fluidity and complexity of the performance of any particular type of regime should lead to a more persuasive account of the ways regimes are enacted and transformed. One question I would like to pose is how to account for the historical transformations behind shifts from the performance of monarchic reigns to the performance of democratic regimes in the West. Are we currently witnessing the kind of changes that could undermine the fundamental conditions that provide the basis for continued enactments of democratic regimes?

Contemplating the monarchic past from within a polity like ours, governed by the imaginary of popular sovereignty and its rich institutional and rhetorical articulations, we can, as outsiders, recognize the fictive and performative foundations of the preceding monarchic political world. But as inhabitants of the democratic order regulated by the imaginary of self-government by the people, it is more difficult for us to recognize the fictive-performative foundations of our own political world. By fictive I do not mean, of course, inconsequential.

I will argue that some political fictions become more real than others, insofar as they function as causes of political behavior and institutions. In the following chapters I define these causative fictions as *imaginaries*. *Political imaginaries*, for our purpose, refers to fictions, metaphors, ideas, images, or conceptions that acquire the power to regulate and shape political behavior and institutions in a particular society. The power of some such political fictions to become politically productive by generating performative scripts that orient behavior and pattern institutions is grounded, among other things, in their apparent congruence with aspects of political and social experience and expectations, their compatibility with norms that appear to legitimate their power, and their (unphilosophical) tolerance for inconsistencies. Although initially political fictions commonly suggest empirically baseless fabrications, some gain sufficient credibility and adherence to attain the status of performative imaginaries that produce behavior that, in turn, affirms them. We shall see that the degree of correspondence between publicly accessible political facts and the hegemonic political imaginaries needed to sustain a particular political world is surprisingly small. Both the technological availability of new mass media and the cultural processes that have undermined conventional modern imaginaries of reality and agency have opened the possibility of a new vocabulary of performative political imaginaries and the deployment of current ones, like democracy, in regions that have persistently resisted political modernism.

Moreover, in our western democratic world, the right of popular sovereignty is upheld by a host of rituals and imaginings to which the actual realities of power and representation only partly correspond. I shall pay much attention in this book to how the yawning gaps between normative imaginaries of politics and its practice have fed the recurrent accusations of theatricality and posturing against politicians. I argue that, to the extent that politics consists of the enactment of imaginaries that legitimate power and authority, theatricality in politics is more often constitutive of politically necessary fictions than a mis-representation of given agencies and realities. Let us consider, for instance, the question of the boundaries and the composition of the people as a democratic agent, and what could constitute its legitimate representation. How is "the peo-ple" construed as the agent of popular sovereignty in contemporary society in comparison to earlier versions of democracy such as Toquevillian America? To what extent may public policies of democratic governments be said to be pub-lic beyond the gloss of political rhetoric and gestures through which they are screened? What could constitute reliable and workable definitions of the public interest as a guideline or criterion for the evaluation of decisions and actions in contemporary demographically, religiously, culturally, and normatively het-erogeneous societies?

Later I explore these and other related questions under the assumption that the difference between monarchic and democratic states, as well as between them and other regime types, lies neither in a difference between a government ruled by fictions and a government upheld by facts, nor between a political order founded on false beliefs and another on true ones validated by empirical reality. I argue that the difference between a monarchy and a democracy, as well as other regimes, is not so much a difference between fictive or real polit-ical grounds as one between alternative reality-producing fictions, between types of regulative political imaginaries.

In politics, that which is collectively imagined produces real political facts, although, as I have indicated, only some of these facts are likely to correspond to the imaginary.[1] Alexis de Tocqueville observed in his *Democracy in America* (1835) that, whereas many of the political institutions and cultural forms of America are the products of a powerful hegemonic collective imaginary of equality, there are signs suggestive of a link between the American imaginary of equality and trends leading to despotic centralization of power. I shall devote much attention in this book to this ironic paradox, whereby values seemingly compatible with particular political imaginaries may contradict the values to which the political facts, produced by these very imaginaries, correspond.

The structure of the political order is always in a process of becoming, of dialectical and ambiguous relations to the imaginaries that sustain it and to the actual or potential imaginaries that subvert it. Given that this book focuses on the traits and shifts of the democratic political imagination, including its most recent turns, we, from within this political world, must negotiate our tendency to ignore the origin of what we experience as the facts of our common polit-ical reality by naturalizing products of our own collective political imagina-tion. In order to better perform this task, we must first examine more closely

---

[1] For instructive discussions of such discrepancies see Edward L. Rubin, *Beyond Camelot: Rethinking Politics and Law For the Modern State* (Princeton: Princeton University Press, 2005) and Stephen P. Turner, *Liberal Democracy 3.0: Civil Society in an Age of Experts* (London: SAGE Publications, 2003).

how the collective imagination works in politics and account for the power of some political imaginaries to become institutionalized and sustainable despite a flimsy correspondence to our experience while others remain unnaturalized or even unnaturalizable fictions.

In politics, as in life, we cannot think, reason, speak, or act, or even begin to experience the world without engaging the faculty of imagination. We imagine when we think, when we look, when we remember, and when we feel. By means of the imagination we transform and fix in our mind past experiences, shape our present ones, structure and focus our future orientations, postulate the theoretical entities we use to conceptualize, enjoy art, escape to utopias, or enter new worlds of meaning. The common equation of the imaginary with the merely fictive and illusory stems from latent ideological commitments deeply embedded in modern western culture that divide human experience between the real and the unreal.

The faculty of imagination does not recognize such boundaries.[2] Reflecting on reality and the imagination, Wallace Stevens says that "reality is life and life is society and the imagination and reality; that is to say, the imagination and society are inseparable."[3] The very division between the imaginary and the real is in itself a product of the creative, transcendent imagination as an all-encompassing human meta-faculty. The still widely held separation in our culture between reason and imagination, including the Cartesian or Kantian versions of the autonomy of rational reasoning and the subordination of the imagination to reason, are in themselves products of the imagination understood as a composing, decomposing, and recomposing faculty.

The devaluation of the imagination in relation to reason was often accompanied, especially during early modernity, by a description of the imagination as a mere material faculty activated by emanations from the body. By contrast, echoing the Platonic hierarchy between reason and imagination, reason was conceived as part of the immaterial mind and thus enjoyed a higher status. Both Descartes and Kant can be regarded, from our perspective, as the principal myth makers of the Enlightenment, similar to Augustine and Dante in relation to Christianity and to Wordsworth, Schelling, and Fichte in the creation of Romanticism.

The imagination may be divided into separate spheres, which correspond to different modes of imagining and to distinct types of imaginaries. Art and science can be regarded as such distinct spheres of the imagination. Art openly, even self-reflexively, performs as a natural domain of the imagination, free therefore to employ illusions beyond the span of common experience. Science constantly aims to conceal or erase the participatory creative and patterning

---

[2] See the insightful reflections on this point in David Ames Curtis (ed.), *The Castoriadis Reader* (Oxford: Blackwell, 1997), pp. 196–217 and 319–37.

[3] Wallace Stevens, *The Necessary Angel: Essays on Reality and the Imagination* (London: Faber and Faber, 1951), p. 28.

role of the imagination in the shaping of its foundations, its theories, and its very conceptions of phenomena, objects, and other facts.

Imagining, then, is a faculty that participates in the shaping of a multitude of interacting forms of human experience, including the experience of the real. The faculty of imagination is inescapably engaged in cognitive acts of perception and representation, as well as in acts of invention and speculation. The trend to "physiologize" important aspects of the mind and its operations has increasingly narrowed the perceived gaps between sensing, feeling, imagining, cognition, and reasoning. This more materialistic orientation toward the mapping of the links between human faculties and the brain has undermined the conventional dichotomy between the human body and what was once regarded as the divine, disembodied faculty of the human mind. Moreover, it has effectively dispensed with the belief that our senses can reliably record external facts without mediation.

In the field of visual perception, for instance, the complexity of the interactions between world, eye, brain, and expectations makes it unreasonable "to talk of some kind of preliminary retinal perception that is truer because closer to the actual world that casts its images on the back of the eyeball." There is no such thing as "an untutored eye."[4] It has become widely recognized that by means of the brain, the imagination participates in the transformation of our inherently muddled sensory experience of the world into patterned forms, consolidated objects, and organized pictures, and that what we experience as objectively external is significantly shaped by both our organs and our culture.

I have already suggested that an important aspect of the imagination's unique power resides in its capacity to move back and forth, often indiscernibly, between the realms prior operations of the collective imagination had previously demarcated as the culturally antithetical spheres of fantasy and reality. It is precisely the omnipresence and the multiplicity of roles played by the imagination in the shaping of our consciousness, conduct, culture, and institutions that largely account for its elusiveness. Born into a universe already furnished by institutionalized products of the collective imagination inherited from past generations, we are seldom aware of the role played by this remarkably creative human faculty in the formation of the objects and agents that populate our world and inhabit our experiences of time and space.

One of the most intriguing and potent qualities of the imagination lies in its ability to cover its own steps, to erase its own traces, and often to cause us to experience the created as a given. We are, therefore, very surprised and often also disconcerted on discovering footprints of the imagination on what we had long experienced as hard facts. This sense of disturbance indicates the importance humans ascribe to the distinction between fact and fiction in the mapping and distributing of cognitive and emotional resources.

---

[4] William C. Wees, *Light Moving in Time: Studies in the Visual Aesthetics of Avant-Garde Film* (Berkeley: University of California Press, 1992), pp. 63–5.

One of the main purposes of this book is to describe and analyze the often hidden political uses of this capacity of the imagination to conceal its role in the shaping of our experience and in furnishing conceptions of political reality. Moreover, the imagination is probably the most neglected form of power in the field of modern political science and, in particular, in political theory. One of my main concerns is with the question of how the restoration of the imagination to its rightful place in our understanding of politics could and should affect political theory, political arguments, and, most importantly, our interpretations of political practice. It is because the political imagination is indispensable to the creation of the political order while also inherently dangerous to its very stability that it constantly problematizes the political. I believe that a theoretical perspective that can apprehend the nature of political imaginaries and their role in politics is likely, among other things, to support illuminating partly revisionist readings of the ideological clashes between socialism and liberalism in the nineteenth and twentieth centuries, as well as subsequent conflicts between liberal individualism and communitarianism.

The imagination does not, of course, create our worlds ex nihilo. Its creativity lies not merely in inventing, but also in reconfiguring and restructuring the fabrics of our experience and thought, and in its capacity to modify earlier modes of imagining. It combines the separate, separates the previously fused, commensurates the formerly incommensurable, fixes that which moves, and unsettles that which was long conceived of as stationary. When we encounter terms such as *God, nation, state, the world*, and *the individual*, we are seldom aware of the ways in which the imaginative faculty has participated in their birth, sustenance, or decline. This assertion is unlikely to seem reasonable to those for whom the word *imagination* means mere fantasy, in contradistinction to reality. Obviously the state or the individual, as well as other working imaginaries, are not illusions in the strict sense of the word.

In this book I use the term *imagination* in a wider or richer sense. I try to show that the narrow equation of the imaginary with the illusionary or the fictive is associated with the Enlightenment's ideological tendency to separate science from religion, reason from the human body and emotions, and politics from the arts. It is precisely this dichotomy between facts and fictions that, while serving the diverse projects of modernity, has also obscured the unique potential of the imaginary to be both fact and fiction.[5] It is precisely this dualism, this coexistence of the real and the illusionary in the imaginary, that has empowered the imagination to become, in many respects, the hidden shaper of politics. Hence, although I usually use terms like *reality, facts*, and *objectivity* without quotation marks, the argument of this book basically questions the givenness of their signified referents.

In the following chapters of the book I attempt to persuade the reader of the analytical advantages of the concept of the performative political imagination

---

[5] I discuss the enormous significance of this dualism further in Chapters 1, 2, and 3.

over more conventional terms like *myths*, *ideas*, and *political knowledge* in linking the normative, cognitive, and emotional components of politics.

This book focuses specifically on the democratic political imagination, on imaginings or fictions (such as "We the People," self-government, rational politics, and freedom) on which modern democratic political worlds have been based and which they have tried to embody, and their recent transformations. Therefore, I concentrate initially on the principal features of the modern democratic political imagination and later on the changes that seem to be altering them profoundly. As we shall see, these changes are bound to raise a host of questions: Can democracy as a form of political life survive the seemingly recent radical transformations of political practice that contradict the democratic political imagination? Is the particular configuration of moral, political, and institutional orders we recognize as approximating the principles of democracy sustainable despite the erosion of the collective political imaginaries that have come to be implicit in our commonsense political notions of agency, accountability, political causality, freedom, public opinion, and the public sphere? In this book I make some preliminary moves toward the elaboration of fuller responses to this and related questions.

Following these introductory comments on the creative powers of the political imagination, the book is divided into four parts and thirteen chapters. The first part (Chapters 1 through 4) contains four interrelated discussions of the intellectual resources and the theoretical perspectives that shed light on my approach to the analysis of politics in terms of collective imaginaries. Chapter 1 discusses the contest over the rightful cultural place of the imagination. Chapter 2 examines the great contribution of the Italian thinker Giambattista Vico (1668–1744) to the understanding of the role of the people's creative imagination in the making of political regimes and his legacy for contemporary political thought. Chapter 3 offers an analytical classification of modes of imagining and an exploration of their interrelations and the role they play in shaping the fabric of politics. Chapter 4 examines the examples of "naturalization" and "historicization" of political matters as two of the principal strategies employed by the political imagination. Part Two is divided into three chapters (5 through 7), which trace the relations between the modernization of the political imagination and the emergence of new democratic political imaginaries. Chapter 5 focuses on the historical impact of science on common sense, which stands for the socio-epistemological *Agora* of democratic publics. Chapter 6 discusses the impact of modernized imaginaries of politics on attributions of causality and responsibility in democratic politics. And Chapter 7 focuses on the arts and the sciences as the respective domains of the undisguised and the disguised imagination. It examines the special role of the transparent artistic imagination in affirming by contrast the existence beyond the professed sphere of artful illusions of the sphere of real – often scientifically certified – facts as the domain for the performance of modern democratic politics. Part Three (Chapters 8 through 11) examines the specific imaginings of political causality and political agency in the democratic universe. This part focuses on one of the principal themes of the book – the fear of theatricality and deception in democratic politics – and the repeated attempts to overcome it by recruiting science and epistemological materialism to support claims of transparency and accountability. Chapter 8 concentrates on the specific historical attempts to evolve observable materialistic political imaginings of causes and events as part of the democratic commitment to resist theatricality and institute transparency. Chapter 9 examines early and modern versions of the individual as a political agent. Chapter 10 discusses the place of the individual in liberal and illiberal incorporations, and Chapter 11 discusses the key role of the arts in cultivating and ontologizing the interior self and its political implications. Part Four and the book's final two chapters explore the postmodern turn in the democratic political imagination. Chapter 12 analyzes the role of the electronic mass media in the ultimate failure of the democratic resistance to political theatricality and the profound implications of this failure for contemporary imaginaries of political reality and agency. Chapter 13 concludes the book with discussion of the possible ethical bases of political choices in the universe of postmodern politics. In this last chapter I raise the following questions: If politics is driven by fact-producing imaginaries (which consist of metaphoric and both cognitive and emotional elements) rather than by arguments, which of these imaginaries is more likely to enhance nonviolent human life and promote the democratic experience of freedom and equality? And what is the role of the political imaginary in future political theory?

PART ONE

NECESSARY FICTIONS OF THE POLITICAL AND THE REALITY OF POLITICAL FICTIONS

I

The Contest over the Rightful Domain
of the Imagination

Historically, the term *imagination* possessed a dual meaning as a cognitive faculty (for example, for recalling and representing past experiences) and as a potentially deceptive faculty. This duality has related to the view that acts of our imagination, unlike those of our senses or our reason, depend neither on distinctly discernible activities of the body nor on deliberate or conscious activities of the mind.

In order to physically see, we must open our eyes, but we imagine with our eyes both closed and open. We can imagine sound or touch without using our ears or hands. We have less distinct indicators to assess our being in a state of imagining than in a state of tasting, seeing, listening, touching, smelling, or reasoning. Since our imagination works, shapes, and creates simultaneously with our acts of seeing, listening, touching, and so forth, it is intriguing to consider how much harder it is to be aware of or to discern its specific contributions to our sense experience. Anthropologists, sociologists, psychologists, and cultural analysts have long since noticed how diverse vocabularies of the imagination shape and signify similar sense experiences by weaving them into distinct patterns of causation, narrative, emotion, and meaning. The largely involuntary or unreflective character of such mental processes partly accounts for the sense that imagination often works within us as a secret agent.

One does not have to subscribe to the radical thesis that the individual is not master of his or her own mental processes[1] to recognize that at least some operations of our mind, including those of our imagination, can be unconscious, habitual, and involuntary. This special capacity of the imagination to conceal its role in framing the contents of our mind, in generating and consolidating the images and the metaphors that give form and meaning to our ideas and experiences, has been very consequential. It has empowered the creative human mind to act as an unacknowledged producer of much of what is generally perceived as real. Its elusive yet crucial role in shaping our experience of

---

[1] Michael S. Gazzaniga, *The Mind's Past* (Berkeley: University of California Press, 1998).

the world and of other people renders the imagination a particularly flexible and versatile factor in generating our notions of reality and fantasy.

This capacity of the imagination is augmented in the respective contexts of religious and political world making because religious and political authorities are deeply invested in convincing their publics of the reality of particular events, objects, and agents that are either inherently invisible or beyond the apprehension of ordinary sense experience in some other way. The capacity of the imagination to play concurrently in the domains of the real and the fictive, to operate where objects and agents are taken as unshakable givens and when they are regarded as ephemeral, shaky, and alterable, has rendered the imagination a particularly valuable and therefore contested means for influencing religious and political beliefs and behavior.

One of the most common and powerful strategies of employing this dual capacity of the imagination to simultaneously create, produce, and represent that which is regarded as a given reality alongside that which is regarded as invented or fantastic has been the cultural isolation of the former. Beyond the realms of art and religion, perceived realities are elevated to the realms of science, reasoning, and politics. The term *imagination* designates mostly the fantastic, the very opposite of the real. This attitude, in fact, splits the imagination into two parts: One is self-denying, self-effacing, or *self-concealing*; the other is *self-proclaiming* or transparent. (See Chapter 7 for further discussion of this point.)

As I indicated earlier, the self-proclaiming imagination is more typically found in the realm of the arts, where the imagination resides openly and honestly as a creative capacity employed by artists and consumers of art, freely engaged by the first in creating and by the latter in experiencing illusions of reality. The self-concealing imagination is most typically found in the realm of science, in which imagination has been commonly regarded as a disturbance at worst and, at best, as having pedagogical, aesthetic, or heuristic functions, facilitating but not substantially influencing the shapes of theoretical abstractions, logic, mathematics, and rationally controlled observations.

Only relatively recently has the role of the cognitive function of the imagination in constructing scientific knowledge in the physical as well as in the social sciences and the humanities been openly acknowledged and discussed. Ernan McMullin, a philosopher and historian of science, maintained that "the theories of the physicist are in their own way as much works of the imagination as are the poems of Wallace Stevens or the paintings of Pablo Picasso."[2] Obviously, in the context of science, imaginings must be subject to numerous specific empirical, conceptual, and other tests in order to endure as parts of acceptable theories or theoretical entities which, like "black holes" or "strings," become legitimate building blocks of scientific models of the world.

The tests that determine the selection of the imaginary in poetry are profoundly different, although in their own way no less demanding. Similarly,

---

[2] Ernan McMullin, "Enlarging Imagination" in *Tijdschrift voor Filosofie* 58 no. 2 (June 1996).

what makes a Picasso painting work is still another set of conditions for the selection of visual imagery.[3] The fact that the imagination plays such a central role in science, as well as in poetry and painting, suggests that, in this respect, the conventional division between science and the arts, as well as between the domains of reason and imagination, is not only simplistic but also utterly untenable intellectually.

The denial of the role played by the imagination in science is no trivial matter. Until the advent of postmodernism, it has been a major though tacit theme in western culture. The consequences for the role of science as non-imaginary or even anti-imaginary in the evolution of the modern political, particularly the democratic, imagination have been profound. The dual capacity of the imagination to represent and invent has played itself out differently in religion and politics than in science and the arts.[4] While the arts have often professed to their creation of an illusion of the real rather than its accurate and reliable representation, religion and politics resemble science in their zealous claim to anchor in and represent the real rather than the fantastic or the fictitious.

Precisely because religious and political beliefs depend largely on the habit or the willingness to regard as real objects and agents that lack a self-evident visual manifestation (or other direct stimuli of sense experience), religious and political authorities are always eager to use the cultural resources at their disposal to establish and indirectly sensualize, concretize, and generally enhance the reality or the presence of entities and events such as God, angels, revelation, incarnation, transfiguration, hell, paradise, prophecies, the people, the nation, the state, the promised land, the founding fathers, the free market, the individual. Hence it is not surprising that, as in the context of science, in the contexts of religion and politics we encounter the workings of the self-concealing imagination, which attempts to ontologize and present its products as incontestable facts. What warrants the reality of Jesus, or the God of the Bible, or the tangibility of the nation or the state in any particular society depends on the effectiveness with which the rich cultural resources that produce reality effects in any given society are engaged.

It is not surprising that the capacity of the imaginary to oscillate between the real and the fictive has been mobilized in support of contesting strategies used in power struggles among competing religions or ideologies. In such conflicts, much of the effort is directed toward convincing the larger public to accept particular dichotomies between facts and fictions and consequent distributions of trust, authority, and power, which in each case favor one group over another. Each group or faction attempts to anchor its worldview in the sphere of reality, that is, in products of the self-concealing imagination that pose as objects

---

[3] The discussions of Nelson Goodman on this point are very illuminating. See his *Ways of Worldmaking* (Indianapolis: Hackett Publishing Company, 1978) and *Languages of Art* (Indianapolis: The Bobbs-Merrill Co., 1968).

[4] It is noteworthy that in Hebrew the word for reality, *metziut*, and the word for invention, *hamtza'ah*, share the same root.

of the perceptual-cognitive faculties, objects belonging, according to common sense, in the world of hard and fixed facts. Opposing worldviews of adversaries are categorized within the fragile, deceptive imagination that generates illusions, myths, metaphysics, utopias, and the like.

Cultural resources that can produce reality effects – the sense of experiencing reality in the minds of the citizens – are scarce and politically contested in every society. These resources are borrowed from different cultural contexts in which distinctions between reality and fiction are well developed and elaborated in particular ways. "*Physica Gloria*," the physics used as evidence for the existence and glory of God as the arch-engineer of the cosmos, is such an example.[5]

Neither religion nor politics have remained indifferent to the potential uses of practices developed in science, poetry, literature, art, theater, or philosophy to manipulate reality effects in order to lend imaginaries the status of unchallengeable reality in the popular mind. Any inquiry into particular historical configurations of the political imagination cannot ignore, therefore, the syncretic genealogy of the political imagination and its inherently profligate relations with diverse fields of human culture and endeavor.

Karl Marx's effective denaturalization and politicization of the market, in particular his attempt to expose the "truer" reality of social and power relations behind the production and distribution of commodities, is illustrative of the strategy of reframing the facts of an adversary ideology as fictions. "The commodity form," he famously argued:

> is nothing but the determined social relation between humans themselves, which assumes here, for them, the phantasmagoric form of relations between things. In order, therefore, to find an analogy, we must take a flight into the misty realm of religion. Here products of the human head appear as endowed with a life of their own, entering into relations both with each other and with humans. This I call fetishism.[6]

Evidently Marx's own scheme, his own ideology, his distinction between facts and fictions, were also based on a distinct set of phantasmagoric visions and fetishistic objects. Beyond the particular political needs that arise in any ideological war, such a derogatory attitude toward the "phantasmagoric" is deeply entrenched in the western tradition.

One of the sources of the distorted view of the role played by the imagination in modern politics lies in the great impact of the generally ahistorical philosophical and scientific discourses and methodologies on perceptions of politics and claims to truth. The (often unconscious) denial of the historicity of philosophical notions of truth and knowledge and the role of the creative imagination in the formation of philosophical ideas have always been among the main hidden sources of the rhetorical power of philosophical arguments.

---

[5] Frank E. Manuel, *The Religion of Isaac Newton* (Oxford: Clarendon Press, 1974).

[6] Karl Marx, *Capital: A Critique of Political Economy*, vol. I, Ben Fowkes (trans.), (first pub. 1886; New York: Penguin, 1976), pp. 165, 186–7.

Gabriel Motzkin reminds us that "a discourse obtains the greatest aura of reality when it does not use time categories, and this is not a cultural fact: it is a result of the tendency to identify reality with constancy."[7] Moreover, Giambattista Vico, the great modern thinker who apprehended early in the eighteenth century the crucial role of the popular imagination in the life and history of politics, philosophy, science, and other human enterprises, observed that the poetical and, from a philosophical perspective, the illogical, imprecise, eclectic traits of what we have called the "political imagination" partly account for philosophers' unfamiliarity with the tools and habits of thought adequate to capture its significance and modes of operation.

This is not only because philosophical preoccupations with logic and coherence are seldom relevant to the analysis of the structure and workings of the political imagination. Since Plato, it is clearly also due to the fact that traditionally, although not always consistently, philosophers have led the campaign to downgrade the cognitive role of the imagination and label it as a fierce enemy of reason, logic, and rationality. Since the early beginnings of the western philosophical tradition, philosophers have become passionate border guards of the demarcation line between reason and imagination, protecting the faith in the superior authority of the former.

This attitude has characterized philosophy's condescending attitude toward common lay consciousness. Alongside this tradition, however, developed another view, later reinforced by Spinoza, Vico, Rousseau, Herder, Burke, and others, according to which reason, unaided by the imagination, cannot serve humanity in creating and understanding the artificial structures on which society, language, the legal system, morality, money, the market, and the state rest.[8] We can, argued Vico, have knowledge of politics and of the state precisely because these are artificial human creations, unlike nature, which, existing beyond human creation, sets inherent constraints on human knowledge. But because our very capacity to imagine gods and states, as Amos Funkenstein observed, depends also on "our constructive imagination," and because, as Vico suggested, the imagination is the driving force of history, it is beyond truth and error.[9]

One can infer, hence, that the works of the constructive or productive imagination are also, in some respects, prior to a strictly philosophical discourse. Vico observed that, since the foundations of modern politics are based on ancient "poetic archetypes" created by poets such as Homer, it "is clear that

[7] Gabriel Motzkin, *Time and Transcendence: Secular History, the Catholic Reaction and the Rediscovery of the Future* (Dordrecht: Kluwer Academic Publishers, 1992). See chapter 4 for his full discussion of constancy and discontinuity.

[8] See in this connection Georg Simmel, *The Philosophy of Money*, T. Bottomore and D. Frisby (trans.) (London: Routledge & Kegan Paul Ltd., 1978); Marc Shell, *Money, Language, and Thought* (Berkeley: University of California Press, 1982); and Yaron Ezrahi, "The Theatrics and Mechanics of Action: The Theatre and the Machine as Political Metaphors," *Social Research* 62 no.2 (Summer 1995): 299–322.

[9] Amos Funkenstein, *Theology and the Scientific Imagination from the Middle Ages to the Seventeenth Century* (Princeton: Princeton University Press, 1986), see particularly chapter 5.

no mind civilized and refined by philosophy could have succeeded in inventing such similes, which are truly incomparable."[10] By implication, according to Vico, the incapacity to invent sets limitations on the capacity to understand as well. I will show in greater detail that Vico understood that, while philosophers debased poetry as the work of *fantasia* (imagination), they positioned themselves on another wing of the vast territory of the imagination, on the wing of the self-concealing imagination that endorsed the particular philosophical worldview or metaphysics from which they launched their criticism.

Whereas the Enlightenment gave birth to thinkers who appreciated the role of the imagination in politics, much of the rhetoric of the period was, as Lorraine Daston observed, directed against the "diseases of the Imagination."[11] Precisely because so many of the thinkers and advocates of the Enlightenment were preoccupied with constructing the world as a body of observable facts, their massive investment in emancipating and perfecting the sense of sight as a tool of science and reason uncorrupted by the imagination betrayed a considerable anxiety lest vision shatter the control imposed on or by the codes of scientific or rational discipline and join the unruly imagination in rendering the perception of the fantastic as real.

Such concerns played a considerable role in the development of the modern science museum and of illustrated encyclopedias. These modern cultural institutions were meant to serve as means to discipline the popular eye and guide it to experience and accept the world as a given entity that would lend itself to representation through science.

These efforts to channel and shape the popular imagination were, however, only partially successful. The history of modern science's relation to society and to polity is fraught with examples of the difficulties entailed in defending the line that separates a seemingly detached and, therefore, objective gaze from a gaze often dismissed as fantastic, poetical, or in many other ways undisciplined, capricious, and deceptive. Hobbes, for instance, thought mathematics and geometry safer sentries of rationality than empirical observations and, therefore, thoroughly distrusted claims made by Robert Boyle concerning the results of experiments performed before a group of witnesses.[12] Boyle, for his part, could only trust witnesses considered gentlemen who, therefore, in his opinion, were capable of comprehending experience, unlike men whose "sensuality and lusts and passions darkened and seduced their intellects."[13]

---

[10] Giambattista Vico, *New Science* (Harmondsworth: Penguin, 1999).
[11] Lorraine Daston, "Enlightenment Fears, Fears of Enlightenment" in Keith Michael Baker and Peter Hanns Reill (eds.), *What's Left of Enlightenment?* (Stanford: Stanford University Press, 2001), pp. 116–28.
[12] Steven Shapin and Simon Schaffer, *Leviathan and the Air-Pump: Hobbes, Boyle, and the Experimental Life* (Princeton: Princeton University Press, 1985).
[13] Robert Boyle, "The Christian Virtuoso" in Thomas Birch (ed.), *The Works of the Honourable Robert Boyle*, (Hildesheim: Verlagsbuchhandlung Georg Olms, 1966), p. 514.

FIGURE 1.1. Francisco de Goya y Lucientes, *The Sleep of Reason Produces Monsters* (1799). Etching, aquatint, and burin. Courtesy of the Metropolitan Museum of Art.

Francisco de Goya expressed similar anxiety regarding the inability of reason to control imagination in a famous etching that depicts the imagination as the adversary of reason. The etching and aquatint entitled *The Sleep of Reason Produces Monsters* (1799, Figure 1.1) has been generally interpreted as a critique of or a warning against imagination unrestrained by reason.

Fear of the imagination was induced during the religious wars of the seventeenth and eighteenth centuries by association with religious enthusiasm, political radicalism, and violence. Michael Heyd observed that "from [the] 1660s onwards, however, the new natural philosophy offered itself as a more reliable antidote to the danger of enthusiasm than scholasticism and humanism had been."[14] One of the ways in which science engaged in debunking the religious imagination of the enthusiasts who attributed their visions to divine inspiration was to "medicalize" enthusiasm by defining it as a pathological phenomenon like melancholy, a consequence of alterations in the blood and spirits, which balance the material imagination.[15] This tendency to disparage the imagination endured for hundreds of years in a vast range of contexts, including the employment of psychology and psychoanalysis to "pathologize" the conduct of dissidents such as Roy Medvedev in the Soviet Union.[16]

The anxiety concerning the fragility of scientific and factual claims could not be eradicated; the experimental as well as the abstract theoretical strains of science could not be severed from their deep roots in the diverse domains of the imagination. Our knowledge of the multiple ways in which realism, empiricism, and experimentalism – no less than theoretical abstractions – depend on mediation by the productive imagination was unavailable to the scientific intellectuals of earlier centuries. There were, of course, a few important exceptions. Rationalists such as Hobbes and Leibniz had a deep awareness of the powers and scope of the imagination and its subversive potential to weaken the imagined capacity of reason to fix immutable truths. Both considered the benefits of actually harnessing the nonrational force of the imagination to strengthen the grip of science and reason on the popular mind.

Hobbes's effort to enlist the popular imagination for the sake of a rational construction of the state represents the inherent dilemma of the philosophical approach to politics, the complex interrelations and interdependencies between the imagined and the rational, and the indispensability of both for political persuasion. Quentin Skinner suggests that Hobbes's conception of civil science in the *Leviathan* assumes that "reason is of small power in the absence of eloquence." He further notes Hobbes's endeavor to guide his readers to visualize the state as a machine rather than an organism, as an artificial man that moves mechanically, a mechanism operated by springs and wheels. "These metaphorical transformations," writes Skinner, "are crucial to Hobbes's argument, helping as they do to underpin his claim that commonwealths can in no sense be regarded as God-given creations or natural occurrences. They are wholly man-

---

[14] Michael Heyd, *"Be Sober And Reasonable": The Critique of Enthusiasm in the Seventeenth and Early Eighteenth Centuries* (Leiden: E. J. Brill, 1995), p. 278.

[15] Ibid., pp. 95–6.

[16] Zhores A. Medvedev and Roy A. Medvedev, *A Question of Madness* (Harmondsworth: Penguin, 1974). Zhores A. Medvedev, a biologist and a critic of Stalinism, was involuntarily committed to a psychiatric hospital where he was reprimanded and medicated for imagining that he could dare move beyond the limits of his scientific expertise to criticize the government and advance reforms in the USSR.

made contrivances, mechanisms we construct with the sole aim of furthering our own purposes."[17]

The machine is only one of several metaphors, including the Leviathan, that Hobbes employed in his political writings. The point is that by directing and shaping the political imagination, such metaphors privilege certain claims and political arguments about the principles, the legitimacy, and the structure of the state, while undermining others. The logic of the political argument, which may be presented as autonomously and rationally compelling, is largely subordinate to such constitutive metaphors.

Spinoza's well-known critique of religion and the credibility of revelation and miracles was not directed so much against Scripture as a bundle of humanly contrived imaginaries that can usefully induce legal and civic discipline and elicit obedience from laymen. An admirer of Lucretius, Spinoza directed his criticism more against the claims of theology to be a path to the truth while adamantly privileging instead the claims of philosophical and scientific knowledge accessible only to the intellectual elite.[18]

Leibnitz also appreciated the role of the public's imagination as a resource that can be used to evoke respect and support. His project was to hold a public exhibition of scientific inventions in order to dazzle the lay imagination and elicit support for science. He shared the sense, prevailing among intellectuals in the period, that the failure to direct the nonrational popular imagination would lead to the marginalization of science and rational knowledge in the political, social, and cultural contexts. Paradoxically, as the very thinker who devoted himself so fruitfully to pure logic and mathematics, Leibnitz did not hesitate to promote the use of spectacles, optical wonders, fireworks, rare instruments, and amazing machines to enhance popular respect for science and its works with the secular equivalent of miracles.[19]

If one observes the forms of politics from the perspective of a thinker such as Vico, human creations of the imagination are neither a distraction from reason nor a pedagogic device intended to make reason and knowledge more palatable to laymen. They constitute the deep underlying structures, the very substance of any period's conceptions of knowledge, reason, and politics and of their trajectories and transformations in the course of time.

---

[17] Quentin Skinner, *Reason and Rhetoric in the Philosophy of Hobbes* (Cambridge: Cambridge University Press, 1996), pp. 376, 387.

[18] Spinoza, *The Theological-Political Treatise*, Samuel Shirley (trans.), 2nd ed. (Indianapolis: Hackett Publishing Company, 2001); and his *Political Treatise* in *Spinoza, The Political Works*, A. G. Wernham (ed. and trans.), (Oxford: Clarendon Press, 1958); see also Steven B. Smith, *Spinoza, Liberalism, and the Question of Jewish Identity* (New Haven: Yale University Press, 1997), pp. 30–2, 83.

[19] Philip P. Wiener, "Leibniz's Project of a Public Exhibition of Scientific Inventions," in Philip P. Wiener and Aaron Noland (eds.), *Roots of Scientific Thought: A Cultural Perspective* (New York: Basic Books, 1957), pp. 460–8.

2

The Revival and Contemporary Legacy of Giambattista Vico (1668–1744) as a Modern Theorist of the Political Imagination

[A]ll the principles of metaphysics, logic, and ethics originated in the public square in Athens.[1]

– Giambattista Vico, *New Science*

An attempt to understand the role of the political imagination in the making and unmaking of political worlds and their histories can benefit immensely from analyzing the foundations laid by Giambattista Vico in his *Scienza Nuova* (*New Science*), first published in 1726. Vico held that the driving force behind the rise of the civil order and the history of politics lies in the creative popular imagination as it initially expressed itself in its purest form in the poetical works of the earliest epic poets. These poets, according to Vico, shaped and fixed the basic vocabulary of the popular imagination in terms of which civic life subsequently evolved and developed. "Poets," wrote Vico, "are the teachers of the masses, and the aim of poetry is to tame their savagery" (782).

Vico maintained that civic history developed in stages characterized by the people's imagined conceptions of the primary agents that shape the organization and guide the direction of collective life. "First," Vico wrote, "came the myths of the gods, which were histories from the crudest age of pagan civilization, when people believed that all institutions necessary or useful to humankind were deities" (7). Human history developed from this age of gods, through the age of heroes, to the modern age of men.

The heroes, the main agents in the second age, were, according to Vico, mostly military leaders whose status was reinforced by belief in their divine origin and, therefore, in their superiority to the plebeians. While the law of these heroic aristocracies was the law of force, religion continued, in Vico's view, to function as a bulwark against the unlimited use of force. The third age, the age of men, brought the recognition of the equality of human nature

---

[1] Giambattista Vico: *New Science* (c. 1744), David Marsh (trans.), Anthony Grafton (intro.) (London: Penguin Books, 2000).

and the development of a more conscious human judgment, which led to the establishment of more humane governments such as democracies.

Each of these ages had its own variations, exemplified in the transformation from a pagan to a monotheistic religious imagination. "The first pagan people," Vico observed, "conceived ideas of things using imaginative archetypes of animate beings, or personifications" (431). The religious imagination of Christianity was profoundly different in that it combined, according to him, civil, natural, and revealed theology (366). In different times and places, different peoples have conjured disparate images of divinity and developed in their epic poetry and myths distinct notions of superhuman heroes such as Hercules, Achilles, and Ulysses who, as heroic archetypes, symbolized and embodied the values, traits, and deeds they sought to venerate. "The gods, heroes, and men all originated at the same time, for it was after all men who imagined the gods and who believed that their own heroes were a mixture of divine and human natures" (446). Until human beings could imagine themselves the agents of their own history, their imagined gods and heroes, thought Vico, served as the principal means of taming the masses and inducing the necessary discipline to create and maintain the political order.

Vico regarded religion as possibly the primary bond of orderly civic life, regardless of the kind of political order. "Once warfare has made a people so fierce that human laws no longer have a place among them, religion is the only means powerful enough to subdue them ... in their fear of this imaginary divinity, they began to create some order in their lives" (177–8). This is why, claimed Vico, the first governments based "themselves on religion, which alone made the state of families possible. Next, as they developed into heroic civil governments, or aristocracies, religion clearly provided the principal stable foundation. Then, as they advanced to popular governments, religion likewise served as the people's means of attaining democracies." Finally, he continued, "in monarchical governments ... religion must be the shield of rulers." Vico then summed up his point: "If people lose their religion, nothing remains to keep them living in society. They have no shield for their defense, no basis for their decisions, no foundation for their stability and no form by which they exist in the world" (1109).

The Italian thinker had a cyclical view of history that posited that, following the initial invention of religion and the age of gods, "in every age and in every nation, it is the plebeians who have changed the government from aristocracy to democracy and from democracy to monarchy" (1017), and all these regimes adapted religion as a shield. One may wonder what Vico would have thought of the emergence, later in the eighteenth century, of public opinion as a novel political imaginary in democracies, serving, as we shall see, as a shield and a threat, an amorphous yet powerful means of legitimizing or undermining an incumbent government.

One need not accept Vico's theory of historical ages or be constrained by his reference to providence to recognize the crucial role he assigned to the collective popular imagination in political world making. Anticipating modern political anthropology, Vico suggested that we study the repertory of the popular political imagination and its expressions, not only in religion but also in poetry, metaphysics, mythology, and science, discerning the ways the imagination works in constraining violence, building authority, and channeling human fears and emotions.

Insisting that the collective popular imagination is the engine of political history, rather than individual authors, Vico sought to establish, for instance, that Homer did not exist as the historical individual who composed the great Greek epic poetry but "was an idea or heroic archetype of the Greeks who recounted their history in song" (873). This assumption, of course, would enhance the significance of the role played by Greek epic poetry such as the *Iliad* and the *Odyssey* in understanding the popular political mind and life of ancient Greece. Whereas Machiavelli thought it "more proper to go to the real truth of the matter than to its imagination,"[2] Vico thought the truth of the political matter primordially embodied in, not beyond, the popular imagination. More precisely, Vico held, as we shall see later in greater detail, that the fabric of political realities consists of imaginary configurations that, in any particular context, are selected from a range of possibilities as hegemonic frames and regulators of political behaviors, institutions, and meanings.

Vico understood that the importance of the political imaginary lies not in the degree of its correspondence to reality but in its role as a cause of political reality – the real effects and consequences of its popular credibility. This is why poetry could assume such importance in Vico's conception of the pagans (383). "The poets" were, for Vico, an expression of the people in their creative capacity. He thought that these origins developed further and gave rise to the civic order and to other human social and cultural endeavors. Hence, he concluded, it is the site, the actual place in which people met and socially engaged, the "public square in Athens," for instance, that gave birth to metaphysics, logic, ethics, democracy, and philosophy (1043). Rejecting the assertion attributed to Polybius that if there were philosophers in the world there would be no need for religions, Vico insisted that "if there had been no religions, and hence no commonwealths, there would have been no philosophers in the world" (ibid.). The philosophical imagination cannot create and uphold a commonwealth, according to him, without the aid of some form of faith. "For even the most brilliant nations arose from ... worship, while no nation in the world has ever been founded on atheism" (518).

The primacy Vico granted religion over philosophy is, in fact, applicable to all forms and expressions of the popular imagination. This position, which has had enormous influence on the rise of the modern social sciences and humanities, provides a basis for his massive criticism of the excessive influence of philosophy on the perception of politics, especially its underestimation of the crucial role played by the popular imagination. The very fact that, as

---

[2] Niccolò Machiavelli, *The Prince and the Discourses* (New York: The Modern Library, 1950), p. 56.

Donald P. Verene observed, Vico tried to generate understanding from images rather than from rational categories renders his work particularly useful for consolidating a theoretical perspective from which major shifts (such as those between religious and scientifically inspired political imaginaries, or between modern enlightened rational and cinematic ones) can be fruitfully discerned and compared.[3]

Whereas Plato and his successors, particularly rationalist philosophers who launched relentless attacks against poetry, regarded the image at best as a pedagogical device subordinate to the concept, Vico maintained that thinking originates from images that shape our initially chaotic sensations. Even concepts or rational arguments are founded on these primary configurations of the imagination. Verne captures the gist of Vico's idea when he observes that "in Vico's thought, images are not images of something; they are themselves manifestations of an original power of the spirit which gives fundamental form to mind and life."[4] From this perspective, Vico can criticize the philosophers for failing, particularly as political theorists, to consider and appreciate the crucial role of the nonrational and nonpropositional in political world-making.[5]

To confine one's approach to politics to the rational analysis of reasons, norms, or interests, while dismissing or ignoring imaginaries and other nonrational components of the fabric of politics like fear or pride, is to commit what I would define as "the fallacy of misplaced rationality"; to use reason as a weapon to kill the very subject of understanding. Rather than the philosopher's abstract discourse about politics, limited to propositional knowledge, to generating propositions about propositions that refer to yet more propositions, Vico's approach is to discern, analyze, and discuss the images and vocabularies of what I have called imaginaries by which humans become a people and a people creates its political world and organizes its communal life. Vico's scholars have suggested that one of his most significant contribution was to the transformation of classical rhetoric practiced in ancient Athens and Rome as immediate interaction between speaker and audience into a practice of effective impersonal communications by means of metaphors and figurative imaginings that travel in culture beyond the particular space and time in which they originated.[6] In many respects this new conception of political communications transcends the local participatory politics of the city-states of early modernity and anticipates the emergence of political ideologies and imaginaries as means for the creation of common sensibilities and institutions in the modern state and the larger political units of later centuries. The shift to impersonal modes of authoritative communications also anticipates the increasing role of

---

[3] Donald Phillip Verene, *Vico's Science of the Imagination* (Ithaca: Cornell University Press, 1991), p. 19.

[4] Ibid., p. 33.

[5] Joseph Mali, *The Rehabilitation of Myth: Vico's "New Science"* (Cambridge: Cambridge University Press, 1992), pp. 50–1, 258.

[6] See for instance the instructive book of David L. Marshall: *Vico and the Transformation of Rhetoric in Early Modern Europe* (New York: Cambridge University Press, 2010).

the authority of science in the politics of legitimation, particularly in modern democracies.

By insisting that one should focus on how people actually behave rather than basing deliberations on political life on axioms about how people should behave, Vico contextualized political philosophy within the frames of what eventually emerged as the modern social and political sciences and humanistic studies. He did not think that philosophy has no important role in human affairs, only that "if philosophy is to benefit humankind, it must support us as frail and fallen beings, rather than strip us of our nature or abandon us to our corruption" (129). Vico criticized philosophy as an elite, esoteric intellectual enterprise with only a small impact on human affairs. He held that only in a fully advanced and refined society can the philosophical perspective have a grip on the popular mind.[7] He pointed out the gaps between the political imaginations of the philosophers and of the people and their practical implications.

By vindicating the political imagination of the people as a force in history, as a cause in human affairs, Vico framed a democratic theory of political knowledge that locates valid accounts of politics and history not in the ideas and feats of unique individuals or heroes, but in the creative imagination and conduct of the people. I devote special attention to the great potential of this theory, as well as to its limitations, toward the end of this book.

Vico further regarded the single-mindedness of some philosophical schools as positively dangerous to public life. He was keenly aware that a working public political imaginary cannot rest on the extremes of skepticism and hedonism. Neither "the Stoics, who tell us to mortify our senses ... [nor] the Epicureans, who make them the rule of life" can provide guidance. "The Stoics let themselves be dragged by fate: whereas the Epicureans abandon themselves to chance" (130). Vico also directed his criticism toward Hobbes, Descartes, and natural law theorists for evolving ideas rooted in abstract, idealized notions of human nature and rationality and thus cut off from a complex historical context.

Vico's emphasis on the crucial role played by popular metaphysics in shaping the political world is reinforced by his conception of common sense (*sensus communis*), by his theory of political knowledge, and by his theory of action. For Vico, who in this respect continued the tradition of Bacon and Hobbes, humans can have a far better knowledge of things they create than of things given by nature. Because men make their own history and politics, they can also deeply know and understand them. This intimate knowledge of manmade things enables the development of a science of history and politics.

---

[7] Also Alexis de Tocqueville held the idea that, on the whole, intellectuals do not have much impact on popular beliefs. He thought, however, that the influence of men of letters on the masses prior to the Great Revolution and particularly their successful attacks on religion were unique to France. See his *The Old Regime and the French Revolution* (first pub. 1856; New York: Doubleday Anchor, 1955).

Human beings are deprived of a real knowledge of nature, a knowledge possessed only by the divine agency that created the universe. If science is an advanced form of human knowledge, then political history is clearly, according to Vico's view, a more scientific enterprise than physics. But the possibility of understanding history and politics does not necessarily facilitate deliberate action or control.

Unlike the study of human history and politics, their production is not exactly a rational human enterprise. It evolves in the epistemological sphere of the popular imagination, located in the territory of the common sense Vico characterized as "an unreflecting judgment shared by an entire social order, people, nation, or even all human kind" (142). Placing history and politics in the sphere of effective commonsense judgment entails situating it beyond conventional philosophical discourse, while stressing the nonphilosophical hidden operation of the political imagination in the popular mind. It also implies the unreflective dimension of collective political action.

Vico's approach raises, therefore, the question of whether unreflective human judgment and action in politics leaves room for deliberate human influence on political affairs and consequently for ethics of political judgment and action. In his treatise *On the Study of Methods of our Time* (c. 1709), Vico stated his belief that what we may define as proper or functional common sense does not grow spontaneously, but must be inculcated among the young. Such common sense is essential for the future of the young as well as for their later conduct as citizens. Common sense must be inculcated and protected against corruption by influences such as premature philosophical training in abstract speculative thinking.[8]

Philosophers might be tempted to follow such a course, led by the misconception that in the education of the young for future citizenship, reason should be privileged over common sense. But Vico recognized that while not all people can exercise reason and master logic, all people use their senses and their imagination. Common sense is, therefore, more inclusive, more accessible, and hence also more politically consequential than reason. The nature and orientation of the educational inculcation of common sense may thus affect the matrix of politics and the political imaginaries of the civil order.

Beyond the question of how educators can foster social stability and growth of common sense among both young and adult citizens, Vico's approach raises a host of questions, some of which will engage us in the latter part of this book: What is common sense – is it a historical variable? Is the emergence of a reflexive common judgment and action in politics possible? Does the historical record support such an expectation? Can the emergence of such reflexive judgment in politics be in itself part of a shift in the character of common sense and

---

[8] Giambattista Vico, *On the Study of Methods of Our Time*, Elio Gianturco (trans.) (first pub. 1709; Ithaca, NY: Cornell University Press, 1990), p. 13, cited in Mark Lilla's *G. B. Vico: The Making of an Anti-Modern* (Cambridge, MA: Harvard University Press, 1994), p. 50. Vico obviously anticipates here Rousseau's and Pestalozzi's influential ideas on education.

the popular political imagination? Do such changes mark developments we associate with the postmodern condition? And finally, how can such changes influence or transform the dynamic relation between political imagination, ethics, and action?

While philosophy has traditionally attempted to capture and fixate the political within an unchanging, atemporal set of truths and universally valid propositions, Vico made the bold move of historicizing philosophy itself as well as politics.[9] Both philosophy and politics, however, are rooted in the changing configurations of the popular imagination, philosophy lacking the power and authority to bind and entrench, and politics being inherently unstable and contingent. Although Vico insisted in his writings that the popular imagination is not a wild force, that it is led by a providential guidance aimed at promoting the well-being of humanity, this position in no way diminishes the radical import of his insights and his grand theory of the popular imagination.

For our purposes, Vico's historical political anthropology is no less detachable from such theological statements than Newton's physics from his theology. The last words of Vico's monumental *New Science* read as follows: "[I]n sum, all the observations contained in this work lead to one conclusion. My New Science is indissolubly linked to the study of piety; and unless one is pious, one cannot be truly wise." Whether Vico believed it or not, the later influential secular reading of his historical political anthropology with its radical intellectual and political implications has remained intact. The force of his move to anthropologize religion, to elaborate on the various human imaginings of God, and of his many observations on the political uses of religion as social bond, remains undiminished.

It is ironic, however, that following his insistence on the disruptive influence of philosophical skepticism on the *sensus communis* that upholds the civil order, Vico, by historicizing and relativizing philosophy, showed the way not only to relativizing religion itself but also the very science on which he sought to found his "rational civil theology." In the postmodern era, historicization has become perhaps the principal strategy with which to batter and anachronize, among other things, the legacy of Plato's idealistic political philosophy and Vico's own cyclical view of history.

The power of Vico's argument lies in the synthesis he achieved between the claim that the imaginary is one of the main, crucial factors in politics, and the understanding that it is subject to historical change. Vico believed that in each community, the true and the real in the civil order are embedded in the historically changing "poetics of politics," in the founding metaphors in terms of which what is real or unreal in politics is defined. Perhaps his clearest formulation of this view on the relations between imagination, reality, and truth is articulated toward the end of *New Science* in the context of his discussion of ancient Roman jurisprudence:

---

[9] See on this point Lilla, *G. B. Vico*, p. 209.

[A]ncient jurisprudence was thoroughly poetic. It imagined the real as unreal, the unreal as real, the living as dead, and (in cases of pending legacies) the dead as still alive. It introduced many empty masks without subjects, *iura imaginaria*, rights invented by the imagination. Its entire reputation depended upon the invention of myths which could preserve the dignity of the laws and administer justice to the facts. Thus all the fictions of ancient jurisprudence were masked truths.... In this way all Roman law was a serious poem acted out by the Romans in their forum and ancient jurisprudence was a severe kind of poetry. (1036–7)

The elasticity Vico introduced into the discourse on politics by replacing notions of an unchanging human nature, or preconceived ahistorical philo-sophical ideas with a historicized political imagination, with "serious poem(s) acted out" by the people in the public arena, highlights the significance of the diversity of the imaginary political universes enacted in history, and of the major historical shifts in the political imaginary. Thus Vico saw a relation between the heroic character of the regime in Japan, its "fantastic religion of fierce and terrible gods, all armed with deadly weapons," and the Japanese resistance to the idea of equality. "By contrast, the emperor of China rules with a mild religion, is devoted to literary studies, and is very human" (1091). In Europe, Vico traced a relation between Christianity, the cultivation of science, and democratic forms of government (1092). Discussing the ancient Greek and Roman polities, Vico noted that the plebeians, influenced by Solon's plea that they should imagine themselves equal to the nobles, changed the common-wealths from aristocracies to democracies (415).

These observations interest us less in themselves than as illustrations of Vico's science or theory of how the popular imagination works in shaping the political universe. Thus the content and temper of a religion that fashions any given popular imagination, the extent to which science enters as a factor, and the dissemination of anti-hierarchical beliefs in universal human equality are all-important in influencing the shape of the civic order, its rise, and its decline.

Furthermore, the idea that a poetic politics and a poetic jurisprudence underlie the edifice of the civic order provides a more congenial frame for recognizing the instrumental, regulatory, and therefore real functions of legal and political fictions as "masked truths," in Vico's terms, as well as the role of words such as "reality" and "fact" in conferring a privileged status on selected fictions and slices of experience. Joseph Mali aptly characterizes Vico's argu-ment about "the mythopoetic constitution of human reality" as "the rehabili-tation of myth."[10]

It was precisely the fragile demarcation between reality and fiction, between what society can take for granted and what it classifies as fictive or imaginary that Enlightenment thinkers attempted so relentlessly to defend. Although the question of whether there are such valid criteria for distinguishing between reality and fiction is, of course, a philosophically interesting query, it does not

---

[10] Mali, *The Rehabilitation of Myth*, pp. 86, 201, 206, 211.

concern us here. What concerns us is whether, or in what ways, the widespread Enlightenment faith in the clear, unmediated accessibility of nature or objective reality to common human knowledge and in the dichotomy between facts and fictions has given rise to specific political worlds, especially to a particular version of democratic culture and politics.

These, I would like to show, are different from those versions of democratic culture and politics that emerged from either the pre-Enlightenment or post-Enlightenment political imaginary and that deny the clarity and certainty of such ideas and distinctions. From this perspective, as I indicated in the preface, one can regard Descartes himself as a preeminent myth maker of the Enlightenment contributing to the rise of a distinct kind of civil order that rests on the welding together of a particular notion of rational individualism and knowable reality.[11]

It is possible to apply Vico's insights on the role of the imagination in the creation of the civil order to transcend his own criticism of Descartes. Vico dismissed Descartes' disapproval of the study of languages, history, and poetry, while approving the study of his own metaphysics, physics, and mathematics, which Vico did not think made any significant contribution to ethics.[12] But if one considers Descartes an influential myth maker of modern reason, if one – to use Vico's vocabulary – regards him as a poet of an ahistorical, socially unsituated, rational individualism, it is precisely in his rejection of the relevance of history and in his disregard for the sociocultural context of thought, as well as in his focus on procedural reason and on rationality as "an internal property of subjective thinking rather than consisting in its vision of reality"[13] that Descartes provided influential support to the modern imaginary of the individual that proved so crucial to the emergence of liberal democratic politics and institutions.

By introducing his notions of self-evident truths and of what constitutes clear and distinct ideas, Descartes contributed to a modern shift to modern commonsense conceptions of fact and fiction and their differentiation. Through his wide impact and, especially, due to his influence on French culture and education, Descartes was clearly one of the key shapers of the political imaginary of the Revolution and of the modern political universe at large. In the following chapters I discuss why and how, in the context of public affairs, such distinct approaches as Descartes' and Vico's to facts and fictions, or to the real and the imagined, constitute very consequential alternative modes of political imagining. But first we turn briefly to the ideas of several innovative contemporary thinkers who, like Vico, recognized and further advanced our understanding

---

[11] See Yaron Ezrahi, "Modes of Reasoning and the Politics of Authority in the Modern State" in David R. Olson and Nancy Torrance (eds.), *Modes of Thought: Explorations in Culture and Cognition* (Cambridge: Cambridge University Press, 1996), pp. 72–89.

[12] Vico, *The Autobiography*, pp. 130, 137–8.

[13] Charles Taylor, *Sources of the Self: The Making of the Modern Identity* (Cambridge, MA: Harvard University Press, 1989), p. 156.

of the central historical and social role of the human imagination in framing and orienting political experience. The revival of Vico's theory of the political imagination should be understood partly against the background of the decline of the Enlightenment program of culture and politics and the growing reflexive awareness of the voluntary and involuntary processes by which humans coproduce their experience of the world and of themselves as agents.

One can start with the centrality of the term *Gestell* (enframing) in Martin Heidegger's lecture (November 1953) on "The Question Concerning Technology." Heidegger's employment of this term can be interpreted as granting that, as a creative power, the human imagination enables us to bring into being diverse potential manifestations of humanity and the world. Technology is one expression of this power. Like Vico, Heidegger does not confine the creative act of enframing to a particular sphere of life, but sees it as all-encompassing in science and technology as well as in society and politics. Technology, according to Heidegger, is a human enterprise that by prior framing or ordering of the world in a particular way generates a host of what I call performative scripts, that is, of procedures, methodologies, and operations that we recognize as science and technology. By such framing, for example, the earth formerly experienced as just an object "reveals itself as a coal mining district, the soil as a mineral deposit."[14] Heidegger's enframing, as exemplified by technology, does not suggest the kind of radical constructivism according to which (wherever a person turns or whatever a person does) one encounters oneself everywhere. Man should be warned of the illusion of exalting himself as lord of the earth.[15] The instrumental orientation of science and technology also exposes the constraints that the world imposes within the frames set by humans.

The Heideggerian objection to a dichotomy between the human subject and the world is echoed in the works of a series of modern and postmodern thinkers. Bruno Latour, for example, criticizes what he regards as the myth of sharp boundaries between objects and subjects. He sees a connection between this myth (and particularly its stress on an external world, on nature as an object that imposes limits on mankind) with the relentless political search for an idea or a principle of constraint. This myth seems to him to reflect moralists' attempts to "avoid falling prey to mob rule." He wants to find an alternative way "to fend off the people ... to shut the mob's too many mouths."[16] Like Heidegger, Latour insists that rejecting the dichotomy between nature and culture does not necessarily lead to a relativist strategy. Humans do not simply invent the world in their minds. Ian Hacking wisely suggests avoiding the culture wars provoked by radical juxtapositions of realism and relativism. "I have no doubt that our discoveries are 'objective,' simply because the styles of

---

[14] Martin Heidegger and David Farrell Krell (ed.), *Basic Writings: Martin Heidegger* (New York: Harper and Row, 1977), "The Question Concerning Technology," pp. 288, 296.

[15] Ibid., p. 308.

[16] Bruno Latour, *Pandora's Hope: Essays on the Reality of Science Studies* (Cambridge, MA: Harvard University Press, 1999), pp. 13, 18.

reasoning that we employ determine what counts as objectivity.... [T]he very candidates for truth or falsehood have no existence independent of the styles of reasoning that settle what is to be true or false in their domain."[17]

This discussion is clearly relevant to our concerns that the central place we accord the political imagination in the history of the metapolitics and intrapolitics of regimes commits us to vulgar relativism and the view that all power is arbitrary. My argument is that hegemonic political imaginaries are neither arbitrary nor deterministic modes of framing the political order. Within their respective domains, they imply styles of legal and political reasoning, concepts of causality, agency, and reality disciplined by the overall frame. Political imaginaries are configurations rich in cognitive content and internal structural constraints. Enframing the material world in ways that bring into existence new, partly artificial, material facts and objects like machines or socio-medical facts like prolonged life expectancy does not correspond to inventing or creating the very material starting points of such human interventions. What is attributable to these material natural starting points and what is attributable to their human framing and interpretations is very much the subject of heated debate. When Donna Haraway criticizes the link between the dichotomy of nature and society and the subordinate social position of women, she seeks an alternative metaphysics, an alternative enframing or political imaginary within which this subordinate position does not appear an objective, naturalized fact or a given condition. "Animal societies," she writes, "have been extensively employed in rationalization and naturalization of the oppressive orders of domination in the body politic."[18] Haraway supports "the political and epistemological effort to remove women from the category of nature and to place them in culture as constructed and self-constructing social subjects in history...."[19]

Both Haraway and Latour are concerned with switching from enduring hegemonic imaginaries of order to alternative imaginaries that for one reason or another can better adjust the production of knowledge and the social order to current shifts in values and interests. By contrast, Benedict Anderson and Charles Taylor focus on how collective political imaginaries create and disseminate certain political entities.

Anderson famously sees nationalism as a cultural artifact that evolves from "imagined communities" and rests on a measure of self consciousness, shared language, beliefs, symbols, and emotional solidarity.[20] He sees the embodiment of nationally imagined communities as partly a result of the declining automatic legitimacy long granted to hierarchies and the symbolism of the monar-

---

[17] Ian Hacking, *Historical Ontology* (Cambridge, MA: Harvard University Press, 2002), pp. 160–1.
[18] Donna J. Haraway, *Simians, Cyborgs and Women: The Reinvention of Nature* (London: Free Association Books, 1991), p. 11.
[19] Ibid., p. 134.
[20] Benedict Anderson, *Imagined Communities* (London: Verso, 1991), pp. 50–1.

chies of western Europe, particularly since the seventeenth century and later, somewhat differently, after 1914.

Charles Taylor regards what he calls "modern social imaginaries" as "the ways people 'imagine' their social existence ... [and] their social surroundings.... Social imaginary is that common understanding that makes possible common practices and a widely shared sense of legitimacy."[21] In Taylor's opinion, the rise of modern social imaginaries was enabled by the dwindling appeal to contemporary publics of magic and spiritual forces, the increasing delegitimation of hierarchical orders and authority since late modernity, the social disembeddedness of the modern self, the conception of the individual as an entity prior to and independent of society, and the shift from the imaginary of society as a moral association to its conception as an economic system.

Acknowledging the influence of Anderson, Taylor regards the rise of democratic imaginaries as the result of the trend toward "radical horizontality," by which he means the shift from religious to secular conceptions of time stressing the present over the eternal, and the horizontal access to networks of communications that strengthen lay individuals and groups in their relations to their governments.[22]

My early work on the impact of the scientific revolution on the rise and practices of modern democracy differs from Anderson and Taylor's work in both focus and approach. I share their willingness to acknowledge the constitutive powers of the collective imagination, but while Anderson concentrates on the embodiment of nations and Taylor on the constitution of modernity and the rise of the "modern moral order," I focus on the political imaginaries that enable democracy. Whereas Anderson is interested in the influence of imaginaries of tribes, territorial homeland, and shared group traits as components of the wider composition of the imaginary of the nation, my concern is with the fundamental role of imaginaries of the democratic individual, common forms of knowledge, and notions of political causality that enable the overall imaginary of the democratic state. I share Taylor's concern with modern and postmodern imaginaries of the individual and the public realm, and his critique of the impact of economic imaginaries of contemporary societies. However, Taylor (as a communitarian philosopher) regards the shift to imaginaries of the socially disembedded individual as basically a regressive shift, while I regard it as a progressive shift, provided democratic citizens are not reduced to flat economic men. "To be an individual," Taylor writes, "is not to be a Robinson Crusoe, but to be placed in a certain way among other humans. This is the reflection of the transcendental necessity of holism...."[23] I argue that what is required for an individual to be placed as a liberal democratic citizen among other such citizens is not the "transcendental necessity of holism" but rather

---

[21] Charles Taylor, *Modern Social Imaginaries* (Durham: Duke University Press, 2004), p. 23.
[22] Ibid., p. 157.
[23] Ibid., p. 65.

particular cultural forms and compatible performative political imaginaries of individual and society.

From my point of view, disembedded individualism is a necessary fiction for the evolution of liberal democracy and its moral and legal order. When culture, society, and politics elevate this fiction to the status of a regulatory imaginary, it enables such things as individual autonomy, human rights, and voluntary association of strangers, along and across the bonding of primordial tribes. The difference between the two approaches is not merely a matter of alternative conceptions of how individuals fit within the social whole and of the desirable moral order. It also concerns different views of how collective imaginaries work to fashion such individuals and their consciousness. If the collective modern imaginary of the disembedded or unencumbered self is a creative sociocultural instrument for fashioning the self-performance of a certain kind of people that fit the liberal democratic order, discussions of a "correct" genealogy of the contemporary individual and its correspondence to or deviation from a particular conception of the "essence" of humans are either secondary or utterly irrelevant. The whole point of the concept of the performative political imagination (see my next chapter) resides in its creative power to open up and embody new possibilities of personhood and human association. Contemporary political imaginaries are not necessarily supposed to correspond to past sociopolitical realities if their manifest or latent function is to help bring into being new ones. In the case of liberal democracy, resistance to normative holism as well as promotion of the imaginary of the unencumbered self have been clearly congenial to drawing a line of defense and defiance against the imperial coercive forces of centralized authoritarian government and the despotism of the collective.[24]

With respect to the public realm I, of course, agree with Taylor that it has to be imagined in order to exist, but in the latter part of this book I examine the impact of scientism on the rise of what I call the moral epistemology of the democratic order, which has actually enabled the liberal democratic public realm and its transformations since late modernity.

Finally, unlike Taylor, I see in the rise of the modern capitalist economic imaginary of society not only a loss, the decline of participatory public-regarding democratic civic culture, but an almost inevitable materialization of social and political interactions as a response to the shift from hierarchical religious to secular horizontal paradigms of politics and its new principles of transparency, accountability, and the depersonalization of power. I return to these issues in later chapters.

As Sheila Jasanoff has indicated in her remarkable works in the field of science, technology, and society studies (STS), one of the most fruitful ways to understand the relations between knowledge and politics is through the

---

[24] See on this issue chapter 5, "Self-narration as Self-defense," in my book *Rubber Bullets: Power and Conscience in Modern Israel* (New York: Farrar, Straus and Giroux, 1997).

concept of their coproduction.[25] "Scientific knowledge," observes Jasanoff, "is not a transcendent mirror of reality. It both embeds and is embedded in social practices, identities, norms, convention, discourses, instruments and institutions – in short, in all the building blocks of what we term the *social*."[26] As the works of Jasanoff demonstrate, science, technology, and society studies combine a wide range of research strategies that attempt to overcome the entrenched dichotomy of studies in science and society guarded so long by the anachronistic, formerly hegemonic imaginaries of the Enlightenment at a high cost to human self-understanding.

In my book *The Descent of Icarus* (1990), I attempted to show the close association between the scientific revolution and the rise of the modern democratic order, and their declining partnership since the last decades of the twentieth century. In analyzing the role of the political imagination in politics, it is useful to distinguish between the processes by which a society shapes itself in a mix of intuitive and conscious selection of constitutive mega-imaginaries that coproduce knowledge and the social order and the processes by which second-order imaginaries are selected to regulate the flow of the internal political life of an already established order. Obviously, in almost all states we encounter partly mixed systems of first-order as well as second-order imaginaries. In an essay on "The Civil Epistemology of Democracy,"[27] I define the concept of civil epistemology by analogy to Rousseau's idea of civil religion in his *Social Contract* (chapter 8) as the positive dogmas of civil faith within a democratic society that are necessary, in his view, to make good citizens and loyal subjects. My significantly different focus there was mostly on the civil epistemology that defines such things as the codes of democratic visual culture, the conditions that determine what lay democratic publics can accept as facts, and the complementary capacity of citizens to function as participant-witnesses of the process of governing. Jasanoff has gone further, developing her concept of "civic epistemologies" designated as the culturally specific ways by which a nation's citizens know things in common and apply their knowledge in the conduct of politics.[28] She regards civic epistemology as including "the institutional practices by which members of a given society test and deploy knowledge claims used as a basis for making collective choices."[29] In her landmark detailed comparative study of the local civic epistemologies of several European countries,

---

[25] Sheila Jasanoff, "The Idiom of Co-Production" and "Ordering Knowledge, Ordering Society" in Sheila Jasanoff (ed.), *States of Knowledge: The Co-Production of Science and the Social Order* (London: Routledge, 2004), pp. 1–45. See also the pioneering insights in H. Nowotny, P. Scott, and M. Gibbons, *Re-Thinking Science: Knowledge and the Public in the Age of Uncertainty* (Cambridge: Polity, 2001).

[26] Ibid., p. 3.

[27] See *Inquiry: An Interdisciplinary Journal of Philosophy* 35, nos. 3/4 (September/December 1992): 363–76.

[28] Sheila Jasanoff, *Designs on Nature: Science and Democracy in Europe and the United States* (Princeton: Princeton University Press, 2005), p. 9.

[29] Ibid., p. 255.

Jasanoff shows how their civic epistemologies differ in framing and handling sensitive biological and biotechnological knowledge and its applications.

In the final analysis we return to Vico's early original insight about the coproduction of knowledge and the social order, his perception that "all the principles of metaphysics, logic, and ethics originated in the public square in Athens" (1043).

3

Modes of Imagining: Elements of a Theory of the Political Imagination

As Vico observed, the historical record demonstrates humanity's capacity to imagine and historicize diverse forms of civic order. Hence, an inquiry into the modern democratic political imagination and its forms and transformations must first distinguish the political imagination from other types of imagination and examine both its particular forms and its relations to human behavior and institutions. My principal purpose in the following is therefore to provide an analytical framework for the extensive use I am making throughout this book of the expression: "the performative political imagination."

I regard the process of imagining as basically that of composing, decomposing, and recomposing the fabrics of images, metaphors, narratives, symbols, metaphysics, fantasies, commonsense facts, popular views of science, social values, shared fears and emotions, and other cultural and experiential materials – a process that continually produces configurations that fulfill diverse needs and functions. These configurations, these imaginaries, which from a philosophical perspective may appear as accidental, half-conscious, eclectic, and muddy assemblages of incommensurable elements, constitute, as we will see, a valuable form of public knowledge that differs in processes of assemblage and validation from those strictly associated with scientific or philosophical knowledge.

The ways in which lay persons learn to imagine and know things collectively usually does not and cannot involve formal procedures, systematic theoretically guided observations, or sophisticated methodologies. Instead, tacit social and political knowledge is engaged and expressed in informal yet discernable commonsense ways of assembling the world and acting in it. It is precisely because imaginaries (unlike theories) can bind together and bring into relation diverse elements (such as fictions, facts, and emotions) that their effects on collective behavior, as Vico realized, are greater than those produced by philosophical ideas.

In order to facilitate our discussion, I limit the use of the term *political imaginaries* to signify only those configurations, imagined authorities, individual and collective agencies, actions, events, and situations that have acquired regulatory powers and causal links to processes of shaping, enacting, and maintaining the political order. I argue that political imaginaries constitute the fabric of political world making, the core of the political order, and the clue to its formal architecture and informal dynamics. In this context, social and political imaginaries are considered neither pure fantasies nor representations of a given external reality, although, as I have indicated, they may employ both modes of imagining. What renders such political imaginaries consequential is their capacity to generate performative scripts that orient political behavior and the making and unmaking of political institutions. This is why it is appropriate to regard fictions that are selected and realized as hegemonic regulatory imaginaries as politically performative.

Generated by the creative collective imagination, political imaginaries (like myths of origin that have evolved in diverse human societies) become powerful tools that, when performed, can produce social and political facts. Their pertinence to our discussion is not their correspondence or fidelity to what is conceived as reality or to some conception of truth, but their power to generate some modes of politics. As we will see, this power is often enhanced by the inconspicuous or concealed nature of their causal relations to the social and political order and by their veneer of familiar givens.

The performative imagination is a universal human capacity that operates in many different spheres of life. The collective performative political imagination as a special version of this general capacity is the principal conceptual instrument I use here to try to cope with the questions of how political worlds are made, sustained, and decline. In order to sharpen the concept of performative political imagination as a fruitful analytical tool, I concentrate on the special capacity of the performative imagination to subdivide into three distinct modes: the reflective, the fantastic, and the instrumental. The reflective or representative usually relates to external empirical references, the fantastic is more manifestly creative and usually unaccountable to a common external reality, and the instrumental is usually deliberately geared to advancing particular goals. In the political context, each of these versions of the collective performative imagination has different functions. My aim is to explicate the ways these variants of the performative political imagination work and interact in the production of democratic politics.

While, as we will see, there can be overlap and close connections between these modes, the analytical distinction is useful. We can better characterize the ways in which the political imagination works in building and upholding the political order.

One of the unique features of the imagination that is particularly effective in the political arena is the capacity to simultaneously induce a sense of the real and the fantastic, or to sequentially alternate between them. The simple classification elaborated later in this chapter illuminates the ways in which shifts between modes of imagining mediate between what is socially accepted as real and unreal and occasionally blur the boundaries between facts and fictions.

I begin with a brief discussion of each of these modes of imagining and their fundamental interrelation.

The *reflective* imagination is characteristically conceived and employed as a reconstructive power at play in the conjuring of representations of past experiences. It concerns the efforts to recall, remember, or form an image of external objects, agents, events, and experiences in the collective past not immediately or currently accessible to sense experience. Typically, the reflective mode of imagining, like the attempt to imagine the face of a particular person or to recall vividly and accurately a particular landscape or event, involves concern with verisimilitude or similarity.

The reflective imagination is always selective, most frequently interpreting past experiences in light of present interests, moods, and emotions; it is always partly involuntarily inventing the past and combining remembered sense experiences with images and narratives subsequently introduced. The imagining subjects, however, are seldom aware of the input of their own minds and cultures into the shaping of the narratives and representations that constitute their imaginings of the past. In particular, we are usually unaware of our common tendency to ignore the selective functions of factors such as the brain, the neurological system, personality, and inherited or entrenched ethical or ideological perspectives in the productions of the reflective imagination.

The reflective imagination works within the boundaries of what constitutes common sense in a particular society or culture. In the commonsense world of ordinary lives we do not usually question the reality or the objectivity of the familiar things we recall. In modern western societies, the reflective imagination seems to operate within the frame of what I have called "commonsense realism," a concept on which I elaborate in Part Two of this book. If one recalls a particular place, the assumption is that this place can be found or, if it has been altered (say by a war or development), its previous form or shape (what the subject recalls) can be reconstructed by other witnesses or records. The close relation between the reflective mode of the composing imagination and commonsense realism, its power to frame and regard as real objects, events, and agents not immediately present to the senses, affects the uses of the reflective imagination in politics. The reflective imagination also operates in "live time" in our electronic age. We summon past and present experiences, including images we associate with politics, to construe our ongoing composition of what we regard as current political realities.

As we see in Chapters 5 and 6, commonsense reality means neither a distorted nor a vulgar version of reality, as philosophy or science would tend to define it, nor is it an arbitrary invention. In any particular sociopolitical context, commonsense reality is a complex, historically changing, and politically consequential cultural product. It may be influenced by sense experience consciously or unconsciously mediated by religion, by metaphysical, philosophical, and scientific ideas, or by culturally available metaphors, but it is never merely derivative of any of these frames.

The reflective imagination and commonsense realism may be two aspects of the same power, playing complementary and converging roles in the fashioning of reality in politics. Both collaborate in upholding a sense of continuity and notions of elementary causal regularity or predictability without which modern political worlds are inconceivable or uninhabitable.

In contrast to the reflective imagination, the *fictive* imagination, insofar as it is conceived of as creating fantastic worlds, is quite literally unaccountable to commonsense realism. When the fantastic imagination performs Pegasus as an artistic work, one would not expect its embodiment in life. The fantastic imagination is pervasive in the domain of the arts, in the deliberate performance of illusions or fictions. A product of the fantastic political imagination such as a utopia is usually recognized by its obvious deviation from the world normalized for us by commonsense realism. As such, performing fantasies of alternative worlds can function as a gloss over criticism of the present order or as a means of influencing collective aspirations by animating and emotionally empowering nonexistent alternative (perhaps even possible) worlds. The fantastic imagination, therefore, often uses the mode of the representative imagination as a genre for the purpose of creating reality effects. Commonsense realism orients us to currently lived, widely shared social and political worlds, which are in themselves historico-cultural products whose presence appears, in some sense, continuous within recent and distant worlds construed by our reflective imagination.

Obviously, the very borders set by our political commonsense world between the politically fictive and the politically real are in themselves bound by contextually embedded imaginaries or meta-imaginaries. These meta-imaginaries underlie what is cast within each political universe as real power and authority and what is classified as a mere product of the fictive imagination that refers to nonexistent things. But from a scholarly perspective, political imaginaries such as the divine right of kings, popular sovereignty, or the nation, which may not have referents in the real world but nevertheless were or are sufficiently believable to produce real political institutions and practices, are causes and therefore not merely fantastic fictions. Imagining popular sovereignty or a nation is not like imagining a flying horse. The flying horse is a compositional product that combines elements of common experience into a fictive entity presumably devoid of an external reference, normative force, or political sense to gain the powers of potential embodiment in ordinary life experience. However widely present in our minds fictive entities such as Pegasus, the Little Prince, or Hamlet may be, they cannot function as productive, self-realizing fictions like the nation.

In politics, the presence or reality of fictive persons, events, or objects is therefore of a different order. Entities such as God, the sovereign, the people, or the nation, may, as we will see, oscillate between the fictive and the real, often becoming more politically real than fantastic. Ernst Kantorowicz demonstrated how the imaginary of the monarch combines the king as a mortal human being with the image of the king deified by grace as a Christ-like though immortal god.[1] Obviously, the flesh-and-blood king would have had a very different political reality without the image of the king deified by grace.

Questions abound regarding the processes through which fictive agents, abstract ideas, or fantasized objects are reified in political contexts. The issue becomes even more complicated when it is not clear that people distinguish between fictive and real entities and when fictive persons or objects are perceived or related to as real. Under such circumstances, fictions may be socially or politically transformed into causes of or constraints on political behavior. Vico's distinction between manmade collective political or legal realities and natural realities that are allegedly given is relevant here in its emphasis on the dependence of the former on civic normative and perceptual tests of admittance into the sphere of the politically real and their historical character.

The form of any specific configuration of the political imagination may be limited, but its sources are extremely diverse. They can include almost anything from poetry, painting, television programs, and architecture to historical experience, organic nature, religion, and philosophy. In any case, by processes of selection and reconfiguration, the residues of earlier products of the political imagination always play an important role in shaping current ones.

The status of the merely imaginary or invented has allowed fanciful literary fictions to serve politically subversive, as well as elite, political goals. These include communicating, by indirection, secret thoughts or unconventional ideas; suggesting alternative political worlds; proposing new identities; or opening possibilities that would have been censured if perceived as seriously intended. Hence the unique potential of fictive imaginaries to surreptitiously screen transgressions under cover of art, theater, and literature, and to transpose them into the commonsense zone of the real (where they can be "confirmed" as objects of the reflective imagination) is politically important, even crucial. Greek dramatists like Sophocles knew very well, and Plato famously feared, the power of the fantastic imagination to become part of the performative political imagination and subvert the existing order.

That which is self-consciously imagined as fictive facilitates a playful, freer, experimental approach to possible worlds and identities. Particularly in oppressive regimes like those of prerevolutionary France or the Soviet Union, fictional novels, operatic works, political utopias, and science fiction played a significant role as vehicles of subversive and critical political consciousness. But also in free societies, ostensibly fictional works may be transformed into the frames of our lived world. Wallace Stevens observed that "what makes the poet the potent figure that he is, or was, or ought to be, is that he creates the world to which we turn incessantly and without knowing it and that he gives to life the supreme fictions without which we are unable to conceive of it."[2]

[1] Ernst H. Kantorowicz, *The King's Two Bodies: A Study in Mediaeval Political Theology* (Princeton: Princeton University Press, 1997).
[2] Wallace Stevens, *The Necessary Angel: Essays on Reality and the Imagination* (London: Faber and Faber, 1951), p. 31.

In any society, then, cultural treasures of fictive fantastic imaginings, produced over time by poetry, literature, the arts, religion, and philosophy, often become significant components of the active political imagination that shapes the aesthetic, normative, and behavioral clusters of the political world. From this perspective, we are interested in the realities of political fictions, in political fictions as social facts, and in the social diffusion of fictions that acquire the status of performative imaginaries, that is, of causes and building blocks in politics.

In addition to the reflective and the fictive modes of the performative political imagination, the third mode is that of the *instrumental* imagination. This mode or type involves deliberate acts of imagining or of selecting imaginaries aimed at serving some specific goal or purpose. The status of imaginings in this context is that of a means to achieve specific ends. Comprising elements of both the reflective and the fictive imagination, the general instrumental imagination composes and selects images or metaphors aimed at fulfilling functions in a variety of fields, including scientific research, pedagogy, military strategy, commercials, ideology, philosophy, and, of course, politics. For instance, archeology has been politically instrumental for cultivating imaginaries of the past in modern Israel, grounding specific national territorial claims. The imagery employed in physical science to frame and fashion theories is another case in point. Gerald Holton observes that:

[O]ur pool of imaginative tools [is] characterized by a remarkable parsimony at the fundamental level, joined by fruitfulness and flexibility in actual practice.... Since Parmenides and Heraclitus, the members of the thematic dyad of constancy and change have vied for loyalty, and so have, ever since Pythagoras and Thales, the efficacy of mathematics versus the efficacy of materialistic or mechanistic models. The (usually unacknowledged) presuppositions pervading the work of scientists have long included also the thematic couples of experience and symbolic formalism, complexity and simplicity, reductionism and holism, discontinuity and the continuum, hierarchical structure and unity, the use of mechanisms versus teleological or anthropomorphic modes of approach.[3]

The history of science is largely a record of the processes whereby imaginings of the kind designated by Holton as *themata* are either adopted or discarded as intellectual tools in the construction of scientific explanations. There is, of course, an ongoing debate among realist and antirealist philosophers and scientists concerning the status of the metaphors used in science. The realists insist that the metaphors and images woven into successful scientific theories belong, in some sense or another, to the products of what I have called the reflective imagination, which they conceive as rich in cognitive content; their view is that figurative language, metaphors and images, corresponds in some literal sense to natural phenomenal referents. The antirealists, however, would classify them with the scientifically useful products of the fictive imagination.[4]

---

[3] Gerald Holton, *Thematic Origins of Scientific Thought: Kepler to Einstein*, revised edition, (Cambridge, MA: Harvard University Press, 1988), p. 17.

[4] For a more detailed discussion see Richard Rorty's *Philosophy and the Mirror of Nature* (Princeton: Princeton University Press, 1979); Nelson Goodman, *Ways of Worldmaking* (Indianapolis:

Regardless of their respective positions, both view the metaphors and images employed for the purpose of representing and generating scientific explanations as belonging to the instrumental orientation of scientists aiming at advancing knowledge. Because the imaginings selected and used respectively by science and philosophy serve profoundly different intellectual goals, the instrumental imagination in science may usefully disregard imaginings instrumental in the field of philosophy.

Scientists often tend, for instance, to believe that they can safely ignore the philosophical debate on the ontological status of theoretical entities. They adopt or eschew metaphors and images of entities used in theory building not on the grounds that they conform to or contradict the criteria of the real or correspond to commonly experienced reality. They tend to regard as real that which works, which satisfies multiple professional criteria such as theoretical value, predictive value, consistency, mathematifiability, simplicity, theoretical applicability, or fertility. Scientists, therefore, are not likely to produce images of reality that are not theoretically, technologically, or at least heuristically productive.

Contrary to the ethos of science, particularly to "scientism" as a major component of modern common sense, a close examination of the actual practices of science can only problematize conceptions of reality.[5] One cannot merely claim that specific metaphors or theoretical entities signify reality while nonscientific, commonsense ones do not. Moreover, no unanimity exists among scientists as to what to classify as real. Such disagreements are, however, likely to reflect different approaches to the question of which specific concepts, images, or metaphors are more instrumental to or supportive of the advancement of a particular scientific claim, or more generally, which are more instrumental in the advancement of the body of knowledge under consideration.[6]

Differences among scientists often reflect diverse approaches to questions of where or how exactly to slice phenomena and bind it as an object of scientific account. Their controversies also reflect questions about the instruments employed, the perspectives they presuppose, and the validity of methodological considerations. Mara Beller notes that in the case of quantum physics, in the debate on the theoretical and ontological status of metaphors or theoretical

Hackett Publishing Company, 1978); Ian Hacking, *Historical Ontology* (Cambridge, MA: Harvard University Press, 2002); David Bloor, *Knowledge and Social Imagery*, second edition (Chicago: University of Chicago Press, 1991); Sheila Jasanoff (ed.), *States of Knowledge: The Co-Production of Science and Social Order* (London: Routledge, 2004); and Bruno Latour, *Pandora's Hope: Essays on the Reality of Science Studies* (Cambridge, MA: Harvard University Press, 1999).

[5] See, for instance, Ian Hacking's *The Social Construction of What?* (Cambridge, MA: Harvard University Press, 1999); note also the works of Bruno Latour and the angry responses, mostly from natural scientists, to his constructivist approach to "scientific reality" in his and Steve Woolgar's *Laboratory Life*, Jonas Salk (ed.) (Princeton: Princeton University Press, 1986) and Latour's *Science in Action* (Cambridge, MA: Harvard University Press, 1987).

[6] See the discussion on the relations between the intellectual and the organizational division of labor among scientific disciplines in Richard D. Whitley, *The Intellectual and Social Organization of the Sciences* (Oxford: Clarendon Press, 1984).

entities, significant differences sprang up between mathematical physicists such as Heisenberg and Born on one hand and physicists like Bohr on the other over the criteria that would qualify theoretical concepts as real. For the former, theoretical and mathematical considerations are important, whereas Bohr's "intuitions about what is 'real' and what is not," says Beller, "are connected with the possibility of visualizing conceptual notions, not with the possibility of observing them."[7]

The instrumental criteria of working scientists have ensured that theoretical entities or images that have lost their explanatory powers, like phlogiston, ether, spontaneous generation, and catastrophic geology, have disappeared from professional scientific discourse. Beller argues that "for Schrödinger, the indistinguishability of particles, implied by the new quantum statistics, signified the total bankruptcy of the concept of a particle, and the continuing use of particles concepts offended his theoretical sensibilities."[8] Obviously, as Born claimed, scientists tend to ascribe the status of real to observables and to conceptual entities important to them.[9] This position is also compatible with Beller's observation that, in addition to the internal scientific criteria for ontologically privileging a theoretical entity or a metaphor, scientists who are continually involved in controversies and endless series of dialogues also assign the status of reality for rhetorical reasons. Realistic representation is a strategy of persuasion "whose significance can only be grasped within the definite sociohistorical circumstances in which it is used."[10]

Clearly reality claims are engaged as potent rhetorical devices in some contexts. With respect to the rhetorical strategy of using a selective attribution of reality to reinforce one's position, there is not much difference between scientists and laymen (although they tend to use vastly different conceptions and criteria serving different goals). Galileo resisted the pressure exerted by Cardinal Bellarmine to moderate the reality claims respecting the scientific imaginings of the earth's place in relation to the sun; Einstein refused the pleas of Henri Bergson and Maurice Merleau-Ponty to reconcile his concept of time with that of time as imagined in the commonsense world in order to allow physics to "freely develop its paradoxes without authorizing unreason."[11] Both were unwilling to make rhetorical concessions to the reality claims of the period's commonsense imaginings, which appeared important to the stability of the contemporary frames of social interaction and order in the eyes of their critics.[12]

---

[7] Mara Beller, *Quantum Dialogue: The Making of a Revolution* (Chicago: University of Chicago Press, 1999), p. 180.

[8] Ibid., p. 233.

[9] Ibid., p. 187.

[10] Ibid., p. 186.

[11] See Yaron Ezrahi's essay "Einstein and the Light of Reason" in Gerald Holton and Yehuda Elkana (eds.), *Albert Einstein: Historical and Cultural Perspectives – The Centennial Symposium in Jerusalem* (Princeton: Princeton University Press, 1982), pp. 262–6.

[12] Ibid.

The point here is that the products of the reflective and fictive imaginations are often appropriated as resources by the instrumental imagination, which subordinates them to its specialized goals and tests. Obviously, the often esoteric professional considerations of the instrumental political imagination differ from instrumental scientific, pedagogic, commercial, or economic imaginations. In each case, formal and informal or "tacit knowledge" concerning the choice of effective metaphors or images is often a matter of a specialized, valuable, and only partly formalizable knowledge.[13]

Against this background, it is instructive to examine, as we will later, the ways in which laymen's common sense appropriates and edits scientific metaphors in order to adapt them to extra-scientific uses in everyday life. At this point, it will suffice to note that whereas metaphors, theoretical entities, and other imaginings are subject to continual and sometimes revolutionary changes in the sciences, laymen have usually expected science to provide a reliable guarantee of the stability, even the unassailabilty of referents. This expectation that science would mirror immutable nature has long been a crucial ground for lay approval of science and its special authority in social and political discourses.

There are, of course, many other interesting illustrations of the workings of the instrumental imagination. Every expert and teacher knows how often an idea, a body of knowledge, or a technique one wishes to impart to students requires the ability of students to use metaphors as lenses to transform x into y. In the field of military strategy, simulations of the enemy, based on the ability to imagine his values, purposes, ways of thinking, or modes of operation are common practice. Competition in sport has been widely used as a metaphor for explaining political contests or rivalries among business firms and political parties.

Envisioning the body as a machine has been a widespread, enormously productive although theologically problematic medical practice at least since William Harvey's discovery of the circulatory system and conceptualization of the heart as a pump.[14] Darwin and other evolutionary biologists were aware that their scientifically instrumentally productive images of nature as a warfare among species similarly challenged the theological imaginings of nature as a harmonious system.

Strategies of instrumental imagining have also been extremely valuable aids to performers in art, sports, and technology. Years ago, my ski instructor gave me useful advice to overcome my fear of falling while taking a steep path. He said to "ignore the visual information which you process as 'I am about to fall' and imagine that you are bound to the ground by a gravitational force."

In city planning, the guiding image of design and construction, the relevant norm underlying its goals, makes a difference. It matters whether that

---

[13] On the concept of "tacit knowledge" in science see Michael Polanyi, *Personal Knowledge* (Chicago: University of Chicago Press, 1958).

[14] For modern uses of the body as a source of metaphors see Mark Johnson, *The Body in the Mind: The Bodily Basis of Meaning, Imagination, and Reason* (Chicago: University of Chicago Press, 1990).

image is an organically unified community, an aggregate of a multitude of free and separate individuals, or an assortment of several different, haphazard, and potentially adversarial communities. In the case of Vienna, such diametrically opposed images instrumentally disciplined and directed overall planning and construction efforts to different ends. Writing about politics and culture in *fin-de-siècle* Vienna, Carl E. Schorske describes the struggle between architects Camillo Sitte and Otto Wagner over the architectural design of the famous Ringstraße as a clash between two deeply opposed modes of imagining representing very different value orientations. One stressed community, historical legacy, integration, coherence, and organic unity; the other functionalism, rational systems, transparency, equality, and uniformity.[15] One was concerned with the danger of losing the whole in the parts while the other was concerned about losing the parts in the whole. Such opposing value orientations yield different parameters for the selection of imaginaries that are instrumental in guiding and regulating construction of the envisioned city.

In television commercials, the viewers' imagination is engaged to instigate purchase of particular products or services. Their promoters take great pains to idealize them and render them appealing by working on the spectators' imagination. (Successful commercials are those that clearly tilt consumers' buying habits in favor of advertisers' products.) It is not surprising that advertisers tend to exploit the ambiguity between the reflective and the fictive imaginations for their purposes. Misled to believe that the idealized fictive attributes of a product are real, consumers may be tempted to buy it.

W. J. T. Mitchell provides a very instructive illustration of this insidious strategy.[16] His example is a commercial entitled "Moviemakers" created by Sprite, a Coca-Cola subsidiary. Mitchell describes the commercial as starting off with a scene from "a brainstorming session of a team of 'creative' advertising, media, marketing, and filmmaking professionals" discussing the creation of a new advertising image and emphasizing the need to produce a new commercial film for the product. Following that, Mitchell continues, "an authoritative voice-over concludes, 'Don't buy the Hollywood hype. Buy what you want … not what image-makers want you to want.'" This is accompanied by the texts: "Image is nothing. Thirst is everything. Obey your thirst." A bottle of Sprite is then "staged as the Real Thing … the object of authentic desire."

Particularly interesting for us in what Mitchell characterizes as this "anti commercial commercial," or a commercial that denies its own commerciality, is the use of images as anti-images, that is, as self-concealing images whose construction is guided by the desire to exploit the only means available to advertisers on the screen – images. These images are then used to create reality effects that take on the image of the product, turning it into "the Real Thing."[17]

---

[15] Carl E. Schorske, *Fin-de-Siècle Vienna* (New York: Alfred Knopf, 1980), pp. 24–115.
[16] W. J. T. Mitchell, *What Do Pictures Want? The Lives and Loves of Images* (Chicago: University of Chicago Press, 2005), pp. 77–81.
[17] Ibid.

This strategy of the instrumental imagination is widely used in marketing political candidates as well, although the conditions of reality effects in politics are different.

Because idealization and deception can be very rewarding in the commodity and political markets, many governments authorize regulators to protect viewers from gross violations. In some areas such as commercial advertising, the state and its agencies are invested in restricting the capacity of the fictive imagination to pose as its reflective counterpart. In other areas, the state may become the primary perpetrator, exploiting its own (i.e., public) resources in order to present idealized, fictive descriptions of issues (such as the state of the economy, the state of national security, or the state of public health) as realistic and normative.

As a rule, governments opt for notions of causality that credit their policies with favorable consequences while ascribing adverse states of affairs to causes beyond their control. Attribution of the destructive effects of earthquakes on houses to nature and domestic economic distress to global economic forces are common practice. In general, the modern state has enlisted the rhetoric of statistics, city planning, social engineering, and rational holism to persuade the public to accept the concentration of power at the top and to justify massive use of that power in shaping and directing collective life.[18] In all these instances, goal-directed, politically instrumental (usually distinct from substantive or technically instrumental) considerations shape behaviorally productive imaginings and the desired composition of the fictive and reflective elements.

Probably inspired by Plato's memorable allegory of the cave, philosophers have employed imaginaries instrumental in framing, communicating, and teaching philosophical ideas. From the perspective of our discussion, perhaps the most important meta-imaginary of the modern western philosophical tradition has been the imagination itself as a distinct faculty of fantasies and illusions separate from the faculty of reason. This move has served many goals, the first of which consists of setting philosophy apart from the arts and from religion, and protecting philosophy and philosophical discourse from the intrusion of laymen and priests. It has also enabled delineation of concepts such as truth and knowledge while obfuscating their inherently contingent, affective, normative, instrumental, and sometimes aesthetic aspects. The professionally instrumental philosophical denial of the central role of the imagination in philosophical thought and discourse has served the ethos of philosophy as a foundational intellectual discipline and its claims of knowledge particularly in the fields of ontology and epistemology. This denial has also delayed the realization, central to this book, of the continuities between human experience inside

[18] Yaron Ezrahi, *The Descent of Icarus: Science and the Transformation of Contemporary Democracy* (Cambridge, MA: Harvard University Press, 1990); James C. Scott, *Seeing Like a State: How Certain Schemes to Improve the Human Condition Have Failed* (New Haven: Yale University Press, 1998); Theodore M. Porter, *Trust in Numbers: The Pursuit of Objectivity in Science and Public Life* (Princeton: Princeton University Press, 1995).

and outside Plato's cave. While Plato sought to confine the public imagination to his cave in order to protect philosophy and the philosopher-king from the mob, Vico's recognition that the reign of the common imagination extends to the vast world beyond the cave, where it acquires the power to constitute political universes, has been gradually restored since late modernity with the erosion of the Enlightenment vision of politics. This trend has been reinforced by anti-elitist postmodern sensibilities and the deepening irreverence toward authority induced by waves of democratization.

I argue that the reflective, the fictive, and the instrumental imaginations, as subdivisions of the performative political imagination, acting separately or jointly, play a role in shaping the political imagination and influencing the ways it works in political practice. As I indicated in my opening remarks, every political order, whether monarchic, fascist, communist, or democratic must be performed in order to exist. The performance or enactment of a political regime requires a central coordinating imaginary and affiliated imaginings. In our time, when mass politics mediated by television has rendered the staged political gesture, the cultivation of the image, and the various skills of stage-craft an integral part of statecraft, it is easy to recognize the inherently performative character of the political imagination. But it is precisely those aspects of the political order that do not appear to be staged but seem natural or given that are the most effective products of the performative political imagination. The performative imagination is most effective in shaping political behavior and institutions when it works through the codes and scripts of the reflective imagination to naturalize its products.

For the insiders of diverse political regimes, the performative political imagination, which is latently constitutive, is manifestly merely reflective of political reality. Close examination reveals the extent to which monarchic, democratic, or fascist regimes, for instance, differ as particular productions of the performative political imagination and the ways in which the reflective-descriptive political imagination contributes to the normalization of an almost always fragile, precariously constructed domestic political world.[19]

The performative political imagination is not only responsible for those aspects of the existence of a political order that are manifestly performative, involving parades, shows, or public rituals, but mainly for the many that are latently performative. Spectacular public rituals comprise, no doubt, an important part of the performance or the enactment of the political imaginary, but they only constitute a part. By performative political imagination, I refer to a far more fundamental process in the making of politics, which encompasses activities not usually identified as either performative or political.

---

[19] On the role of architecture, painting, and the theater in the production of the monarchy of Philip IV, see Jonathan Brown and J. H. Elliott, *A Palace For a King: The Buen Retiro and the Court of Philip IV* (New Haven: Yale University Press, 1980). On the performative features of fascism see, for instance, Mabel Berezin, *Making the Fascist Self: The Political Culture of Interwar Italy* (Ithaca: Cornell University Press, 1997).

In order to clarify this point, it is useful to briefly consider the ways in which the term *performative* is used in the influential works of philosophers of language such as J. L. Austin and his follower, John R. Searle.[20] In his early work, Austin suggested a distinction between utterances that are just "sayings" (constatives, statements, assertions, and the like) and utterances that are themselves a kind of action (promises, bets, warnings, and so forth).[21] In Austin's early work, only the latter class of utterances is seen as performative. He thought that only those situations in which "we do things with words," such as getting married or appointing a chairperson, belong in the class of performatives. He also distinguished between written words that are performative, like a shopping list, and more strictly descriptive texts. But, as John Searle notes, the distinction between performatives and other kinds of utterances was rejected in Austin's later work when he realized that "making a statement is as much performing an illocutionary act as making a promise, a bet, a warning, or what have you. Any utterance will consist in performing one or more illocutionary acts."[22]

Though subject to all the necessary qualifications, I am using the expression "performative (political) imagination" analogically, encompassing not only acts deliberately aimed at achieving specific political effects. I am not restricting this expression to deliberate acts that introduce images, texts, rituals, utterances, and sounds, such as those associated with coronations or state funeral ceremonies in the public sphere in order to promote specific behavioral (political) effects such as promonarchic or pronationalist attitudes. In the following discussion, I stress my use of the category of the performative political imagination to cover also the production, articulation, dissemination, and institutionalization of imaginaries such as those of reality, agency, and time, which act indirectly and often also surreptitiously, but are nevertheless crucial for the production of configurations of regime-supporting behaviors and institutions. It is in this context that the concept of the coproduction of knowledge and the sociopolitical order is particularly fruitful. Take, for example, the sociohistorical correspondence (to be discussed at greater length later) between the imaginaries of the scientific community and the liberal democratic society as aggregates of free rational individuals. In both contexts, this imaginary of the community as a voluntary association of autonomous individuals legitimates knowledge and politics as their respective products. This is also why concepts of reality evolved respectively between individual scientists and between individual citizens can partly converge in rendering politically legitimate the imaginary of reality produced by commonsense realism.[23]

---

[20] See, for example, J. L. Austin, *How To Do Things With Words*, J. O. Urmson (ed.) (Oxford: Clarendon Press, 1962), and John R. Searle, *Expression and Meaning: Studies in the Theory of Speech Acts* (Cambridge: Cambridge University Press, 1979).

[21] Searle, ibid., pp. 17–18.

[22] Ibid.

[23] See for instance Michael Polanyi's classic essay: "The Republic of Science" in *Minerva* 1 (Autumn 1962): 54–73.

I would like to emphasize that, in particular, political reality in itself is not accessible unless mediated by social conventions of discourse and action. Regardless of whether the "objectively real" is fixed or fluid, the ruling desire underlying convention is to perform the real as a constant reified referent, a safe anchorage for human cognition and behavior. It is precisely this sense of stable relations between signifiers of the real and the assumed fixity of the signified, or between the performativity of political referents and the stability of their matching references, which is disrupted when political realities undergo revolutionary change.

Sandy Petrey has instructively developed the insight of the Russian philosopher of language, V. N. Vološinov, that in different political contexts "any current truth must inevitably sound to many other people as the greatest lie. This inner dialectic quality of the sign comes out fully into the open in times of crises or revolutionary changes."[24] The French and Russian revolutions provide a host of illuminating examples for the disruptive and creative effects of radical sociopolitical change on conventional languages and discourses of social and political reality. Petrey focuses on the role of portentous moments such as the decapitation of the king of France, which disrupted the givenness of standard references to "the present King of France," and on the shift from voting by order to voting by head in the Estates-General, which destabilized references to the "Third Estate" that had begun to converge with references to the "French Nation."[25]

These and other revolutionary experiences reversed the causal order between facts and language; "instead of propositional content corresponding to the world," argues Petrey, "the world was brought to correspond to propositional content."[26] Such fateful events led to the realization of the instability inherent in the imaginaries of the politically real and the languages that institutionalize them in any current public discourse. In other words, the solidity as well as the instability of political agencies and realities – as referents of the discourse of the socially and the politically real – have been widely recognized in modern times as a product of shifts between competing power configurations and their matching political imaginaries.

In terms of our discussion, successful political imaginaries are those that, by means of power shifts, can affect the transformation from potential into actual political referents. Since in such cases the sign precedes the signified, we can say that the referent is derivative of the performative, that designative language refers to the products of the performative language of political imaginaries, or simply that realism in political language and action implies a culmination of

---

[24] V. N. Vološinov, *Marxism and the Philosophy of Language*, L. Matejka and I. R. Titunik (trans.) (New York: Seminar Press, 1973), pp. 23–4; Sandy Petrey, *Realism and Revolution: Balzac, Stendhal, Zola, and the Performances of History* (Ithaca: Cornell University Press, 1988).

[25] Petrey, *Realism and Revolution*, pp. 17–36.

[26] Ibid., p. 27.

the achievement of the performative imagination in creating the illusion of the given and concealing its own creativity.

When the aforementioned creative process of the composing imagination is hidden from the public eye, its efficacy in presenting the imagined as real may significantly increase. Political history suggests that the power of the public critiques launched by intellectuals such as Rousseau, Marx, and Paine derived from their ability to persuasively redefine the "naturalized" grounds of the regimes they criticized as willful works of imagination and arbitrary power.

From a political perspective, imaginaries generated by fantastic imagination and those by reflective imagination would usually work differently in the political context of an existing regime. The former could produce performative scripts that either idealize the regime or subvert it by radically transcending existing political practices. The latter would characteristically generate performative scripts that behaviorally confirm hegemonic legitimating imaginaries of the regime or debunk them by focusing on political facts that seem to disconfirm them or on flaws the regime tries to conceal.

In some respects, all three modes of imagining can converge in the performative process, particularly when it works toward the overall shake-up or enactment of a regime. Very often each of the three subcategories would be typically associated with a particular area or institutional section of the "system." Thus, in a liberal democratic context, the reflective political imagination describing the individual as a free agent would combine with the instrumental imagination in promoting this image in the educational and legal systems. Literature and the arts would then project, deepen, and emotionally, aesthetically, and ethically plot this individual type as real and appealing within the overall performance of the liberal democratic regime. In a collectivist nationalist context, the reflective political imagination is likely to focus on naturalizing the agency of the nation and combine with the instrumental imagination in promoting the primacy of the collective in the educational and legal systems. History, literature, and the arts would typically reify the collective as a being, an agency, a moral authority, and object of emotional identification and glorify it aesthetically.

Conformist and dissenting poets, writers, musicians, and painters are often inescapably drawn into these wars between competing political imaginaries of agency and reality as well as alternative performative scripts of same or similar collective political imaginaries in the same political context.[27] In more general terms, we can say that the very robust collective political imaginary of democracy tends to be socially and politically contextualized in various societies by means of different performative scripts adaptable to local values, beliefs, and traditions. Despite relatively common terms like *freedom, equality, separation of powers*, or *the rule of law*, democracy and its performance trigger

---

[27] I am grateful to Sheila Jasanoff for suggesting the use of the concept of performative scripts to describe modes of translating fictions or imaginaries into political facts.

and engage different political rhetoric, behaviors, institutions, and meanings in each society.

To reiterate, the performative political imagination acquires special powers when its products are experienced as part of a given reality or its accurate representation, rather than a deliberate contrivance, a means of furthering a political purpose. This power is reinforced by the ability of the imagination to divide itself. It can publicly project a separation between the self-concealing imaginaries of the real and the products of what the public identifies as the fictive and the instrumental imaginations. As we will see, it is precisely the acknowledged projection of the fantastic imagination as the specific producer of contrived illusions of reality and agency that indirectly supports, by contradistinction, the credibility of the reflective imagination.

Machiavelli alerted the Prince regarding the tendency of the lay public to interpret his actions in moral terms, which are alien to the instrumental imagination that should guide his actions, including the selective use of violence, to stabilize the kingdom. The Prince was advised to conceal the instrumental motives and considerations behind his moves as a governor behind a façade of piety and generosity. Machiavelli's point can be interpreted as suggesting that, at times, transparent governmental instrumentalism is counterproductive to the legitimacy and stability of the regime.

The rise of the capitalist state encouraged the transference of this dualism between the moral and the instrumental onto the spheres of economic and social policies. Modern democratic ideology and practice constitutes, to some extent, an attempt to heal the split identified by Machiavelli between moral and instrumental imaginings of governmental actions by rendering their instrumentalism consistent with liberal democratic values of rationality, transparency, accountability, free choice, and competitiveness.[28]

The relations between imagining and acting, or between forms of the political imagination and structures of political behavior and institutions, have been the subject of extensive research in fields such as sociology, political science, and anthropology. A good part of this research and its political implications have been insulated within local internal disciplinary discourses and their agendas. I do not intend to systematically extract the many insights hidden in these specialized sites of knowledge. For now I will draw selectively on a particularly instructive few.

It seems self-evident that the performative imagination has a powerful impact on individual behavior in diverse contexts. The individual erotic imagination may be clearly performative in several senses of the word. What one imagines in the context of sexual intercourse and how one imagines a sexual partner obviously affects one's voluntary and involuntary behavior. In his essay "Of the Force of Imagination," Montaigne explores his belief that impotence is a pathology created by the tyranny of the imagination. His view is that, con-

---

[28] Ezrahi, *The Descent of Icarus*, especially pp. 9–127.

sciously or not, different kinds of imaginings produce different forms of sexual behavior.

Experience may suggest that at least much of the erotic imagination that affects the behavior of sexual partners is spontaneous, non-deliberate, or unconscious. This distinction between deliberate or undeliberate or unreflective imaginings is important for the distinction between the instrumental and the reflective performative modes. This applies also to other contexts. How one imagines a business partner, a co-worker, or one's superior, as well as who these people "really" are or how they respectively imagine the other, will often become loaded with performative effects on their interactions and the social reality that these interactions generate.[29] Such interactions consist of unreflective spontaneous elements combined with a measure of potential self-direction. They may involve the simultaneous workings of the individual reflective, fictive, and instrumental performative imaginations.

In the context of the collective performative imagination as well, the relation between what is imagined and how groups behave and institutions grow and function is essentially hidden, as in the cases of religion and the economy. This stems from the fact that the performative efficacy of imaginary configurations that uphold religious or economic systems depends, to some extent, on unreflective public acceptance, that is, on a public tendency to hold a view of the system that overlooks the public's own imaginary as an essential factor in the system's very existence.[30]

Characteristically, the performative imagination in the domains of religion, the economy, and, I argue, politics cultivates imaginal frames that erase or underplay its causal traces to the relevant popular imagination. Obviously, the fact that, as products of the performative imagination, religious and economic systems are produced and sustained by a multitude of ongoing individual and institutional actions naturalized by hegemonic imaginaries only contributes to public unawareness of their causal links. This kind of unawareness can, of course, be spontaneous. But in many sociohistorical contexts, it is reinforced by elite-determined policy driven by the fear that lay awareness of its own powers and often passive collaboration in constituting and sustaining the regime could destabilize its foundations.[31]

---

[29] See on this subject the works of Erving Goffman, *The Presentation of Self in Everyday Life* (Garden City, NY: Doubleday, 1959); *Strategic Interaction* (Philadelphia: University of Pennsylvania Press, 1969).

[30] Donald MacKenzie in his brilliant book *An Engine, Not a Camera: How Financial Models Shape Markets* (Cambridge, MA: MIT Press, 2006) has shown how financial markets of the kind that collapsed in September 2008 are created and sustained by imaginaries whose public credibility is reinforced by scientific economic models and mathematical elegance that exceed their sustainable performativity.

[31] The September 2008 collapse of Wall Street and its aftermath have had precisely such effects of shaking the very foundations of the financial market, revealing public credulity and ignorance of how it works.

In many respects, this is also the case with regard to the legal system. Public perceptions of the law, the courts, and the judicial process are usually oblivious of the extent to which the law and legal institutions hinge, as Vico observed, on certain imaginary universals. First-year law students are often surprised to learn that moral principles and justice are rarely useful in elucidating the ways in which the legal system works. Furthermore, whereas people are usually aware of the fact that in democratic systems the legislative process consists of political battles that obey political logic, they seldom stop to wonder how the law, the product of such intense and evident political struggles, suddenly becomes apolitical as a consequence of legislation. What is the mechanism whereby people change perception and regard the law as apolitical, expecting the judicial process to be generally free of political considerations?

Despite the profound differences between religious and public economic discourses, references to entities and issues such as God and revelation or, conversely, to market and inflation are hypostatized in both contexts. By contrast, legal discourse is much more consonant with a deliberate language of (legal) fictions in relating anthropomorphically to entities such as the sovereign or the business corporation.

Generally, it seems that in the more esoteric circles of theologians, economists, scientists, jurists, and other professional circles insulated from the public gaze, the necessity of fictions as institutional building blocks and regulatory devices is more readily acknowledged. It is mostly in these confined group contexts that reflexive critical orientations that admit the strict instrumentality, plasticity, and fragility of constitutive or regulatory fictions may be engaged without disrupting their sociopolitical performative efficacy.[32] Representatives of the established order are always on guard against what they perceive as the danger that elements of this esoteric, elite culture of skepticism, criticism, and reflexivity will permeate the public sphere and disrupt the performative efficacy of the imaginaries upholding the system.[33]

Censorship is only one of the most obvious instruments at the disposal of governments, as well as of other organizations, to protect an unreflective near automatic acceptance of the imaginary at the basis of their respective systems. Social thinkers such as Karl Marx, Émile Durkheim, and Michel Foucault

---

[32] Legal theorist Laurence H. Tribe has criticized the tendency to relate to the law or the state as kinds of given objects or reified pre-legal entities. He believes that a more plastic view of the law and the state that recognizes the normative-political underpinnings of such givens would be more hospitable to the judicial protection of human rights and freedom. See his "Curvature of Constitutional Space: What Lawyers Can Learn From Modern Physics" in Theodore L. Becker (ed.), *Quantum Politics: Applying Quantum Theory to Political Phenomena* (New York: Praeger, 1991), pp. 169–99.

[33] Yaron Ezrahi, "The Distribution and Redistribution of Political Reflexivity in Contemporary Democracy" in *Reflecting on Reflexivity*, Terry Evans and Don Handelman (eds.), (forthcoming). See also my "Modes of Reasoning and the Politics of Authority in the Modern State" in David R. Olson and Nancy Torrance (eds.), *Modes of Thought: Explorations in Culture and Cognition* (Cambridge: Cambridge University Press, 1996), pp. 72–89.

exposed the use of far subtler sociocultural strategies for maintaining a hegemonic order, strategies that do not necessarily entail the use of naked force, rather utilizing education, medicine, science, law, psychology, ideology, and the arts.

Societies may, nevertheless, experience instances in which the general imaginal structure and foundations of the world in which they live are suddenly exposed. Such rare sudden revelations can be precious moments in which opportunities for social and individual choice are discernible. The chain reaction triggered by the Tunisian revolt of early 2011 in several Arab countries illustrates the contagious potential of an event that suddenly induces a sense of new, formerly unthinkable, political possibilities of choice. In the field of finance, a collapse of the banking system of the kind that took place in the United States in September 2008 and its aftermath have had precisely such effects of shaking the very foundations of the financial market by exposing to the public its own credulity and ignorance of how the system really works. Part of the revelation was that it has been largely this public ignorance that has helped this faulty system to operate. For better or for worse, such crises of practice usually entail similar crises of faith. Public faith in the progressive character of industrial developments has been shaken by growing evidence of its deleterious effects on the environment and on human health. Such revelatory erosion of public trust has been dramatically demonstrated by the impact of leaking nuclear reactors in Japan and elsewhere on public faith in this novel source of energy. Similarly, in some circles, trust in fundamental elements of religious imaginary has been shaken by the efficacy of modern medical treatment of acute illnesses.

By repudiating established religious doctrines and practices and instating alternative ones, the Reformation generated many situations in which parts of society could recognize the fragility of the religious imagination that was hypostatized and institutionalized in earlier periods, triggering an ongoing war of religious imaginaries of order.[34] In our own times, acknowledgment of the flimsiness and contingency of a hegemonic imaginary and of its underlying belief system may lead sectors of the public to realize its involuntary, unconscious previous adherence to the creations of its own imagination. Mary Douglas observes that "in most forms of society hidden sequences catch individuals in unforeseen traps and hurl them down paths they never chose."[35] What Douglas describes here is precisely the workings of the performative imagination when unhindered by reflexivity and by awareness of the possibility of choice and the risk of disaster.[36]

---

[34] See John B. Knipping, *Iconography of the Counter-Reformation in the Netherlands: Heaven on Earth*, 2 vols. (Nieuwkoop: De Graaff, 1974).

[35] Mary Douglas, *How Institutions Think* (New York: Syracuse University Press, 1986), p. 42.

[36] An example from antiquity is that famously only following three hopeless rebellions against Roman rule in Palestine between 66 CE and 132 CE did the Jewish minority shift from messianic visions of triumph to pragmatic adjustment to the limits of its power against Rome.

The capacity to unreflexively reify and hypostatize imagined objects and agencies bespeaks the workings of the performative imagination at the peak of its powers. Instead of regarding labels such as "public opinion" or the "public sphere" as imaginaries that despite their fictive origins produce political facts, individuals and communities imagine them as preexisting socio-institutional givens in the external world. This acceptance without questioning is largely what grants commonsense imaginaries of reality immense power as social and political coordinating devices. It is noteworthy that primarily (though not exclusively) in authoritarian regimes, one can often discern a large gap between officially endorsed and popular imaginaries of the political and moral orders. When such gaps become extremely wide, they create a progressive legitimacy deficit that, if not contained by fear of violence, can lead to unrest and revolution.

We can conclude that the performative function of the political imagination is conceptually all-encompassing. The very division of the composing imagination into reflective, fictive, and instrumental modes and the dynamics of their interaction grounds its potential for performing a wide repertoire of scripts and strategies for the creation of diverse domains of human creativity and experience.

The sense of experiencing the real world, or of having an experience of the real is usually reinforced by a host of factors geared for the production of what is often referred to as "reality effects." These factors include repetitions that foster a sense of familiarity and fulfilled expectations and also offer a temporal framing of events and agents (particularly in the mass media) as simultaneous social experiences that thereby appear to listeners and spectators as external facts.[37] These reality effects, in particular the materialistic externalization of events and agencies as objects of actual or possible sense experience in political space-times, are necessary for creating the imaginary of an objective sociopolitical world as a guide to and constraint on individual and group behavior. The reality status of political events and agents depends on successful inhibition of a potentially contaminating reflexive-reflective public awareness of the role played by the performative imaginations in generating the sociopolitical world, not just its verisimilitude.

Of particular significance in this discussion are those reality effects produced by behavioral indicators or by the assumption on the part of each individual that other people are coparticipants-witnesses to the same events and objects that one experiences. Albert Einstein was keenly aware of the importance of this social factor in the commonsense construal of physical facts or events as objective. He thought that such socially generated reality effects, which create the popular imaginary of the objective world, may block lay understanding of scientific notions of the world. To illustrate his point, Einstein proposed the example of the common experience of lightning as an objective external event.

[37] See Daniel Dayan and Elihu Katz, *Media Events: The Live Broadcasting of History* (Cambridge, MA: Harvard University Press, 1992).

He observes that, at first, the experience "it is lightning" seems personal. But when a person who experiences the sensation of lightning also experiences the behavior of other people who seem to relate to his own experience of lightning, then, argues Einstein, that experience is

no longer interpreted as an exclusively personal experience, but as an experience of other persons.... In this way the interpretation that "it is lightning" which originally entered into the consciousness as an "experience," is now also interpreted as an [objective] "event." It is just the sum total of all events that we mean when we speak of the "real external world."[38]

While he was critical of this process of construing commonsense reality, Einstein's insight is very valuable for our purposes. If even a singular physical experience such as lightning can be externalized as an objective event merely by virtue of its perceptual socialization when discrete individuals located in different places experience *each other* as having the experience of lightning simultaneously, an ostensibly similar mode of sensory social sharing of images can also generate commonsense imaginaries of objective, external political realities.[39] No wonder Einstein's own physics greatly contributed to the progressive mutual disengagement of common sense and scientific imaginaries of the real world, to the widening gap between, in Einstein's own words, what is "seen" and what is actually "happening."

Mindful of the role of the popular imagination in producing self-embodying imaginaries, Benedict Anderson has associated the imagination of socially simultaneous events and agents with the very creation of society and the objectification of the nation. Drawing on Walter Benjamin, Anderson stresses the role of the secular modern concept of "homogeneous empty time" as enabling a sense of socially experienced simultaneity which is "transverse, cross-time, marked not by prefiguring and fulfilment but by temporal coincidence measured by clock and calendar." He assigns the modern novel and modern mass newspapers the role of creating images of simultaneously socially experienced events that coproduce the events themselves as well as the community that experiences them as objective.

Whereas Charles Taylor sees the simultaneous experience of co-occurring events as an aspect of the profanization of time in modern societies, a process that in his opinion has despiritualized and disenchanted modern politics, Anderson sees it as the very basis for the construction of modern society. His example is taken from a case appearing in Filipino literature, according to which a particular social event such as a party is "discussed by hundreds of unnamed

---

[38] Albert Einstein, *Relativity: The Special and the General Theory*, R. W. Lawson (trans.), fifteenth edition (New York: Crown Publishers, 1961), p. 123. For a wider discussion of Einstein's conceptions of common sense and scientific notions of reality see Yaron Ezrahi, "Einstein and the Light of Reason" in Gerald Holton and Yehuda Elkana (eds.), pp. 253–78.

[39] See Yaron Ezrahi, "Einstein's Unintended Legacy: The Critique of Common-Sense Realism and Post-Modern Politics" in Gerald Holton, Peter L. Galison and Silvan S. Schweber (eds.), *Einstein for the 21st Century* (Princeton: Princeton University Press, 2008).

people, who do not know each other, in quite different parts of Manila, in a particular month of a particular decade [thus] immediately conjur[ing] up the imagined community."[40] In other words, each experience of an event or a fact as public combines the fashioning of the objects of perception with the construction of society as a perceiving agency. This process transmits the sense of experiencing objective events or entities to the individual encounter.

In the course of time, the widening gap between common sense and scientific imaginings of the real noted by Einstein has rendered contemporary common sense particularly vulnerable to the resurgence of powerful influences of religion, anti-Enlightenment popular beliefs, and the cinematic imagination. As we will see by the end of this book, the combination of these old and new influences has been very significant for the shaping of the postmodern political imagination and its role in the making of postmodern politics. The power of commonsense perceptions of simultaneous social sharing of events and other facts plays a major role in generating contemporary imaginaries of reality and democratic politics. The powers of electronic and printed mass media have been pivotal to the expansion of a sense of simultaneity, transcending spatial barriers. In many respects, these developments contribute to the process of globalization. The relations between the globalization of horizontal mass communication systems and the snowball impact of local political and economic events on the global system is obvious but not yet sufficiently understood. If governments do not succeed in significantly controlling these processes, they are likely to radically change the power relations between publics and their governments and generate new kinds of local and global politically performative imaginaries.

It seems that, despite new obstacles and setbacks, the modern western tradition of equating the publicly visible with the real has persisted and even been reinforced by contemporary mass media, although the actual image of the real and the process of making images of the real have been profoundly altered. When the electronic visual mass media reports on events and actions, the awareness that everyone else is either watching or can watch the same televised event lends an often merely virtual and sometimes only partly real event, at least momentarily, the status of a solid external fact. But in the contemporary fast-moving media environment, consecutive events, each of which may be granted a momentary status of being real, add up neither to a coherent nor a stable picture of factual reality.

I have argued that popular conceptions of reality are characterized by unreflective acceptance of certain aspects of experience as given, compelling facts, as uncontestable parts of commonsense reality that leave no room for choices. I show, however, that while a process of historic change in commonsense imaginaries of the real has typically involved mere shifts between equally uncritically accepted imaginaries, the most recent transition from modern to postmodern

---

[40] Benedict Anderson, *Imagined Communities: Reflections on the Origin and Spread of Nationalism* (London: Verso, 1996).

versions of common sense may have produced an unprecedented awareness of the actual possibility of choice between alternative imaginaries of reality as well as an apprehension of their eclectic composition. But popular awareness of the possibility of choice undoubtedly depends on the workings of imaginal clusters or meta-imaginaries that encourage the coexistence of multiple repertories of political world-making programs of the kind advanced, for instance, by writers like Donna Haraway and Bruno Latour.

The introduction of alternatives and choices implies the possibility that some such imaginal clusters be considered as particularly emancipatory, that is, as enlarging the range of political possibilities. This will bring us later to the performative imaginaries of freedom, which constitute a major part of the political imagination of democracy. But now I turn to examine the workings of competing strategies of political imagining.

4

Naturalization and Historicization as Strategies of the Political Imagination

Political worlds are made by human groups layering mostly unconsciously selected self-realizing, self-institutionalizing imaginaries naturalized by the performative political imagination. As we will see, an adjective such as *naturalized* is in itself but a fragment of a political imaginary that had constituted nature as the epitome of the external-real and that still carries some of its former force.

One may wonder why only some imaginings or fictions become imaginaries, that is, acquire performative power in the political sphere, or why certain shifts in the status of key metaphors correspond to certain changes in patterns of behavior. I am not sure I can respond to these questions satisfactorily. In the course of this book, I suggest that a number of fictions, those selected as behaviorally productive regulating imaginaries, often seem more consistent with prevailing values, memories, interests, and aspirations, and are often more effective in evoking emotional attachments. Obviously the very idea that, as a political order, democracy rests on an identifiable number of necessary fictions is a heuristic assumption for the exploration of the role of the political imagination in the making and unmaking of democratic regimes.

Legal, religious, or political world making involves the enactment of elaborate systems of classifications and divisions.[1] Imagined objects, agencies, and processes can be classified or framed as natural, artificial, causal, fictive, abstract, visible, invisible, parts, wholes, historical, sacred, ethical, unethical, legal, private, public, and political. There are, of course, other such categories to which I shall devote some attention, such as poetic, aesthetic, universal, organic, and so forth.

Obviously, the imagined agents, objects, and processes that populate any religious, political, or other kinds of worlds are selectively fixed and interwoven within established frames or classifications. Internal relations among various classified imaginings and the shifts in their boundaries may have great

---

[1] On the enactment of classification systems and the ritual construction of imagined worlds see Don Handelman's *Models and Mirrors, Towards an Anthropology of Public Events* (Cambridge: Cambridge University Press, 1990).

performative political significance. Examining how such categorizations are formed, embedded, and slackened, how they interrelate and are used in the context of social interactions, may yield valuable insights into the evolution and deterioration of political worlds.[2] Lorraine Daston observes that:

[I]t is one of the oddest oddities of current intellectual life that nature, once the battering ram of social criticism (think of Condorcet), and history, once the bulwark of tradition (think of Burke), have exchanged political valences. History now purportedly subverts the status quo with the counterexamples; nature purportedly shores it up with stubborn facts.

To this analytical assertion, Daston adds her personal view that "we need a politics which can argue honestly as politics – without nature, without history."[3] Daston's discussion provides a very useful point of departure for our brief exploration of strategies employed by the political imagination because it simultaneously engages three such strategies: naturalizing, historicizing, and politicizing. While I am doubtful that there is, as Daston seems to think, anything like pure politics as politics unmediated by naturalizing, historicizing, legalizing, or other imaginal frames, I think she is quite right in suggesting that naturalizing and historicizing have switched places over time as principal strategies for legitimizing and delegitimizing the established order, although both continue to coexist in some spheres of the same society.

As resources of the political imagination, nature and history consist respectively of multiple layers of meanings revealed in their etymology. In some cultures, the image of nature is primarily instrumental, while in others it is divine or poetic. A mechanistic scientific image of nature may, as the record shows, easily reinforce a utilitarian view of nature as a resource to be exploited and harnessed for human ends. A religious perspective of nature as a divine script, or a poetic perspective of nature as a sanctuary for the solitary individual soul, or a utopian depiction of nature as the embodiment of a primordial harmony and a model for a moral society, may discourage instrumental utilitarian orientations. Many of the elements developed and used in the different perspectives of nature are preserved in the "genetic" fabric of its imaginary and may be invoked or applied to any given context.[4]

---

[2] For an illuminating study of the ways in which classification systems are translated into working "bureaucratic logic" in Israeli society, see Don Handelman, *Nationalism and the Israeli State: Bureaucratic Logic in Public Events* (Oxford: Berg, 2004), especially pp. 21–32.

[3] Lorraine Daston, "Enlightenment Fears, Fears of Enlightenment" in Keith Michael Baker and Peter Hanns Reill (eds.), *What's Left of Enlightenment?* (Stanford: Stanford University Press, 2001), p. 128.

[4] On the tensions between instrumental and moral or poetical orientations toward nature see, for instance, Sheila Jasanoff, *Designs on Nature: Science and Democracy in Europe and the United States* (Princeton: Princeton University Press, 2005), pp. 171–202; Herbert L. Sussman, *Fact into Figure: Typology in Carlyle, Ruskin, and the Pre-Raphaelite Brotherhood* (Columbus: Ohio State University Press, 1977); Martin Wiener, *English Culture and the Decline of the Industrial Spirit, 1850–1880* (Cambridge: Cambridge University Press, 1982).

Similarly, as a resource of the political imagination, historical time has proven extremely elastic. Time frames may be cyclically closed or linearly open to an infinite future; time may be imagined as cosmic, historical, religious, secular, social, biographical, or as a combination of such frames. It may be fractured into small particles such as seconds or gathered into large units such as centuries, millennia, and so forth.

Obviously, any such time frame will have different connotations depending on the contextual narrative. The movement of time may signify entropy or progress, deterministic or voluntary processes, repetition or regeneration. Time frames may be synchronized to match the movements of celestial bodies, to account for the rise and fall of nations, or to convey the stream of individual consciousness.[5]

These different perspectives have yielded a wealth of versatile natural and temporal images that have been woven into the fabric of opposing political imaginaries such as those of liberal individualism and racism, aristocracy and democracy. For instance, Edmund Burke describes the aristocracy as "the great oaks that shade a country," using a metaphor of robust and majestic nature to buttress the legitimacy of the monarchic-aristocratic class. Thomas Paine, however, uses a negative image of nature to support the attitude of the French populace, who "began to consider aristocracy as a kind of fungus growing out of the corruption of society that could not be admitted even as a branch of it."[6] Burke attaches a corresponding image of time to his naturalization of the aristocracy. He observes that the English way is

always acting as if in the presence of canonized forefathers, the spirit of freedom, leading in itself to misrule and excess, is tempered with awful gravity.... We procure reverence to our civil institutions on the principle upon which nature teaches us to revere individual men; on account of their age; and on account of those to whom they are descended.[7]

This Burkean use of time to legitimize aristocratic genealogies clearly differs from the use of time implicit in Tocqueville's observation that in America, democracy not only "makes every man forget his ancestors, but it hides his descendants and separates his contemporaries from him. It throws him back forever upon himself alone and threatens in the end to confine him entirely within the solitude of his own heart."[8] In contrast to Burke's attempt to enlist

---

[5] See Reinhart Koselleck, *Futures Past: On the Semantics of Historical Time*, Keith Tribe (trans.) (New York: Columbia University Press, 1985); Gabriel Motzkin, *Time and Transcendence: Secular History, the Catholic Reaction, and the Rediscovery of the Future* (Dordrecht: Kluwer Academic Publishers, 1992).

[6] Burke is quoted in Keith Thomas's *Man and the Natural World: A History of the Modern Sensibility* (New York: Pantheon Books, 1984), p. 218. For Paine, see his essay "The Rights of Man" (1791–2) in *The Thomas Paine Reader* (Harmondsworth: Penguin, 1987), p. 241.

[7] See Burke's "Reflections on the Revolution in France" in Jerry Z. Muller (ed.), *Conservatism: An Anthology of Social and Political Thought from David Hume to the Present* (Princeton: Princeton University Press, 1997), p. 93.

[8] Alexis de Tocqueville, *Democracy in America*, Harvey C. Mansfield and Delba Winthrop (trans. and ed.) (first pub. 1835; Chicago: University of Chicago Press, 2002), p. 484.

both nature and history to reinforce the political imaginary of aristocracy, Tocqueville discerns in America the uses of ahistorical naturalization as a strategy to delegitimize historical rationales for hierarchy and political authority and to rationalize instead democratic equality. A contemporary Communitarian philosopher, Charles Taylor, has regarded this as a regrettable shift stemming from the fact that "the modern social imaginary no longer sees the greater translocal entities as grounded in some other, sometimes higher, than common action in secular time."[9]

While the particular political imaginaries of democracy have obviously varied with time and context, drawing upon different nuances of naturalization and historicization, there is some basic continuity in their thematic foci. As strategies of the democratic political imagination, naturalization and historicization have usually been mobilized for the sake of diverse goals such as criticizing the centralization of governmental power, empowering the individual or the community as political actors and sources of authority vis-à-vis the government, substantiating voluntaristic notions of politics, voluntary obedience to the law, and voluntary associations. They have also been pivotal tools for building an imaginary of freedom as a creative and potentially progressive human capacity.

Basically, naturalization was a powerful democratic weapon against antidemocratic conventions, while historicization proved to be the ultimate foundation of the democratic imaginary of politics as a human enterprise. Whereas nature was often conceived of as the provider of the program, the basic rationale and principles of a free society of equals, history was regarded as the record of human struggles to achieve it. The naturalization of rights and laws was a means to consolidate them as the foundations of a new set of conventions to be performed in historical time by revolutions, reforms, and legislation.

Already in the fourteenth century, Marsiglio of Padua, running the risk of persecution by the Inquisition, composed his very influential work *The Defender of the Peace* (1324), in which he asserted that the natural and the supernatural are to be thought of as completely separate spheres, thus relocating politics and government within the sphere of rationally intelligible nature. By invoking Aristotelian nature as the cause of the state, and by redefining the law as manmade rather than conceived by a divine legislator, he framed a dualistic political imaginary that proved instrumental in the processes whereby the power and authority of the Christian Church were increasingly restricted. It is of course ironic although not surprising that, whereas Marsiglio endorsed the naturalization of the state as a means of circumscribing the powers of religious authority in civil affairs, many centuries later the strategy of naturalization was applied to individual human rights largely in order to limit the authority and powers of the modern state.

In the western democratic tradition, summoning nature in order to redefine the rights of man as primordial, presocial, and prepolitical, and also to define

---

[9] Charles Taylor, *Modern Social Imaginaries* (Durham: Duke University Press, 2004), p. 155.

the law as impersonal and objective, had the effect of redefining the meaning of "obedience to the law" from "following a command" to "following one's own reason as guided by the laws of nature." The dualism between nature and culture, between the given and the artificial, has provided the bedrock for a powerful modern critique of social, legal, and political practices and institutions. This dichotomy has proved essential for the eventual grounding of the democratic demand that governmental actions be transparent like the open "Book of Nature," and for reconciling the idea of nature as a whole created by a divine intelligence with the imaginary of society as a system, the free interplay of whose parts, like those of a mechanical clock, lead not to chaos but to order and harmony.

The constant anxiety surrounding the need to legitimize and authorize the law has often encouraged a simultaneous appeal to diverse, even seemingly incompatible imaginaries as sources of authority. It is not surprising, therefore, to find a coexistence of naturalization, humanization, and deification of the origins of the law in one and the same context. Perhaps one of the most striking examples is the concurrent emergence of these three strategies of the imagination as explicit and implicit frames of the law during the French Revolution. The revolutionary cult of the law combined, in its presentation, the imaginary of (Rousseau's) general will, stressing the *natural* grounds of the rights of men and citizens as well as commitments to freedom and equality; *humanizing* politics through the historical act of revolution and *iconographically* and rhetorically embodying the Declaration of the Rights of Man and Citizen in the image of the Mosaic tablets.[10]

Jonathan Ribner surveys many examples of visual representations of French revolutionary law in the shape of engravings in stone or metal within the conventional iconography of the Ten Commandments, the rounded Mosaic tablets. He notes that the final article of the 1793 constitution explicitly states that the texts of the constitution and of the Declaration of the Rights of Man and Citizen are "engraved on tablets in the midst of the assembly and public places."[11] Ribner points out that "the theme of divine legislation actually crossed political boundaries. Moses and the Ten Commandments and the legendary lawgivers Numa and Lycurgus were invoked by revolutionary republicans, Napoleonic authoritarians, Restoration ultra-royalists, and Orleanist constitutional monarchists."[12] Similarly, the imaginary of nature with its multiple layers of meanings has also been mobilized and integrated into diverse and often contradictory political imaginaries.

The grounds for construing an image of nature as extra-social and therefore as a source of authority external to and potentially above human, social, religious, or political authorities, were likely established by the Epicureans and the

---

[10] Jonathan P. Ribner, *Broken Tablets: The Cult of the Law in French Art from David to Delacroix* (Berkeley: University of California Press, 1993).

[11] Ibid., pp. 6, 8, 10, 13, 15, 18.

[12] Ibid., p. 4.

Stoics, who conceived of phenomena in merely physical terms, that is, as devoid of any relation to human conduct. For the Epicureans, the idea or knowledge of nature was not so much aimed at understanding, but was regarded as part and parcel of a philosophical way of life in which human beings could achieve tranquility and pleasure.[13] Peace of mind in relation to natural phenomena meant, in this context, reducing the anxiety concerning natural catastrophes or extraordinary events such as eclipses, which were interpreted as signs of the gods' wrath and divine retribution for human insurrection.

The Epicureans sought to fashion an image of nature that would allay human fears of celestial and natural phenomena. This benign image of nature drew on the physics of Democritus and that of other pre-Socratic materialist Greek philosophers and eventually found its way into a more elaborate mechanistic image of the universe. The Stoics also appropriated an image of nature that could foster inner tranquility, even though, by comparison to the Epicureans, they fashioned nature as the embodiment of universal reason operating through a system of necessary causes.[14]

While Greek philosophers, such as the disciples of the school of Mellitus at the beginning of the sixth century B.C., propagated images of nature as more narrowly theoretical entities instrumental in achieving their central aim of understanding and explaining the world, the images disseminated by the Epicureans and the Stoics were apparently intended to be more psychologically and ethically oriented toward the performance of particular forms of life. They taught their followers that imagining nature as indifferent to the gods or as an autonomous causal system would induce the inner states of serenity and modes of conduct they aspired to attain.

Epicurus's idea that physical knowledge can liberate humans from false fears that natural disasters constitute divine retribution for their transgressions was preserved in a very evocative didactic poem, "De Rerum Natura" ("On the Nature of Things"), written by a Roman poet-philosopher named Lucretius almost two thousand years ago.[15] This magnificent poem, the manuscript copies of which disappeared during centuries of Christian hegemony, was rediscovered around the end of the fifteenth century and effectively transmitted secular Epicurean notions of nature's indifference to humanity to early modern thinkers and writers like Machiavelli, Montaigne, and Shakespeare. Thomas Jefferson's library contained several copies.

During the modern period, imaginaries of nature deriving from these Greek traditions were geared toward the fulfillment of manifold goals, such as the advancement of objective scientific knowledge and the fashioning of a vision

---

[13] Pierre Hadot, *What is Ancient Philosophy?* M. Chase (trans.) (Cambridge, MA: The Belknap Press of Harvard University Press), pp. 113–26; ibid. pp. 126–39.

[14] Ibid.

[15] Titus Lucretius Carus, *De Rerum Natura*, W. H. D. Rouse (trans.), Loeb Classical Library 181, second edition, Martin Ferguson Smith (ed.) (Cambridge, MA: Harvard University Press, 1975).

of technology as a neutral ameliorant of nature. In the political sphere, such images have also been employed to buttress the constitution of anti-monarchic, anti-hierarchical legal and political systems grounded in presocial human rights. More recently, a green image of nature often redefined as "environment" has featured as a buffer against technological-industrial society and as a constraint on an expanding ruthless global industrial capitalism.

Each of these images of nature has become a key component of a distinct modern performative political imaginary. The change in the status of science that has taken place in the postmodern era is partly related to the fact that the clustered imaginings of nature and science, while still instrumentally powerful, have lost much of their former performative efficacy in the spheres of culture, ethics, and politics.

The Greek idea of nature as a system independent of society has given rise to a host of later developments crucial to the emergence of new modes of democratic imagining and shaping politics. As a primordial given, intelligible to human reason yet associated with pagan and Christian imaginaries of cosmic harmony, nature was later invoked as a powerful means to induce consensus, resolve conflicts, and rationalize individual and social claims against established governments. Above all, it became an emblem of necessity, circumscribing human freedom and politics.[16]

Considering its role in the rhetoric of modern revolutions, natural law has functioned also as an emancipatory imaginary. It has been suggested that if it were not "for natural law there would probably have been no American and no French revolutions, nor would the great ideas of freedom and equality have found their way into the law-books after having found it into the hearts of men."[17] The expression "the hearts of men" obviously evokes Rousseau's famous assertions at the end of the First Discourse that, prior to society, the principles of virtue are "engraved in all hearts" and that "freedom is a gift [of] nature" to every individual. Rousseau insists that society, government, and even parents have no right to divest individuals of their natural freedom.

Rousseau's remarkable influence on the political imagery of the French revolutionaries attests to his exceptional ability to fashion perhaps the most morally and emotionally persuasive rhetoric of freedom and equality in modern times. By idealizing the virtues of presocial man and by anchoring the rights of human beings in the "state of nature," Rousseau carved an image of nature that would – as the historical record indicates – serve as a continual source of revolutionary and reformatory energy and as a basis for effective criticism of social and political institutions. By naturalizing freedom and equality while socializing and historicizing private property and inequality, he anticipated modern ideologues such as Paine and Marx, who exploited the idea of

---

[16] Judith N. Shklar, *Legalism: Law, Morals, and Political Trials* (Cambridge, MA: Harvard University Press, 1986), pp. 67–8.

[17] A. P. d'Entrèves, *Natural Law: An Historical Survey* (New York: Harper and Row, 1951), p. 13.

nature as an unconventional political weapon in their arsenal, and he contributed to the fashioning of the most effective slogans of the American, French, and Russian revolutions.

In the course of time, and despite the influence of the poetic Romantic imaginary within some circles – part of which can also be attributed to Rousseau, much of the moral-political authority of nature transferred to the field of science, but only insofar as it could be perceived as a believable representation of the presocial, extra-social, and prepolitical laws of the objective world. This authority declined, as I hinted earlier, when the imaginary of nature was largely replaced by the imaginary of the environment, reflecting the emergence of an interactive imaginary of nature and society and a growing convergence between the authority of science, particularly technology, and that of social and political values and interests.

As a normative image that induces society and government to respect fundamental social rights, nature appears almost at the very beginning of the French Declaration of the Rights of Man and Citizen of 1789: "The representatives of the French people convened in the National Assembly ... have resolved to set out in a solemn declaration the natural inalienable and sacred human rights." The French insisted on the separation of church and state, stressing the secular character of the latter and, unlike the Americans, refraining from reference to God the Creator, yet bestowing the attribute of sacredness to natural human rights, thus revealing the religious imaginal layer underlying the imagery of a primordial nature.

These twofold religious-secular connotations conferred upon nature indicate the extraordinary power elicited by the modern democratic political imagination, power aimed at revolutionizing old regimes and limiting the powers of new ones. As the expression "sacred human rights" suggests, the revolutionaries constructed an idealized, religiously suggestive image of nature that drew much of its political revolutionary force from the Greek and Roman paradigmatic contrast between nature and convention, a binary opposition that privileged the former and reinforced it by divine sanction.

The particular powers of a more explicit divine "sacralization" of nature in America were acknowledged by the framers of the American constitution. The Declaration of Independence of July 4, 1776 states that the "the laws of Nature and Nature's God entitle them" (the people of America) to assume the power to separate from the British empire. Then follows the famous declaration: "We hold these Truths to be self-evident, that all Men are created equal, that they are endowed by their Creator with certain unalienable Rights that among these are Life, Liberty, and the pursuit of Happiness." Naturalization of rights is explicitly supported here by sacralization.

While naturalization and sacralization of the laws and the people's power respectively reflect the urge to anchor the organization and management of common life in transhuman grounds, the powers of secular and sacral naturalizations are, indeed, philosophically or conceptually incompatible. The ability to surmount such contradictions and draw upon antithetical worlds of ideas and images demonstrates the unique political power of the political imagination to contain contradictions and its advantage over reason as a political resource.

The case of natural rights provides a good illustration of such a *Concordia/discordia*. On one hand, rights that have been naturalized through the prism of a secular-mechanistic image of nature suggest the enforcement of extra-human limitations on political power, will, or convention. On the other hand, natural rights, when portrayed as the gift of God's nature, are endowed with special spiritual and moral force. In a society in which secular and religious citizens must coexist, and in which even the secular citizens are (consciously or not) prompted by moral ideas and aesthetic forms inherited from the imaginaries and metaphysics of a medieval religious universe underlying secularized imaginaries and rhetoric, the laminated character of the imaginary of nature has a clear performative advantage.

Even such a material-secular envisioning of nature as an amoral, indifferent system carried a substratum of religious vestiges that supplemented the natural imaginary with a moral-spiritual dimension. This subliminal undercurrent played a major role in the endorsement of human agency, in the affirmation of man's rights to participate in the political order – stressing man's superiority to beast – and in the delegitimizing of slavery. This tendency has been essential for idealizing democratic politics, for shaping the political as combining elements of naturalization, sacralization, and humanization.

By creating a divide between creatures chained by the inexorable, causal laws of nature and human beings who can freely use nature to transcend its limitations, the imagination also laid the basis for the implementation of categories of classification geared to support nondemocratic hierarchical political orientations. Such a manipulative use of the imagination is demonstrated in man's creation and perpetuation of a slaveholding society. Categories that cast "native," "primitive," or "savage" peoples as belonging to nature were instrumental in the colonial endeavor to fashion a conception of indigenous peoples as belonging in an inferior, material, precivilization sphere. These aboriginals were then juxtaposed to European or, more generally, western peoples considered a higher species of human beings dwelling in the sphere of history.[18] Another example, as I intimated earlier, is the use made of the dichotomy of nature and history and animal sociobiology to rationalize the subordination of women to men. Donna Haraway criticizes feminist writers like Shulamit Firestone for attributing the subordination of women in the body politic to the organic demands of reproduction, thus opting for a historical materialist

---

[18] See the fascinating juxtaposition of the presuppositions of the respective exhibitions of primitive peoples still bounded by nature in the close company of the animal world and the exhibition of the art of "superior" peoples who live in history and supposedly belong at the top of the evolutionary ladder in Mieke Bal's comparison between the exhibitions of The American Museum of Natural History and The Metropolitan Museum of Art, "Telling, Showing, Showing Off," *Critical Inquiry*, vol.18, no. 3 (Spring 1992): 556–94.

account that turns the female body into the "ultimate enemy" rather than one that focuses on social and political forces.[19]

Alongside the hierarchical image of man's superiority to other natural creatures, extended in the colonial period to include primitive communities (which must be ruled or civilized by advanced human beings), the dividing line between society and nature also generated an idealized imaginary of natural man. The "Noble Savage" represented an archetype of primordial human innocence, of man untainted by the corrupting influence of society, culture, history, and politics.

These often coexisting yet antithetical images of nature as both limiting and/or empowering, lofty and/or debased, innocent and/or predatory were invoked or emphasized in different contexts, thus investing the strategy of naturalization with alternating binary meanings.

Despite the flaws and inconsistencies of the modern naturalization of the political order, that is, imagining this order as founded on and constrained by natural law – by laws deriving, as it were, from nature rather than man – it was a crucial strategy of the democratic political imagination. Insofar as the laws of nature and subsequently also natural rights were assumed to be transparent to natural reason, the political strategy of naturalization combined two different imaginaries of nature: nature as the realm of presocial universal and necessary causes and nature as the transhuman, partly divine source of the principles of a constitution to which all reasonable human beings could voluntarily adhere.

The welding of impersonal necessity and volitional human conduct, modeled after nature's laws, endowed western law with unique performative powers. As A. P. d'Entrèves notes, the law of nature rested on the claim that the validity of the law does not hinge on force but on reason: "It was an appeal to the intrinsic dignity of the law, rather than to its power of compulsion."[20] This imaginary of the law in which the external, the divine, the immutable, and the necessary were combined with human obedience enfranchised by natural reason sheds light on the grounds whereby, even in its most secular contexts, the declining force of imaginaries that entrench rights and laws in nature could not impoverish them.

There was something uniquely powerful in clustering together, in a single imaginary, contradictory principles or attributes such as necessity, voluntarism, secular universality, and sacrality, contradictions that enabled one to uphold in a flexible, dynamic way the mystic authority of the law and the dignity of man as a free citizen. Such a cluster facilitated the achievement of a balance that later became unsustainable when this configuration fell apart.

This multilayered, fecund integration of politico-legal imaginaries may largely account for the performative efficacy of the belief that:

---

[19] Donna J. Haraway, *Simians, Cyborgs, and Women: The Reinvention of Nature* (London: Free Association Books, 1991), p. 10.

[20] Ibid., p. 18.

[W]ritten constitutions, upheld by judicial bodies, can effectively constrain the tyrannies of both executive force and populist majorities.... [The Founders of the American nation] had the imagination to perceive that there is a sense, mysterious as it may be, in which human rights can be seen to exist independent of privileges, gifts, and donations of the powerful, and that these rights can somehow be defined and protected by the force of law.[21]

In the context of the imaginal layers that frame the beliefs and perceptions of the Founding Fathers, they may seem, I think, less "mysterious" than Bailyn considers them. The dualism between nature and human will, between necessity and freedom, between fear of arbitrary power and the desire to render power democratically legitimate, generated a uniquely democratic imaginary of power. It "could be created and constrained at the same time."[22] As Bailyn notes, the modus operandi of this constitutional plan was not the result of a grand theory or a coherent ideology but of a myriad of compromises, adjustments, and modifications.

Furthermore, the multiple imaginings that had been brewing for hundreds of years in the West, available at that historical moment, were to be welded into an eclectic configuration clustered into a constitution and a set of institutions that, though fraught with ambiguities, formed one of the most performatively effective and enduring political regimes in modern political history. A crucial factor behind this feat was the fashioning of a normative imaginary of nature that allowed, particularly in North America, the development of a vision of a political order whose principles were free from the burden of history and the European legacy of hierarchies, privileges, and wars. These tenets derived much of their strength from a common perception of a divinely sanctioned nature untainted by civilization and not yet challenged by Darwinism.

The naturalization of law, power, and political action in a democratic context could entail the expectation of or demand for transparency in governmental procedures. This was obviously related to the legacy of the Christian notion of "the open Book of Nature," a view of God's nature as a universally legible divine script. Writing about American visions of landscape painting, Robert Hughes observed that "if the presiding metaphor of the landscape experience was that of God as supreme artist, it need only be a short step to the idea that artists were seers or priests.... If American nature was one vast church, then landscape artists were its clergy." Hughes further pointed out that "[b]etween the first Presidency of Monroe and the death of Lincoln, most writing about art in America tended to be rapturously pietistic, evangelical, and full of a breathless conviction that the visual arts could change the moral dimension of life."[23] One of the main themes of nineteenth-century American painting was

---

[21] Bernard Bailyn, *To Begin the World Anew: The Genius and Ambiguities of the American Founders* (New York: Alfred A. Knopf, 2003), pp. 4–5.

[22] Ibid., pp. 54–5.

[23] Robert Hughes, *American Visions: The Epic History of Art in America* (New York: Alfred A. Knopf, 1997), p. 139.

FIGURE 4.1. Frederic Edwin Church, *Twilight in the Wilderness*, 1860. Oil on canvas, Courtesy of the Cleveland Museum of Art.

the "distillation of light as a concretion of divine presence" (see Figure 4.1 for a popular example of this trend).[24]

In this context, to naturalize, to make governmental actions appear legible as nature, could mean to simplify and render them transparent to the public. Such association of nature, transparency, and legitimacy is prevalent in Paine's influential rhetoric. Whereas monarchic governments, he insists, rest "on the puppet-show of State and aristocracy," in "a democratic government,"

whatever are its excellences or its defects, they are visible to all. It exists not by fraud and mystery.... Nature is orderly in all her works; but ... [The monarchy] is a mode of government that counteracts nature by contrast ... the representative system always parallels with the immutable laws of nature, and meets the reason of man in every part.[25]

By naturalizing representative democratic modes of government and denaturalizing the monarchy, Paine aims to subsume an imaginary of nature comprising layers of religious, moral, and secular scientific semes of meaning into an emancipatory democratic political imaginary. The power of this move benefits from such a simultaneous spiritualization and materialization of the idea of democracy as consisting of mutually reinforcing strategies of the political imagination.

[24] John Wilmerding, *American Light: The Luminist Movement 1850–1875* (Princeton: Princeton University Press, 1989), p. 17; Barbara Novak, *American Painting of the Nineteenth Century: Realism, Idealism, and the American Experience* (New York: Praeger Publishers, 1969).
[25] Paine, "The Rights of Man," pp. 214, 283.

Democratic citizens can thus "see" their government with their own eyes and perceptibly experience the abstraction of popular sovereignty as (or as if it were) a tangible fact. Paine insisted on the materialization of democracy as a real thing, a perceptually accessible object, therefore demanding that a constitution be "not just a thing in name only, but in fact.... Wherever it cannot be produced in visible form, there is none."[26]

Naturalization, or nature as a resource of democratic political legitimizing, was also closely associated with holistic imagery of society and the state. Whereas the imagined relation between cosmology and polity was undoubtedly central in the Greek tradition, its legacy was edited into and perpetuated by Christianity and a few of its key elements were preserved further in modern secular versions of holism in science and society.[27] The idea of political society as a whole, as a system, was, from its earliest Greek beginnings, associated with the postulation of an inherent and transcendental harmony.[28] In both their ontological and analogical versions of the naturalizations of society and polity, Greek philosophers usually implied that individuals and smaller groups are just fractions of a larger whole whose place in the political order is regulated by a systemic logic usually beyond the ken of individual partial perspectives.

Such a privileged synoptic perspective to which the whole system revealed itself was, in different contexts, preserved either for god in a theocratic or religious state, for the king in a monarchy, for the philosopher in Plato's *Republic*, and finally for the scientist or the city architect in what we regard as a typically advanced society.[29] Roland Barthes suggests that the main function of the Eiffel Tower was to give Frenchmen a panoramic vision of Paris, thus materializing the imagined city as a "concrete abstraction," a whole.[30] The only way in which democratic citizens in an egalitarian society can actually see the system from a bird's-eye view or a godlike vantage point is to gaze at the city from the top of a tower, a skyscraper, or an airplane.

In the modern democratic political imagination, a secular-mechanistic metaphor of the political system could do away with the privileged synoptic

---

[26] For the previous citation and for an extensive discussion of transparency as a democratic norm, see Yaron Ezrahi, *The Descent of Icarus: Science and the Transformation of Contemporary Democracy* (Cambridge, MA: Harvard University Press, 1990), especially pp. 108–17.

[27] On the religious sources of the metaphysics of modern social and political holism see Edwin Arthur Burtt, *The Metaphysical Foundations of Modern Physical Science* (Garden City, NY: Doubleday, 1954) and Frank E. Manuel, *The Religion of Isaac Newton* (Oxford: Clarendon Press, 1974).

[28] Leo Spitzer, *Classical and Christian Ideas of World Harmony*, Anna Granville Hatcher (ed.), (Baltimore: Johns Hopkins Press, 1963).

[29] See, for instance, Yaron Ezrahi's "Modes of Reasoning and the Politics of the Modern State" in David Olson and Nancy Torrance (eds.), *Modes of Thought: Explorations in Culture and Cognition* (Cambridge: Cambridge University Press, 1996), especially pp. 72–3; Louis Dumont, *Essays on Individualism: Modern Ideology in Anthropological Perspective* (Chicago: University of Chicago Press, 1992).

[30] Roland Barthes, "The Eiffel Tower" in *A Roland Barthes Reader* (London: Vintage Classics, 1993), pp. 242–3.

perspective, while granting instead credence to the claims of scientists or experts to know the logic and the regularities of the system and, therefore, to be entitled to advise the government and to rationalize its interventions in apolitical instrumental terms.[31]

But the main latent function of the appropriation of holism by a modern democratic imaginary might have been to protect the emergent imaginings of individual freedom from the widespread fear that such freedom necessarily leads to fragmentation and chaos. In its earlier modern forms, the imagination of political freedom could entail the mere freedom of the parts to find their right place within the whole. It could later shift from traditional pyramidal hierarchies with the king at the top, followed by the aristocracy and the clergy with the common people at the base, to modern hierarchies in which the whole, a collective such as the nation or society, is above the individual or the voluntary groups conceived as its components. In such modern hierarchies, there has often been greater leverage and equality among the parts themselves.[32]

There have been respectively liberal, democratic, and anarchistic versions of this idea of freedom, constrained by the imagined systemic laws or regularities of the whole, which seemed to guarantee that individual freedoms could be compatible with harmony, stability, equality, dignity, and, above all, preservation of the integrity of the collective. Replacement of a class hierarchy with an impersonal hierarchy in which an abstract whole, such as an imagined nation, is positioned above individuals or smaller groups viewed as its components, marked a far less radical change than the emergence of the individual, since late modernity, as a whole unto himself.

One can argue that replacement of the coherent or integrated holism of modernity by fragmentary individualism and the incoherent eclecticisms of postmodernism reflects, and appeals to, profoundly different imaginaries of freedom. Because it has also involved a break with normative and ontological holism, such a shift constitutes, in many respects, a greater departure from the past (including eighteenth- and nineteenth-century democratic political imaginaries) than the shift from medieval to modern holisms.

The aspects of naturalized holism appropriated by the modern democratic political imagination as a metaphor for society or for the political community have, undoubtedly, been very different from those assumed by authoritarian nationalist regimes. In the latter, the integral logic has been conceived in terms of a far stricter conception of the relations between whole and part, granting greater leverage to the agencies representing the whole to fit the parts together and exclude elements perceived as incompatible with the system.

Characteristically, although not without important exceptions, such imaginings tended to fashion the whole in terms of organic rather than mechanistic metaphors, thus accentuating the hierarchically fixed relations among parts. In the conservative sociopolitical context, therefore, naturalization has often

---

[31] Yaron Ezrahi, *The Descent of Icarus.*
[32] See, for instance, Dumont's *Essays on Individualism.*

constituted a strategy for justifying privileged groups, validating the confinement of women to their natural procreative functions in the private domain, and excluding those who do not belong to the tribe. The very expression "the rights of man" offers an instructive illustration of the special gendered status given to man as representing humankind.

In addition to the organic naturalization of holism, of inequality, and hierarchy, conservative naturalizations expanded to include the naturalization of different versions of determinism as opposed to voluntarism (in human affairs), including the naturalization of war. Naturalized determinism has been a predominant conservative political strategy employed to denaturalize and derationalize the right to freedom of the weak, and to rationalize the claims of the strong to rule.

As a strategy of the political imagination, historicization, like naturalization, has served authoritarian, conservative, and democratic political objectives. To historicize, as well as to naturalize, can mean different things in different contexts. In the framework of religious communities, to historicize figures such as Moses, Jesus, or Muhammad has often meant strengthening religious faith by the psychological effects of realism.[33] Similarly, it is possible to discern many direct and indirect attempts to historicize miracles and mythological narratives. Such uses of the historical frame as a means to embody the sacral in the world of material, sensorially accessible facts is connected with the particular force that historicization draws from the imaginary of the humanly real. Here the continuities between the imaginary of the real, the concrete within the respective worlds of the religious, the mythological, or the modern "scientistic" (rather than scientific), is no less instructive than the unsurprising discontinuity. Strategies of historicizing have been chameleon-like in justifying or debunking claims to territory, the right to govern, or the right to rebel.

Historicization as an emancipatory political strategy has typically been combined with an imaginary of stages progressing from slavery to freedom, from darkness to light, from corruption to justice, or along any other path leading from a wretched state to redemption. Modern politics has interwoven a twofold temporal scheme: the eschatological time of the religious imagination (focusing on the final destiny of the human soul and mankind and on apocalyptic visions such as the Day of Judgment and the roads to hell or paradise) and the time frame of human history.[34]

Obviously, the historical time frame and the imaginary of the redemptive path of a nation would differ significantly from that of the emancipation of a society conceived as a collection of individuals. Hence historicization as a

---

[33] On attempts to historicize Jesus, see for instance Albert Schweitzer, *The Quest of the Historical Jesus*, John Bowden (trans. and ed.) (Minneapolis: Fortress Press, 2001); Gerd Theissen and Annette Merz, *The Historical Jesus: A Comprehensive Guide*, John Bowden (trans.) (Minneapolis: Fortress Press, 1998). See also David Flusser, *Jesus* (Jerusalem: The Hebrew University Magnes Press, 1998) [Hebrew].

[34] On the relation between theological and historical time see Motzkin, *Time and Transcendence*.

political strategy of nationalism diverges from historicization as a political strategy of liberal democracy. In the latter, the individual lifespan is privileged, reflecting present time's normative superiority over past or distant future. It is related (as we will see in Chapter 13) to the divergent attitudes of nationalism and liberalism toward war and the perils of individual life. The transition between the fashioning of firm genealogies of collectives (imagined as organic wholes) to looser collectives (featuring aggregates of individuals) has often been accompanied by an increased humanization of time.

For Vico, to historicize civil life implies recognition of its poetic foundations in the creative faculties of the human spirit, humanizing it, politicizing it, and making it a legitimate object of human (scientific) knowledge. "Still in the dense and dark night which envelops the remotest antiquity," writes Vico:

there shines an eternal and inextinguishable light. It is a truth, which cannot be doubted: The civil world is certainly the creation of humankind, and consequently, the principles of the civil world can and must be discovered within the modifications of the human mind. If we reflect on this, we can only wonder why all the philosophers have so earnestly pursued knowledge of the world of nature, which only God can know as its creator, while they neglected to study the world of nations, or civil world, which people can in fact know because they created it. (331)

This remarkable observation, which in some ways anticipates the thinking of both Rousseau and Kant, plays a significant role in the emergence of historicization as a fundamental mode of the modern and postmodern political imagination. As such, historicization has become a useful modern political strategy for the framing of politics as an autonomous human enterprise, thus often undermining transcendental and naturalistic genealogies of the civil order. Historicization can, then, be enlisted for a variety of purposes including destabilizing monarchic and aristocratic governments, denaturalizing market mechanisms, and challenging the subordinate place of women in the family and the polity. R. G. Collingwood made the pertinent observation that "the desire to envisage human action as free was bound up with a desire to achieve autonomy for history as a study of human action."[35] Historicizing in this sense, assuming a view of individuals and groups as agents of history, meant to simultaneously moralize and voluntarize politics or, in other words, to frame the modern democratic emancipatory conception of politics.

As strategies of the political imagination, the aforementioned modes of naturalizing and historicizing can interchange domains and functions, compete over the framing of the same political events and entities, and, at times, converge and reinforce one another within a wider and a more complex strategy. Burke exemplifies the workings of such a convergence:

[T]hrough the same plan of the conformity of nature in our artificial institutions, and by calling in the aid of unerring and powerful instincts, to *fortify* the fallible and fee-

---

[35] R. G. Collingwood, *The Idea of History* (London: Oxford University Press, 1967), p. 319.

ble contrivances of reason, we have derived several others, and those no small benefits, from considering our liberties in light of inheritance. (my emphasis)[36]

In general, the convergence of strategies of naturalization and historicization has manifested itself in cases in which subversive genealogies, publicly deployed to challenge official genealogies of authority, have worked jointly (albeit not coherently) to resist the established order by fashioning imaginaries of natural rights.

Consistent with the orientation advanced by feminist theorists mentioned earlier, a particularly instructive contemporary reversal has taken place between the naturalization and the historicization (which often meant in this context also politicization) of the inequality of women, both in the family and the polity. The increasing leveling of gender roles in the family milieu, as well as the growing constraints imposed by the modern state on parental control of children, reveals the erosion of conventional naturalization patterns that succeeded in perpetuating the subordinate status of women and the unprotected position of children over many centuries.

The feminist movement has been able to make considerable changes in the status of women by effecting a shift naturalizing a gender-inclusive concept of universal rights reinforced by sociopolitically historicizing gender inequality. Obviously, such an effective feminist movement could not have flourished in cultures lacking repositories of natural and historical imaginaries like those available to the western political imagination. The relevant questions in this respect relate to the kind of images of history and nature that reside in the latent or manifest repertory of the political imagination of any particular political universe, to their modus operandi, and to their interrelation as elements of the performed regime. Sheila Jasanoff provides a most illuminating account of how imaginaries of nature and history combine differently in different societies to provide hybrid performative policy scripts and institutional practices rooted in locally specific imaginaries of nature and history. Discussing the controversies around genetically modified food and stem cell research and development, she shows how these issues played out differently in England, the United States, and Germany (with its memories of Nazi eugenics).[37]

A further comparison between earlier ideological/political uses of nature and history in different societies can be instructive. Whereas for conservatives such as Edmund Burke to historicize politics meant to celebrate continuities and block revolutionary change, for revolutionaries such as Thomas Paine, to naturalize politics meant "to begin the world anew."[38] For a substantial part of American history, before the emergence of the "machine in the Garden,"[39] before the massive introduction of technology problematized Americans'

[36] Burke, "Reflections on the Revolution in France," p. 93.
[37] Jasanoff, *Designs on Nature.*
[38] Bailyn, *To Begin the World Anew.*
[39] See, for example, Leo Marx's *The Machine in the Garden: Technology and the Pastoral Ideal in America* (New York: Oxford University Press, 1967).

relation to nature, America's paradisiacal landscape had been suffused with an ahistorical religious, spiritual, and moral aura. Naturalization could thus serve to obliterate the past, severing ties with Europe, giving birth to a new nation, and creating a new political system. If for America's founders, naturalization meant to ideologically dehistoricize society and politics and embark on a new beginning, for Zionists active during the late nineteenth century and throughout a large part of the twentieth century, nature was not considered a normative alternative to history. Their main imaginary was not so much that of a new beginning but of a return. Hence in the Zionist–Israeli case, nature did not conspire with religion to dehistoricize, but on the contrary, to ground and substantiate a sacred as well as a secular history. The centrality of the desert in both the Jewish religious tradition and Zionist Israel is one such example.[40]

As Handelman and Katz point out, the modern Zionist calendar of Israel conflates history and nature, forming a particularly powerful political imaginary. The state adopted the Hebrew calendar (yearly cycle), embedding in it, in close temporal proximity, a sequence of festivities and remembrance days starting a few days after Passover, continuing through the Memorial Day for the victims of the Holocaust, followed by the Memorial Day for soldiers fallen in Israeli wars, and concluding the sequence with the celebration of the birth of the state of Israel on Independence Day.

The Zionist narrative of progression from catastrophe through sacrifice to freedom is thus inscribed in the yearly cycle. This narrative is reinforced by an overlapping cosmological sequence from winter to spring, as well as by the symbolic Passover sequence celebrating the passage from slavery in Egypt to liberation in the Land of Israel.[41] One of Israel's early prime ministers, Levi Eshkol, put it succinctly on Memorial Day 1964:

The Martyrs and Heroes' Memorial Day falls between the ancient Festival of Freedom [Passover is often called "spring festival"] and the modern day of independence. The annals of our people are enfolded between these two events. With our exodus from the Egyptian bondage, we won our ancient freedom: now, with our ascent from the depths of the Holocaust, we live again in an independent nation.[42]

As Handelman and Katz observe, this sequence from exile through return to redemption hinges on a metaphysic of becoming. The coexistence of natural, historical, religious, and ideological strata in this hegemonic, multilayered,

---

[40] See for instance Yael Zerubavel, "The Desert and the Settlement as Symbolic Landscapes in Modern Israel" in Julia Brauch, Anna Lipphardt, and Alexandra Nocke (eds.), *Jewish Topographies: Visions of Space, Traditions of Place* Heritage, Culture and Identity Series (London: Ashgate Press, 2008), pp. 201–22. See also her *Desert in the Promised Land: Nationalism, Politics, and Symbolic Landscapes* (Chicago: Chicago University Press, forthcoming).

[41] See Don Handelman and Elihu Katz's "Sequencing the National: Opening Remembrance Day and Independence Day," in Don Handelman (ed.), *Nationalism and the Israeli State: Bureaucratic Logic in Public Events* (Oxford: Berg, 2004), pp. 119–42. Other sections of Handelman's book comprise an invaluable discussion of these issues.

[42] Ibid., p. 97.

Zionist imaginary is, however, no guarantee of harmony. In the educational context, for instance, it is easy to discern tensions between progressive Zionist educators drawing upon Bacon, Rousseau, and Pestalozzi in their aim to raise Israeli children in a new culture of objective nature conceived as an alternative or corrective to the preaching of traditional religious texts, and religious Zionists, who sought to find in regional landscapes archaeological evidence for the accuracy of the biblical text and, conversely, textual evidence for the divinization of local nature and politics.[43]

While secular and religious Hebrew cultures clashed constantly even before the birth of Zionism, the drive to weld elements of the two cultures has progressively increased since the establishment of the state in May 1948. Not surprising, Israeli zoo curators have created a popular Biblical Zoo in Jerusalem, and philologists, botanists, and Bible scholars have continually engaged in discovering or inventing a continuum between Jewish history, culture, religion, language (ancient and modern Hebrew), and nature in the Land of Israel. For many Israeli archeologists, nature has been conceived as a thin, relatively recent layer covering archeological treasures of thousands of years.

America and Israel represent, therefore, diametrically opposed appropriations of nature and history by prevailing political imaginaries, as well as different ways of interrelating them. The one uses nature to dehistoricize politics and make a new beginning; the other employs religious or secular versions of holy history to historicize and appropriate nature.[44]

In the more recent history of Israel, tensions between naturalization as a strategy of founding democracy on natural birthrights for freedom and historicization as a strategy for defining the legitimate collective within strict religious-ethnic boundaries forced a compromise. In 1992 and 1994, the Israeli legislature introduced a definition of the state as both "Jewish and Democratic" in Israel's basic (constitutional) laws. This legislation was achieved by a momentary controversial compromise. On one hand were those for whom to historicize the Israeli collective as a Jewish state is to promote Israel as a nation-state, which downgrades the status of non-Jewish individuals and communities; on the other hand were those for whom democracy means equal natural rights for all. For the ethno-religious nationalists, the legitimacy of Israel and its actions (including the occupation of the West Bank) derives mainly from the past, from the genealogy, the traditions, and the classical texts of the Jewish people. For liberal democrats, the authority of the state derives from the natural freedoms of the living. The Israeli polity thus embodies a conflict between foundational collective political imaginaries, between past and present, history-based and nature-based politics. The dual constitutional commitment to both visions

---

[43] On this educational approach, see the introduction to *Shi'urei Histaklut Vidiat Hamoledet (Object Lessons and Knowledge of the Homeland* – in Hebrew), by Ozrakovski, Krichevsky (Ezrahi), and Yichieli (Jaffa: Kohelet, 1912).

[44] For an illuminating discussion of Israeli and Palestinian archeology and ideology see Magen Broshi, *Bread, Wine, Walls and Scrolls* (New York: Sheffield Academic Press, 2001).

can also be interpreted as inviting Israelis to negotiate a working coexistence between two political programs without setting a deadline.[45]

The respective authorities of science and history appear to be sharply separated. The predominance of the mechanistic metaphor of nature in modern science has widened the gap between natural science, perceived as knowledge of nature, and history, conceived as knowledge of the evolution of human ideas and actions. Yet Darwin's evolutionary theory has blurred the distinction between them by providing a scientific version that historicizes nature. Although the temporal span of evolutionary theories extends far beyond the temporal span of human history, at the level of the popular political imagination this development has, among other things, encouraged the emergence of racism as a political strategy that draws on the naturalization of the history of human groups' diversity.

One of the most glaring and devastating manifestations of such strategies of political imagining was Nazi ideology and politics. This doctrine endorsed politically induced violence, exclusion, and extermination on the grounds of biological scientism, thereby imposing on human beings a "natural" hierarchy of "essential" group traits and group differences. In the modern democratic polity, occasional attempts to naturalize human cognitive or moral traits are usually resisted.[46] Nevertheless, there obviously are many differences in the drawing of boundaries between nature and history (or between nature and society) by the political imaginaries of democracies such as England, France, post-World War II Germany, the Netherlands, Israel, and others. These differences could undoubtedly provide important clues to the contours and the performative political effects of their respective political imaginaries.

In the final section of this book, I return to a discussion of the role of historicization in the erosion of the Enlightenment project, the decline of nature as a liberal democratic political resource, and the emergence of a radical critique of foundationalism. In Part Two, I discuss the crucial role of modern conceptions of reality and the individual in the emergence of the modern democratic political imagination. I hope to account for the reasons whereby modern reality and the modern individual as historical products have played such an important role in the emergence of democratic political imaginaries and institutions since the late eighteenth century, and to explain why their transformation in our time has been so consequential for the postmodern shift in politics.

---

[45] See how the strained coexistence of these two distinct imaginaries destined to shape the Israeli polity was already evident in Israel's Declaration of Independence of May 14, 1948.

[46] See for instance Yaron Ezrahi's "The Jansen Controversy: A Study in the Ethics and Politics of Knowledge in Democracy," in Charles Frankel (ed.), *Controversies and Decisions: The Social Sciences and Public Policy* (New York: Russell Sage Foundation, 1976), pp. 149–70.

PART TWO

MODERN COMMON SENSE AND THE RISE OF MODERN POLITICAL IMAGINARIES

5

The Historicity of Common Sense and the Role of Scientism in the Modern Political Imagination

Politics shares with religion its dependence on the public's readiness, conscious or not, to regard invisible entities as real. The nation or the state are not essentially more visible or concrete than God or angels. Likewise, both politics and religion depend on the willingness of people to grant human beings transcendence beyond their physical bodies. In their various manifestations, they both seek to establish the reality of intangible entities such as human souls, narratives, authorities, genealogies, beliefs, conscience, memory, and spiritual legacies. Both politics and religion, therefore, are driven by an urge for self-concretization. But as we will see, in the case of modern (particularly democratic) politics, whereas this urge has generated a commitment to a visible materialistic imaginary of political causality and accountability in public affairs, spiritual causality has persisted in religion. An important reason for the popular appeal of the ensemble of modern performative democratic imaginaries of politics has been their break with religious epistemology and ritual.

Like religious worlds, political worlds have to be collectively imagined in order to historically exist. Politics, perhaps more than any other sphere, confirms Clifford Geertz's apt observation that "the real is just as imagined as the imaginary."[1] I would push this point further and propose that the real is no less dependent on the performance of the imaginary of the real than on the performance of the imaginary of the unreal. In other words, the performance of either the real or the fictive usually simultaneously entails the performance of its imagined opposite.[2] Moreover, in both religion and politics, that which is imagined as real extends beyond the sensuously experienced, although the category of the sensible may be mobilized to validate claims or beliefs respecting the insensible.

---

[1] Clifford Geertz, *Negara: The Theatre State in Nineteenth-Century Bali* (Princeton: Princeton University Press, 1980), p. 136.
[2] During the French Revolution, both the realities of the power and the powerlessness of the king of France were created by behaviors that simultaneously performed divergent imaginaries.

In both religion and politics, as well as in some areas of science, sensory experience is engaged and elaborated in a variety of ways in order to establish the existence of both sensible and insensible entities. The imaginaries of the real fluctuate across temporal and spatial dimensions. Their variations provide important clues as to the structures of culture, society, and politics.

In each case, imaginaries of the real provide a particular link between causal and moral orders and establish basic parameters of what can be known, what needs to be known, and how knowledge can be obtained and verified. Furthermore, they also shape the possibilities and meanings of action. In ancient China, where the political mandate of the emperor was believed to be divinely ordained, momentous celestial events such as eclipses assumed political significance and were associated with the authority of the Chinese emperor. The pursuit of legitimacy required the emperor's anticipation of such events and his engagement in actions and rituals that reinforced his purported role as mediator between heaven and earth.[3] Though differing in both structure and meaning, the causal and the moral-political orders are also interrelated in the modern state. In later chapters, I discuss in greater detail the ways in which the normative order of democracy is linked to specific imaginaries of the causality that underlie social and political orders.

In our culture, common sense is a fundamental, elementary layer of the imaginary of the real. As an inclusive frame of social perception and interpretation, it also provides or certifies, in each sociohistorical case, the native or folk imaginaries of the political that constitute the fabrics of political world making. In this chapter, I discuss the relations between the rise of democratic politics in the West and the emergence of materialistic commonsense realism, which I define as a modern form of common sense influenced by the rise of modern science. In his observations on American democracy, Tocqueville seems to regard egalitarian individualism as the principal cause for the pervasiveness of a discernible "taste for the tangible," a bias for unmediated contact with the facts of experience and in favor of the normative superiority of the practical over the theoretical among the citizens of democratic America.[4]

However, the causal relations between democratic egalitarianism and modern commonsense realism seem to me to be more reciprocal. I argue that only within the epistemological frame of Western commonsense realism could the novel imaginaries (and metaphors) of political causality and the agents that constitute the democratic participatory political order emerge.

My discussion focuses solely on the relations between common sense and the political imagination in European democracies, and on the cultural and

---

[3] See for instance Geoffrey Lloyd's "Science and Antiquity: The Greek and Chinese Cases and their Relevance to the Problems of Culture and Cognition" in David R. Olson and Nancy Torrance (eds.), *Modes of Thought: Explorations in Culture and Cognition* (Cambridge: Cambridge University Press, 1996).

[4] Alexis de Tocqueville, *Democracy in America*, Harvey C. Mansfield and Delba Winthrop (trans. and ed.) (first pub. 1835; Chicago: University of Chicago Press, 2002), pp. 433–9, 459.

political configurations to which it gave rise in America and in a few other countries under the sway of European legacies. Although many elements of commonsense realism can be traced to earlier times and remote places, in its manifestation as a fairly coherent cluster of orientations toward experience, it is a culture-specific feature of societies that have undergone the scientific revolution or were subject to its impact. As comparative cognitive anthropologists and cultural analysts have pointed out, although some similarities may be found in the imaginaries of reality across different cultures, the differences are significant enough to warrant doubts about sweeping generalizations regarding the existence of a universal elementary human cognitive layer of common sense, but not sufficient enough to warrant cultural relativism.[5]

This issue and the related debate are indeed pertinent to any discussion of the potential and actual diffusion of Western commonsense realism and its affiliated democratic political imaginaries across the globe. But this is not our main concern in this book. My principal purpose is to examine the particular ways in which modern political imaginaries have framed novel relations between causality, agency, and political order in modern Western societies.

This discussion of commonsense realism eschews the debate on whether modern common sense is more advanced than earlier "primitive" popular beliefs, or whether there is a linear cognitive-cultural progress from primitive states to more advanced ones. As I have already noted, the actual connections between causal and moral (or political) orders may vary across different democratic as well as nondemocratic regimes. Moreover, even within the general boundaries of any particular culture or society, commonsense realism and its associated imaginaries of causality and agency may not be equally pervasive.[6] In modern societies, there are recognizable domains of folk psychology, folk physics, folk biology, folk religion, folk metaphysics, and folk politics; some mixed with scientism and some not. As Scott Atran argues, "[h]uman minds seem to be endowed with fundamentally distinct domains of causal schema for thinking about the world."[7]

Although there may be important links among such diverse domains of folk beliefs, significant shifts between or within any such domains can have profound political consequences. What guides my interest is precisely the influence of scientism on my notion of commonsense realism and, consequently, on folk politics – the common imaginaries of the political order – in modern Western democracies. In other words, I am interested in the role of modern folk physics, for example, of physics modified by scientism, in the transformation of folk politics, and in its relation to the emergence of modern democratic politics. I argue that, in modern Western societies, commonsense realism has played the role of an epistemological *Agora* that enabled and facilitated the rise of

---

[5] See David R. Olson, "Introduction" in *Modes of Thought*, pp. 1–6.
[6] See Scott Atran, "Modes of Thinking about Living Kinds: Science, Symbolism, and Common Sense," ibid., pp. 216–17.
[7] Ibid.

modern democratic politics; that it constituted a cognitive-perceptual space in which the normative and ontological dimensions of democratic politics could converge.

A crucial part of this ostensible development stems from a demystification of the political and its descent from heavenly to earthly spheres through processes of "visualizing" or, in a larger sense, "materializing" political causalities, events, and agents in the sphere of commonsense perception. This shift of political epistemology was indispensable in upholding the fiction of popular participation and the visible accountability of democratic governments, despite the paucity of facts that lent it verisimilitude or reality within the domain of modern common experience.

Regarded as a particular historical configuration, modern democratic political epistemology has emerged from the accumulated effects of a multiplicity of developments that took place throughout earlier centuries. The profound changes that such epistemology has undergone in recent decades are, I believe, bound to influence the survival and shape of future democracies.

I shall now discuss some salient indications of increasing scholarly acknowledgment of the importance of the historicity and transformations of the popular imagination, as well as some of the intellectual obstacles such recognition has had to overcome in order to recognize the causal productiveness of the modern popular imagination and its underlying commonsense realism.

Vico's emphasis on the creative powers of the popular imagination and his notion of *sensus communis*, of common sense, as a universally shared "unreflective judgment" are closely related. In the context of their ordinary, everyday engagements, people are usually unaware of the relations between objects, hypostatized causes and agents, and the creative popular imagination. The existence of alternative imaginaries of causation and agencies is rarely acknowledged; people are generally unaware that the ways they classify people, objects, animals, and so forth may relate to and be causally influenced by their beliefs and their social position. The more unreflexive our commonsense notions of the world and our engagement in its affairs, the more concealed the role of the creative popular imagination in the making of the very universe we inhabit. Whereas the unreflexive and unreflective character of modern popular orientations toward the political is, from a philosophical perspective, a great weakness of the popular mind, this very "weakness" has actually empowered such popular orientations in shaping collective life and influencing individual behavior.

Hence the performative political imagination that shapes the imaginaries that furnish our political world, creating our sense of the politically real and regulating our institutions, is inherently the unreflective or self-concealing imagination. Vico's view of the historicity of the popular imagination and his acknowledgment of its crucial role in shaping the history of politics goes hand in hand with his readiness to privilege the creativity of the people and the products of the popular imagination above the imaginaries and ideas of philosophy. This is the reason for his insistence that "[a]ll the principles of metaphysics, logic, and ethics originated in the public square of Athens" (1043). Vico could, therefore, argue that the philosophical imagination is at best a derivative refinement of or abstraction from the popular imagination (934, 1043).

In the final analysis, Vico's view that political history is largely the consequence of the creative development of the popular imagination is his most radical contribution to democratic theory. This aspect of Vico's theory, and of that of his followers, has been overlooked primarily because historians and philosophers have tended to associate politics driven by the popular imagination with the rejection of rationalism, generating the politics of fascism or totalitarianism and mob violence. The culturally and institutionally disembodied character of much modern political philosophy has heavily influenced this distorted perspective.[8] These ideological and intellectual tendencies have hindered the recognition that, since popular political imaginaries shape the political order and direct its politics, the difference between authoritarian and democratic regimes does not lie in a dichotomy between politics based on imagination, deception, and violence, and politics based on rationality, facts, and deliberative processes. The opposition is rather between competing clusters of the popular imagination and their institutional and political consequences. An understanding of the political imagination's role in political world making might be very helpful in our assessment of the versions of democracy emerging after modernity. In his work on multiple modernities, S. N. Eisenstadt notes the diverse forms of contemporary democracies and the specific modes of the coproduction of knowledge and politics exemplified in each.[9]

REASON AND THE COMMON IMAGINATION AS CAUSES IN POLITICAL HISTORY

The special powers of common sense usually originate in an unreflective view of the physical and social worlds, a view experienced by the subject as natural and unproblematic. As such, common sense normalizes and naturalizes the structure of our experience and guides our practical actions. This derives from the presumed status of common sense as a universal frame of the perceptions and practices through which human beings ordinarily encounter the world and conduct themselves in everyday life. Given its intrasocial inclusiveness (sometimes more presumed than actual), common sense derives its authority from the fact that subjective experience is confirmed by the experiences of others. This is largely why states invent and deploy maps, calendars, official statistical tables, or fixed standards that shape and articulate the experience of the multitude and constrain subjective constructions of reality.

For reasons to be discussed later in this chapter, especially in the modern world, that which is public and widely shared socially is more likely to assume

---

[8] See S. N. Eisenstadt, *Political Theory in Search of the Political* (Liverpool: Liverpool University Press, 2007).
[9] S. N. Eisenstadt, "Multiple Modernities," *Daedalus* (Winter 2000): 11–14, 23.

the status of reality. Furthermore, the engagement of the entire spectrum of our senses grants additional validity to the experience of objects, events, or agents (when what is seen, for example, can also be touched, heard, smelled, or tasted). Early uses of the term *common sense* in the Western tradition tended to identify this term, often equated with the imagination, with the orchestration of all five senses. In the course of time, the validation of a comprehensive or integrated synaesthetic experience, in which each sense confirms and is in return corroborated by the others, was further reinforced by any apparent behavioral indicator that the experience of the individual corresponds with that of others. The development of an experience of the world as a stable and uniform hypostatized object has been supported, then, by the "testimonies" of multiple senses and of the multitude.

One of the prominent interpretations of Aristotle's references to common sense defines it as a complex sense that cannot be reduced to any of the others because it is the sense of the difference and unity of the five senses as a whole.[10] As the fourteenth-century Moslem philosopher-statesman Ibn Khaldun observed in *The Muqaddimah*, the "common sense transfers [the perceptions] to the imagination, which is the power that pictures an object of sensual perception in the soul as it is, abstracted from all external matter."[11]

This notion of the relations between common sense and the imagination may be subsumed in my notion of the reflective imagination (see Chapter 3), which refers to an external world experienced and authorized by common sense. Daniel Heller-Roazen has observed further that as a cognitive faculty shared universally by all men, the modern notion of common sense is a conceptual invention that may be traced to the classical Roman tradition. As such it is associated with *sensus communis* as a capacity associated with what all men can take for granted and regard as self-evident truths. Hebrew, Greek, Latin, and Arabic thinkers tended to attribute common sense to the imagination as well as to other "powers of the soul" such as thinking and remembering, and often linked it to political life.

These early texts and their modern philosophical developments were, nevertheless, usually considered part of a nonhistorical discourse on human capacities. The modern drift to sever the foundations of society and polity from their transcendental anchor in God or nature undoubtedly encouraged a vigorous reorientation of the search for the foundations of a civil order that could be grounded in humans and history. Along the trend to naturalize, one can discern in the Enlightenment's Sciences of Man the early modern beginnings of an appreciation of cultural and historical variability in collective perceptions

---

[10] Daniel Heller-Roazen, "Common Sense: Greek, Arabic and Latin" in Stephen G. Nichols, Andreas Kablitz, and Alison Calhoun (eds.), *Rethinking Medieval Senses: Heritage, Fascinations, Frames* (Baltimore: Johns Hopkins University Press, 2008). See also Daniel Heller-Roazen, *The Inner Touch: Archeology of a Sensation* (Brooklyn, NY: Zone Books, 2007).

[11] Ibn Khaldun, *The Muqaddimah: An Introduction to History*, Franz Rosenthal (trans.) and N. J. Dawood (ed.) (Princeton: Princeton University Press, 1967), p. 76.

of the world. However, the view of man's nature as subject of the new scientific study of nature as a system of unchanging universal laws hindered further recognition of the role of the collective imagination in politics as well as of the historicity, anthropological complexity, and diversity of folk imaginaries of causality and agency. The historical and comparative anthropological insights of Vico, Rousseau, and others gathered momentum only with the subsequent rise and emancipation of humanistic studies, modern jurisprudence, and the social sciences.

In many ways, this conservative legacy of the Enlightenment persisted until very recently. It is intriguing to discover the extent to which contemporary historians such as Jacques Le Goff and Edmund Morgan or a philosopher like Charles Taylor, who were among the first to show appreciation for the historicity of social or political imaginaries and of common popular notions of social and political causality or agency, seem burdened and bounded by their tacit discursive commitments to lingering conventional binaries such as facts/fictions, reality/fantasy, or ordinary/ extraordinary experiences. I do not mean to imply that such distinctions cannot be useful in some discursive universes. But it is certainly unhelpful, for instance, to attempt to understand and explain historical shifts in the very imaginaries, or commonsense frames that in any given context define the boundaries between reality and fantasy, through straitjacketed standards for classifying facts and fictions. Those standards themselves are obviously culture bound. Such an approach can easily commit the "fallacy of misplaced rationality" by eschewing the rich double lives of fictions as political realities, facts, and generators of social and political behaviors and events.

"Over the past several years," wrote French historian Jacques Le Goff in 1985, "I have become increasingly interested in imagination as a dimension of history."[12] While admitting that the term *imagination* is not yet sufficiently worked out conceptually for purposes of investigation, he attempts to overcome this limitation by a series of definitions or classifications that do not seem satisfactory enough to meet the task. For Le Goff, imagination is still primarily a matter of images and representations of reality, still circumscribed to works of art and literature – the permissible niche assigned to the imagination by Enlightenment thinkers. He cannot confidently acknowledge that the imagination is not limited to representing or conferring meaning upon a given reality, but in fact has the capacity to actually create it or participate in its production, especially in public affairs. Still, Le Goff is strongly committed to the idea that "the imagination nourishes man and causes him to act. It is a collective, social, and historical phenomenon. A history without the imagination is a mutilated, disembodied history."[13]

Some strains of the Enlightenment encouraged the assumption that politics can be shaped by socially and politically disembodied abstract ideas or rational theories that descend from the intellectual elite down to popular consciousness

---

[12] Jacques Le Goff, *The Medieval Imagination* (Chicago: University of Chicago Press, 1988), p. 1.
[13] Ibid., p. 17.

or imagination. Philosophers and other intellectuals may, of course, influence the popular imagination. But the process is far from one way and top down. Le Goff provided a more complex yet useful perspective on this issue when he wrote that the "success of a theme of the imagination in any society is related to the degree to which the relation between that theme and the rest of the cultural and mental legacy captures the contemporary context."[14] Le Goff points to the existence of a process whereby some themes of the imagination become successful while others are left out, but he does not elucidate the enigma of what enables some themes of the imagination to capture the contemporary context and thus become successful. Pondering on its prospects, Le Goff expresses the awareness that study of the imagination has a long way to go. "I firmly believe," he wrote in the first French edition of his book on the medieval imagination (1985), "that the imagination will become an increasingly important subject not only of historical science but of science in general."[15] Writing around 1988, American historian Edmund S. Morgan audaciously acknowledged:

I have been troubled by the pejorative connotations attached to the word [fiction], but I have been unable to find a better one to describe the different phenomena to which I have applied it. I can only hope that the readers who persevere to the end of this book will recognize that the fictional qualities of popular sovereignty [the subject of Morgan's book] sustain rather than threaten the human values associated with it. I hope they will also recognize that I do not imply deception or delusion on the part of those who employed or subscribed to the fictions in which they willingly suspended disbelief.[16]

Morgan's anxiety reveals the difficulties inherent in the vestiges of the Enlightenment's dichotomy between reason and imagination in contemporary historiography and culture and its inhibitory effect on attempts to reframe and reconceptualize terms such as *facts* and *fictions*. Since the terms *fiction* and *imagination* were often used in the political context in association with political deception and manipulation, he is driven to assure us that fictions and imaginaries can function as causes that uphold good and not only bad political systems. As he puts it:

[T]he success of government thus requires the acceptance of fictions, the willing suspension of disbelief requires us to believe that the emperor is clothed even though we can see that he is not.... The popular governments of Britain and the United States rest on fictions as much as the governments of [Soviet] Russia and China.[17]

Such difficulties in acknowledging the historical role of the popular imagination in the creation of good political institutions and influencing the course of collective life are discernible throughout the works of many political philosophers. They may, of course, represent an elitist intellectual tradition beginning

---

[14] Ibid., p. 172.
[15] Ibid., p. 13.
[16] Edmund Morgan, *Inventing the People: The Rise of Popular Sovereignty in England and America* (New York: W.W. Norton, 1988), pp. 14–15.
[17] Ibid., p. 13.

with Plato, according to which the ideas of philosophers and other intellectuals not only should but also ultimately do shape the lives of peoples in the course of time. Such a conflation of normative political philosophy and political history has implicitly sustained both an exaggerated belief in the relevance of philosophy to political life and a rationalist conception of politics.

However, any examination of the historical configurations of common sense and its concomitant political and social imaginaries indicates that common sense is not merely a passive recipient of ideas from above and that imagination is not merely a sensuous embodiment of abstract truths for the illiterate. While they may assimilate metaphors and other imaginings circulating or developed in philosophical discourse, common sense and the political imagination are the prime shapers of the folk political worldviews that guide and regulate social and political life.

This is a point some contemporary political philosophers and intellectual historians still tend to underestimate in their analysis of political processes. As I suggested earlier, Charles Taylor is one of the very few in a minority of modern political philosophers who have revised some of their convictions upon realizing the importance of collective imaginaries in the shaping of politics. "The social imaginary," he writes, "is not a set of ideas; rather it is what enables, through making sense of, the practices of a society."[18] Taylor acknowledges that a feature such as the public sphere "can exist only if it is imagined as such."[19] This implies, of course, that the genealogy of the imagination that has rendered a democratic institution like the public sphere plausible is vital.

But Taylor goes only half way. In his conception of the nature of social (or what I prefer to call political) imaginaries, he follows a long tradition that regards the commonsense context of social imaginaries as a mere receptacle of external intellectual input. He is incognizant of the role of common sense as an active, culture-specific, and protean normative-perceptual maker and editor, both creative of and selective in relation to, the "externally available" materials it processes and assimilates.

Moreover, Taylor overly emphasizes the role of philosophy in the historical genealogy of the political imagination, its place in the top-to-bottom version of the origins of social imaginaries and their matching institutions. Unvaryingly oblivious to the role played by the popular imagination and the selection performed by the common sense of each epoch, he predictably thinks it "clear that the images of the moral order which descend through a series of transformations from that inscribed in the natural law theories of Grotius and Locke are different from those embedded in the social imaginary of the premodern age."[20] For Taylor, the change stems from the fact that "this theory has ended up achieving

[18] Charles Taylor, "Modern Social Imaginaries," *Public Culture* vol. 14, no. 1 (Winter 2002): 91–124 (Taylor's approach to social imaginaries is more fully expressed in his book *Modern Social Imaginaries*, published by Duke University Press in 2004).

[19] Taylor, "Modern Social Imaginaries," p. 113.

[20] Ibid., pp. 92–5.

such a hold on our imagination."[21] Whereas he acknowledges that what ordinary people imagine is "carried in images, stories, and legends," and that "social imagery is that common understanding that makes possible common practices and a widely shared sense of legitimacy," he insists on the recognition that "what starts off as theories held by a few people may come to infiltrate the social imaginary, that of elites perhaps, and then of society as a whole."[22]

For the purpose of our discussion, the key phrase used by Taylor is that "images of the moral order descend" from the "theories of Grotius and Locke." Obviously the very concepts of nature and natural law, which thinkers such as Grotius and Locke employed and developed, were partly influenced by earlier elite philosophers like those of the Stoic school in ancient Greece. But for the cultural, political, and legal lives of imaginaries of nature, there were also many other sources, including fragments of popular premodern religious and metaphysical imaginings of nature, formed in Ancient Greece and the Roman Empire, as well as throughout the Middle Ages. These images were widely disseminated by poetry, mythology, theology, education, and religious and legal practices. It is precisely because Vico opposed a top-bottom hierarchical theory of the formation and the diffusion of social and political imaginaries and practices that he regarded *both* the Homeric epics and Homer himself as collective products of the popular imagination and philosophical ideas as its derivative refined abstractions.

The problem, however, goes deeper. Taylor is part of a tradition, epitomized by Plato's allegory of the cave, according to which only a few thinkers can generate the ideas that lead humanity to the truth, provided that either they or the rhetoricians and the politicians succeed in effectively representing these ideas to the lay public and applying them to life. Within this frame, the role of the imagination is at best to represent, transmit, or imitate the truth rather than to create or embody it. In other words, such an attitude tends merely to engage the elite imagination while neglecting the vital influence of the creative performative popular imagination on the institutionalized political order, on common imaginaries of the politically real, and on elite intellectual discourse.

The early as well as the modern philosophical discussion of the imagination is generally confined by the tendency to use the imagination as a tool for educating the masses, a vehicle for the transmission of knowledge and truth from the intellectual elite at the top of the cultural hierarchy to the people at its bottom.

In line with this approach, images, stories, and legends ostensibly constitute masked or only partial truths, not their frank embodiment. They consist of – and this was also Einstein's position in relation to this issue in the context of science[23] – the distorted shadows of the real world from which, as in Plato's

---

[21] Ibid., p. 100.
[22] Ibid., p. 106.
[23] See Yaron Ezrahi's "Einstein's Unintended Legacy: The Critique of Common-Sense Realism and Post-Modern Politics" in Gerald Holton, Peter Galison, and Silvan Schweber (eds.), *Einstein for the 21st Century* (Princeton: Princeton University Press, 2008).

allegory of the cave, some human beings may begin the long, arduous journey from darkness to light. To borrow Taylor's own word, these shadows provide the "background" for our understanding of real truth.

This position underlies the authority assumed by scientists and philosophers as critics of common sense. But eschewing the particular structure and functions of common sense and popular beliefs as the epistemological *Agora* of politics, disregarding the latent functions of the subtle selective processes, these critics often commit what I have called "the fallacy of misplaced rationality." Especially in the modern democratic West, they overlook the role of common-sense realism as the core of the inclusive and therefore moral epistemology of ordinary political life, the moral commitment democratic citizens have, according to Hobbes, for instance as witnesses, to acknowledge shared experiences and not to deny what they "know together."[24]

To be sure, the influence of philosophers and scientists on commonsense notions of experience need not be ignored. Clifford Geertz acknowledges that "the development of modern science has had a profound effect … upon western common sense views."[25] But this influence, including the reification of theoretical scientific entities by the popular imagination, has always been filtered and edited by commonsense classifications and vocabularies acceptable within the boundaries of the local civic epistemology and adapted to the practical political and social needs to which commonsense frames respond. This may also account for the ostensibly commonsensical tendency to preserve reified theoretical entities that initially belonged to already scientifically discarded theories. While their contributions to scientific knowledge have been dismissed, their value to socially working imaginaries and their commonsense frames has persisted. Such discrepancies relate, among other things, to the fact that both the pace of the shifts between alternative imaginaries of the world as well as the reasons for such shifts vary with the respective contexts and orientations of experts and laymen.

In contrast to Charles Taylor, Bruno Latour – a social and cultural theorist – is willing to completely reject the separation between the spheres of knowledge and common sense. Latour maintains that the dichotomy in Plato's allegory of the cave between knowledge and common perceptions of the world, or between philosophers and scientists on one hand and laymen on the other, rests upon a myth that must be replaced by one superior and more valuable that would obliterate or rule out such binary oppositions.[26]

Latour recognizes the centrality of the cluster of nature, factual reality, and science in the construction of the objective world of the modern commonsense system. In his book *Politics of Nature*, Latour seems to suggest that an imaginary

[24] Thomas Hobbes, *Leviathan*, Michael Oakeshott (ed.) (New York: Collier, 1962), p. 57.

[25] Clifford Geertz, *Local Knowledge: Further Essays in Interpretive Anthropology* (New York: Basic Books, 1983), pp. 86–7.

[26] Bruno Latour, *Politics of Nature: How to Bring the Sciences into Democracy* (Cambridge, MA: Harvard University Press, 2004).

that combines rather than separates nature and politics and, therefore, does not resist the politicization and moralization of socially applied knowledge and technology, is far more compatible with a balanced and legitimate order. He seems to have underestimated the extent to which the elimination of this cluster is likely to efface perhaps the most powerful commonsense resources for the creation of a common public world without which the particular form of modern Western democracy, as we have come to know it, is unrealizable.

The other difficulty posed by Latour's view lies in his belief that such a switch between basic political imaginaries is both desirable and achievable almost at will. He provides a glossary of terms and a summary of the argument "for readers in a hurry" in order to facilitate the reception of his new "experimental metaphysics," which is supposed to end the "old regime" of the hegemonic modernist metaphysics that rests on the separation between nature and society, facts and values, subjects and objects, and so forth. In Latour's new universe, the "common world" is to be built with largely different materials and to relate to politics in a profoundly different way.

He does not seem to devote sufficient consideration to the distinct structural and dynamic properties of common sense as a sociocultural system that may very well resist attempts to abruptly abandon such a powerful imaginary as objective nature, and shift from an existing, familiar, and relatively working system of social and political imaginaries to an open-ended experimental and untested one. By demanding a series of radical changes in the cultural and the political imagination, by taking the position of a metaphysician-scholar-teacher or cultural engineer rather than that of a listener-observer-interpreter who follows the nuances of public feelings, images, values, and languages, Latour, in fact, subscribes to a version of the hierarchical Platonic-Taylorean model of politics, shaped by ideas coming from above.[27]

EARLY SHIFTS TOWARD COMMONSENSE REALISM

It is important to reiterate at the beginning of this discussion that popular beliefs about reality and politics were never homogeneous in pagan Greece, Christian medieval, or secular modern Western societies. This point is worth stressing due to an influential ahistorical use of the expression "commonsense realism" by thinkers of the phenomenological tradition who tended to associate it with general notions of everyday experience and basic human responses to it. Alongside the move to historicize, social scientists have also attempted to culturally "anthropologize" and "sociologize" common sense, stressing the particular blends of general human experience and capacities with locally unique patterns of culture, meanings, and practical problems.

These developments can facilitate the understanding of commonsense realism as a historically and culturally specific configuration that coexists with

---

[27] For Latour's later partial reversal of this view, see "Why has Critique Run out of Steam? From Matters of Fact to Matters of Concern," *Critical Inquiry* vol. 30, no. 2 (2004).

other, often more marginal, models of experience. Now, it is more widely understood that every society actually encompasses mixed and often contradictory systems of common practical beliefs. Sometimes such heterogeneity is discernable in separate religious affiliations, sometimes along class divisions, including the rural–urban divide, sometimes through other kinds of gaps such as those between levels of literacy and education. Geoffrey Lloyd perceived the political connotations of such social divisions in imagining the cosmos in ancient Greece:

[F]or some Greeks the cosmos is a monarchy under the benevolent rule of an intelligent craftsman like force, but others represented it as an oligarchy or democracy of balanced powers or even, in the case of Heraclites, as anarchy, since for him justice is strife and war rule. These divergences in the way the cosmos was conceived reflect the equally radical disagreements on political ideals.[28]

A great diversity of popular beliefs also persisted in medieval Europe despite some significant homogenizing effects following the dissemination of Christianity. Since sometimes even extremely polarized worldviews could be found in the same society, it is not surprising to find, for instance, rational quasi-modern scientific attitudes in some thirteenth-century medieval social circles as well as magical or quasi-magical attitudes and practices in some parts of nineteenth-, twentieth-, and even early twenty-first-century societies. Even if we were to hypothetically assume that all human beings bring the same elementary cognitive equipment to their encounter with the world and have access to shared cultural resources, collective and individual variations in the hierarchy of values would have sufficed to account for heterogeneous imaginaries of the cosmic and the political orders, and be associated with correspondingly diverse behavioral patterns and institutions within and between cultures and societies.

Differences in value clusters between those that place the individual at the summit and those that regard the individual as an epiphenomenon or as merely derivative of the group, foster different notions of order, different relations among parts, different cognitive foci, and varied distributions and uses of attention and intellectual effort. Diverse value orientations generate and employ different patterns of time and space as well.[29] Still, within each living society the multiplicity of popular beliefs does not rule out the importance of widely shared orientations, of commonsense frames that facilitate communication and practical actions across subcultures.

The attempt to discern the characteristics of modern Western common sense, the very characteristics that have eroded due to postmodern trends, can benefit

---

[28] Geoffrey Lloyd, "Science in Antiquity: The Greek and Chinese Cases and their Relevance to the Problem of Culture and Cognition" in David R. Olson and Nancy Torrance (eds.), *Modes of Thought: Explorations in Culture and Cognition* (Cambridge: Cambridge University Press, 1996), p. 26.

[29] Gabriel Motzkin, *Time and Transcendence: Secular History, the Catholic Reaction and the Rediscovery of the Future* (Dordrecht: Kluwer Academic Publishers, 1992); Eisenstadt, "Multiple Modernities," *Daedalus* (Winter 2000).

from scholarly work on significant period-specific commonsense cultures, tracing apparent shifts between medieval and modern societies. Among the most important discontinuities discernable between medieval and modern societies are their respective imaginaries of agency and causality. Le Goff observes:

In medieval society the interpenetration between "natural" and "supernatural" agencies and forces, the ambiguous relations between God and Satan as the two super agencies as well as the earthly agencies, the very persons who were believed to be empowered as their delegates, left medieval persons in a state of permanent anxiety. On the one hand individuals in the Middle Ages felt that they were continuously watched by the agencies of good and evil, never left alone, free from "a constant double spy-system." On the other hand they lacked the criteria for distinguishing between good and evil agencies and actions, between black and white magic, miracles and tricks, the ordinary and the marvelous.[30]

Such a modern perspective on premodern medieval culture has often been accompanied by condescending criticism by the "moderns" of the "primitives."

It is interesting to note the ways in which some of the discontinuities between modern and premodern societies surface in the tacit normative assumptions of some of the most important scholarly work. Reflecting on his findings on medieval society, Le Goff observes: "The tragedy of the existence of the common mass of humanity" in the medieval era "lay in not being able to distinguish easily between the good and the evil, in being constantly deceived, and in taking part in the spectacle of illusions and misunderstanding which formed the medieval scene."[31] Of course, the external perspective underlying such an observation reflects the modern assumption that a life unguided by clear distinctions between facts and fictions or between good and evil must be tragic. But from the perspective advanced in this book, the confusions that Le Goff finds in medieval existence stem from an anachronistic retrospective view through a prism of the specific modern imaginaries, which authorize the possibility of setting clear, distinct, objective boundaries between facts and fictions or between dream and reality.

If one shifts perspective again, this time regarding the status of modern demarcation between fact and fiction, viewing the real and the imaginary from a postmodern perspective, one could easily reframe these clear-cut dichotomies as tragic illusions that derive their powers from anachronistic values, practices, and institutions. For postmodern individuals, the tragedy of the existence of the modern person may lie precisely in the belief that the (modern) subject is driven to distinguish too clearly between facts and fictions or between good and evil and to experience an unwarranted confidence generated by such a sense of certainty.

To reverse perspectives again, contemporary moderns, who jealously guard such certainties, may consider as tragic and intolerable the lives of postmoderns

---

[30] Jacques Le Goff, *Medieval Civilization, 400–1500* (New York: Basil Blackwell, 1988), pp. 159–61, 162–4.
[31] Ibid.

who equate freedom with a life emancipated from strictures imposed by such clear dichotomies, a life that entails a radically self-reflexive/reflective existence in which the real and the imaginary are, once more, not clearly delineated.[32]

From our analytical point of view, each of these three universes – the medieval, the modern, and the postmodern – undoubtedly rests on fictions and imaginings reflecting different sets of values, practices (including rituals of legitimation), and institutions. In each, the evidence considered sufficient for purposes of persuasion and action are profoundly different, and in each, individual lives and identities are experienced by means of a very different psycho-cultural repertory. It is instructive that, for a medieval individual like Augustine, dreams were a particularly loaded site of contest for the invisible agents of evil temptations, moral warnings, revelations, and truths. The modern tendency to interpret dreams in medical and psychological terms obviously diminished the power of dreams as carriers of social messages, although their role in the life of the individual persisted and even expanded, as reflected in Freud's pervasive influence.

In a world populated by ghosts, magicians, witches, miracle makers, and prophets – a world in which nature was considered a divine script and natural events were construed as signs from heaven, as punishments or rewards for human conduct, a world in which the individual was usually imprisoned by invisible chains of submission and obedience – it was within the boundaries of common beliefs to expect both natural and supernatural powers from political authorities as well.

There is a substantial body of records and research on the allegedly extraordinary powers attributed to medieval European kings as magicians, miracle makers, healers, and spiritual leaders. Kings themselves were interested in construing the status of kingship as bestowed by the grace of God. Claims to govern by divine grace found ritualistic expression in royal coronations, especially since the ninth century. The liturgy, the prayers, and the symbolism – all indicate the powerful amalgamation of religious and political imaginaries.[33] By contrast to the English monarch, French and German kings tended to lay greater stress on the religious dimension of kingship. Ullmann observes:

[T]he holy oil with which Clovis in the late fifth century was supposed to have been baptized served as a particularly strong factor with which to express the uniqueness of French theocratic kingship. None of the other kings had that distinction which he had. His oil was, as it were, brought down straight from heaven, whilst all other kings had to go to the chemist's shop. He was "the most Christian king" of Europe who possessed ... miracle-working and healing powers by which the royal mystique was considerably fostered.[34]

---

[32] See on this issue Yaron Ezrahi's "Science and the Modern Democratic Political Imagination" in Sheila Jasanoff (ed.), *States of Knowledge: The Co-Production of Science and Social Order* (London: Routledge, 2004), pp. 254–73.

[33] Ullmann, *Medieval Political Thought*, p. 86.

[34] Ibid., p. 155. See also Ernst Kantorowicz's *The King's Two Bodies: A Study in Mediaeval Political Theology* (Princeton: Princeton University Press, 1997).

Also on the level of the mundane life of common humanity it was customary to imagine the course of one's life as reflecting the workings of supernatural causal forces. The basic frame was that life, as Keith Thomas observes, was "not a lottery, but reflected the working out of God's purposes.... [T]he events of this world were not random but ordered."[35] To discern and possibly influence these divine purposes or block the schemes of evil agents such as Satan, premodern persons relied heavily on the authority of mystical "technologies" such as astrology, magic, Kabbalah, and witchcraft.

Common people in particular resorted to a wide variety of magical means to handle misfortune and promote their goals, including healing by means of the king's touch (a power often attributed to him by virtue of his consecration by the holy oil daubed at coronation). Other ends reached by magical means included recovering lost property and identifying thieves, predicting the course of one's future life, the weather, or the harvest, invoking the spirits of the dead, and so forth. Either by eschewing God's help or summoning it in ways unapproved by the official religious channels, popular magic posed a challenge to the authority of Church and clergy. The medieval Church, as Keith Thomas demonstrates, responded "by providing a rival system of ecclesiastical magic to take its place."[36]

Magic, witchcraft, and astrology must have offered the medieval subject some relief from the enormous persistent burden of human suffering. Their eventual decline cannot be attributed exclusively to the cognitive and imaginary aspects of the modernization of common sense or the social diffusion of more sophisticated notions of agency and causation. Neither can it be attributed solely to the rise of experimental science and its cultural and social consequence fomenting distrust of invisible agents and causation in the context of ordinary life. Equally important were socio-psychological transformations that substantially reduced (while not fully eliminating) the fears, anxieties, and tensions that generated the demand for such practices or altered their status across broad social circles. A case in point is the introduction of insurance in England at the end of the seventeenth century. This was in effect a social technique that reduced anxiety triggered by loss or fear of loss, thus weakening the demand for magical means to guarantee safety or recover material loss.[37]

Such cognitive and psychological shifts were connected to the search for another kind of politics not guided by transcendental powers or driven by invisible causality. Politics would be situated within the confines of a modern common sense that encompasses the realm of human agents and ordinary events; a world in which "one had to judge everyday political behavior, for example, against its own set of practical utilitarian rules, and not against

---

[35] Keith Thomas, *Religion and the Decline of Magic: Studies in Popular Beliefs in Sixteenth- and Seventeenth-Century England* (New York: Oxford University Press, 1997), p. 91.

[36] Ibid., p. 331.

[37] Ibid., pp. 779–82.

any prescribed, all-encompassing ethic."[38] Practical utilitarian standards for assessing causality and actions implied a convergence of commonsense realism and politics, which was influenced more by economic and other material and instrumental frames of reference than by spiritual or religious ones.

EARLY MODERN ASSOCIATIONS BETWEEN ATTRIBUTIONS OF CAUSALITY AND RESPONSIBILITY

I suggest that the modern emergence of novel political agents such as the individual and the public was associated with the tendency to experience the world as public reality, and that these developments were related to the emergence of new ways of attributing causality and responsibility in politics. It is obvious that in order to encompass the perceptions and orientations of a multitude of individuals, in order to uphold the very image (or fiction) of the modern public, new images of agency and causality had to replace medieval ones. In the language of cognitive social psychology, the "attribution schemas" employed by ordinary people to anchor and relate imaginaries of agency and causality had to shift.[39]

Lay attributions of causality in the contexts of making, unmaking, or sustaining political power and authority are usually connected with latent attributions of responsibility. In many cases, it can be demonstrated that an agent's desire to exonerate itself of responsibility for unhappy conditions or developments leads to schemes of causes and effects that lay blame elsewhere. The very connections between attributions of causality and responsibility in social and political affairs mean, of course, that any moral-political order presupposes a causal order that enables it.[40]

While many scholars, including Vico, have discussed relations between science and democracy, I devote much attention to the specific ways in which popular versions of scientific, or rather scientistic, notions of causality have been integrated into specifically democratic political norms and practices and their apparent coincidence with schemes of blaming and justifying. Clusters of explanation-accusation-justification and imaginings of causality conceived in terms whereby political agents are either blamed or credited vastly differ among theocracies, monarchies, totalitarian despotisms, and democracies. This

[38] Stephen L. Collins, *From Divine Cosmos to Sovereign State: An Intellectual History of Consciousness and the Idea of Order in Renaissance England* (New York: Oxford University Press, 1989), p. 119.

[39] For key discussions of "attribution theory" see Fritz Heider's *The Psychology of Interpersonal Relations* (New York: Wiley, 1958); S. T. Allison and D. M. Messick, "The Group Attribution Error," *The Journal of Experimental Social Psychology* vol. 21 (1985): 563–79; E. E. Jones and V. A. Harris, "The Attribution of Attitudes," *Journal of Experimental Social Psychology* vol. 3, no. 1 (1967): 1–24; and volume 10 of *Advances in Experimental Social Psychology* (1977).

[40] The vast legal discourse concerning relations between psychological or genetic causalities and the assignment of criminal responsibility provides ample illustration for such links, as well as for the mutual adjustments between notions of causality and responsibility.

point relates to our earlier discussion of the uses and effects of strategies of naturalization and historicization in allotting blame or merit and in attributing causes either to human actions or to nonhuman forces.

We can now be more precise and regard democracy as a novel modern cluster of interrelated causal and moral commitments. I consider the shift from nonhuman to human political agents as closely related to shifts from spiritual and invisible causalities to material ones, facilitating the integration of attributions of human causality and responsibility into publicly accessible frames of commonsense experience. This is, of course, just another way to state that the modern rise of commonsense realism and its lay metaphysics is inseparable from the rise of the social and political norms and practices that form the fabric of democracy. It is also in this connection that I argue at the end of this book that one can speak about an ethics of political imaginaries. Refusal to subscribe to certain imaginings could, for instance, be judged as the rejection of, or the inability to accept, a particular cluster of agents, causes, and responsibilities and, ultimately, the values they presuppose, while subscribing to an alternative constellation of values. I am interested in these issues in connection with the rise of the individual simultaneously as a social or political cause and a moral agent, and particularly the place of the imaginary of individual conscience in modern democracy.

Charles Taylor argues that a new conception of the moral order of society is central to Western modernity,[41] which, as I indicated earlier, he attributes largely to the influence of theorists such as Grotius and Locke. Without denying some such intellectual influences on the popular political imagination, I believe that the combined emergence of the modern commonsense view of reality, of the public, and of the modern individual as political agents – a complex development crucial for Western modernity and democracy – is the outcome of the cumulative effects of a host of developments in such diverse spheres as theology, science, and technology as well as in social structure and values, political interests, emotions, and perceptions. Only by assimilating a multiplicity of such factors could ideas articulated by intellectuals migrate in society, permeating the popular imagination, possessing the power to undermine hegemonic premodern political imaginaries while generating new ones.

The transformation of popular medieval beliefs about causality and agency and the emergence of modern common sense in the West, were, of course, neither sudden nor complete. We are discussing here a cluster of processes that have unfolded throughout a period of several centuries. A substantial body of work on history, sociology, and the anthropology of popular beliefs has illuminated this aspect of modernization in Western societies.[42] My concern is confined in this context to the two key implicit elements of modern commonsense metaphysics fundamental to democratic political world making:

[41] Charles Taylor, *Modern Social Imaginaries* (Durham: Duke University Press, 2004).
[42] See for instance Mary Poovey, *A History of the Modern Fact: Problems of Knowledge in the Sciences of Wealth and Society* (Chicago: University of Chicago Press, 1998).

the constitutive imaginaries of modern reality (including causality) and the individual.

One of the most important early factors affecting the emergence of the modern popular image of reality as a sphere of discernable regularities was the rationalization of God's nature. The view of God as an arch-engineer rather than a capricious performer of miracles and punishments weakened the belief that natural disasters are divine retribution and timely rain is a divine blessing. It is widely acknowledged that Protestantism made a substantial contribution to a view of nature relatively free of magical and spiritual accounts of events.

In the course of the seventeenth and eighteenth centuries, natural causes became more widely acceptable as alternatives to mystical and spiritual ones. "When the Devil was banished to Hell," writes Keith Thomas, "God himself was confined to working through natural causes. Special providences and private revelations gave way to the notion of a Providence which itself obeyed natural laws accessible to human study."[43] The ascendancy of natural theology over magic, he observes, was also associated with a sharp break in the link between guilt and misfortune.

These observations note that such early moves away from premodern notions of agency and causality involved shifts not only in theology but also in psychological and particularly emotional aspects of the individual's relation to the world. Following the rationalization of causation, the emotional need to find an instant panacea for misfortune was apparently tempered by the realization that there is no agent, neither god nor king nor priest, who could instantly redress a situation, contingent on complicity procured by magical or spiritual techniques.

Once the imagery and vocabulary of the emerging mechanistic model of natural causation empowered by modern science expanded to increasingly wide social circles, causation could be conceived as an autonomous phenomenon, even one indifferent to human wishes or, like nature, as a given resource that some agents (such as scientists) could manipulate in the service of human goals. This notion of neutral, independent chains of causation, access to which was not restricted to an esoteric elite of magicians, alchemists, astrologists, or spiritual virtuosi, was essential for the eventual emergence of an image of nature that, as a metaphor for the polity, could uphold a demystified version of transparent political causality. Such a view would link acts of the people or individual citizens in a causal chain that could either empower or disempower the government.

There was no more significant development in shaping the modern democratic political imagination than the psycho-cultural shifts that enabled modern individuals to imagine themselves as a potentially decisive factor in politics,

---

[43] Thomas, *Religion and the Decline of Magic*, p. 765; see also Amos Funkenstein's *Theology and the Scientific Imagination from the Middle Ages to the Seventeenth Century* (Princeton: Princeton University Press, 1986), pp. 117–201.

anchoring the imaginary of the people as the foundation of government. This shift has underlined modern revolutions and movements of liberation.

Mere acknowledgment of natural and legal individual and group rights, devoid of the support of these novel notions of political agency and causality, would not have sufficed to generate such historical events and processes. The relations between the de-spiritualization of nature, the democratization of understanding and human agency, and the partial malleability of material causality evidently required that scientists not merely replace priests as privileged mediators or surrogates of the causality linking the people and the social order. The people had also to perceive itself as a factor, as a cause, and conceive natural and political causality as consisting of processes and events in the sphere of commonsense experience in a disenchanted world.

The history of science as a social institution in Western societies reflects tensions between this commitment to present scientific knowledge as a public resource and the largely esoteric character of scientific practice. Many studies of the history of science record scientists' repeated efforts to depersonalize claims and certifications of knowledge and make that knowledge readily accessible to the public, especially in England and America, but also in other Western societies such as France and Italy. This instigated dissemination of knowledge by means of museums of science, illustrated books, and encyclopedias aiming at mass scientific instruction and public performance of experiments accessible to amateur observers, especially when exploring concepts such as electricity.

Such developments reflected the rise of the public as a more specifically accepted source of legitimation and accreditation of science, and the need of scientists to draw upon this new source of authority in order to support their activities and institutions. Scientists such as Robert Boyle, Joseph Priestly, and Michael Faraday, for instance, took care to belittle their own roles in scientific discovery, thereby encouraging the emergence of more democratic imaginaries of nature, knowledge, and science.[44] In contrast to the claims made by magicians, alchemists, and witch doctors, the claims made by scientists could not rest on an assumption of extraordinary personal powers of the scientist. In increasingly wider social circles, new standards of reliability required that the basis of claims to knowledge be accessible to the lay public (in principle, if less in practice), free of subjective bias and the influence of religion and politics and confirmable by nonprofessional witnessing of work, experiments, and well-ordered specimens.

The shift from believing in invisible agents and effects to trusting visible or tangible ones, from having confidence in the existence of spiritual agency and

---

[44] Steven Shapin and Simon Schaffer, *Leviathan and the Air-Pump: Hobbes, Boyle, and the Experimental Life* (Princeton: Princeton University Press, 1985); Simon Schaffer, "Priestley's Questions: An Historiographic Survey," *History of Science* vol. 22 (1984): 151–7; David Gooding, "In Nature's School: Faraday as an Experimentalist" in David Gooding and Frank A. J. L. James (eds.), *Faraday Rediscovered: Essays on the Life and Work of Michael Faraday 1791–1867* (Basingstoke, NY: Stockton Press, 1985), pp. 105–35.

causality to relying on more material, physical, observable agency and causality was, of course, never complete. But apparently it was sufficiently achieved to enhance nature and science as sources of constitutive imaginaries of modern democratic politics, projecting into politics "physicalist" images of objective causal connections between the citizens, or the people, and the government. The de-spiritualization of commonsense notions of agency and reality facilitated the materialization of politics in the realm of sense perceptions and the evolution of a modern democratic visual culture.

6

Empiricism, Induction, and Visibility: The Moral Epistemology of Democratic Political Power

Democratic visual culture and its epistemological grounds have been essential in shaping the expectations and practices of modern commonsense realism. One of the primary tendencies of modern commonsense realism in the West, particularly in the Anglo-American context, has been the association of the real with the visible, the belief in ocular witnessing as the guarantor of factuality.[1] The tendency to associate this development with the progress and the dissemination of the Enlightenment, which entailed a break with the perceived prejudices and superstitions of the medieval world, has often overlooked the particular relations between the rise in the authority of lay empiricism and the ascendancy of the public as an authority in the legitimation of factual claims about the world.

Partly in reaction to the pervasiveness of "invisibles" in medieval hierarchical cultures of authority, modern political authority and power came to depend for their legitimation on the degree to which politics could be apprehended within the actual or metaphorical frames of "material" and, therefore, "visible" agencies, causes, and effects. Materiality that could ensure accessibility to sensory experience became an important, albeit not a sufficient condition for fulfilling the political requirements of public visibility, participation, and accountability. As Mary Poovey has demonstrated, materiality could be and was metaphorically extended to include invisibles, which often retained only a slight gestural relation with the observables.[2] Until the upsurge of fundamentalism in the late decades of the twentieth century, the latent tendency in modern western political culture was to shift the political focus from religion and spiritual well-being to economic, medical, and other material measures of

---

[1] For a very early modern reference to the power of visible evidence see Othello's plea to Iago: "Villain, be sure thou prove my love a whore/Be sure of it; give me the ocular proof" (III. iii.364–5).

[2] Mary Poovey, *A History of the Modern Fact: Problems of Knowledge in the Sciences of Wealth and Society* (Chicago: University of Chicago Press, 1998).

well-being and to stress the role of technology and statistics in state actions. Instrumentalism, as a pervasive political mode in vast fields of state discourse and action, has drawn much of its extraordinary authority from its implicit gesture toward the public, aimed at materializing the political and placing it within the inclusive epistemological boundaries of commonsense realism.[3]

Thus, not without irony, instrumentalism as an emerging political strategy geared to depoliticizing claims of political power and authority could seem publicly accountable while actually relying on esoteric expert or quasi-expert authorities. This was largely achieved through the social spread of induction as a moral-political gesture, a rhetorical trope flexible enough to accommodate countless ways of evading rigorous empirical methodologies. Its minimal requirement was usually to construe a chain of claims and related actions based on references limited to a few actual or virtual observables in the sphere of commonsense reality.

As I have argued throughout, to regard such practices as merely deceptive is to misperceive the role of such gestures and the functioning of necessary fictions in upholding the democratic political order. Presenting itself as an alternative to hierarchical, arbitrary, and spiritual politics, instrumental politics as a widely endorsed fact-producing imaginary seemed for a considerable length of time to draw sufficiently on pseudo-real or imagined common experience to warrant its claim to public accountability. Although within such a frame the very "facts" that must be rendered public or transparent derive their authority from the presumed trust of a witnessing potentially critical public, they could appear to be just commonsensical descriptions of a given shared external reality.

Again, we can discern here the extent to which the performative imagination underlies perceptions of common sense. By concealing the moral-political sanction of gestural induction, it facilitates the performance of a particular reality as a neutral external given. As such, the reflective mode of the performative imagination is empowered to represent as authoritative factual reality what is largely the product of the concealed creative composing imagination of the community. This process of reality production is further reinforced in the political context where abstract entities like the state, the nation, democracy, or a successful war metamorphose into visual imagery of material facts and events. These "givens" owe much to the effects of the modern imaginary of the presumed continual gaze of the public as the quasi-sovereign (discussed in Chapter 10) that unknowingly composes the very public reality that plays such a vast role as a resource of democratic politics, influencing, for example, the attitudes of the same public toward claims of objectivity and neutrality made by dominant actors. For a long time the journalistic ethos of neutral reporting, including the conventional separation between news and analysis or opinion,

---

[3] I have extensively discussed the rise of instrumentalism in modern democratic politics in my book *The Descent of Icarus: Science and the Transformation of Contemporary Democracy* (Cambridge, MA: Harvard University Press, 1990).

has provided vital support in sustaining the perception of such initially publicly created realities in a kind of spiral loop that recalls Hobbes's observation that men tend to stand in awe of the creations of their own imaginations.

The socio-epistemological ground for determination of a public and commonsensical world of facts has been the almost universal belief that all individuals actually or potentially live in, experience, and see the same external world. This belief has been crucial for the emergence of an imaginary of the world as a naturalized, universally accessible factual reality constituting a neutral referent for the various discourses on truth as well as nonarbitrary political action.

Science, or rather scientism, has obviously played a major role in the emergence and cultivation of this modern commonsense imaginary of reality as a resource of democratic political world making. The term *scientism* is used in this discussion in a nonpejorative sense to describe fragments of scientific knowledge after they have undergone a process of selection and adaptation to the commonsense contexts of epistemological literalism and everyday practical needs. What I have called here gestural induction has actually derived its power from mimicking Isaac Newton's formula when he famously asserted that the

analysis [that] consists in making Experiments and Observations, and in drawing general Conclusions from them by Induction and admitting of no Objections against the Conclusions, but such as are taken from Experiments, or other certain Truths arguing from Experiments and Observations by Induction ... is the best way of arguing which the nature of things admits.[4]

It is easy to see how such assertions made by the supreme authorities of science could be transformed, in the context of common experience, into vulgar apprehension (or to my notion of gestural induction) undisciplined by the methodical observations, experiments, or methodologies sanctioned by science. Acts of making public could thus produce legitimation on the commonsense premise that sheer publicity lends the status of actuality, that assertions about what enters the supposed field of vision of the public eye are no longer subjective or biased.

Thus gestural induction could become a most productive, commonsensical instrument for the generation of modern realities. Commonsense realism, therefore, has come to rest on a form of epistemological literalism, a cluster of orientations and practices that relates to the world as a domain of plain public facts.

If literalism as a textual approach assumes that meaning is inscribed on the surface of language and therefore does not require interpretation, epistemological literalism assumes that facts reveal themselves to simple ordinary observation, that factual truths are inscribed, as it were, on the visible surface of experience. In its methodological approach to both texts and facts, literalism is an all-encompassing orientation that thus seems more democratic and less dependent on expert mediation. Since much of its authority derives from

---

4 Isaac Newton, *Opticks*, Query 31 (London, 1704); Isaac Newton, *Opticks, or, A Treatise of the Reflections, Refractions, Inflections and Colours of Light*, second edition (London: W. Bowyer, 1717), cited in Peter Dear, *Discipline and Experience: The Mathematical Way in the Scientific Revolution* (Chicago: University of Chicago Press, 1995), p. 240.

its directness and inclusiveness, it is potentially a means of empowering laymen against religious, political, and scholarly elites. Literal meanings and literal facts are the ammunition of the common man in confronting the men and women of abstract doctrines, principles, theories, and authority with "the real, simple facts of experience."

Oblivious to the complex ontological, interpretive presuppositions and productive processes that lend texts and facts their self-evident surface and ignoring the role of concepts and theories in the production or corroboration of facts, literalism reduces all compositions and interpretations to mere descriptions. When such descriptions are repeated and integrated within the common experience as signifieds of fixed signifiers, they tend to become reified as information and perceptual social habits. It is, then, the perspective of commonsense realism that makes laymen relate to such descriptions as representations of an independent external reality.

My notion of *epistemological* (and *discursive*) *literalism* is not confined to laymen in the context of ordinary everyday experience. Nelson Goodman points out that the relations between conceptions of reality and perspective are also fundamental in the contexts of science and philosophy. "The physicist," he observes:

takes his world as the real one, attributing the deletions, additions, irregularities, emphases of other versions to the imperfections of perception, to the urgencies of practice, or to poetic license. The phenomenalist regards the perceptual world as fundamental, and the excisions, abstractions, simplifications, and distortions of other versions as resulting from scientific or practical or artistic concerns. For the man-in-the-street, most versions of science, art, and perception depart in some ways from the familiar serviceable world he has jerry-built from fragments of scientific and artistic tradition and from his struggle for survival. *This world, indeed, is the one most often taken as real; for reality in a world, like realism in a picture, is largely a matter of habit.* (my emphasis)[5]

So the literal and the denotative, in the respective contexts of science, art, and common sense, are made of distinct configurations of metaphors, analogies, schemas, perceptions, values, and other elements that coalesce into habits of references to, or designations of, the real in these domains.

Sometimes it is the scientists themselves who, under constant social and economic pressure to be relevant to life, to give guidance, or to publicly justify their claims, authority, and resources, employ commonsense-epistemological literalism as a rhetorical strategy. Encouraging the belief that scientists and laymen inhabit the same world and refer to the same facts, scientists draw power, authority, and trust from the public as omnipotent witness of the facts they represent or interpret. Only in such a context could facts "speak for themselves" or be regarded as self-evident. It has required, undoubtedly, great skill on behalf of scholars and experts to know when to be epistemologically literal and when to distance themselves as agents of a different, more esoteric knowledge. For instance, there is a marked gap between the complex and tacit

[5] Nelson Goodman, *Ways of Worldmaking* (Hassocks, Sussex: The Harvester Press, 1978), p. 20.

knowledge doctors share about the drugs they prescribe and the information and language they use in instructing patients. The point is that their expert status has largely come to depend on the ability to navigate across the culturally demarcated yet unstable boundaries between lay and expert realms, a skill that has become more difficult to attain in our time.[6]

Epistemological literalism among scholars and scientists has nevertheless surpassed the requirements of communication with laymen and the social legitimation of scholarly authority. Within the scholarly community, literal conceptions of facts, detached from a theoretical framework, have been useful to scholars in diminishing controversies, enhancing irenic over polemic styles of discourse and thereby generally promoting civility.[7]

But, as Nelson Goodman suggests, even within the most internal forums of scientific discourse such as that of physics, the status and boundaries of attributions of factuality and the selective reifications of abstractions and theoretical entities have been responsive to shifting and competing conceptual strategies and their corresponding ontological commitments and rhetoric.[8] The fluctuating definitions and boundaries of scientific facts recorded by historians of science illustrate the context-boundedness of factuality. Nelson Goodman's observation that "facts are little theories" applies both to the contexts of science and common sense, while suggesting a greater degree of similarity between the two spheres in relation to the problematics of factuality.[9]

The complex syncretic and elastic processes of defining and handling facts are more conspicuous in the modern social sciences, less constrained than in the traditions of experimental physics. During the latter half of the seventeenth century, William Petty (1623–87), one of the most influential early founders of political statistics and political economics, collected diverse data and measures of land, population, domestic production, and so forth, in order to produce surveys of the state of the kingdom that, he claimed, would improve the efficacy of the government. Like other members of the early Royal Society of London, William Petty was a Baconian who believed in the superiority of persuasion by "examining" and of showing over "telling."[10] His practice, however, was more

---

[6] For an exceptionally instructive study of the authority of experts in public affairs see Sheila Jasanoff, *The Fifth Branch: Science Advisers as Policy Makers* (Cambridge, MA: Harvard University Press, 1990). Also very valuable are Charles E. Lindblom, *Inquiry and Change: The Troubled Attempt to Understand and Shape Society* (New Haven: Yale University Press, 1990), and Mark B. Brown, *Science in Democracy: Expertise, Institutions and Representation* (Cambridge, MA: MIT Press, 2009).

[7] See for instance Lorraine Daston's "Baconian Facts, Academic Civility, and the Prehistory of Objectivity" in *Annals of Scholarship* vol. 8, nos. 3–4 (1991): 337–64; Steve Shapin, *A Social History of Truth, Civility and Science in Seventeenth-Century England* (Chicago: University of Chicago Press, 1994); Poovey, *A History of the Modern Fact*.

[8] See the reference to Mara Beller's *Quantum Dialogue: The Making of a Revolution* (Chicago: University of Chicago Press, 1999).

[9] Goodman, *Ways of Worldmaking*, pp. 91–107.

[10] Lisa Jardine, *Francis Bacon: Discovery and the Art of Discourse* (Cambridge: Cambridge University Press, 1979), p. 15.

complicated than his claim to ground his reports in tangible evidence warranted. As Mary Poovey indicates, "Petty's facts were conjectural rather than observed, and they described abstractions rather than historical events.... [Yet] he claimed for his facts the same degree of epistemological authority that members of the Royal Society claimed for experimental facts" based on collective witnessing.[11]

Poovey argues further that Petty actually made a contribution to the building of professional authority on the "relationship of numbers and impartiality."[12] This, no doubt, was important. But his insistence on basing his assumptions on "only Arguments of Sense, and ... consider[ing] only such Causes as have visible foundations in Nature; leaving those that depend upon ... Opinions, Appetites, and Passions of Particular Men, to the Consideration of others"[13] are a powerful illustration of the attraction of the moral-political-rhetorical force of gestural induction. Especially in the context of discourse on governance, it appealed to the latent legitimating participatory role of the public in the production of facts.

Reliance on numbers, on counting, has been, as Shapin, Shaffer, Dear, Porter, Poovey, and other historians have suggested, inextricably bound to the authority of observables. The point I wish to emphasize is that numbers and quantitative measures were secondary to and derived from a comprehensive notion of the world as a spectacle and of the public as viewer.[14] Even Petty's attempt to serve the monarchy and to reinforce effective control of the centralized government does not contradict the increasing implicit reliance on the authority of the public in attesting to facts. The constitutive democratic imaginary of facts was also perfectly compatible with the gestures made by seventeenth-century monarchs toward the people in order to reinforce the eroding foundations of hierarchic and spiritual authorities by introducing elements bearing a semblance of democratic legitimacy.

Reliance on the authority of visible facts in the course of the seventeenth century signified the early stages of the emergence of a modern democratic political epistemology. One of its most evident manifestations was the aforementioned implicit link between the increasingly popular definition of the world as spectacle, as an observable, orderly assortment of objects and events, and the largely metaphorical conception of the public as a gazing agency. It took at least another century for the public as an imaginary to find sufficient institutional and behavioral expressions to become a robust democratic agent, and for the "celebratory visual orientations" of the king's subjects to be substantially replaced by the "attestive visual orientations" of the emerging, more skeptical, democratic citizens.[15]

---

[11] Poovey, *A History of the Modern Fact*, p. 123.
[12] Ibid.
[13] Ibid. p. 132, from William Petty's *The Economic Writings of Sir William Petty [1662]*, Charles Henry Hull (ed.) (1899; Fairfield, NJ: Augustus M. Kelly, 1986), p. 244.
[14] Theodore M. Porter, *Trust in Numbers: The Pursuit of Objectivity in Science and Public Life*, (Princeton: Princeton University Press, 1995).
[15] See Ezrahi, *The Descent of Icarus*, especially pp. 73–4.

Like the works of other seventeenth-century European social scholars and statisticians such as John Graunt and Henry Conring, Sir William Petty's *Political Arithmetick* constituted an effort to appropriate the language of the empirical sciences of nature and transmute it into a discourse on ostensibly similarly observable social objects and events. These works anticipated and laid the foundations for the rise of the modern social sciences and their massive though often latent extension of the discursive frames of physical scientism onto the sociopolitical sphere. Such a tendency amounted to the discovery of "social physics," in the language of Auguste Comte and other French social scientists, thus certifying various plausible forms of social realism beyond physical commonsense realism.

The ability to expand the authority of gestural induction into vast spheres of social and political life so radically, to persuasively combine scant references to social observables with latent conjectural frames and implicit conceptual abstractions and produce powerful modern imaginaries of social reality, has had profound consequences for the emergence of modern democratic notions of agency and causality. Deriving their authority mostly from virtual public witnessing and naïve epistemological literalism, modern social facts could feature as sheer objective material or substantive givens, thus contributing to objectifying and depoliticizing the supposed grounds of government decisions and actions. These factors rendered many uses of political and bureaucratic powers plausibly impersonal and nonarbitrary while concomitantly warranting the expectation that journalism – the great modern flattener and simplifier of experience – could render the government transparent to freely discriminating citizens.

In the longer run, however, the behavioral and institutional dynamics of democratic politics were bound to limit the power of the social sciences and the bureaucracy to fix definitions of social reality. Particularly in democratic societies, which deny the authority of any privileged synoptic perspective on reality beyond the inherently partial perspectives of a multitude of equal and contesting individuals, social and political definitions of factual reality were bound to remain underdetermined. And it is this inherent indeterminism that has both facilitated the free play of competing political imaginaries of the whole and parts of the political order, and secured its inconclusiveness. A democratic society, a society that performs democratic political imaginaries and therefore constantly interrogates its own rules, foundations, and history, can grant any cluster of social and political facts and values only temporary life. This is partly why democratization has diminished the authority of hierarchical political authorities to define political reality and why journalism, with its short-term perspectives, has largely replaced historical perspectives on social realities and political processes.

Within the context of liberal democratic politics, this inherent indeterminacy of factual reality is a most effective constraint on the tendency to generate sustainable dogmas. In the late seventeenth century, the idea that empirically grounded notions of reality are open-ended and modifiable by ever new testimonies, forwarded, for example, to the Royal Society of London by its fellows from distant lands, already entailed another implicit democratic gesture toward the lay public as an active source of opinion and information, relevant for collective definitions of the real. The eyewitness accounts of laymen at the site of a reported event, and much later of amateur photographers, gradually became authoritative participants-definers of the sociopolitical reality.[16] This process was increasingly augmented by modern technology. During mass protests that broke out in 2011 in countries like Syria, Egypt, Spain, Israel, and Russia, photographs and videos taken by the demonstrators with their cellular phones and transmitted by the mass media enjoyed privileged authority over government or commercial media in defining the situation.

Such attitudes proved crucial for ensuring that the new imaginaries of factual reality would leave cultural and political space for a continual political world making and public fashioning and refashioning of common life. This would not have been the case had modern concepts of truth and reality been bound to the certainties of mathematics and geometry, as thinkers like Hobbes or Spinoza at least provisionally hoped.

Among seventeenth- and eighteenth-century political theorists, the exceptionally accessible contribution of John Locke to the evolution of modern open-ended imaginaries of reality and inconclusive knowledge and their liberal democratic implications warrants special attention. For Locke, a modern political philosopher with uniquely exceptional influence on popular notions of liberal politics, assertions of facts about reality were merely judgments based on probability rather than certainty, that is, on "the appearance of agreement upon fallible proofs."[17] The two crucial words "appearance" and "fallible" suggest a horizontal, interpersonal-relational conception of knowledge. Locke anchors this inherently uncertain mode of knowledge in a balance between individual and social sources of evidence and confidence. It is grounded, he maintains, in "the conformity of anything with our own knowledge, observation and experience (and with) ... the *testimony of others, vouching their observation and experience*" (my emphasis).[18] Whereas probability is just "likeliness to be true," for "which there be arguments or proofs to make it pass, or be received for true,"[19] it is a good enough condition for the ordinary, everyday business of humanity. Consistent with his objection to formalized reasoning and unqualified concepts of certain knowledge, Locke advanced an unmathematical, largely conversational concept of the probable, and therefore provisional, factual knowledge. It is a concept of factual reality based on everyday experience

---

[16] Yaron Ezrahi, "Science and the Problem of Authority in Democracy" in Thomas F. Gieryn (ed.), *Science and Social Structure: A Festschrift for Robert Merton* Transactions of the New York Academy of Sciences, series II, vol. 39 (New York, NY: New York Academy of Sciences, 1980), pp. 43–60.

[17] John Locke, *An Essay Concerning Human Understanding*, II, book IV, chapter XV, § 1.

[18] Ibid., § 4.

[19] Ibid., § 3.

and requiring comparisons among competing propositions and their respective grounds. The mind, according to Locke, needs to:

examine all grounds of probability, and see how they may make *more or less* for or against any proposition, before it assents to or dissents from it; and upon a due *balancing the whole*, reject or receive it, with a *more or less* firm assent, proportionally to the preponderancy of the greater grounds of probability on one side or the other. (my emphasis)[20]

Here Locke narrows the gap between the authority of scientific knowledge and commonsense realism, enhancing the grounds for the participation of the people in both the cultural and political orders. His is a philosophy that conceptualizes and mirrors common ordinary practices and commonsense judgment rather than delegitimizing them on the basis of a theory-based formal and systematic knowledge. Locke certainly attempts to equip laymen with habits of observing and reasoning that would allow them to transcend the naïveté inherent in "epistemological literalism" and resist the dangers of being carried away by their occasional fantasies. Locke thus advanced standards and skills more likely possessed by English gentry than by commoners in his day.[21] But his was a crucial move to translate the commitment to the imaginary of popular sovereignty into specific codes of conduct, to build the normative and epistemological grounds for practices that could give credence to a newly conceptualized order. Such an order would derive its legitimation from the lay public; from the bottom rather than from the top.[22] If we view Locke's elaboration of liberal political epistemology together with his concept of private property as his attempt to hypostatize or embody individual freedom and agency, we may discern a comprehensively orchestrated project of apprehending liberal democratic politics within the coordinates of commonsensical material sense experience.[23]

European merchants provide a particularly instructive illustration of the spread of commonsense realism in some European social circles of the period. Confronting distant societies and cultures and searching for ways to communicate with their native inhabitants, they were driven to reflect on differences between foreign cultures and their own. European merchants also developed and employed modern techniques of counting, measuring, and reporting in commercial transactions and in their social milieu. Their perspective can shed light on their cultural worldviews and commitments. William Pietz observes that "Protestant merchants visiting the [African] coast elaborated a general explanation of African social order as being based on the principles underlying

---

[20] Ibid., § 5.

[21] Ibid.

[22] See Steven Shapin, *A Social History of Truth: Civility and Science in Seventeenth-Century England* (Chicago: University of Chicago Press, 1994). See also the illuminating, comprehensive book by Douglas John Casson, *Liberating Judgment: Fanatics, Skeptics, and John Locke's Politics of Probability* (Princeton: Princeton University Press, 2011).

[23] See also James Tully, *An Approach to Political Philosophy: Locke in Contexts* (Cambridge: Cambridge University Press, 1993).

the worship of Fetissos" (fetishes), which they criticized.[24] Such Protestant criticism probably echoed similar objections long directed against [Roman] Catholic practices such as the Corpus Christi ritual. Pietz notices that

for seventeenth-century European merchants, the economically valuable material object often became the very basis and medium for social relationship ... in associated developments in political and legal argument, material objects came to be identified as proper to economics as opposed to religious activity, so Grotius argued in 1609 when he denied the Pope's right to grant the Portuguese trade monopolies: "Trade has only to do with material gains, and has no concern at all with spiritual matters, outside which, all admit, Papal power ceases."[25]

Seventeenth-century European merchants came, by contrast, to regard the organization of African life as an irrational concoction of fancy, of modes of thought and behavior produced by what I have called the "fantastic imagination." Pietz further observes that

[T]he function of "Fetissos" [fetishes] in oath-taking was of particular importance to European merchants searching for the means to establish permanent and trustworthy trade relations. Many early voyage accounts describe instances of Africans who required the Europeans to take an oath upon some material object before they would agree to trade.[26]

In 1702, Willem Bosman, a Dutch merchant who sailed to the coast of Guinea at a young age in 1688 and eventually became chief merchant for the Dutch West Indies Company, wrote a popular travelogue in which he, like other reporting merchants, charged Africans with living by false religious values, superstitions, and fetishism, with a propensity to animate European technological objects. Particularly pertinent to our discussion is that this kind of criticism of magical causality indicates the social spread of postmedieval/modern materialist conceptions of reality and mechanistic notions of causality since the early seventeenth century.

Less than a century and a half later, in his *Democracy in America*, Tocqueville observed several instances of Lockean democratic politico-epistemological practices: reliance on one's own observations and judgments, distrust of non-observables and extraordinary phenomena and, above all, commitment to an inclusive commonsense realism, the belief "that everything in the world may be explained, and nothing transcends the limits of understanding."[27] Tocqueville associated such developments with the despiritualization and the materialization of the political and with modern imaginaries of individual agency and causality.

---

[24] William Pietz, "The Problem of Fetish, II: The Origin of the Fetish," *RES* vol. 13 (Spring 1987): 23–45. I am indebted to Professor Lydia Liu for calling my attention to this source.

[25] Ibid.

[26] See Jelle C. Riemersma, *Religious Factors in Early Dutch Capitalism 1550–1650* (The Hague: Mouton, 1967), pp. 55–7, cited and discussed in Pietz, ibid., 40–1.

[27] Alexis de Tocqueville, *Democracy in America*, Harvey C. Mansfield and Delba Winthrop (trans. and ed.) (first pub. 1835; Chicago: University of Chicago Press, 2002), pp. 403–7.

Despite the urge to entrench the real and stabilize the objects of our experience, despite the powerful rhetoric of truth, the quest for ideals and for *the* final conclusive theory, science has, in fact, evolved as a continually self-transforming and dynamic process. As such, it has actually reflected a fluid concept of reality. In the practice and culture of experimental science, such a view is embodied in the norm of what Robert K. Merton has aptly defined as "organized skepticism."[28] This aspect of scientific practice and its democratic implications for the authority of science, both within the scientific community and in society at large, was expounded in Michael Polanyi's famous discussion of a feature of scientific practice he labeled "tacit knowledge," signifying the informal and unformalizable character of much of scientific practice.[29]

While scientific notions of reality and causality have probably significantly influenced the emergence of modern commonsense realism, their adaptation to the materialist commonsense context of epistemological literalism has usually necessitated detaching them from their ground in an ongoing theoretical discourse. This process has often been accompanied by an inclination to reify theoretical entities and hypostatize abstractions. In this respect there are interesting similarities in the tendencies of animation and reification between premodern and modern cultures.

Since such a process of reification facilitated in modernity by scientism also applies to political theories and abstract ideas such as the city, the nation, sovereignty, personality, the subconscious, and the public, it is instructive to briefly examine some illustrations of its workings. Charlotte Linde observes:

> As a given explanatory system becomes better known and more widely held, it begins to move closer to common sense and may eventually come to form a part of common sense. As an example, we take the notion of the Freudian slip, which seems to be a part of the general, common sense body of accepted notions and which does not require the support of the Freudian explanatory system to be comprehensible.[30]

This process of selective assimilation involves a shift from complex Freudian theoretical discourse to a popular language that uses only "a very small number of the concepts present in expert Freudian psychology ... those concepts of expert explanatory systems [that] ... do not contradict other popular theories of the mind and the reason for human behavior."[31] Similar processes of diluting

---

[28] For a discussion of Merton's classic article on the normative structure of science see Yaron Ezrahi, "Science and the Problem of Authority in Democracy" in Thomas F. Gieryn (ed.), *Science and Social Structure: A Festschrift for Robert Merton* Transactions of the New York Academy of Sciences, series II, vol. 39 (New York, NY: New York Academy of Sciences, 1980), pp. 43–60.

[29] Michael Polanyi, *Personal Knowledge: Towards a Post-Critical Philosophy* (New York: Harper Torchbooks, 1982); on risk and probability in our time see Ulrich Beck, *Risk Society: Towards a New Modernity*, Mark Ritter (trans.) (London: SAGE Publications, 1992) and Daniel Kahneman's *Thinking, Fast and Slow* (New York: Farrar, Straus and Giroux, 2011).

[30] Charlotte Linde, "Explanatory Systems in Oral Life Stories" in Dorothy Holland and Naomi Quinn (eds.), *Cultural Models in Language and Thought* (Cambridge: Cambridge University Press, 1987), pp. 350, 362–3.

[31] Ibid.

and therefore often also of distorting influential scientific theories in the course of their selective assimilation into commonsense discourse can be traced in scientistic appropriations of fragments of Darwin's theory of evolution and modern economic theory. The scientific authority of the theory of evolution seems to have lent power to commonsensical usage of phrases like "the survival of the fittest" (widely deployed to back up claims of racial superiority) or "the struggle for existence," phrases usually cut off from their rich theoretical context.

Similarly, commonsense use of terms borrowed from economic theory (such as *inflation* or *free competition*) usually simplifies and attenuates them to such an extent that the theoretical qualifications that render these notions meaningful and useful to experts are missing. If commonsense discourse sometimes generates imagery or ideas that experts borrow, refine, and transpose into theoretical concepts,[32] the reverse procedure entails the deracination and simplification of metaphors or imaginings embedded in thick theoretical networks and their conversion into coins in the common discourse.

The discontinuities between commonsense and scientific discourses, combined with the tendency of the former to selectively borrow from the latter, often generates tension and acute controversy. As noted earlier, French philosophers Maurice Merleau-Ponty and Henri Bergson were concerned that transplanting the concept of time developed in Einstein's physics within a commonsense system would produce disruptive paradoxes that could sanction unreason. But while acknowledging the difference between "psychological time" and "the time of the physicist" that he considered independent of ordinary perception and therefore more objective, Einstein declined the request to confine his concept of time to the context of science, detached from the domain of commonsense discourse in the realm of ordinary life.[33]

Another clash evolved in the late 1960s between a group of laymen and educators on one hand and genetic psychologists on the other regarding the correct use of the term *intelligence*. The IQ controversy demonstrates the tensions generated by the double lives of terms such as *intelligence* and concurrent commonsense categories as well as theoretically loaded measurable scientific concepts. This case is particularly illuminating because, as a term used for social classification of people, *intelligence* is implicitly or explicitly engaged in the construction of the moral order. As a concept in a theoretical scientific account of behavior that, among other things, might be useful for measuring human capacities and predicting levels of scholastic performance, it is deliberately stripped of such normative connotations.[34]

---

[32] Stephen C. Pepper, *World Hypotheses: A Study in Evidence* (Berkeley: University of California Press, 1942), especially pp. 39–70.

[33] See for a more detailed discussion Yaron Ezrahi's "Einstein and the Light of Reason" in Gerald Holton and Yehuda Elkana (eds.), *Albert Einstein: Historical and Cultural Perspectives – The Centennial Symposium in Jerusalem* (Princeton: Princeton University Press, 1982), pp. 253–78.

[34] See Yaron Ezrahi's "The Jensen Controversy: A Study in the Ethics and Politics of Knowledge in Democracy" in Charles Frankel (ed.), *Controversies and Decisions* (New York: Russell Sage Foundation, 1976), pp. 149–70.

It is precisely because scientific discourse encourages such separations between causal accounts and their normative contexts that the deployment of scientific or quasi-scientific accounts of social reality could be so rhetorically appealing in a polity deeply beset by controversies over issues of social equality and exclusion. Roy D'Andrade has developed the concept of "cultural schemas" to suggest the cultural means whereby members of a group shape the meaning of their experience and orient their behavior. Such a concept may help discern why and in what ways the respective cultural schemas of folk common sense and of professionals' worlds differ.

D'Andrade indicates further that the schemas that "portray simplified worlds ... portray not only the world of physical objects and events, but also more abstract worlds of social interaction, discourse, and even word meaning."[35] He distinguishes between "simple objects like 'cats' and 'disasters' [that] are things and events in the world ... [and] propositional objects [that] are not 'things' – they are 'thoughts' or 'beliefs,' such as the belief [in a] likely nuclear holocaust."[36] If this distinction is apprehended in its restricted sense, one may claim that, in addition to the central role of imaginaries, part of the objects in politics issue from thoughts or beliefs based on "propositional knowledge" rather than on observables. Hence the intense urge and effort to give them concrete perceptual expression. Films such as Kurosawa's *Dreams* (1990) illustrate the desire to visualize where certain imaginaries can lead.

Another salient discontinuity between commonsense and expert accounts of human behavior concerns the relations between the attribution of causes and the attribution of responsibilities. While in the professional context of the social sciences, explanations are aimed at advancing knowledge, understanding, and sometimes control, in the commonsense context of everyday life and ordinary politics the preoccupation with praise and blame tends to subordinate the attribution of causation to the attribution of responsibility. In descriptions of human behavior, commonsense categories do not usually conform to the demand in the social sciences for a separation between causal accounts or descriptions and the attribution or distribution of moral or political responsibility.

Machiavelli noted this tendency when he warned the Prince that people are inclined to judge the actions of their governors in moral terms. This tendency to uncritically mix moral attributions of responsibility and scientific, or rather scientistic, attributions of causality is manifest in public controversies over questions such as whether destructive floods or mass hunger are caused by nature or by the failure of government policies; whether an epidemic can be avoided; whether a technological disaster such as the explosion of the manned American space vehicle *Challenger II* should be attributed to foreseeable or

---

[35] D'Andrade, "Some Propositions About the Relationship Between Culture and Human Cognition" in J. W. Stigler, R. A. Shweder, and G. Herdt (eds.), *Cultural Psychology: Essays on Comparative Human Development* (New York: Cambridge University Press, 1990), p. 93.

[36] D'Andrade, "A Folk Model of the Mind" in Dorothy Holland and Naomi Quinn (eds.), *Cultural Models in Language and Thought* (Cambridge: Cambridge University Press, 1987), p. 118.

unforeseeable events. In the field of technology, claims such as obliviousness to the laws of nature, a disregard of physics, could form the basis for blaming decision makers for taking unreasonable, morally indefensible risks.

There is a difference between nature as an unpredictable and uncontrollable force, a *force majeure* that absolves human beings from responsibility, and nature as represented by available scientific knowledge. The latter model subjugates nature's uncontrollable force to the domain of the predictable and the knowable while expanding the sphere of potential human intervention and, therefore, responsibility. In many areas, then, scientific knowledge has metamorphosed nature from a pretext or vindication to an imperative.

In his "Minority Report to the Space Shuttle Challenger Inquiry," Richard P. Feynman determined that the probability of failure was high enough to warrant the exercise of far greater precaution on behalf of the decision makers. Their concerns about meeting administrative and political deadlines encouraged a tendency to overlook degrees of uncertainty and danger that they should have taken into consideration. Nature, or reality as represented by scientists and engineers, was thus enlisted by Feynman to make a diagnosis, to determine responsibility for a failure by specific individuals and organizations, and to issue a general warning. "For a successful technology," he argued, "reality must take precedence over public relations, for nature cannot be fooled."[37]

It is noteworthy in this connection that social psychologists have pointed out that differences in the attributions of causality and responsibility may often be related to positional-perceptual loci. Thus spectators observing actors tend to attribute their action to the actor's own personality or inner motives, whereas actors tend to attribute their own behavior to external causes in their environment.[38] Obviously these two perspectives generate distinct accounts of both causality and responsibility.

The previous comments may suffice to indicate that, in every period and culture, common sense, as a context of human action and discourse, has its own particular features, norms, and needs, often including external boundaries, gates, and permits. In the modern democratic state, as the epistemological site of political world making in which the fabric of political imaginaries is shaped and institutionalized, common sense cannot be regarded as a passive recipient of external data or phenomena. It is from this perspective that I have attempted to map the links between the modern consolidation of commonsense realism, influenced by scientism, and the emergence of democratic imaginaries of political agencies and causalities as real public facts.

[37] Richard P. Feynman, *The Pleasure of Finding Things Out: The Best Short Works of Richard P. Feynman* (London: Penguin, 1999), pp. 151–69.
[38] See Chapter 5, footnote 39.

7

The Performing Arts and the Performance of Politics: The Dialectics between the Transparent and the Self-concealing Imagination

With the erosion of the long-standing belief that the foundations of the political order reside in a transcendental divinity, nature, or tradition, modern politics has begun to develop more consciously as a product of human action, dependent on the accumulated creations of the historical political imagination already conceived by thinkers such as Vico, Hume, Rousseau, and Burke. The need to rely on new political imaginaries has derived from the sensed vacuum exposed by the collapse of the conventional grounds of political power and authority. The transformation of new political imaginaries into new political realities was bound to enhance public reflexivity and awareness of the historicity and fragile foundations of the political order. Against the background of this "secret" of the inherent fragility of the grounds of the political order, the utterances and actions of politicians have become more vulnerable to charges of theatricality, hypocrisy, and deception. The inevitability of the theatricality inherent in the very enactment of imaginaries of the political order has been largely created by the absence of a political reality independent of its own performance. The fiction that liberal democratic politics can be realized without its own constitutive theatrics, the enactment of its own imaginaries, has been sustained particularly by the Enlightenment's still somewhat influential vision of politics.

Consistent with this vision, secularized politics tried to distinguish itself from religious culture by adopting rhetorical styles and modes of action compatible with the emerging norms of commonsense realism. Such separation between the domains of religion and politics, anticipated by Machiavelli in the early sixteenth century, was eventually reinforced by the trends to privatize religion, to suspect religious notions of causality in public affairs, and to affix political imaginaries to the popular versions of scientific or quasi-scientific worldviews. These trends gave rise to a novel imaginary of politics as publicly visible and potentially instrumental.

I argue that, like religion, the arts, as a domain of the nonrational and often also of the esoteric imagination, were assigned a place beyond the ordinary modern commonsense universe and its scientistic version of the world. It was from the perspective of this framework of commonsense realism that religion and the arts were, with some important exceptions, widely conceived as belonging in spheres beyond the public rational domain of democratic politics. As such, western democratic politics has come to be suffused with elements of the self-concealing scientific as well as scientistic imagination and gloss over their inescapably fragile roots in the genealogy of the popular imagination.[1]

Ironically, while the loss of a transcendental divine or natural anchorage paved the way to imagining the democratic political order as dependent on the people, the inherent instability and unruliness of the people, particularly the people's political imagination, as the foundation of the political order repeatedly reignites a quest for religious, natural, or other transpolitical reinforcements. While Edmund Burke mourned the collapse of the monarchy as a bundle of "pleasing illusions that made power gentle,"[2] Thomas Paine presided over the inauguration of another bundle of illusions, which eventually (at least during the American, French, and subsequent democratic revolutions) combined nature and rights to render power more popular and constitutional, although perhaps less gentle.

Burke and Paine can be regarded as rival choreographers in the practice of politics as a performative art – the art of shaping and institutionalizing political imaginaries that would produce, from their opposing perspectives, desirable political effects, forms of behavior and institutions that fit their respective visions of stable and legitimate regimes.

The ultimate political skill has remained, however, to entertain, invent, or modify political imaginaries whose roots in the collective imagination are sufficiently concealed and their compatibility with current values and orientations sufficiently close to allow them to command public trust and function as political realities. Throughout western political history, the fragile distinction between the art of acting on the theater stage and the necessary political enactment of imaginaries of order on the political stage induced tensions between art and politics. It is possible to trace a continuum between the dilemmas of maintaining this dualism between the art of the theater and political stagecraft as a necessary dimension of statecraft to which Machiavelli alerted European princes in the early sixteenth century and the dilemmas facing contemporary leaders of enacting the necessary fictions of democracy in the current age of mass electronic visual media. Machiavelli recognized the necessity of such constitutive political theatricality for ensuring the stability of the current government, the need to protect the government's ability to act sometimes cruelly out of reasons of state while maintaining a façade of morality, piety, and generosity. Obviously the imperative of effective and credible gestural and symbolic projections of the hegemonic political (and legal) imaginaries of the political order

---

[1] Recall Vico's brilliant observation that "all the principles of metaphysics, logic, and ethics originated in the public square in Athens" in *New Science* (Harmondsworth: Penguin, 1999), 1043.

[2] Edmund Burke, *Reflections on the Revolution in France*, Conor Cruise O'Brien (ed.) (Harmondsworth: Penguin Books, 1969), p. 171.

in order to enable their translation into working institutions and political facts persists in contemporary efforts to legally, organizationally, and behaviorally embody human rights, equality, freedom, and self-government. Contrary to the short life expectancy of the reality effects that capture theater audiences that cooperate by the suspension of their disbelief, in any regime, I argue, it is rare for subjects and even citizens who conveniently believe in the given political reality of the existing order to suddenly suspend that belief upon realizing that this very reality is the product of their own recursive performative political imagination.

Simultaneously with the marginalization of the public role of religion in the modern secular state, the arts have entered the cultural space partly evacuated by religion and acquired the latent function of, among other things, representing the domain of (secular) fantasies, of the creations of an imagination unaccountable to commonsense experience that by contradistinction have come to support a cultural boundary between reality and illusion. The arts, including the performing arts, by constituting a distinct domain of illusions, contributed to the transmutation of constitutive political imaginaries placed outside that domain into perceived commonsense factual realities. The point I wish to stress is that in liberal democratic societies it is precisely the supposed autonomy of the domain of the fine and the performing arts – their apolitical status as belonging in the demarcated territory of fancy and illusion – that has facilitated, by contradistinction, an affirmation of a separate domain of the real as the sphere of responsible human actions. That which has been presented as deliberately fictive, as merely fantastic or imaginary, or as a purely stylized representation has latently come to confirm, by contrast, the reality of the external natural, social, and political worlds beyond the theater or museum walls.

If art is an honest attempt to use illusions, what, in the period under discussion, is realism in art? In some respects realism in art is, to any spectator or audience that cares to reflect upon this issue, a display of the powers of the creative imagination to use illusion in order to produce reality effects as elements of an aesthetic experience. From our perspective, these powers of art can point also to the potential latent uses of illusion to produce political reality effects that serve the aesthetization and legitimation of power and its application in public affairs. Commonly, however, the public is too preoccupied with the urge to compare a realistic painting with objects or figures in the familiar world of everyday life to ponder the role of the imagination in producing both fantastic artistic and sociopolitical reality effects – albeit from different materials and by means of distinct cognitive processes.[3] Unlike artistic works of the manifestly and deliberately fantastic imagination, realistic art claims to refer directly or indirectly to an outside world and to be its true representation. The apparent

---

[3] This idea is elaborated in Adam Smith's treatise, "Of the Nature of that Imitation which Takes Place in What are Called the Imitative Arts" in Ruth Katz and Ruth HaCohen (eds.), *The Arts in Mind. Pioneering Texts of a Coterie of British Men of Letters* (New Brunswick: Transaction, 2003).

separation between experiencing entities in the world and their representations in the specific sites of the arts tends to obscure the participation of the constitutive unconscious imagination in the shaping of the very objects of our ordinary experience that realistic art attempts to represent. Again we encounter here a genre of the reflective or mimetic imagination that implicitly conceals the prior function of the primary performative imagination that operates recursively to shape the very objects the mimetic artistic imagination represents as illusions that correspond to what is perceived as objective given reality.

In this western liberal democratic world, the self-proclaimed illusionary that pretends to resemble the real world beyond art gives credence to the self-concealing illusionary that poses as real just as the copy recreates the original and the metaphorical shapes the boundaries of the literal. In his writings on realism in nineteenth-century music, musicologist Carl Dahlhaus noted and elaborated on French literary and artistic theory of the 1850s that realism in art frequently breaks the rules of traditional stylization, including that conventionally excluded from artistic works as ugly, tasteless, or low. It also serves as social or intersubjective reference to publicly observable objects or events rather than subjective ones. Indeed realism in the nineteenth century was largely a reaction to the conventions of idealism, classicism, ornamentalism, and romanticism.[4] Although in breaking established artistic paradigms the claim of an artistic work as a true representation was often supported by appearing raw, unstylized, unedited, or unstaged, obviously even raw reality must be stylized as "raw reality" in art just as any other experience mediated by the imagination is, at least unconsciously, partly edited and stylized. Hence Dahlhaus usefully reminds us of the well-known distinction between the aesthetics of the true and the aesthetics of the beautiful. He notes, in this connection, Sir Walter Scott's discrimination, made around 1816 in his observations on Jane Austen's novels, "between the 'romance' in which the marvelous, the improbable, and the extravagant could be indulged, and the true 'novel,' which represented a segment of reality as it really exists in the common walks of life." From our perspective here, however, such reality, whether identified with the beautiful or the ugly, the stable or the unstable, the coherent or the fragmented, is no more than a segment of experience collectively imagined in the "common walks of life" of a particular society as given and hence real.[5] It is not usually recognized that distinctions between the real and the unreal engage different departments of the performative imagination and correspondingly distinct norms for defining facts and fictions, that both the imaginaries inside and outside Plato's cave engage the primary composing faculty of the imagination.

Tendencies in late modernity and postmodernity to stage messy, unstylized, or unstructured ordinary objects or events "as they really are" have developed in several art forms, most saliently in film, as a means of producing reality effects

4 Carl Dahlhaus, *Realism in Nineteenth-Century Music*, Mary Whittall (trans.) (Cambridge: Cambridge University Press, 1985), pp. 60–1.
5 Ibid., pp. 57, 115.

in the various houses of illusion. These techniques later became very influential when deployed in television broadcasts of news, documentaries, political events, and the presentation of personalities. Obviously such a shift from the orderly to the disorderly as conventions of the real demonstrates its own historicity.

THE MONARCHY, THE CHURCH, AND EARLIER ANTECEDENCES OF THE TENSIONS BETWEEN NOTIONS OF THE REAL AND THE STAGED

As noted earlier, in the contexts of political and religious controversies, the process of sharply separating illusions, theatrical gestures, and fictions from sincere behavior or factual truths has been anticipated and influenced by Protestants and critics of the Catholic establishment and the monarchy who attempted to undermine those hierarchic structures by insisting on the theatricality of the spectacles and rituals through which they sought to enhance their legitimation. One is reminded of the lines, written centuries later, in Blake's *Jerusalem*: "What is a Church? & What is a Theatre? Are they Two and not One? Can they Exist Separate? Are not Religion and Politics the Same Thing?"[6] The Church and the monarchy responded with their own antitheatrical strategies. But neither the Church, insisting on the sinfulness of the human imagination and, in the tradition of Saint Augustine, regarding the theater as a false temple that can mislead humanity and undermine the true temple, nor the monarchy, using its powers to impose censorship and sanctions against actors, could afford to dispense with stagecraft in persuasively enacting their narratives and shaping their rituals of legitimation.[7] The problem faced by the Catholic Church was how to deny or conceal the theatricality of religious sacraments and rituals while actually harnessing it to augment the power of the service to engage the congregation.

The inherent theatricality of public religious practices rendered the Church vulnerable to unsettling criticism. During the sixteenth century, "plays ... used the motifs and conventions of medieval devotional theatre for irreproachably, even militantly, Protestant purposes," provoking Catholic concerns about "profaning religious truths by performing them as a play."[8] While the theater was prone to exploit the ambiguous relations between religion and histrionics for its own purpose of heightening the impact of performances upon its audience, the Church was concerned that the same ambiguity, together with a potentially unreserved theatrical appropriation of some features of religious practices, could evoke lay distrust of these practices.

[6] David Erdman (ed.), *The Complete Poetry and Prose of William Blake* (New York: Anchor Press, 1982), p. 207. See also a discussion by Sarah Beckwith in ref. 18.
[7] Jonas Barish, *The Antitheatrical Prejudice* (Berkeley: University of California Press, 1981).
[8] Peter Womack, "Imagining Communities: Theatres and the English Nation in the Sixteenth Century" in David Aers (ed.), *Culture and History 1350–1600: Essays on English Communities, Identities and Writing* (New York: Harvester Wheatsheaf, 1992), pp. 98–9.

Against this background, elements of the Protestant critique of Church practices, the nascent cultures of science and the Enlightenment, and rising democratic conceptions of authority tended since early modernity to converge in their insistence on the separation of the sphere of the arts (and of course religion) from the spheres of science and politics. Above all, the impulse to establish a new kind of political authority, free of and protected from the contaminating effects of artistic illusions used to aestheticize power and authority, was a driving force in the cultivation of modern commonsense realism (discussed in Chapter 5) and in its establishment as the normative epistemological sphere of the new politics.

Strategies of removing the imagination from the political sphere included the evolution of the theater as an autonomous house of fiction, the consequent commercialization of the shows, the increasing focus on entertainment, and the actual segregation of the audience of the theater from the audience of religious and civic rituals. Already during the time of Marlowe and Shakespeare, "sealed off from the order of everyday reality by the walls of the playhouse, the actors lay claim to the autonomy of fiction."[9]

Ironically, however, the very autonomization of the theater and the other arts as belonging to the apolitical sphere of creative illusions rendered the arts a potent reservoir of resources for covert political criticism. Stagecraft in the theater hall could expose the stagecraft in the royal palace and later also in the modern democratic *Agora*. Stephen Greenblatt calls attention to the uses of the theater to expose the theatricality of the monarchy and the Church. Precisely because the theater was an acknowledged house of fiction, the wearing of borrowed or used clerical costumes on the Elizabethan stage could expose the theatrical, contrived illusions of Catholic ritual in seducing the public and eliciting its consent and devotion. Seeing the bishop's robe both on stage and in church, the Elizabethan individual could hardly avoid reflecting on the analogy.[10]

The still commonly accepted dualism between reality and fiction thus has come to function as a vital resource of a wide vocabulary of modern political criticisms and oppositional rhetoric. Regardless of the nature of established power and authority, be it the Church, the monarchy, the totalitarian state, or the democratic state, the imagined dualism between facts and fictions, the divide between the self-concealing and the manifest imagination has created at the heart of the regime an invaluable space for political opposition and resistance. Critics always focus on those areas in a regime in which the gaps between the legitimate and legitimating political imaginaries and rituals of the system, and the imagined political facts of everyday life are glaring.

Given the intuition and sometimes the realization that fictions or imaginaries can produce political facts, those who wanted to change the perception of

[9] Ibid., pp. 108–9.
[10] Stephen Greenblatt, *Shakespearean Negotiations: The Circulation of Social Energy in Renaissance England* (Berkeley: University of California Press, 1988), pp. 94–128.

political realities have naturally gravitated to exploiting the vulnerability of the regime to the occasional public perception of such gaps and seek to promote competing, more credible, behavior-producing political fictions. Even a large part of the scholarly literature that attributes, in the pejorative sense, theatricality to monarchs, for instance, seems to have uncritically inherited the polemical antitheatrical vocabulary of the antimonarchists. Commonly overlooked is that political actors who level charges of theatricality against an established regime are inevitably trying to enact at the same time another genre of imaginaries, to institutionalize the fictions or imaginaries that form the foundations of an alternative political regime.

Periods of transition and revolutions accentuate the tensions between politics and the arts as the contests over symbols and gestures are politically very consequential. This can be illustrated by the plight of the revolutionaries who during the French Revolution were caught up in the double bind between their accusations of the monarchy's theatricality and their own staging of the revolution. The French Revolution has been construed by and large in the western mind as the paradigmatic modern popular revolt. This break with the constitutive symbolism of the monarchy, particularly the massive use of violence by the revolutionaries, required a dramatic and radical transformation from the legitimating political imaginaries of the divine right of kings into those of popular sovereignty. The French were compelled, over a relatively short period of time, to discard as unwarranted fictions those imaginaries that for centuries had upheld the monarchy and to accept the imaginaries of a popular government as their new banners. But this challenge was complicated by the fact that exposing the theatricality of the monarchy not only did not suffice to conceal or deny the theatricality of the revolution but could even accentuate the alertness of the public to its gestural, image-making, and performative dimensions.

From our perspective, the problem was not how to move from theater to reality or from fiction to truth, but how to undermine belief in one set of regime-supporting fictions while suspending disbelief in another. Once again, the hidden workings of the popular imagination required a separation between strategies (mindful of the art of the theater as a house of illusions) of politically discarding the increasingly exposed fictions of the old order and strategies (mindful of the common everyday world outside the delineated sites of art) for the affirmation of new, yet no less self-concealing fictions. The ascendance of the new to a position of hegemony entailed its concomitant rise to the status of believable reality, a rise supported by the kind of means used to produce reality effects in art as indicated by Dahlhaus. Because the politics of the monarchy and the revolution entailed the enactment of rival political imaginaries, their respective practices reflect then the distinction between theatricality as a means to project or at least aestheticize their respective political worlds, and theatricality as a means of exposing and disrupting the alleged deceptive gestures of their rivals.

THE NATIONALIZATION OF THE PUBLIC AND THE ENACTMENT
OF NOVEL CIVIC AGENCIES

With the decline of both the monarchy and the Church, claims for the autonomy of the theater as a house of fiction as well as the autonomy of other arts were associated with the politically significant rise of the public as an independent addressee. Peter Womack argues that this shift toward the cultural and institutional enfranchisement of fiction was linked to the rise of the abstract imaginary of the nation as an invisible and radically more inclusive community, an addressee of the theater increasingly conceived as a national emblem whose audience was regarded as distinct from the more specific local addressees of the Church.[11] A comparable process occurred in the transition from the curiosity cabinets of princes and aristocrats to the public science museums as shrines of the culture of science.[12]

Hence, the emancipation of art from visible or invisible elite royal or priestly controls was associated with the emergence of new agency, a new power – the public or the nation – which has increasingly come to challenge established hegemonic hierarchies. But the nation was, of course, quick to replace religious or monarchic controls with controls of its own. The surface de-theatricalization and autonomy of the political vis-à-vis religion, art, and so forth, was dialectically related to the terms underlying the tacit agreement to grant autonomy to the theater as well as to the other arts and often to science as well in a new political universe in which the national public became the universal addressee of cultural institutions. The public was thus encouraged to imagine politics as belonging to a domain separate from the depoliticized domains of the theater, the other arts, and science addressing different dimensions of the experience of the same collective.[13] Inasmuch as the government in the nation-state claimed to represent the entire public, it was motivated to label as politically partisan and therefore potentially illegitimate and censurable art works (and bodies of knowledge) that appeared to serve only sections of the general public or subgroups that challenged the assumed authority of the government to represent the entire public. Even in relatively open nation-states, then, the autonomy of culture was politically restricted (at least in the sense of not being invincible in the face of damaging soft or bold political controls) by the particular premises of the political order.

---

[11] Womack, "Imagining Communities," pp. 116–37. Theater as an arena for molding the national body was central to Lessing's and Schiller's conception of the theater's cultural role. See Beat Wyss, "*Ragnarök* of Illusion: Richard Wagner's 'Mystical Abyss' at Bayreuth" *October* vol. 54 (1990): 57–78.

[12] Yaron Ezrahi, "Words and Works in the Social Iconography of Scientific Knowledge: A Study in Science as a Cultural System." (Unpublished manuscript, Jerusalem, 1976).

[13] It was the emerging autonomy of science that also gradually empowered scientific authority as an extensively employed political resource for the depersonalization and depoliticization of political authority in the modern democratic state.

Despite the process of secularization and the rise of popular mass politics, the influence of the Church's theatrical techniques of materializing and ritualizing the projection of unity and self-legitimation has persisted well within the symbolism and practices of late monarchies and modern secular postmonarchic nationalism, democracy, and often other mixed political configurations. This link can be illustrated by the processes whereby monarchic and postmonarchic regimes drew on the Corpus Christi cult and its ritual processions in developing their own equivalents of the king's body as a unifying symbol.

As a model for imagining and articulating the sense of the community or the body politic as a whole, the image of the body of Christ that became an emblem of the *corpus mysticum*, the corporate body of the Church, was first transformed – for instance in the French monarchy – into the body of the king as an emblem of the corporate body of the monarchy. The public image of the king's body was undoubtedly a major instrument of governance, and kings danced, acted in their court theater, and played music in projecting themselves as models of mastery, cultivation, and magnificence. Louis XIV memorably employed a host of theatrical techniques to establish and sustain his image as the source of authority. As Jeffrey Merrick observes,

[T]he elaborate etiquette regulating language, gestures, and conduct demonstrated his sovereignty more effectively than impressive but infrequent rituals invested with constitutional significance. The theatrical life of the French court collapsed the mystical into the physical body of the king, who played the role of the sun not only when costumed as such in allegorical ballets but also during daily life from lever to coucher.[14]

Susan Foster describes how Louis XIV, from the earliest years of his reign, "had reinforced the body's role in conveying social status.... He pursued a defectless body through his own dancing, and consolidated rubrics of etiquette and comportment as part of his strategic plan to enhance royal authority."[15] Earlier, the Stuart kings similarly cultivated a court theater that, under a master stage designer like Inigo Jones, produced very effective spectacles and theatrical projections of monarchic authority.[16]

Obviously, before the rise of science-inspired commonsense realism as the epistemological domain of modern politics and the concomitant democratic rejection of overt theatricality in politics, such direct theatricalization of the monarchy was a much less risky strategy. In postmonarchic regimes the picture was more mixed. The theatrical, ritualistic, and symbolic instruments of the

---

[14] Jeffrey Merrick: "The Body Politics of French Absolutism" in Sara E. Melzer and Kathryn Norberg (eds.), *From the Royal to the Republican Body: Incorporating the Political in Seventeenth- and Eighteenth-Century France* (Berkeley: University of California Press, 1998), pp. 17–18.

[15] Susan Leigh Foster, "Dancing the Body Politic: Manner and Mimesis in Eighteenth-Century Ballet," ibid., p. 168.

[16] Yaron Ezrahi, *The Descent of Icarus: Science and the Transformation of Contemporary Democracy* (Cambridge, MA: Harvard University Press, 1990), pp. 71–3, 108–11. See also Stephen Orgel's *The Illusion of Power: Political Theater in the English Renaissance* (Berkeley: University of California Press, 1975).

Church and the monarchy were rejected as illegitimate or partly adapted to the needs of secular civic politics. Mervyn James shows how during the sixteenth century the dramatic power of the Church's sacraments and the subsequent ritual procession of the elites in order of status were privatized and transformed into both theater plays and civic rituals.[17] The model drama of Corpus Christi was perpetuated beyond the sacralization of the king's body in the context of the movement of many towns toward their formal incorporation as towns. The politicization and secularization of this and of related church models and rituals for embracing and binding the scattered parts of society or the polity into a whole unified *corpus civicum*-like body of the community coexisted with the more specifically theatrical enactment of the drama of Jesus' sacrifice and his embodiment in the midst of the congregation on the stage as a mystery play. This combination constructed the dualism between the manifestly theatrical within the theater hall and the hidden theater that originated the projections or enactments of the civically or politically real outside the theater walls. The preservation of such apparent yet fragile dualism between the sphere of fantasy and the sphere of secularized symbolism was propitious for charges of idolatry and magic both against the Church and rival political authority, while often fomenting the links between antitheatricalism, anticlericalism, and antimonarchism.[18] Whereas theatricality in its concealed unreflexive mode was bound to remain a necessary dimension of the enactment of religious as well as secular political imaginaries of order, its exposure as theatricality in the pejorative sense remained a principal strategy of delegitimizing any religious or political establishment.

As Thomas Paine advocated, by contrast to the "pupit [*sic*] show of [state and] aristocracy,"[19] in a democratic political universe political agents are expected to present themselves to the gazing public as truthful, sincere, rational, and free, capable of taking technically effective actions undistorted by fictive or ostensibly theatrical representations. The "subversive" idea that this alternative political program is supported by just another vocabulary of politically productive albeit favored make-believes, and that the performative political imagination has obviously been latently present all along, could, of course, encourage the counterproductive view that politics in democracy, like in the monarchy, is a form of deception, a view based on the false conventional classification of theatricality not as a necessary dimension of embodying a particular political imaginary of order but as the polar opposite of authenticity and sincerity in politics. (This view, influenced by contemporary mass media, has

[17] Mervyn James, *Society, Politics and Culture: Studies in Early Modern England* (Cambridge: Cambridge University Press, 1986); see especially pp. 1–47.

[18] Sarah Beckwith, "Ritual, Church and Theatre: Medieval Dramas of the Sacramental Body" in David Aers (ed.), *Culture and History 1350–1600: Essays on English Communities, Identities and Writing* (New York: Harvester Wheatsheaf, 1992), pp. 65–89; Barish, *The Antitheatrical Prejudice*.

[19] Thomas Paine, "The Rights of Man" in Michel Foot and Isaac Kramnick (eds.), *Thomas Paine Reader* (Harmondsworth: Penguin Classics, 1987), p. 214.

spread widely in our time.) Because adversary political groups and institutions commonly charge their rivals with posturing while denying their own, the convergence of antitheatrical and antipolitical prejudices amplifies perceptions of insincerity. Against this background, the eventual relocation of political authority in the field of simple, transparent, human, constitutional, and political causality, ostensibly free of fantasy and theatricality, has been vital for the attempt to save the normative and epistemological grounds of civic virtues in participatory democratic politics. The invention of modern democratic politics was inseparable, then, from the invention of the concept of objective public factual reality where virtuous citizens can assemble to make reasonable choices. From a critical-analytical perspective, the difficulty has been to enlist the culture of science and the professions to render politics and government more accountable and credible while capitalizing on the lay public's ignorance of the foundational role of the particular imaginaries and disputable presuppositions that underlie and enable any particular scientific discipline, the more general enterprise of science and technology, and the authority of expertise. At the end, the ever precarious attempt to conceal the omnipresent theatrical, aesthetic, ritualistic, and gestural substance of politics as a system of human communications and actions performed in a supposedly real world of objective, transparent facts could only partly be sustainable. The rising normative status of commonsense realism as the frame of legitimate political claims did not spare leaders of modern democratic governments the need to protect themselves from charges of posturing and deception by glossing over their failures with false reports and the diffusion of misinformation framed in the rhetoric of scientific and technical expertise. While the stability of democracy has depended on an inherently plastic configuration of facts, fictions, values, experiences, and imaginaries whose capacity to mobilize the community and elicit its compliance is constantly threatened by even slight gaps or rearrangements of these components, democratic leaders have discovered that in the short run they can buy the minimal necessary public credibility through a choreography of accountability rather than transparency of substantive investments in problem solving. What in the final analysis makes a regime reasonably democratic in such circumstances is the constant anxiety of the rulers that the public or its unofficial agents might inadvertently glimpse backstage and see how politics is actually fashioned. Such a glimpse could easily disrupt the public's suspension of disbelief that secures the instrumental political efficacy of a sometimes carefully contrived performance played out and displayed at the front of the stage. The main actors in the regime, the very agencies that must continually negotiate the interplay between the logic of back and front stage, between contrived political realities and political appearances in order to survive, are the ones most prone to recognize or intuit the potential political costs they may incur when the public comes to believe that what is actually happening does not correspond to what is presented.

When such awareness, such reflexivity, permeates even parts of the larger population, unmasking these fictive elements or questioning their relationships to what the public perceives as the facts of common experience can shake any concept of political reality. As Judith Shklar notes, the genealogies of hegemonic authorities are fraught with cracks easily exploited to subvert the regime. That is why, as she observes, thinkers such as Hobbes, Kant, and Burke believed that too close scrutiny of the origin of any authority by, or on behalf of, the lay public may plant the "most effectual seeds of death of any state," to quote Hobbes.[20] No wonder rulers have used all the materials available: law, history, nature, science, poetry, literature, myth, and theater to consolidate and imprint their official genealogies in the popular imagination.

From the perspective of this book, then, that which is often labeled theatrical or fictive (in the sense of deceptive) in the demeanor of kings, presidents, prime ministers, and other magistrates has often reflected critics' intuitive or deliberate attempts to exploit the fact-fiction dualism as a political strategy to expose to the public what in fact are the fragile grounds of all political establishments as but the unique weakness of a particular government.

THE DUALISM OF FACTS AND FICTIONS AS A NECESSARY CONDITION FOR A CULTURE OF POLITICAL CRITICISM

Viewed from an analytical perspective then, neither the dances of Louis XIV nor Inigo Jones's theatrical productions for the Stuart court were just theatrical. They were reifying performances of hegemonic political imaginaries, not decorations but realizations directed by the performative scripts of particular monarchic political worlds. As fact-producing fictions, they were real political forces, manifestations of the political ontology of these monarchies. We witness here the operation of the constitutive performative political imagination in its fullest power. Hence the term *theatrical* (with its critical connotation of illusion or deception), applied to describe the political behavior and actions of the monarchy, reflects the penetration of the sensibilities of democratic revolutions and their alternative epistemology and vocabulary of commonsense realism. It also reflects our critical attitude toward the ancient regime, formed within the distinct imaginary of democracy, which is hostile to it. To reiterate, our culture-bound vantage point clearly constrains our understanding of the inherent role of theatricality and more generally of the performance of collective imaginaries in all forms of politics, including in our own democratic politics.

Insofar as the fictive or theatrical is part of the fabric of every political universe, gestures, images, parades, plays, frescos, music, and architectural works can be conceptualized in three categories: those that perform, articulate, socially concretize, and generate the realities of a particular power and authority structure; those debunking such existing political configurations by labeling their enactments deceptive while presenting their own as real; and finally those partly politically innocent (but not inconsequential) self-proclaimed

---

[20] Judith N. Shklar and Stanley Hoffmann (eds.), *Political Thought and Political Thinkers* (Chicago: University of Chicago Press, 1998), pp. 132–3.

artistic and theatrical make beliefs in the service of pleasure, aesthetic experience, entertainment, and general culture. Their frequent coexistence reinforces the perceived or alleged distinctiveness of each as strategies that constitute the building blocks of the specific, often conflict-ridden, political universe. As related components of the same political universe, the real, the deceptively real, and the artistic illusionary are modes of imagining that respectively correspond to the self-concealing, reflective, and manifestly creative modes of the political imagination that fashions the rich vocabulary of politics and culture in monarchies as well as in democracies.

Because all political regimes depend on the performance of collective imaginaries, monarchists of earlier periods could probably join contemporary conservative critics in leveling charges of theatricality as deception against democratic governments for their extensive use of external signs, gestures, and languages of science and technology. They could claim that such regimes employ props including scientific language, statistics, genres of research reports, and the symbolic import of technology as external garments for the legitimation of policies and actions while disregarding actual scientific knowledge and facts. But as I try to show in Part Three, this kind of attitude rests on a misperception of the crucial latent pseudo-scientific functions embedded in the performative political imagination of modern democracies, the way in which this theatricality of the real, this political scientism is a necessary political strategy of concretizing and legitimating particular democratic imaginaries of political causality and agency and political uses of power. These imaginaries require the utterances and actions of political authorities to be impersonal, transparent, empirical, and nonhierarchical. Elsewhere I have tried to show that the rise of the modern genre of instrumental politics, modeled after the technological adaptation of means to ends, had the politically useful latent import of depoliticizing and depersonalizing the exercise of political power.[21]

Only when we recognize the importance of such shifts in the genres of the performative political imagination can we appreciate the significance of what we perceive as monarchic theatricality as in fact a creative strategy for idealizing and factualizing the king's body and person aimed at perpetuating the regime. The charge of theatricality by its critics does not diminish its fundamental constitutive function in embodying the political imaginary that regulates the regime. Similarly, one can appreciate the significance of the role of science and scientists as a political resource for the theatricality of the antitheatricality that facilitates the lay perception of the utterances and actions of democratic political agents as apolitical, impersonal, and instrumental, thus granting them legitimacy. I should note, however, that, whereas charges of theatricality from a critical stance outside a regime are prone to overlook theatricality as part of the process of politically and institutionally embodying a particular hegemonic political imaginary, when theatricality is a charge of deception made from within the system and its imaginary framework against deviation from

---

[21] Ezrahi, *Descent of Icarus*, particularly pp. 15–40.

that very imaginary, then the charge of theatricality in the pejorative sense as deception or posturing makes sense. One can, of course, challenge Al Gore's use of scientific authority to buttress his claims about global warming as deliberate or indeliberate posturing but not the relevance of the authority of experts to legitimate policies within the political imaginary that rules America. In other words, one should make a distinction between intra-system and extra-system uses of theatricality as a charge against authority.

Scientific-public-policy controversies are often examples of intrasystemic opposition. Unlike government scientific advisers, scientists working for oppositional political forces perform the counter-role of unmasking political actors charged with using false data to cover their political motives or goals with the rhetoric of objective scientific facts consistent with the imaginary paradigm. These can be effective political strategies as long as a supportive political imagination and culture can sustain the dualism between reality and fiction, valid and false evidence.[22] In more monistic or fragmented political universes, in which separate categories of the fictive and the factual are rendered meaningless, such scientific legitimizing or criticizing of government would be ineffective.

The ideological chasm between the illusionary domain of the arts and the real domain of politics is, of course, implicit in the democratic critique of fascism as the practice of aestheticizing the political. Conversely, it is reflected in the critique of the rise of the mass media's theatrical political style in the contemporary democratic state. Paradoxically, such criticisms (while useful in liberal democratic political wars against rival imaginaries) are themselves based on the powerful Enlightenment fiction that liberal democratic politics is devoid of its own theatrics. Again this meta-imaginary suggests that such a political system can thrive and evolve in a world in which divisions between fact and fiction, reason and emotion, are deemed natural.

Artists and other advocates of the freedom of art who have struggled against censorship in order to protect creative art from the encroachment of political power have often ignored the fundamental point that the autonomy of art is in fact the centerpiece of an alternative political program, the liberal democratic political program, that has attempted to confine art to a separate domain and to temper its powers to aestheticize power and relocate politics in a sphere in which the pomp, the splendor, and the dignity of those at the top of the pyramid are replaced by nonhierarchical, unglorified agents. Such a genre of unadorned politics consisting of deaestheticized actions and utterances was supposed to be performed by political agents whose record is open to scrutiny with reference to transparent ordinary public facts and instrumental assessments.

The autonomy of reason (especially its perceived but false claim of independence from values and emotions) and faith in the weight of the deliberative process in politics have themselves depended on sets of imaginaries that have long proved indispensable in liberal democratic political world making. In Chapter 5, I argued that commonsense reality is usually a tacit social construct

---

[22] Ezrahi, *Descent of Icarus*, pp. 17–27.

with its own syntax of fictions, its separation between fictions that are recognized as such and therefore are excluded, and fictions that are regarded as facts, or at least as probable realities, and therefore are included or absorbed. One of the most politically consequential effects of the mass media on the contemporary political imagination has been to socially redistribute reflexive social and political consciousness between elites and laypersons.[23] In the early twenty-first century it has become more difficult to rely on a sustainable credulity of the large publics that have been exposed for a long time now to the tricks of the visual electronic mass media. The social spread of political skepticism is apparently one of the reasons for the decline of political parties and authority, and the fragmentation of democratic political systems. (I discuss the specific impact of the mass media on democratic political epistemology in Chapter 12.)

Recognizing the elastic and historically unstable boundaries between that which is taken for granted as real in any particular sociopolitical world and that which is regarded as imaginary or fictive raises the question of whether it is necessary for a liberal democratic universe to situate politics in the realm of reality in the modern sense of the word as a world of publicly accessible facts, while consigning religion and the arts to the realm of fictions and illusions. Is such a separation a necessary condition for the split between private and public spheres, situating politics, but not religion and art, in the latter? Furthermore, can democracy survive the recent expansion of public reflexivity and awareness of the difficulty of sustaining clean or solid concepts of facts in politics given the conditions of the contemporary media environment?

There are, of course, important examples of earlier blurring of boundaries between the political sphere and the domain of illusions and fictions in modern democracies. We can discern many instances of convergence of the political, the aesthetic, the theatrical, and the deliberately illusionary. Political representation, as we have seen, is often an obvious example of posturing as a substitute for governing. Still, the insistence on literalizing or hypostatizing the political along the parameters of commonsense realism, scientism, and what I referred to in Chapter 6 as "democratic moral epistemology" has become one of the pivotal elements of liberal democratic culture and values, as its early analysts and expositors (such as Thomas Paine and Alexis de Tocqueville) so aptly noted.

To reiterate, from our perspective, that which liberal democratic citizens have regarded as binding political facts has, in some sense, depended on the wide acceptance of such imagined abstractions as the public sphere, the observing public, the general will, the public interest, or the sovereignty of the people as meaningful categories of a given political reality that replaced, for instance, the divine right of kings as a politically anachronistic abstraction. The democratic imaginings of causation in politics as a participatory public process

---

[23] See in this connection also Yaron Ezrahi, "The Distribution and Redistribution of Political Reflexivity in Contemporary Democracies," in T. M. Evans and D. Handelman (eds.), *Reflecting upon Reflexivity* forthcoming.

reflect the desire to envelop politics within the sphere of commonsense realism and the consequent need to anchor political imaginaries, authority, power, decisions, and actions in a sensory-material world of visible public facts accessible to all. It was in this connection that the modern liberal democratic separation between the arts and the sciences into the respective spheres of illusion and reality made so much sense as a meta-political commitment underlying the very definitions of the political in the liberal democratic state. It was also in this context that the political uses of the plastic arts, theater, and cinema to influence political behavior was so often regarded as an illegitimate, nondemocratic strategy of persuasion characteristic of the Catholic Church, monarchic regimes, the fascist state, and corrupt democratic politics.[24]

This need to create a hypostatized public world and subsequently to reframe the political in terms of such a world of public facts and causality sustained the fictions of self-government by a collective of discrete individuals. Despite inherent constraints imposed on lay demand for certainties by probabilistic frames of scientific knowledge, the autonomy of individuals as citizens endowed with independent judgment was assumed to depend on certifiable public facts that rendered science, or rather the social authority of science, an indispensable political resource of the modern liberal democratic state.

Both the perception of a demystified physical world as the ostensible object of public knowledge and the perception of the modern political world as a similarly demystified object of an attestive, inquisitive public gaze supported by the logic of transparent democratic causality have confirmed the rise of the modern public, conceived in liberal democracy as an aggregate of free individuals, as a political agency.[25]

Instrumental bureaucratic as well as expert authorities could be widely deployed and justified in modern democracies because of the belief in the existence of an objective, universally accessible, public reality as a stable coordinator of the orientations and actions of a multitude of autonomous individual agents. Public acceptance of this view of reality appeared to make it a "solvent" that would render decisions in matters of public affairs neutral, transparent, rational, impersonal, and potentially consensual. This modern connection between the rise of the perception of aggregates of individuals as a perceiving public agent and the rise of a materialized, transparent, hypostatized political power as an object of observation has been destabilized since the latter half of the twentieth century by the fluidity of the public as a political agency and the ambiguity of the political world as its transparent and readily accessible object.

---

[24] On fascism and aesthetic politics see Walter Benjamin's "The Work of Art in the Age of Mechanical Reproduction" in Hannah Arendt (ed.), Harry Zohn (trans.) *Illuminations* (New York: Schocken, 1969), especially pp. 241–2; see also Garry Wills, *Reagan's America: Innocents at Home* (New York: Doubleday & Company, 1987).

[25] The public as a modern democratic political agency is extensively discussed in Chapter 9. On the "attestive" as juxtaposed to the "celebratory" gaze see Ezrahi, *Descent of Icarus*, 74–87; for the simultaneous rise of the viewing subject and the world as object see Martin Heidegger, "The Age of the World View," *Measure* vol. 2 (Summer 1951): 277–9, 282.

John Dewey had this connection in mind early in the twentieth century when he drew a direct link between the public's inability to discern the relations between cause and effect in politics and its own deterioration into a walking and talking "ghost."[26]

---

[26] Yaron Ezrahi, "Dewey's Critique of Democratic Visual Culture and its Political Implications" in David Michael Levin (ed.), *Sites of Vision: Discursive Construction of Sight in the History of Philosophy* (Cambridge: MIT Press, 1997), pp. 319–22.

PART THREE

MODERN IMAGINARIES OF DEMOCRATIC POLITICAL AGENCIES AND CAUSALITY

8

Voluntary Action, the Fear of Theatricality, and the Materialization of the Political

In line with his insistence that "life is no argument," Nietzsche observed:

We have arranged for ourselves a world in which we are able to live with the postulation of bodies, lines, surfaces, causes and effects, motion and rest, form and content:
without these articles of faith nobody could now endure to live! But that does not yet
mean they are something proved and demonstrated.[1]

I have argued that the point about such "articles of faith" in the political arena,
characterized in this book as the imaginings that constitute political imaginaries, is not their validity or veracity; rather, it is their latent functions and
consequences for the political order. Our concern in this chapter, therefore – to
paraphrase Nietzsche's words – is the ways in which, as modern individuals,
we "have arranged for ourselves" a democratic political world based on the
imaginings of political causes and effects conducive to democratic concepts of
political participation, responsibility, and accountability.

I argue that the most crucial difficulty faced by the evolving democratic
political causalities in modern states is twofold: tensions between moral-political commitment to a voluntaristic theory of political action and commitment
to the materialist-sensory political epistemology of political action as a necessary condition for the agents' freedom, efficacy, and accountability. At one
level, the voluntaristic notion of political agency and the materialist epistemology of democratic political action have been complementary. As a political
agent, the voluntary individual is expected to act in the world of commonsense
realism in which his or her actions are visible to other agents as public facts.
However, the very materialization of political action can encroach on its invisible source – the volition of choice. The tensions are between the moral-political
requirements of voluntarism rooted in the human interior on one hand and the
epistemological requirements of transparency and accountability on the other.
In other words, the latent function of a materialist political epistemology is
to check the potential degeneration of the freedom to act into unaccountable,

---

[1] Friedrich Nietzsche, *The Gay Science* (Leipzig: E. W. Fritzsch Verlag 1887), p. 121.

arbitrary actions. These tensions are often expressed in a clash between the tendency to attribute actions to persons and the tendency to project actions onto external circumstances, necessities, or other involuntary factors.

Since the dawn of the Renaissance, the belief in the individual as a source of action, fundamental to the imaginary and behavioral practices of a participatory democratic political order, has been accompanied by anxieties over the potential freedom of political agents to deceive, to posture, and to engage in other ways of corrupting democratic transparency and mandates. In his historical study, Walter Ullmann has observed that tensions arising between the individual personality and the requirements of office have increased since the early unfolding of the Renaissance humanistic tradition, which emphasized the forces of human personality and freedom.[2]

Alexis de Tocqueville's discussion of "tendencies particular to historians in democratic centuries" provides a valuable source of insight into modern developments in framing democratic political causality and related problems.[3] Tocqueville distinguishes between aristocratic and democratic accounts of political history:

Historians who write in aristocratic centuries ordinarily make all events depend on the particular wills and humors of certain men, and they willingly tie the most important resolution to the least accidents. With sagacity they bring out the smallest causes, and often they do not perceive the greatest. Historians who live in democratic centuries show altogether contrary tendencies. Most of them attribute almost no influence to the individual over the destiny of the species or the citizens over the fate of the people. But in reverse they give great general causes to all the little particular facts.[4]

Fashioning an image of historical political causation, Tocqueville argues that it "perceives first of all a very few principal actors who guide the whole play." The "great personages, who are kept at the front of the stage" and "arrest [the historians'] sight and fix it" are, of course, an image of a political causal order consistent with that of a monarchic or aristocratic moral order.[5] We have here a kind of aristocratic personalization of political history that encourages such historians to "apply themselves to unveiling the secret motives that make them act and speak," while tending to "forget the rest."[6] But in an age of masses (rather than of aristocratic individualism), with the sheer multitude of individual citizens, the distribution of the power to act among the masses diminishes the influence of each individual while increasing the power of aggregates or groups, according to Tocqueville. In his view, this warrants attribution of special weight to general causes. Whereas aristocratic individualism limits influence to a few privileged individuals, democratic individualism involves the

---

[2] Walter Ullmann, *Medieval Foundations of Renaissance Humanism* (London: Paul Elek, 1977).

[3] Alexis De Tocqueville, *Democracy in America*, Harvey C. Mansfield and Delba Winthrop (trans. edit. intro.) (Chicago: The University of Chicago Press, 2000) vol. 2, ch. 20 pp. 469–72.

[4] Ibid., p. 469.

[5] Ibid.

[6] Ibid.

motives and acts of a large number of individuals, thus problematizing attribution of causality to single individuals.

This dilemma was bound to create tension between the normative primacy that liberal democrats grant the individual citizen as a political actor and the actual supremacy of the complex political consequences of a multitude of individual agents as a political cause of government and its actions. But if, as Tocqueville argues, only "[r]easons acting separately on the will of each citizen, in the end produce the movement of the people,"[7] such an abstract imagining of the political process in a democracy could easily undermine the vital voluntary component of democratic imaginings of political causality. Following such an orientation, Tocqueville warns that "one is tempted to believe that this movement (of the people) is not voluntary and that without knowing it, societies obey a superior, dominating force."[8] Tocqueville expresses his concern that:

[H]istorians who live in democratic times, therefore, not only deny to a few citizens the power to act on the destiny of a people, they also take away from peoples themselves the ability to modify their own fate, and they subject them either to an inflexible providence or to a sort of blind fatality.... Historians of antiquity instruct on how to command; those of our day teach hardly anything other than how to obey.[9]

Tocqueville's critique of historians in the democratic age is based on the assumption that the difficulty of distinguishing the motives behind or the reasons for the acts of each separate citizen from those of a "movement of the people" paradoxically invites a democratically subversive conception of causal determinism.

I think that such reflections indicate that Tocqueville was keenly aware of the danger that deterministic notions of political causality would undermine the popular commitment to voluntarism and individualism as vital parts of the democratic political imagination of action and encourage political indifference and even fatalism, which would corrupt the foundations of political initiative and participation. These concerns relate to his well-known preoccupation with the potential of democracy to breed despotism of the majority as well as a centralization of power. Referring to the doctrine of causal determinism, Tocqueville insists that "such a doctrine is particularly dangerous in the period we are in; our contemporaries are only too inclined to doubt free will because each of them feels himself limited on all sides by his weakness, but still willingly grant force and independence to men united in a social body."[10]

To rephrase in our terms, then, the issue is, given the practical constraints, how to protect voluntarism as a key component of the democratic political imaginary, an orientation that even when it does not fully correspond to accounts

---

[7] Ibid., p. 471.
[8] Ibid.
[9] Ibid., pp. 471–2.
[10] Ibid., p. 472.

of the political process has behavioral consequences that strengthen it. To reiterate, Tocqueville's response to this dilemma is twofold: on one hand, to avoid the reduction of political causality to an aristocratic version of the volitional causal role of a few privileged individuals; on the other, his notion of "general facts" or "general causes" that correspond, to some extent, to "methodological collectivism," a phrase coined by social theorists to account for social or political phenomena that attribute primary agency or cause to a collective rather than to an individual or an aggregate of individuals. The remedy, according to Tocqueville, is to imagine general causes and particular (individual) influences as coexisting. The sole difference between democratic and aristocratic contexts is the relative weight assigned to these factors.

As a matter of both theory and fact, I believe that it is precisely the irresoluble tension between particular and general causes, the interplay of individuals and collectives as political agencies, and the mix of personal and impersonal abstract agents that characterize democratic imaginings of political causality. J. S. Mill, and later John Dewey, Karl Popper, and Jürgen Habermas confronted this dilemma from a more liberal perspective in an attempt to protect the integrity and position of the individual as the ultimate source of political judgment and authority in relation to the collective. Despite their differences, they expressed great confidence in the individual as a free participant in a collective political discourse that blends diverse individual contributions into widely shared preferences of policy and action. They and kindred thinkers attempted to protect liberal individualism (as the foundation of democratic politics) against privileged aristocratic individualism. They believed that reason, as a guide to a public discourse based on open-ended and uncertain human experience, could bridge individual and collective actions without falling into the trap of empowering abstract entities such as the nation or the people, or other nonliberal democratic agents.

The discovered potential political uses of the apolitical authority of experts and technology for integrating knowledge-based, voluntary action into visible materialistic democratic causality could respond in some respects to Tocqueville's dilemma. He was concerned about generating accounts of democratic action that allow voluntary policy choices without resorting to aristocratic individualism or abstractions of unreflexive movements of the masses that undermine the democratic premise of government by a free, deliberative people. This approach has generated a host of strategies whereby democratic political actors have attempted to project their actions as honest, dispassionate, objective, apolitical, transparent, and public-oriented. They were quick to discover, for instance, the rhetorical efficacy of science and technological instrumentalism in depersonalizing and depoliticizing their conduct, claiming to harness their skills to the public will and allaying charges of deception and theatricality.

Historically, two other major means of building up the people as an agency of democratic action, as a cause of the rise and sustenance of democratic regimes, have been violence by, of, and for the people and elections. In the following two sections, I discuss the problems raised by violence and elections as two forms of public enactment and legitimation of democracy, and the social perceptions respectively of violent and electoral events as material human causes in democratic politics.

DEMOCRATIC CAUSALITY – THE AMBIGUOUS STATUS OF VIOLENCE

In the course of the early decades of the fifth century B.C., Athenians erected and reerected a group statue depicting citizen warriors in a heroic gesture of tyrannicide in the *Agora*, the Athenian public square (Figure. 8.1). This statue apparently expressed the Athenian celebration of the killing of a tyrant, which led to the creation of democracy.[11] The Athenians also honored a later armed resistance by citizens fighting for their freedom against the rule of oligarchs. In his history of the Jewish War, Josephus (37–100 C.E.) actually praises popular violence when he describes Jewish resistance to Roman dominion, preferring death to slavery.

The assassination of Julius Caesar on March 15, 44 (B.C.E.), one of the most memorable and controversial political events of antiquity, has been the subject of an ongoing debate regarding the moral justification of tyrannicide and revolution. At the center of this debate lies the question of the necessity to resort to violence in order to save the republic. A related dilemma is whether the act of assassination should be judged in reference to republican goals and the public assessment of Brutus and Cassius's respective intentions or with regard to its contribution to the chain of events that led to the destruction of the Roman republic.

Had the use of violence been preceded by a public appeal to the people and their accord, rather than by a conspiracy, would the assassination of Caesar have appeared more defensible in light of republican values? What are the criteria for distinguishing a republican from a tyrannical leader? Is it sufficient for an authoritarian leader to actually pursue the public good in order to be classified as non-tyrannical and even republican? These and related questions have been raised with special urgency particularly since the latter decades of the sixteenth century against a background of religious intolerance and the oppression of religious minorities in European countries.

The issue of whether violence can be defended on the grounds of serving republican and democratic values was discussed in detail in a very influential Huguenot tract entitled *Vindiciae Contra Tyrannos*, first published in Latin in 1579 and then translated several times into English in the course of the seventeenth century as *A Defense of Liberty against Tyrants*.[12] The basic argument in

---

[11] Josiah Ober, *Athenian Legacies: Essays on the Politics of Going On Together* (Princeton: Princeton University Press, 2005), pp. 212–27.

[12] I am using here the 1689 translation with an historical introduction by Harold J. Laski (London: G. Bell and Sons, 1924); http://www.constitution.org/vct/vind.htm and http://www.constitution.org/vct/vind_laski.htm.

FIGURE 8.1. Roman copies of statue group of Harmodius and Aristogeiton (original 514 B.C.E.). Courtesy of National Archeological Museum, Naples.

favor of resorting to violence in order to overthrow a tyrant is that "kings are chosen by God and established by the people."[13] This meant that the authority of kings derives from two related sources and that the people's act of confirming

[13] Ibid., p. 76.

the king's authority is part and parcel of the causal constitution of kingship. Kings have no authority to compel God's people to disobey God's law and become idolaters. Moreover, kings are crowned for the good of the people and are therefore judged with reference to their service to the people. Tyrants violate their covenants with God and with the people, and consequently the people are no longer bound to obey. The author of the *Vindiciae* compares the king to the pilot of a ship:

In a commonwealth commonly compared to a ship, the king holds the place of a pilot, the people in general are owners of the vessel, obeying the pilot, whilst he is careful of the public good; as though this pilot neither is nor ought to be esteemed other than servant to the public.... But let us suppose, that in this our ship of state the pilot is drunk, the most of his associates are asleep ... the ship ... instead of following her right course ... is ready rather to split herself. What should a master's mate, or some other officer do, who is vigilant and careful to perform his duty?[14]

The author of the *Vindiciae* does not think that individual subjects should act as private persons, because the people, not individual persons, confirmed the king and have a contract with him. Nevertheless, he fully acknowledges the impracticality of assembling the people for the purpose of joint action due to their large numbers. He resolves the problem by placing responsibility for the use of force on the magistrates' shoulders by virtue of their accountability to the public good. The magistrates, as "master's mates," are then entitled to use force on behalf of the people, the owners of the vessel, to save the ship of state.

In the course of modern political history, the weight of the rationale for overthrowing a tyrant shifted from an assessment of his liability (according to his adherence to the covenant with God who elected him) to an appraisal of his accountability (in accordance with his adherence to or violation of his contract with the people who confirmed him). This shift toward more earthly tests of the legitimacy of governmental uses of power, including the material welfare of the people, entails changes in both the normative and the epistemological frames of politics materializing the political power of the sovereign people as the source and cause of government, as well as the warrantor of its ethical foundation. An important part of these changes stemmed from the tenet of God's orderly nature as a publicly visible source of political norms and as a metaphor for the ideal political order.

Whereas the *Vindiciae* is cautious about a right of popular revolt, regarding the use of popular violence mostly as a deterrent, it is unambiguous in praising the republican heroes of tyrannicide. It refers to them as a host of "liberators from tyrants; as Harmodius and Aristogeiton at Athens, Brutus and Cassius in Rome, and Aratus of Sycion. To these by a public decree were erected statues, because they delivered their countries from the tyrannies of Pisistratus, of Caesar, and Nicocles."[15] The *Vindiciae Contra Tyrannos* concludes that in

---

[14] Ibid., p. 32.
[15] Ibid., pp. 66, 72.

cases of a "questionless tyrant by practice ... the officers of state may judge him according to the laws. And if he supports his tyranny by strong hands, their duty binds them, when by no other means it can be effected by force of arms to suppress him."[16]

In late sixteenth-century England, reflection on tyrannicide and on the status of republican values was very much in the air, as Shakespeare's play *Julius Caesar* (1599) indicates. The play represents a complex view of the assassination of Caesar as motivated by and serving both republican and anti-republican values. It depicts Roman republicanism as too fragile and degraded to be rescued by a conspiracy.[17] The historical chain of events has indeed led to fiercer tyrannies and to the misuse of public republican rhetoric to justify dictatorship. Ian Donaldson points out that:

[A]ny play concerned with conspiracy, political ambition, and the assassination of a ruler was bound to be of absorbing interest to audiences of England in the late 1590s, who would no doubt have seen some broad resemblances to their own time in the political uncertainties and jockeyings for power in Republican Rome.[18]

Hadfield maintains that *Julius Caesar* "charts the power struggles of an elite which clearly resembled those taking place in the last years of Elizabethan England and exposes the uncertainty of the succession."[19]

Whereas the imaginary of popular sovereignty emerges in this period as a rationale for holding the king accountable to the people, the actual historical materialization of the people's power to establish and disestablish the monarchy by resorting to republican or democratic violence will become a fact only with the great revolutions that would follow.

In order for an act of violence to be regarded as a cause of a democratic government, it first must be a distinct event – or a series of related events – and then it must be associated with the goal and effects of creating or protecting a democracy. The former concerns the material epistemological perception of an event as a cause that produces certain political effects, whereas the latter concerns the normative framing of cause and effect. The historical record is, of course, full of examples of incongruencies between the causal and the normative conditions of democratic violence.

In antiquity, certain kinds of violence against oppressors were regarded as democratic and laudatory, though the violence that liberates from tyranny or oligarchy does not necessarily produce a democracy, nor can it constitute the moral basis of a democratic regime. The question is: In which instances does bloodshed that liberates from tyranny purporting to engender democracy become antidemocratic? If there is a notion such as democratic or popular violence, at which point does it cease to be democratic and turn into the opposite?

---

[16] Ibid., p. 76.
[17] Andrew Hadfield, *Shakespeare and Republicanism* (Cambridge: Cambridge University Press, 2005), pp. 154–83.
[18] Ibid., p. 182.
[19] Ibid.

Is there a line that divides democratic and antidemocratic popular violence? These questions formulate the overarching dilemma that has haunted many revolutions and political theorists.

The customary response to this problem has been that popular revolutionary violence, or violence endorsed by republican values, must bring about a constitution and a legal system that represses violence in the name of the people who initiated the revolutionary violence establishing the rule of democratically legislated laws. According to this approach, lawless violence can potentially be democratic when the motives and results of the use of force correspond to the promotion of freedom and self-government, that is, when force is directed against tyranny at a prelegal stage and is followed by the rule of democratic laws that it must produce. This of course is nearly an ideal situation. But it clarifies the point that even when it can be established as democratically motivated, popular violence that breeds terror or dictatorship rather than a constitutional democracy can hardly be classified as democratic. Once a democratic revolution leads to a constitutional democracy, the only sanctioned democratic violence is that authorized by law. Sheldon S. Wolin observed that "Greek theorists developed a critique of democracy and then constructed a conception of a constitution as a means of demonstrating how democracy might be domesticated, rendered stable, orderly, and just."[20]

Within a constitutional democracy, periodic elections are intended to replace popular violence as events that cause and constitute democratic governments, a means of overthrowing bad governments and keeping reasonably good ones responsive and accountable. Evidently, such arrangements never ensure a neat transition between extralegal revolutionary violence and a constitution. Moreover, in some democracies, the potential for popular violence may persist as a significant deterrent against authoritarian governmental measures that would undermine democratic politics.

Despite the possibility that the idea of democratic violence may be inherently problematic, and despite the considerable complexities, ambiguities, and horrors of the violence that erupted, for instance, during the American and French revolutions, the modern democratic political imagination has succeeded in canonizing these revolutions as constitutive democratic events.

In the following section, I discuss some of the issues involved in framing violence as a democratic political cause. I argue that, like authoritarian political power, democratic political power gravitates toward the uses of physical force as a means of materializing or corporealizing its presence and transforming itself from an idea or a fiction into a fact. In other words, I contend that the use of lethal force by or on behalf of democratic as well as nondemocratic political agents can be at least partly explained as a response to the general fear of unmasking their elusive foundations. From this perspective, then, the sheer

---

[20] Sheldon S. Wolin, "Norm and Form: The Constitutionalizing of Democracy" in J. Peter Euben, John R. Wallach, and Josiah Ober (eds.), *Athenian Political Thought and the Reconstruction of American Democracy* (Ithaca: Cornell University Press, 1994), p. 35.

fact of using violence to substantiate political power cannot be identified as the *differentia specifica* that distinguishes different political regimes. Other factors such as the modes, the limits, and the narrative frames of the uses of violence are more relevant to making such distinctions. One of the central problems faced by democratic revolutionaries in the modern era is how to convince the people as well as themselves that there is a difference between royal violence, which they consider illegitimate, and murder or democratic violence "for the sake of the people," which they regard as legitimate.

Such a problem arose when purportedly democratic violence was not directed only against the king, his family, his close aristocratic supporters, his officials, and army, but also against wider circles of individuals and groups considered part of the people or part of the vanguard of the revolutionaries themselves. Such a crisis was embodied in the predicament of Georges Jacques Danton and Jacques-René Hébert, widely and highly regarded prior to their execution by their former corevolutionaries as revolutionary patriots who had acted on behalf of the people.

The ability to establish a distinct form of democratic violence, a kind of aggression that ostensibly serves to institute a democratic legal system – an event that functions as a cause of a democratic political order – has constituted a colossal challenge given the contradiction between the right to resist oppression by violence and the value that democrats accord individual life, unforced persuasion, voluntary self-government, and the rule of law. I would argue, however, that even when a society has undergone a transition from an authoritarian regime to a constitutional democracy by means of a revolution or other violent event, the incentive of hegemonic political agency to engage in lawful killing persists as a means to project the continued concrete presence of the abstract power of "the people."[21] Even in a constitutional democracy, killing may remain the ultimate strategy of materializing and naturalizing political power in the sphere of commonsense reality. With the elimination of the death penalty in most democracies, this observation may still be relevant to occasions in which democracy goes to war or uses violence against external targets.

Political bloodshed may be particularly pliable in corporealizing claims to power and authority in times of radical regime change, as during the American and French revolutions. In the French revolutionary context, in addition to the instrumental goal of destroying the monarchy and instituting a republic, the use of violence, especially the terror exercised by the Committee of Public Safety (note the name) headed by Robespierre and Saint-Just, must have also fulfilled the somewhat covert role of protecting that new authority from a

---

[21] The questionable substantive existence of "the people" in the liberal-democratic or republican state, of course, complicates the attribution of such violence and its legitimation. On the questionable ethical and empirical substance of "the people" as a unified agency see for instance Seyla Benhabib, *The Rights of Others: Aliens, Residents and Citizens* (New York: Cambridge University Press, 2004).

popular perception of the revolution as a mere fleeting theatrical gesture. The revolutionaries' concern regarding the ostensible theatricality of their own actions reflected both their contempt for the theatricality of the monarchy as well as their vulnerability when subjected to similar charges stemming from the inescapable theatrical dimensions of their own acts.

One of the curious manifestations of the anxiety over political theatricality on both sides of the political spectrum issued from suspicions regarding the political activities and performances of professional actors in the public arena. It was resolved by efforts to exclude professional actors from politics.[22] Paul Friedland observes that "in almost every instance in which actors crossed over onto the political stage, they were lambasted by journalists and pamphleteers who were quick to unmask these migrations as evidence of both the insatiable political ambitions of dangerous clowns and the inherent theatricality of the revolution itself."[23] He further alludes to pamphlets "in which the entire National Assembly was unmasked as a troupe of actors in disguise and election results were printed in the form of a cast list. Invariably, denunciations of political figures sought to portray them as unscrupulous actors, deceiving the people with their all too believable performances."[24]

Against this background, the massive executions performed by the revolutionaries, especially during the Reign of Terror, may be attributed at least in part to the force whereby politically ordained execution could resist the frame of theatricality. Involuntary death as an irreversible fact is the consummate antitheatrical act, the end of all posturing, the ultimate reality principle. When actual death occurs – even by accident – on the theater stage, the illusionary or the theatrical are bound to be suddenly disrupted by the real.

The terror and the mass executions disseminated fear and deterred the actual and imagined enemies of the revolutionary radicals among the monarchists and moderate revolutionaries. Visible mass murder may also have served the revolutionaries as a powerful means to ground what might have appeared to many as merely gestural and rhetorical politics in a firm, new (albeit terrifying) reality of power. Death, which could irrefutably be attributed to a new revolutionary agency ostensibly operating on behalf of or for the sake of the people, probably facilitated the efforts of the revolutionaries to overcome the paradoxes, ambiguities, and therefore also the anxieties of establishing the new political imaginaries of the revolution as a real alternative to the monarchic imaginary. The concomitant reconfiguration of physical force and political power over the ruins of the dying monarchy constituted an attempt to harness violence for the sake of the rhetoric of a new political vision. Whereas mass murder may have constituted a potent means of persuading the French people

[22] Paul Friedland, *Political Actors: Representative Bodies and Theatricality in the Age of the French Revolution* (Ithaca: Cornell University Press, 2003).
[23] Ibid., p. 170.
[24] Ibid., p. 2.

of the reality of the revolution, Robespierre's famous and infamous defense of democratic terror is still a subject of passionate debate.[25]

Following similar lines, Elaine Scarry traces a direct link between torture, war, and death in the urge of power to corporealize itself. Regarding torture, she argues that "the physical pain is so incontestably real that it seems to confer its quality of 'incontestable reality' on that power that has brought it into being. It is precisely because the reality of that power is so highly contestable, the regime so unstable, that torture is being used."[26] Also in a period of war, she observes, "a made world of culture acquires the characteristics of 'reality,' the process of perception that allows invented ideas, beliefs, and made objects to be accepted and entered into as though they had the same ontological status as the naturally given world."[27] She thinks that war tends to begin "when the system of national self-belief is without any compelling source of substantiation ... when a country has become to its population a fiction."[28]

Against the background of such observations, the debate among theorists and historians concerning the sources of revolutionary terror may be illuminating. I note specifically Lefort's observation that the purges were "motivated by a desire to furnish proof of the reality of the Revolution in the shape of the death of its enemies, to conjure up an actor and to give him a face."[29] "Without the operation of the Terror," Lefort asks, "what would become of the real?"[30] I would add the question whether political imaginaries of a government of and by the people could at all succeed in acquiring the privileged status of an acknowledged political fact without lethal violence attributed to the agency of the people. How else could these new imaginaries be established as shapers of the institutions of the postrevolutionary order and regulators of novel public-political expectations and behavior?

The point obviously goes beyond the French or other modern revolutions. It concerns the relations between political fictions and political power. Since democracy may also need its confirming epic moment, a dramatic victory of the people against tyranny, violent resistance, or revolution may appear to be a desirable material manifestation of popular sovereignty, a condition for the projection of the presence of the *Demos* as an agency and its later institutionalization. More precisely, the historical record shows that political murder and violent events can play a formative role in the political validation and establishment of a democratic system of political imaginaries and their continued sustenance.

[25] Maximilien Robespierre, *Virtue and Terror*, Slavoj Žižek (intro.), Jean Ducange (ed.), John Howe (trans.) (London: Verso, 2007).

[26] Elaine Scarry, *The Body in Pain: The Making and Unmaking of the World* (Oxford: Oxford University Press, 1987), p. 27.

[27] Ibid., p. 125.

[28] Ibid., p. 131.

[29] Claude Lefort, *Democracy and Political Theory*, David Macey (trans.) (Oxford: Polity Press, 1988), p. 83.

[30] Ibid., p. 84.

This issue raises a host of important questions: Are political fictions (including democratic ones) more effective in covering up their imaginary roots when they "murder"? How far can one regard a politically induced death as a conscious or unconscious means of concealing the ever-shaky, ontologically undecidable foundations of power and authority? Does it latently serve to shift public attention from the problematic genealogy of power to the self-empowering import of its actual manifestation? Does the fictional layer inherent in the foundations of any democratic (and nondemocratic) political order imply that an increased awareness of this fact is likely to encourage the use of physical force or other visible means to generate events that can animate and reify political agencies and inscribe material democratic political causality on the shifting imaginary and perceptual fabrics of politics? Can the shocking impact of terror be attractive as an effective or necessary revolutionary means to extricate a people from the entrenched habit of accepting their slavery as natural and preparing them for an alternative emancipatory imaginary of political order? Aren't we sensing here an especially curious and paradoxical symbiosis between statecraft and stagecraft, between violence and theatricality in the very creation and sustenance of democratic or republican political order?

The motivations as well as the effects of acts of violence performed by leaders of a democratic revolution or a government are different from those that seem to emerge more spontaneously from below. The very imaginary of such "popular violence" is an extremely complex phenomenon. John Walter, one of the most careful and insightful historians of crowd behavior during the English Revolution points out: "Clearly crowds are complex, polyphonic phenomena. Any crowd contains within it groups and individuals with varying motives. Crowds are events and their intentions may change over time. In this sense there can never be one correct reading of crowd action."[31]

This state of affairs obviously complicates the historian's task. But more significant for our present discussion, it invites competing political appropriations of an event such as crowd riots or violence by the political imaginaries and the adjunct narratives of contesting groups and interests.

As in the case of modern revolutions, historians often play an important role in substantiating or criticizing such narratives. Marxist historians tend to define and endorse violence in terms of class struggle, and monarchist historians attribute it to plunderers and criminals, whereas liberal democratic historians frame it as popular violence informed by a politics of rights. This remark does not intend to belittle the explicit contributions made by ideological historians to our understanding of the past, or to praise the special virtues of the great works of professional historians who attempt to insulate their personal preferences from their work and establish links and causal relations that may contradict their individual preferences. But even in those instances, the authority assumed by historians as guardians of the real past to draw a line between

---

[31] John Walter, *Understanding Popular Violence in the English Revolution: The Colchester Plunderers* (Cambridge: Cambridge University Press, 1999), p. 342.

facts and fictions is always exploitable by agents of competing political imaginaries in order to fictionalize the claims of their opponents' works and certify the material factuality or reality of their own.

John Walter's treatise can further contribute to clarifying the point. In his very meticulous study of popular violence during the English Revolution, he warns that many of the original primary reports available to historians of these events of popular violence expressed an elite's unsympathetic bias against the rioters, whom they characteristically described as "plunderers." Others, among them historians, he argues, tended to frame these events of popular violence as "food riots," connoting a narrowly instrumental and locally focused uprising. In contradistinction, Walter observes that a series of factors, including supporting evidence from parliamentary and Puritan preaching, suggest that what initially appear to be local events (such as the plundering and vandalizing of noble and gentry households in the counties of Essex and Suffolk) should rather be regarded as forms of popular political violence associated with a process of politicizing the masses in the early 1640s, as well as with the development of a parliamentary popular culture. Instead of aiming to account for these riots on the grounds of local economic distress or class hostility, he recommends that we "take seriously the politics behind the crowd's actions.... It would be a mistake to over-explain crowd action. But the actions of the crowds in 1642 were informed by a politics of rights, not least the right of the people to take action in their defense."[32]

Walter's study is undoubtedly a very useful resource for those seeking to integrate the riots of the 1640s into a narrative of democratic violence, which also animates the public as a real agency. But Walter actually rejects "grand narratives which use particular episodes of crowd actions to support larger theses ... if they ignore or suppress the contexts within which those actions took place."[33] Despite historians' limited control over such slips, omissions, and suppressions, they are often driven by a powerful need to produce grand narratives of democratic and antidemocratic political causalities.

The first Palestinian Intifada (the wave of violent protests that broke out in Gaza on December 8, 1987 and quickly spread to the West Bank) provides a contemporary illustration of the contest over the framing of popular violence. Benjamin Netanyahu, serving as Israel's representative to the United Nations, voiced the official Israeli version of those events: The Intifada was terrorist agitation induced by the Palestine Liberation Organization (PLO) from its Tunisian headquarters. Foreign journalists, impressed by the magnitude of the demonstrations and their unorganized patterns, reported instead a spontaneous grassroots uprising. Obviously, this view framing the Intifada as a popular revolt or spontaneous democratic violence was more legitimizing and effective in inviting international condemnation of the Israeli occupation.

[32] Ibid., pp. 339, 352.
[33] Ibid., p. 352.

Sometime later, the PLO, attempting to take credit for the demonstrations, which earned broad international support, ironically came closer to the official Israeli version that insisted on its expatriate role in organizing the Intifada. The Intifada, which lasted for a few years, had of course gone through different phases – sometimes manifestly led by local groups and individuals, sometimes by outside leaders. These and competing attempts to frame the Intifada as a political, emotional, and organizational resource reflect no qualms about appropriating or distorting the already complex facts of the situation in order to justify their respective political narratives.

Since the late 1990s, waves of violence and suicide bombings have focused attention on the question of whether random killing of civilians could be regarded as a legitimate violent response to oppression, or more generally, on the nature of the relations between the motives and purposes of violence and its forms. The religious dimension of suicide bombing has complicated this debate, which has highlighted huge cultural differences between East and West in coding such forms of violence.

A more democratically legitimate form of resistance erupted in the Arab world during the early months of 2011, when persistent mass nonviolent demonstrations succeeded in toppling Arab dictators. This wave of Arab revolts signified the dramatic emergence of a new kind of Arab hero: the unarmed Arab freedom fighter whose willingness to risk his or her life for the cause of democracy captured the imagination of the Arab masses and eclipsed the heroic martyrdom of the Arab suicide bomber. The willingness of dictators to defend their regimes by shooting many of the protesting civilians only reinforced the epic democratic luster of that moment.

The peaceful performative phase of embodying the suasive political imaginaries of democracy in an actual system of rules and institutions is, of course, quite another matter. The energies of the protesters can be, and often are, misdirected. They must be properly channeled in order to enable the long, arduous odyssey of evolving democratic institutions for the nonviolent regulation of conflicts, developing democratic civic culture that can generate trust without suppressing criticism and skepticism, and the self-fashioning of tolerant citizens who can cope with the inherent instabilities and uncertainties of democratic politics. The collective popular imaginary of democracy is considerably more coherent and one dimensional than its performative phase. The struggle for freedom is usually more focused and galvanizing than the use of freedom momentarily obtained to generate the democratic institutions that can preserve it and the behaviors that embody it. Yet, at least initially, the advent of a wave of partly successful, nonviolent Arab revolts on such a scale compares favorably with some of the great democratic revolts of the past, recalling the French Revolution that generated some of the classic modern examples for massive revolutionary violence in the name of democracy.

While complex events of popular violence do not easily lend themselves to generalization in terms of grand political narratives, in certain cases some of the most salient features of a violent event are already fraught with democratic rhetorical force. The seizure of the Bastille by a Paris crowd on July 14, 1789 and the execution of Louis XVI on January 21, 1793 are obvious examples. Obviously, the attempt to frame as democratic the violence of the terror, the execution of thousands of "enemies of the revolution" by the "revolutionary government" between September 1793 and July 1794 is far more problematic.

While the Bastille – a medieval fortress that served as a prison for a mere seven inmates released by the crowd – was not a particularly memorable site, the future framing of this event in the democratic political imagination of France, the West, and beyond would benefit from the conjunction of factors such as popular anger over the rise of the price of bread and the fact that the troops guarding the Bastille fired into the crowd. The timing, the site, the opposing forces, and the image of the people breaking into the prison through the lowered drawbridge and overwhelming the firing guards generated a powerful image that the radical press apparently rushed to exploit, transforming it into the celebrated, paradigmatic event of the revolution. The fall of the Bastille became a symbol for the people's democratic resistance to absolute monarchy, a significant icon of the people's power to liberate itself and fight for a democratic republic.

Considering the fact that the revolutionary events spanned a period of several years, the ability to translate the seizure of the Bastille into a paradigmatic symbol of democratic violence was undoubtedly crucial to the long-term power of the revolutionary rhetoric, despite the continuing debate over the character and import of this event. One can distinguish some nuances between the manifold accounts by noting whether the assailants of the Bastille are referred to as a "mob," "crowd," "workers," "the people," or "The People." There are but few examples in modern history of an event that has become so momentous in the popular political imagination.

The execution of King Louis XVI almost three and a half years later constituted another example of constructing the act of killing outside positive law as a paradigmatic democratic use of violence. On December 3, 1792, Robespierre, who was against putting the king on trial, argued before a divided convention that the king was already condemned by virtue of his crimes against the people and humanity. He insisted that following the overthrow of the monarchy on August 10 Louis could not be judged. "[E]ither he is already condemned or the Republic is not acquitted." "To put Louis on trial ... would be to regress towards royal and constitutional despotism." Robespierre insisted that "Louis must die because the homeland has to live."[34] Robespierre here defends democratic violence both outside the dying legal system of the Ancien Régime and before the passing of the new constitution.

Rhetorically or theatrically, this event could not have been staged in a more effective manner to convey the message that political force and violence are transformed into power exercised by and for the people and in their name. An eyewitness report written by Henry Edgeworth, an English cleric (and

---

[34] Robespierre, *Virtue and Terror*, pp. 57–65.

vicar-general of the Diocese of Paris, confessor of Louis XVI) invited by the king to accompany him, recorded details crucial to later canonization of the event as a most powerful expression of democratic violence. Referring to the king's short trip between his prison and the site of the execution, Edgeworth reported that the streets were "lined up with citizens, all armed." Later the king had to undress. He "untied his neck cloth, opened his shirt, and arranged it himself." Then, Edgeworth recalled:

[S]eizing with violence the most virtuous of kings, they dragged him under the axe of the guillotine, which in one stroke severed his head from his body. All this passed in a moment. The youngest of the guards, who seemed about eighteen, immediately seized the head, and showed it to the people as he walked around the scaffold; he accompanied this monstrous ceremony with the most atrocious and indecent gestures. At first an awful silence prevailed; at length some cries of "vive la Republique!" were heard. By degrees the voice multiplied and in less than ten minutes this cry, a thousand times repeated, became the universal shout of the multitude, and every hat was in the air.[35]

An unarmed king must expose his body at the scaffold in the midst of armed citizens. Now they could all see, as Edmund Burke distressingly wrote, that "a king is just a man." The king's decapitation destroyed two bodies at once – the mortal body of flesh and the immortal body of the king as the embodiment of the entire French nation, the unifying principle of the Ancien Régime. The king was dead and the monarchy too, but the French Republic was newborn and very much alive. Hence the significance of the grotesque brandishing of the king's severed head accompanied by an increasingly triumphant chorus crying "Vive la République!"

By comparison with what came to be established as democratic violence at the Bastille and the public beheading of the king as ritual regicide – like the tyrannicide commemorated in the public square of ancient Athens – the raging violence of the Reign of Terror between September 1793 and July 1794 posed far greater quandaries regarding its classification as democratic violence. Here some of the massive killing, ostensibly aimed at eliminating "enemies of the revolution," was channeled against self-declared revolutionaries such as Danton, who disagreed with the dominant revolutionary factions. Since after the fall of the monarchy terror was exercised by an extremely centralized revolutionary government, and because it was directed by The Committee of Public Safety (CPS) and rationalized as violence necessitated by the state of emergency, the question of whether it was unconstitutional or not provoked continual debate over its legitimacy. To further enhance these ambiguities, during the Reign of Terror, government forces were employed to repress the peasant army, insurgents, and other circles that saw themselves as moderate revolutionaries but were treated by the Jacobins of Paris as dangerous royalists who must be eradicated.

---

[35] Henry Edgeworth, quoted in J. M. Thompson's *English Witnesses of the French Revolution* (first pub. 1815; Oxford: Blackwell, 1935).

Beyond the particular circumstances of revolutionary violence there is, of course, the perennial issue of the status of domestic violence employed by a democratic state when it declares a state of emergency and suspends ordinary laws and norms in a way that exposes citizens to the lethal force of the state. Is this kind of an act a constitutionally defensible "state of exception" or is it a more inherent and continual aspect of the modern state even when it is a democracy, as Giorgio Agamben, for one, claims?[36] I am inclined to agree with Agamben but, in line with my earlier observations, I tend to attribute the materialization of state violence to the powerful drive to epistemologically hypostatize and ontologize state power as the embodiment of a ruling political imaginary, especially when governors feel vulnerable to oppositional forces or to lay perceptions of the fragile foundations of the regime's legitimacy.

Given the role of murder and of the naturalization of state power in the psycho-historic grounding of political fictions, one may ask, with particular reference to the democratic state: How much or how far can any given historically working configuration of the democratic imagination tolerate such ambiguities in the attempt to use force against citizens before it provokes countermeasures or collapses into dictatorship? What is the status of the often professed demarcation line between a revolutionary force used to establish a democratic state and a legalized force domestically employed by the postrevolutionary-constitutional state in order to maintain order and public safety?[37]

As the case of modern Israel may suggest, the line dividing revolutionary constitutive from postrevolutionary and, in this case also, an occupying force may not only be unintentionally ambiguous – such an ambiguity may actually be the consequence of a deliberate policy. For many years, Israeli authorities maintained a fair amount of order within the Green Line dividing the territories that constituted Israel before the 1967 war from those occupied during that war, while at the same time politically, financially, and administratively backing a largely extralegal or extraconstitutional force of settlers seeking to root themselves on the West Bank of the Jordan River. Those settlers, or *mitnachalim*, defined their struggle as a continuation of the 1948 War of Independence.[38] Throughout this period, the State of Israel used force delegated to the Israel Defence Forces as the carrier of the sovereign powers of the

---

[36] Giorgio Agamben, *Homo Sacer: Sovereign Power and Bare Life*, Daniel Heller-Roazen (trans.), (Stanford: Stanford University Press, 1998); and his *State of Exception*, Kevin Attell (trans.), (Chicago: University of Chicago Press, 2005).

[37] The clashes between the Iranian government and millions of citizens peacefully protesting election fraud, the government charge that the mass demonstrators are "enemies of the people," and the use of live fire to repress the demonstrations in order to "protect the people's choice" illustrate the characteristic tendency of dictatorships to act against the citizens in the citizens' own name.

[38] See Talia Sasson's official report on the illegal settlements in the occupied territories, 2005. This report records the massive illegality of the settlement enterprise. See also *Lords of the Land: The War Over Israel's Settlements in the Occupied Territories, 1967–2007*, Idith Zertal and Akiva Eldar (eds.), (New York: Nation Books, 2007).

state over the occupied territories to protect its citizen-settlers from Palestinian violence, but largely ignored its legal responsibility to equally protect native Palestinians against the Israeli settlers' violence in the occupied territories.

Whereas the revolutionary violence that preceded the establishment of the state of Israel on May 14, 1948 was followed by deliberate, massive efforts to constitutionalize the new state and subordinate the use of violence by citizens, police, and soldiers to the rule of law, the culture of illegal action and violence cultivated within the framework of the state in the occupied territories following the 1967 war disrupted the domestic process of constitutionalization. In many respects, Israel emerged as a classical dual colonial system under which a fairly proper legal system restraining arbitrary use of power within the pre-1967 border coexists with a massive system of settlements illegal under international law on occupied territories in which settlers' violence is informally (and sometimes also legally) tolerated by a government unwilling to risk its political support by the Israeli right.[39]

The picture becomes more complex when we consider the issue of covert use of force by secret security agents of the modern democratic state, a tendency considerably reinforced in response to international terror. The dramatic emergence of mega-terror on the international scene since September 11, 2001 has led anxious democratic publics to consent uncritically to an excessive and overarching implementation of anti-terror measures. Such measures often seem to expand readily beyond targeting terrorists engaged in random mass killings of innocent civilians. This expansion also targets popular violence that can be construed as resistance to foreign invasion, occupation, or other forms of massive oppression. These developments have demonstrated the persistent elasticity of the rhetoric of governmental care for "public safety," coined by French revolutionaries engaged in terror and adapted to modern conditions by contemporary governments.

In addition, democratic states not infrequently engage in covert operations whose secrecy is defended more strictly on instrumental grounds as a requirement of operational efficacy. It is precisely because of the high political cost of flagrant violations of the constitution or the laws of the democratic state that governments seek to maintain an ambiguous policy on the simultaneous employment of legal and illegal or extralegal means. Obviously, a considerable part of the efforts of modern democratic states to present their use of force as circumscribed within the legally warranted and mandated defense of their citizens entails the use of secrecy to conceal aspects of their illegal, excessive use of force from the public eye. In several democracies, this freedom is constrained by the accountability of secret services to special parliamentary committees. This, however, has apparently seldom proved effective.

[39] See ibid. and Yaron Ezrahi "The Impact of the Occupation on the Israeli Democracy" in Daniel Bar-Tal and I. Schnell (eds.), *Impacts of Occupation on Occupiers: Lessons from the Israeli Occupation of the West Bank and Gaza Strip* (Oxford: Oxford University Press, forthcoming).

The democratic commitment to replace violence with peaceful modes of action, such as elections, legislation, and judicial procedures is undoubtedly kept within the memory of the costly prestate revolutionary violence that gave birth to the state and an imagined violence as the implicit anarchistic alternative to the current rule of law. Between these two poles, legally authorized violence effected by the police combines the necessity of maintaining the law with the conversion of prelegal or preconstitutional violence into constitutionally and legally sanctioned forms, in the shadow of the fear of the ominous alternative – the collapse of order and the reeruption of formless violence.

Democratic violence always justifies itself as an alternative to nondemocratic or antidemocratic violence. So ironically but realistically, there are no peaceful democratic means, no democratic laws unrelated to past, present, and anticipated violence. As Walter Benjamin observed, "in the exercise of power over life and death, more than in any other legal act, law reaffirms itself."[40]

Many of these ambiguities and their concomitant questions emerged during the French Revolution, particularly following the Reign of Terror. Since during the Terror revolutionaries were also engaged in killing other revolutionaries, it is not surprising that the difficulty of whitewashing it even to themselves as "democratic terror" or, as Robespierre called it, "the despotism of freedom," permeated their own consciousness. Lefort thought that perhaps no one expressed this ambiguity more poignantly than Saint-Just when he opined that the magistrates responsible for the terror might perhaps secretly have told themselves: "we are not sufficiently virtuous to be so terrible."[41] Lefort suggests that the terror implied that "the terrorists must recognize one another as individuals who are equal before the law – the law of which the terror is said to be the sword but which it embodies in fantasy." Operating in the still uncharted zone between the political imaginaries of the falling monarchy and of the not yet formed republic, the revolutionaries who were required to take responsibility for the terror without the backing of a reliable general system of power and its legitimation probably felt fearful that their power was too hollow to kill.[42]

In order for domestic violence to seem democratic, it must not be contaminated by personal or partisan political interests. The force of the law cannot even begin to pose as democratic if it does not appear to represent the people rather than its own agents. This thought must have guided Robespierre when he declared in his speech defending the execution of the king before the National Convention: "Yes, the death penalty [in general] is a crime" ... I myself abhor the death penalty ... and for Louis I feel neither love nor hate; I just hate his crimes."[43] When democratic violence is carried out or authorized

---

[40] Walter Benjamin, *Reflections: Essays, Aphorisms, Autobiographical Writings*, P. Demetz (ed.), E. Jephcott (trans.) (New York: Harvest/ HBJ, 1978), pp. 286, 277–300.

[41] Lefort, *Democracy and Political Theory*, pp. 86–7.

[42] Ibid.

[43] Robespierre's speech before the Assembly on the trial of the king on December 3, 1792 in *Maximilien Robespierre: Virtue and Terror*, p. 64.

by the people rather than by self-appointed or partisan agents, however, the ambiguity inherent in the very definition of "the people" and, therefore, also in definitions of the "public interest" or the "public good" implies that, unless strictly confined to the use of force authorized by the law, "democratic violence" is likely to be an oxymoron.

It is hard to envision such a term without sensing a contradiction. In some respects, this relates to the problem previously discussed regarding Tocqueville's observation about the tension between the democratic tendency to reject the aristocratic attribution of action to a few individuals only and the need to preserve the voluntary component of democratic action while concomitantly privileging the abstraction of the people or the public as the primary democratic agent. Lefort notes the difficulties confronted by the French revolutionaries, particularly by Robespierre, in their attempts to depersonalize and depoliticize the pursuit and voluntary exercise of power. In order to achieve "the symbolic security of a mind free from doubts," maintains Lefort, "everyone who sought power was under an obligation to disappear as an individual."[44]

The record of the modern democratic state indicates the often mixed appeals to popular imaginaries of power, grounded in and restrained by morality, legality, images of nature, public safety, reason, and even tradition, setting boundaries and giving shape to violence. I submit that such imaginaries are not necessarily fictions merely devised to legitimate that which is in fact nothing but the arbitrary personal and political use of force. I do not believe that choreographies of virtue, legality, and rationality are all there is, or that threats to public safety are not sometimes sufficient to warrant the use of violence against parts of the public to protect the public. My purpose is to indicate tensions between the positive rhetorical and epistemological functions of violence in rendering democratic power tangible to the lay public and its adverse moral import. Great constraints, therefore, hamper any attempt to imagine the possibility of democratic violence and of integrating violence into sustainable imaginaries of democratic causality.

From the point of view of democratic political imaginology (the theory of the relations between political imaginaries and politics), this difficulty constitutes a pivotal feature of democracy. By contrast to republican democracy, which so readily relapses into crass nationalism and a moralization of the sacrifices of the individual in favor of the group, the liberal democratic commitment to the value of each individual life, to the individual lives of citizens, soldiers, and, in genuine liberal democracies, also of enemies, exerts enormous pressure on democratic rulers to account for any use of domestic and, to a lesser extent, external state force.

The strength of democratic political imaginaries regulating a democratic polity fluctuates over time, and modern democracies are largely mixed systems in which nondemocratic and antidemocratic political imaginaries can, at least temporarily, occupy center stage. It is therefore not surprising that regressive

---

[44] Lefort, *Democracy and Political Theory*, p. 87.

shifts in the performance of democracy are reflected in periodic massive uses of force by the democratic state both internally and externally.[45]

It should be clear, then, that, notwithstanding the difficulties inherent in the very possibility of democratic violence, the minimal requirement for beginning to consider a violent event democratic is that it can be legally restrained or, alternatively, produced by a politics of popular rights aimed at defending freedom, removing violent tyrants, stopping repression, instituting the rule of law, or, in more general ways, bringing about or restoring a democratic order. But retrospectively such events may or may not be judged democratic depending on who judges and when. This means that (especially domestically) the classification of illegal violent dissent as democratic means that more widely it must be political in the sense of being the only alternative to absent legal-political routes of participation and protest. It must be a widely supported measure of last resort intended to stop oppression and promote democratic institutions and practices.

Obviously, such large-scale and prolonged eruptions of violence as those recorded during the English, American, French, Russian, and Arab revolutions included thousands of sporadic violent events, some of which came close to furthering democratic causes while others were clearly antagonistic to any democratic principle, idea, or practice. But the democratic political imagination has often tended to ignore these fine distinctions and rather lump together, codify, and appropriate multiple and largely contradictory events as coherent acts of popular insurrection. The need to ground the genealogical narrative of the democratic regime in a material factual cause, in a clear and distinct originary event, has often proven stronger than the need to represent or acknowledge the complexities and ambiguities of past affairs. By construing and fashioning revolutions and events of similar magnitude as epic narratives signifying monumental historic turning points, and by composing and codifying them as transmittable collective historic memory, democratic political imaginaries have aimed at converting themselves into sustainable believable realities. The performative political imagination that has combined fragments of experience

---

[45] A debate on whether such a regressive shift occurred during Israel's military action in Gaza between December 27, 2008 and January 2009 began immediately after the clashes. This operation was intended primarily to weaken Hamas's military arm and diminish its capacity to fire rockets indiscriminately into towns in southern Israel. The large number of civilian Palestinians killed and injured in this operation provoked acrimonious domestic and world debate on the moral code and practice of the Israeli army. Were basic commitments to protect enemy civilians kept despite their deliberate use by Hamas as human shields? Did Israeli soldiers take appropriate measures to discriminate between armed and unarmed Palestinians, those wearing civilian clothes as camouflage and genuine noncombatants? The controversy revealed marked differences between liberal democratic and republican right-wing voices. The former insisted that the IDF was not sufficiently discriminating, that despite recognition of the operational difficulties in urban war, the army employed excessive force violating basic norms of a democratic army; the latter defended the practice. The former used language focusing on the value of individual life as a universal norm while the latter concentrated on the antagonism between the two groups, seeing membership in the enemy collective as incriminating even civilians.

and public desire into constitutive democratic events has (usually effectively) transmuted not only mass violence but also occasionally equally ambiguous and inconclusive peaceful events such as elections into definitive causes of democratic governments.

DEMOCRATIC CAUSALITY – THE PROBLEMATIC STATUS OF ELECTIONS AS CONSTITUTIVE POLITICAL EVENTS

Democratic ambivalence toward political violence has contributed to the emergence of electoral events as a nonviolent means of establishing, legitimizing, and changing governments. In contemporary democracies, electoral campaigns and elections have become major political and media events attracting massive public attention both domestically and internationally. In many countries, election day has become a holiday, voting accompanied by an atmosphere of festivity. Despite trends in some countries indicating periods of marked decline in the percentage of citizens' participation in elections and the fact that, due to the often large stretches of time between elections their power to legitimate incumbent governments tends to decline over time, elections have retained their status as the democratic act par excellence, as the culminating moment of democratic political participation by both the individual citizen and the people. This remains true even in the face of the current proliferation of new modes of legitimating and delegitimating power facilitated by dramatic advances in accessible technologies of instant horizontal communications.

Furthermore, as the ultimate political cause in democracies, as the indispensable requirement for a state to be democratic, the status of elections has been sustained despite ambiguities inherent in key components of the election process such as political participation, representatives and representation, majority, election results, and political mandate. Obviously, the pressure to establish elections as a political cause, the need to embody the political imaginary of popular sovereignty, was usually sufficient to mask these ambiguities and produce the appropriate measure of observable behaviors supportive of a persuasive performance of democracy as a political reality.

In ancient Athens, the meaning of democratic political participation was qualified by severe restrictions imposed on the right to citizenship. The *demos* included Athenians born to Athenian parents but excluded women, slaves, freedmen, and foreign residents. Nonetheless, in the direct democracy of Athens, participation was not usually mediated by the election of officials but by direct participation in decisions that, in the general assembly of the citizens, were often passed by a majority following a debate in which every citizen had the (usually inoperative) right to speak. Allocation of official positions was by drawing lots, a way to avoid privileging the rich and block aristocratic access to power, as well as to curb the temptation to buy power through bribery.

Elections were usually limited to the selection of generals and officials in charge of finance. Nevertheless, the central role of elites was usually beyond dispute. The role of elites was even more pronounced in the politics of ancient

Rome. Alexander Yakobson observes that the historians' debate on the Roman political system focuses mostly on the degree in which the *populus* influenced the results of ongoing competition among aristocratic families or oligarchs. Although senatorial positions were mostly limited to privileged families, the leverage of the voting populace in choosing from competing candidates was apparently considerable.[46] There has been an ongoing debate on whether to classify the Roman political system as an oligarchy or as a republican democracy. Quite a few historians, however, seem to agree on regarding republican Rome as a mixed system based, in Yakobson's words, on an

interplay between popular and elitist elements … [in which] elections were a meeting place between the ambitions of the "oligarchs" and the voting power of the people. By the very act of exercising their suffrage, the people gave power to the "oligarchs"; at the same time, the ambitions of the "oligarchs" could not be fulfilled without resort to popular suffrage.[47]

In addition to deference to superiors, bribery of voters and patronage were very significant elements in Roman elections. A mixed picture emerges of serious constraints on elections as the expression of free choice together with significant elements of genuine elections as a competition among nobles for voters' support and secret ballots.[48] Yakobson further suggests that "the fact that Republican tradition included popular and even revolutionary elements may well have strengthened its resistance to the idea of a genuine revolution."[49] Such republican symbolism, more than actual electoral republican practice, was deployed in later eras. For instance, in the *Vindiciae* a fairly large number of monarchs sought to integrate elements of the political imaginary of popular sovereignty in order to compensate for the declining powers of the imaginary of the divine right of kings and royal family genealogies as sources of legitimation.

As the record of political history indicates, the idea that elections can function as an effective political strategy in legitimizing hierarchical structures has had great appeal even in advanced democratic republics like the United States. But whether in democracies or in republics, the imaginary of a government by the *demos* has always been loftier than its partial and muddled practice. Tocqueville's recognition of the precariousness of elections as a means of installing a new leader or renewing the mandate of an existing one led him to observe that one can "consider the moment of the election of the president of the United States as a moment of national crisis.… The factions at that time redouble their ardor; in that moment all the factitious passions that the imagination can create in a happy and tranquil country become agitated in broad

---

[46] Alexander Yakobson, "The Roman People, the System and the Elite – Continuing Debate," quoted from an English version by the author of "Il popolo Romano, il sistema e 'l'élite': il dibattito continua," *Studi Storici* 47/2 (2006): 377–93.

[47] Ibid. p. 7.

[48] Ibid.

[49] Ibid., p. 22.

daylight."[50] The fragility of American democracy is related to the fact that "[t]he government of the Union rests almost wholly on legal fictions. The Union is an ideal nation that exists so to speak only in the minds, and whose extent and bounds intelligence alone discovers."[51] Because of the innumerable difficulties of enacting such a system of fictions and living well with the dualities and paradoxes implied in turning legal or political fictions into a functioning political system, it requires a good deal of collective wisdom to perform democracy. Tocqueville turns somewhat ironic in this connection when he writes: "I never admired the good sense and the practical intelligence of the Americans more than in the manner by which they escape the innumerable difficulties to which their federal constitution gives rise."[52] In these and other such observations Tocqueville highlights the importance of political culture in enabling the complicated task of performing democratic political and constitutional imaginaries.

Edmund Morgan has made the apt observation that what upholds political fiction, what gives it the power to orient or rationalize modes of political discourse and action, is not an accurate correspondence to the reality it refers to, but a partial, sometimes only symbolic "closeness to the facts." He describes a good part of the seventeenth and eighteenth centuries' struggle in England between royalist advocates of the fiction of the divine right of kings and antiroyalist supporters of the fiction of popular sovereignty in terms of their respective efforts to narrow the gap between each adopted legitimating fiction and popularly acknowledged facts, while discrediting the other's facts as wholly fictitious.[53]

As I indicated earlier in this book, it is always easier to recognize and analyze political imaginaries or fictions structuring political worlds distant from us in time or place than to perceive our own. From within one's own polity, the successful products of the performative political imagination are usually implicitly confirmed as real by the practices of the reflective imagination that relates to them as external givens. Morgan realizes the difficulty of recognizing the fictive layers behind the political realities of one's own political universe. He observes that the "fiction that replaced the divine right of kings is our fiction, and it accordingly seems less fictional to us. Only the cynical among us will scoff at Lincoln's dedication to 'government of the people, by the people, and for the people.'"[54]

In a sense, we are always shifting between fictions that have solidified in our culture as facts and those that have not (or not yet) so crystallized. When the hypostatized fictions of other cultures or societies do not converge with

[50] Tocqueville, *Democracy in America*, p. 127.
[51] Ibid., p. 155.
[52] Ibid., p. 156.
[53] Edmund Morgan, *Inventing the People: The Rise of Popular Sovereignty in England and America* (New York: W. W. Norton, 1989).
[54] Ibid., p. 38.

ours, we more readily see them as "soft" facts or recognize them as fictitious. Western publics tend to accept the sovereignty of the people or of human rights as givens that must be universally acknowledged, although they are never satisfactorily acted upon or fully practiced. When a political fiction like that of the sovereignty of the people acquires such a degree of credibility, it becomes apparent that it is, at least partly, viable.

Reiterating our earlier observations, a winning political fiction is one that has succeeded in superseding other political fictions and usurping their privileged status as real, normative, and regulatory. Thus the performative political imagination induces changes in the common experience of political-constitutional facts by causing socially selected political fictions to be experienced as facts, and by recasting yesterday's facts as today's fictions. In some respects, political history is a record of attempts made by competing agents to establish their preferred fictions as reality. Morgan records and interprets this process, which led, at least in England and America, to the historic shift from monarchic rule based on divine rights of kings to a democratic regime. He shows how a configuration of several central democratic political fictions was able, aided by favorable circumstances, to produce enough novel political facts to render these fictions sufficiently credible to be sustainable and partly institutionalized.

However, as we noted in the French case, at no time have such fictions as the existence of a discernable general will of the people, democratic violence, the representativeness of legislators, or the validity of elections as expressions of public choices ceased to be, at least in part, fictions. Take, for example, the imaginary of the people. "The sovereignty of the people," observes Morgan,

is a much more complicated, one might say a more fictional fiction than the divine right of kings. A king, however dubious his divinity might seem, did not have to be imagined. He was a visible presence, wearing his crown and carrying his scepter. The people, on the other hand, are never visible as such. Before we ascribe sovereignty to the people we have to imagine that there is such a thing, something we personify as though it were a single body, capable of thinking, of acting, of making decisions and carrying them out, something quite apart from government, superior to government, and able to alter or remove a government at will, a collective entity more powerful and less fallible than a king or than any individual within it or than any group of individuals it singles out to govern it. To sustain a fiction so contrary to fact is not easy.[55]

I agree with Morgan on the difficulties of imagining "the people" as a material, visibly embodied entity. We have already noted the enormous leaps of political imagination the French had to make around the time of the revolution with respect to the imaginary of the people. This difficulty inheres in the recognition that while in a monarchy (as Morgan states) power was embodied in the person of the king, the locus of power in democracy is an abstract, barely definable entity. Calling it "the people" does not render it a visible and specifically discernable agent. Claude Lefort refers to this shift from monarchy to democracy

---

[55] Ibid., p. 153.

as involving the "disincorporation" of power whose periodic generation and distribution is subject to relatively stable rules.[56]

But the difficulty of imagining democratic agency (which I discuss extensively in the next chapter) does not diminish the difficulties inherent in the sustainability of the fiction of a divine right of kings. The fact that the king wore his crown, a visible emblem of sovereignty, did not (contrary to Morgan's view) ease matters. When people looked at the king, they saw first of all an individual person dressed like a king. To imagine such a particular person as a king required that people view him as more than just a man or an actor posturing as king.

We have discussed many situations in which such tensions between appearance and reality in politics have destabilized the political imagining of the king, epitomized in Edmund Burke's poignant apprehension of the fragility of this imaginary once the public discovered that [a naked corpse bespeaks that] "a king is just a man." As writers such as William Makepeace Thackeray and Hans Christian Andersen[57] or historians like Ernst H. Kantorowicz realized, the gap between the individual person and the king, between the king as a naked individual and a monarch fully dressed in his majestic garments, is precisely one of those things that made the political fiction of the monarchy and the divine right of kings so vulnerable.[58]

Beyond the vulnerability of the king's majesty and honor, imagining an individual person as embodying the body politic was both empowered and problematized by its complex theological roots in the Christian cult of Jesus' body as the embodiment of the Church. Transference of versions of this religious model onto the king or the modern secular sovereign was loaded with potentially exploitable contradictions.

Though related to the previous model, the difficulties entailed in imagining the people as a collective person were different. Rousseau's struggle to conceptualize the "general will" and the attempts to realize it, especially since the French Revolution, are well known. So is the continual debate among political

---

[56] Lefort, *Democracy and Political Theory*, p. 179. For the view that the disincorporation of monarchic power was followed by the reincorporation of democratic power in the flesh of the individual citizens who compose the "Body Politic" and the problems entailed by this shift, see Eric L. Santner, *The Royal Remains: The People's Two Bodies and the Endgames of Sovereignty* (Chicago: The University of Chicago Press, 2011).

[57] For a more extensive discussion of this point and these writers see Yaron Ezrahi, *The Descent of Icarus: Science and the Transformation of Contemporary Democracy* (Cambridge MA: Harvard University Press, 1990), pp. 108–17.

[58] See also the paradigmatic example of Shakespeare's *King Lear*. LEAR: "Thou art the thing itself: unaccommodated man is no more but such a poor bare, forked animal as thou art. Off, off, you lendings! Come, unbutton here" (III. iv). And Thomas Carlyle's mordant "[n]o man can be a Grand-Monarque to his valet-de-chambre. Strip your Louis Quatorze of his king-gear, and there *is* left nothing but a poor forked radish with a head fantastically carved; admirable to no valet"; see Thomas Carlyle *On Heroes, Hero-Worship and the Heroic in History*, Michael K. Goldberg (notes and intro.), Michael K. Goldberg, Joel J. Brattin, and Mark Engel (text) (Berkeley: University of California Press, 1993).

theorists regarding the question of the real in our image of the people. Is it just a legal construct issuing from the fiction of a social contract or is it a real entity?

In the course of the twentieth century, many social scientists demonstrated the logical constraints and the impossibility of constructing collective choices or the "people's will" by adding up individual preferences.[59] Ernest Gellner and Benedict Anderson shed light on the fictive basis of modern nationalistic mystifications of the people, on the ways nations, their histories, as well as sacred boundaries, traditions, and their related features, are invented and materialized in the popular mind.[60] Anderson does not conceal his wonder at the willingness of so many people to voluntarily murder and "die for such limited Imaginings."[61]

Skeptical about the possibility of compiling individual choices into collective preferences and the very idea of a public will, contemporary social scientists were already anticipated by seventeenth-century observers who noted that what ostensibly constitutes "the people" is in a state of continual flux, and its composition is perpetually reconfiguring. The wishes of particular individuals did not show much correspondence to those promoted as expressing the general will.[62] That gap between fiction and experience repeatedly raised the possibility that actual, though inherently heterogeneous, popular wishes could be suppressed in the name of a reified popular sovereignty.

The objection, widely shared among political theorists, to endorsing referenda in modern democracies is often linked with the fear that a referendum would easily become a mere political strategy for manipulating public credulity by reifying the fiction of a people's choice. By means of this ritual, an individual or a few individuals can draw enormous power to speak and act on behalf of the people from the fiction of the popular will. On behalf of the fictive voice of public opinion as an abstract agent that can neither speak nor act, John Dewey's "ghost" "obscures, confuses and misleads governmental action in a disastrous way."[63] Even if we suppose, contrary to the opinion of leading experts, that an answer of the people to the specific question formulated in a referendum can be deduced by compiling the individual answers of a multitude of individual citizens, surely the public mood and orientation on referendum

[59] Kenneth J. Arrow, *Social Choice and Individual Values* (New Haven: Yale University Press, 1951); W. H. Riker, *Liberals against Populism* (Illinois: Waveland Press, 1982); John Elster and A. Hylland (eds.), *Foundations of Social Choice Theory* (New York: Cambridge University Press, 1986).

[60] Ernest Gellner, *Thought and Change* (London: Weidenfeld and Nicolson, 1964); Benedict Anderson, *Imagined Communities* (London: Verso, 1991).

[61] Ibid., p. 7. See also Yaron Ezrahi, *Rubber Bullets: Power and Conscience in Modem Israel* (Berkeley: Berkeley University Press, 1998).

[62] Morgan, *Inventing the People*, pp. 61, 82.

[63] John Dewey, *The Public and its Problems* (Chicago: Swallow Press, 1954), p. 125; see also Yaron Ezrahi's "Dewey's Critique of Democratic Visual Culture and its Political Implications" in David Michael Levin (ed.), *Sites of Vision: The Discursive Construction of Sight in the History of Philosophy* (Cambridge, MA: MIT Press, 1997), pp. 315–36.

day can change radically within just a few days in response to changing cir-cumstances or new information.

Neither can the shape of personal will or that of a collective be conceived of as freezing in time. This is even more evident when a referendum is held on a very specific question. Because general elections are periodically held on a wide range of issues, their results are much less prone to such rapid fluctua-tion. But, as the record of democratic elections shows, frequently the ostensible mandate produced by elections can peter out within only a few months. Yet no president or prime minister will concede a mandate supposedly granted to him or her merely because there might be evidence that "the people" has changed its mind, or that the government's answer to the question posed is no longer relevant. Still, one must acknowledge that, as a vehicle for the establishment of the people as the cause of government, as a political fact (to use Morgan's language), elections aid in bringing the fiction of popular sovereignty closer to reality. Precisely because an election event seems to simultaneously perform the imaginary of popular sovereignty and individual freedom, enacting the apparent interdependence of the choices of individuals and the choice of the people, it can gloss over the liberal democratic dilemma of harmonizing indi-vidual and collective freedoms. Yet as a ritualistic performance of the believ-able impossibility of aggregating multiple individual choices into a meaningful collective choice, election events project a much more balanced and persuasive appearance of the cause of a legitimate democratic government than popular violence.

While largely a ritual, elections have curiously combined premodern and modern features in an apparently congenial way, which has further rendered fictions of popular government and public choice seemingly real. Obviously, the idea of the people's election of the government was anticipated in many places before actual elections were held, including by kings like the aforemen-tioned Frederick the Great, who invoked the idea of being servant of and part of the people to compensate, among other things, for a legitimacy deficit. Not surprisingly, those who could begin to imagine the king or the ruler as the crea-tion of the people were often precisely those who could no longer regard either as a sacred person. Discussing the erosion of the fictional underpinnings of the monarchy, Edward Muir observes that in eighteenth-century France

[T]he waning of Catholic observances undercut the evocative power of the Eucharist, which had been the most powerful model for sacralizing the body of the king. The Jansenists, moreover, found the notion of sacred kingship blasphemous. To them the Holy Ampulla was a fraud, the king's touch indecent, and the coronation ceremony at Rheims a farce. They argued that the coronation should represent the election of the king by the people. Rather than making the king a consecrated person, the ceremony should merely ask God to ratify the people's decision.... "Public opinion" no longer found kingship mysterious, admirable, or intimidating.[64]

---

[64] Edward Muir, *Ritual in Early Modern Europe* (Cambridge: Cambridge University Press, 1997), p. 273

Not only did these trends contribute substantially to the French Revolution, they also created space and demand for a new, more secular, repertoire of acts and rituals that would articulate, institutionalize, and celebrate the periodic and (in some respects) continual role of the people as the primary cause or source of the government. Many important elements of old rituals survive to this day in ceremonies of celebration of elected leaders and in state funerals in prominent European states and in the United States.

But no less intriguing is the fusion into election events of even earlier elements of popular culture. Edmund Morgan, for example, finds many traits of medieval or early modern carnivals in the phenomenon of elections. In both, popular culture is engaged and the people's participation is often accompanied by violence; in both, the usual hierarchical social order is momentarily suspended, giving the common people a sense of power and participation; in both, such a reversal of roles and positions makes superiors appear dependent on the common people; and in both there is often a characteristic suspension of the usual structures of the social order, and the possibility of chaos becomes more palpable.[65]

In contrast to the carnival, the religious procession, and other premodern rituals, modern attempts to enact a credible chain of causes leading from the people to the government do not rely on imaginaries that derive their power from faith in magical, spiritual, or mystical causalities. Democratic imaginaries pay tribute instead to some modern imaginings of earthly agency and causation in secular time. This innovation includes the concrete modern procession of masses of individual voters casting their votes in certain limited, legally regulated sites and times; the procedure of an objective counting of the votes; the open decision and declaration of winner and loser. Those modern rites legally and psychologically create a directly accessible apparent causal link between a concrete election event and the actual event of establishing a new government.

The narrowing of these reiterative causal links specifically to the political process as a relatively distinct, even autonomous system of causes and effects has contributed to the modern differentiation of politics from religion and to the recasting of relations between politics and the law. A ritual is, according to Don Handelman, a means designed to produce a specific result within certain parameters. "The ritual," he observes, "contains the generative processes of the social world.... The human being ... moves from the virtuality of ritual into 'actuality,' re-enabled to continue to generate the practices of humanness and sociability that the ritual re-initiated."[66]

Elections may be regarded as a specific means of generating a persuasive, partly self-actualizing imaginary of participatory collective political choice. Thus the invisible God who, supported by religious rituals, is the original

[65] Morgan, *Inventing the People*, pp. 202–8
[66] Don Handelman, *Models and Mirrors: Towards an Anthropology of Public Events* (Cambridge: Cambridge University Press, 1990), pp. xxvii, 10–11.

cause of monarchic governments and who could be momentarily concretized or observed as conferring his grace upon a new king (by means of a privileged birth and the holy oil of the coronation ceremony) is replaced by the no less invisible people, whose status as a momentarily reified agent acting as a cause of legitimate government is concretized in the ritual of elections as a humanly contrived event, a public, observable, nonmystical, legally rational, patterned act. Unlike election by God, election by the people is a public event that takes place in the epistemological territory of everyday political experience. This event provides laypersons a simple, readily available commonsense explanation for the legitimate selection of a particular leader in terms of objective, quantifiable election results.

The apparent simplicity of legitimating the choice of a leader or a parliament by a majority vote glosses over an enormously complex and ambiguous bundle of facts, assumptions, and fictions. Particularly important here is the fiction that a majority choice is the people's choice, an expression of the general will. Pierre Rosanvallon has pointed out that "today there is no simple identity between 'the people' and 'the greater number,' a definite, palpable mass of individuals. The boundaries of 'the people' shift constantly as this or that group protests a lack of recognition, a denial of rights.... Hence the term has lost its connection with the monolithic numerical notion of the majority. On the contrary, 'the people' is often conceptualized today in terms of minorities.... The people exist as a narrative, a collection of stories, rather than a fixed voting bloc."[67] Benjamin Constant, in his defense of the independence and autonomy of the liberal individual, challenged the claim of the electoral majority to stand or act for the whole community, which he regarded as an elusive abstraction.[68] He complained that political writers commit the error of viewing the majority as "a real being" despite the fact that "it is common for a part of yesterday's majority to become today's minority. To defend the rights of the minority is therefore to defend the rights of all.... To grant unlimited authority to the majority is thus to offer up the people taken one by one as a sacrifice to the people taken as a mass."[69]

In the course of time, statistics, as one of the modern sciences, would further endow popular elections and their results with the status of an objective majority choice. The temporal sequence between the event of elections and the various gestures, rituals, and signs surrounding a new government has been equally important in public imaginings of popular elections as the cause of government. One of the main features of the frame of commonsense realism is

---

[67] Pierre Rosanvallon, *Democratic Legitimacy: Impartiality, Reflexivity and Proximity*, Arthur Goldhammer (trans.) (Princeton: Princeton University Press, 2011), pp. 70–1.

[68] Stephen Holmes, *Benjamin Constant and the Making of Modern Liberalism* (New Haven: Yale University Press, 1984), pp. 96–7.

[69] Cited in Rosanvallon, *Democratic Legitimacy*, p. 71. In the cited translation from the original edition of Constant's *Principes de Politique* (1806), edited by Etienne Hofmann, the word *holocaust* is used; I chose instead the word *sacrifice* because of the extra connotations the former word acquired after World War II.

the transformation of temporal succession of actions and events into a causal chain.[70] Preceding the ascent of a new political authority, elections are perceived as its cause.

I do not wish to contend that, under certain circumstances, elections cannot actually contribute to the causes that establish, change, or renew governments or their political mandates. I argue, rather, that the imagining of elections as a popular choice that creates governments and policies is a gross simplification that overlooks their complexity as a special compound of facts and fictions, including the fiction of being a simple, visible process. Clearly then, like the fiction of popular sovereignty, the fiction of the people's choice by means of free elections could never be fully literalized.

Alongside the apparent gestures, rituals, actions, and rhetoric that seem to bring these fictions closer to reality, Morgan points out the numerous facts and practices that contradict them. Reviewing English and American elections of the seventeenth and eighteenth centuries, he questions the meaning of the voters' choice while noting the persistence of voters' deference to social superiors in England and, to a lesser extent, also in America. This is reflected in the consistent exclusion of women and in extensive practice of bribery and other maneuvers that compromised the reliability and validity of claims to representation.[71]

Such discrepancies between facts and fictions were apparently not sufficient to destroy the capacity of fictions to further produce supporting facts, while also ensuring a measure of political stability. The balance between fictions and supporting facts was generally sustained in some democracies in the face of periodic crises. Although elections entail a reification of the paradigmatic imaginary of democratic causality, their inherent vulnerability to exposure of such discrepancies is a continual source of anxiety during, and sometimes after, election day. The stability of a regime depends to a large extent on a smooth transition of power between governments and on the power of election events to generate sufficient legitimation for a new government or, at least, its initial policy.

The deadlock in the 2000 U.S. presidential elections, broken only by a Supreme Court ruling issued a considerable time after the elections, and the shock waves it produced in that usually solid democracy, provide a rare insight into the problematic relations between the fictive and the factual layers that constitute election events. During a period of thirty-six days following election day, the choice of the president was fraught with uncertainties that could be resolved only by providing evidence beyond doubt that one of the candidates had won most of the votes in the state of Florida. The fact that, following an arduous campaign, televised debates, and an avalanche of commercials, the electoral machinery failed to produce a clear-cut election event as the cause of

---

[70] Albert Michotte, *Perception de la Causalité*, second edition (Louvain: Publications Universitaires de Louvain, 1954).

[71] Morgan, *Inventing the People*, pp. 174–208.

the next government, that the election did not yield an unambiguous result that could appear to be the people's choice; that in the end it was the court and not the people that *appeared* to decide the outcome, could not constitute the kind of fact that brings the fiction of the people's choice closer to reality.[72]

Even more damaging and dangerous was the fact that the apparent inconclusiveness of the election results ushered in a close legal and media interrogation of the electoral process, thus bringing to public attention gaps, uncertainties, contingencies, and facts that are usually the concealed facets of every election, and that can, when thus brought to light, undermine public confidence in the reality of elections as a trusted transparent process with an irrefutable closure. In other words, the 2000 elections failed precisely in the be-all and end-all of an election event: rendering the appearance of a final, unambiguous result that provides for a stable transference of power.[73] This fact haunted the entire presidency of the candidate who finally made it to the White House.

A minute examination of the electoral process, therefore, is always likely to reveal details that might undermine the popular imaginary of the election event as a legitimate cause of government. Seventeenth-century English satirist Jonathan Swift illuminated the link between close-up examination and disenchantment. Poking fun at the aristocratic English ladies who turned a standard version of the microscope into a fashionable toy, he claimed to have used it to closely examine the face of the most beautiful woman in England only to discover the shocking holes in her skin and other ugly imperfections concealed behind the cosmetics that make up the illusion of beauty. Every close-up has this disruptive potential.

In the case of the American elections discussed here, close scrutiny showed the precariousness of both automatic and human vote counts, flaws in the work of observers responsible for supervising the process, the incompetence of people involved in managing and coordinating the process, and issues of fixing and applying standards for interpreting ballots and irregularities.[74] It is not surprising, therefore, that judges who appreciate the instrumental value of necessary (legal) fictions would tend "to avoid detailed investigations of electoral practice, unless enough votes are in question to alter the outcome."[75] In the case of the 2000 presidential elections:

[T]he political/legal judgment of the Court did not decisively resolve the objectivity of the final vote count or even the final electoral outcome....

---

[72] Israeli democracy also repeatedly suffers from inconclusive election results due to a combination of social divisions and a multiparty system of proportional representation. In this system the democratic principle of fair representation is maximized at the cost of governability.

[73] See the illuminating article by Clark A. Miller, "Interrogating the Civic Epistemology of American Democracy: Stability and Instability in the 2000 US Presidential Elections," *Social Studies of Science* vol. 34/4 (August 2004): 501–30.

[74] Ibid.

[75] Ibid., p. 521.

The Court ruled on the basis of "finality," explicitly acknowledging that it has chosen not to pursue a more accurate vote count. The discrepancy between the Electoral
College and the popular votes totals, which favored Gore (over George W. Bush) by
nearly half a million voters, certainly did not reinforce the message that the candidate
who had won most votes nationwide was accorded electoral victory.[76]

Still, despite the loss of legitimacy, the fiasco of the 2000 U.S. presidential elections did not inflict a fatal blow to the status of democratic elections in America
and even contributed somewhat to the sense that the American constitution
provides a partial remedy in case the election process fails to produce an unambiguous outcome. In the end, hegemonic political imaginaries are stronger than
the facts that may challenge them.

One can easily recognize here the extent to which democratic rituals of legitimation could function effectively – to a considerable extent, independently
of the actual processes and practices that contradict them – provided the gap
is not manifest regularly, and that it is neither too large nor too apparent.
Historical and contemporary evidence of this kind supports the realization
that, in many respects, the political imagination is a reality unto itself, a self-
creating reality that can supersede other realities, thus constituting a major
part of the political universe.

Attempts to at least partially hypostatize the people as an agent and the elections as democracy's paradigmatic act have become only a part, albeit a central
one, of a host of moves intended to reify components of the democratic political imagination within the epistemological framework of a modernized commonsense realism. I suggest that we can discern specifically modern democratic
imaginings of causation in politics, which are different from both the premodern ones, typical of monarchic and theocratic regimes, and modern ones such
as nationalist or communist regimes. This implies that the ways in which the
public imagines political causation are inseparable from established forms of
the political imagination and their (not necessarily internally coherent) moral
and legal dimensions.

These notions of political causation or processes are partly subsumed by
the image of the machine as a political metaphor used to describe ways in
which the state and its constitution work in impersonal, apolitical, instrumental terms. The decision to use machines in voting and vote tallying, as in the
American elections, is closely associated with the mechanistic imaginary of the
state and its links to rhetoric of objectivity and neutrality. Scientism, mechanism, instrumentalism, and factual realism in politics have latently functioned
as a powerful protection against suspicions of deception and fraud.

Closely associated with transparency, honesty, and accountability, instrumental realism seemed to constitute a powerful measure against political theatricality and to resist the exposure of the imaginary foundations of political
reality. As such, until its partial demise in late modernity, it constituted an

---

[76] Ibid., p. 522.

effective self-concealing imaginary. It has also instigated the emergence of a new visual culture in the political sphere that actually relates to and frames governmental policies and actions as observable and reportable facts and the citizens as their potentially critical, attestive witnesses.[77] This latter development has been well apprehended by redefinition of governmental decisions as "*public* policy" and of governmental bureaucratic organizations as "*public* administration," and by materialistic political metaphors like "the *machinery* of the government." The shift to democratic political regimes is thus inextricably linked to shifts in the hegemonic political imagination that include – and this is most important for our discussion – changes in imaginaries of political causation, as well as a host of rituals, gestures, and facts that sustain them.

Further developments contributing to the evolution and institutionalization of modern democratic imaginaries of political causation have included the rise of professional scientific authority as a frequently exploited resource for justifying governmental action or non-action and the massive permeation of simplified, sometimes even vulgar versions of social science vocabularies into public political discourse.

Each of the several branches of social science has made a distinct specific contribution to the reification of democratic political imaginaries as discernable spheres of observable and rationally analyzable facts. Economics and statistics have been particularly salient in materializing, quantifying, and depoliticizing sociopolitical descriptions of the conditions of the people, empowering the rhetoric, gestures, and decisions of governments and conceptualizing relations of multitudes of individuals. Political science has more directly framed politics as a legitimate object of objective scientific observation and analysis; sociology has contributed to reifying the democratic fiction that society is a distinct whole, a system of voluntary actions that commonly add up to regularities separable from, and independent of, the state; and psychology has facilitated the ontologization, or commonsense reification, of the individual as a largely non-derivative, demystified, and therefore discernable system unto itself, possessing its own logic of inner forces and their external manifestations. Undoubtedly, in each of these social science disciplines, one can find schools of thought and theories subversive to their own liberal democratic ideological imports. Still, these and other social sciences have steadily contributed to the institutionalization of democratic modes of imagining and have related to politics as a domain of observable factual relations between agents, causes, and effects. The social sciences have made important contributions to modern commonsense social realism, to the ways in which human beings imagine each other, and to their modus operandi as agents and causes in social and political life.

These moves and processes share one effect crucial to democratic political world making: All, in one way or another, have contributed to the externalization of human agents and actions in an actual, or virtual, visible public space, and within the frame of actual human temporality. All have attempted, in some

---

[77] Ezrahi, *The Descent of Icarus*; see especially pp. 73–4, 91, 102, 132.

sense, to objectify or materialize the political in the perceptual space of commonsense realism and, as such, have supported democratic (and sometimes also nondemocratic) modern fictions of mass popular political participation in the establishment and maintenance of the political order. The uniqueness of these modern political imaginaries and their enactment is particularly salient against a background of the premodern universe, populated by invisible agents and magical or spiritual forces operating from a distance.

The manifold externalization of the political process facilitated the emergence of transparency as a major democratic requirement, a central component of democratic political imaginaries and practices. Publicity came to have the power of legitimizing the government, if not by divine grace or holy oil, at least by the people's mandate. Actual or virtual visibility could function in democratic states as a way to create a sense of an informed public participating in what actually remained the rule of the few over the many in most democracies, most of the time.[78]

By appearing to render its subject an object of public knowledge, any act of publicity tacitly reconstitutes and reconfirms the democratic public as a gazing agent. I suggest that while modern democracies have often achieved a greater degree of decentralization of power than their predecessors, on the whole they have exemplified less a radical break with the principle of hierarchy and the rule of the few over the many than the revolutionary transformation of the political fictions that uphold the political order would suggest. In some respects, the latent functions and effects of performative democratic imaginaries of order have only legitimated more moderate, porous, accountable, and changeable hierarchies. Over time, however, the behavioral and institutional effects of the regulatory imaginary of popular sovereignty have engendered successful enough efforts that, leading to a partial narrowing of the gap between ruling democratic political fictions and the popular political experience, have rendered this complex system sustainable.

The process of democratization has largely consisted of marshalling multiple moves and procedures of externalizing and materializing political power, rendering it public and transparent enough to enable the rituals and practices of participation and accountability that constitute actual vehicles of legitimation and some limited modes of control. Because the new liberal democratic sensibilities and imaginaries rejected the principle of hierarchy in politics, it was necessary to assume or imagine a world in which, perhaps, the most powerful means to legitimate the unavoidable, though more moderate, modern hierarchies (of the courts, the army, the bureaucracy, the political elite, or the experts) in democratic terms was based on imagining the political order and its hierarchies as emerging from the bottom up.

Political theorists such as Hobbes, Locke, and Rousseau, among others, reflected these new orientations in their view of the social contract as the source of state legitimation and the limits of the citizen's obligation to obey.

---

[78] See Ezrahi, *The Descent of Icarus*, pp. 217–36.

Attempts made to literalize (at least partially) the fiction of the social contract required not only that persons could envision themselves as the source of the authority of state and government, but also that they could imagine how (without resorting to the power and authority of superiors) they, as a multitude of equal individuals, could act and cooperate to overthrow the old regime, create a new political order, renew their contract with their rulers by means of periodic elections, and hold them permanently accountable. It was precisely on account of this perceived shift of authority to the people that popular conceptions of agency and causality had to be reframed and readapted to accommodate the imaginary of citizenry, the perception of the public as an aggregate of free individuals and voluntary groups rather than an organic individual entity, and the self-perception of the individuals themselves as the ultimate political agents.

It is partly due to the objective constraints on the realization of the ideals of self-government and democratic decision making that hierarchy as an organizational-structural principle has survived in practice in modern democracies, robed in entirely new garments. The necessity of imagining the new political order as rising from the bottom up and of envisioning the government as constantly accountable to the public are the reasons that publicity and transparency have become such important norms of modern democratic politics. Claims of visibility in the new democratic regime have become inextricably linked with the willingness to believe in the possibility of horizontal collaboration, coordination, and responsibility.

To reiterate, modernized common sense, the new "scientist realism" of the western populace, in its distrust of invisibles, provided the perceptual and normative underpinnings of the modern democratic political imagination and supported the persistent public actions and gestures that could impose it on political reality. Obviously, the reception and assimilation of the normative and epistemological cluster of commonsense realism and its matching democratic expressions in the requirements of political transparency and accountability have been uneven in different societies. Observers of Russian political culture, for instance, have frequently noted that the conspiratorial orientations and the invisibility of power so characteristic of Russian politics from Stalin through Putin and beyond resemble the surrealistic worlds imagined by writers like Dostoyevsky, Gogol, and Bulgakov. A systematic juxtaposition, not undertaken here, between norms and orientations toward agency and political reality, relations between the literary and the political imagination, and the character of journalistic cultures in the United States and Russia (as well as in other societies), may yield valuable insights into variations in the social and historical conditions of commonsense realism as an infrastructure of modern democratic political culture in different societies.[79]

[79] See, for instance, Nina L. Khrushcheva's column "Russia's New Inspector General" on Russian democracy in the age of Putin, *New York Times*, August 10, 2007.

The emergence of the requirements of publicity and transparency as necessary, if not sufficient, conditions for authority and credibility in modern democratic politics developed in the postmodern context in very different and surprising directions. Still, within the modern context, normative publicity and transparency as well as their ritualistic embodiments have provided the basis for a conception of politics that could appear all-inclusive without necessarily being participatory. The appearance of being public, as a precondition for the perception of factuality, was a deeply politically loaded development since it implicitly granted the public authority to draw a line between facts and fictions, and between the political and the apolitical. The political came to belong to a sphere in which claims were publicly contested against a background of commonsense facts, whereas the apolitical gravitated toward a sphere of self-evident, uncontested factual claims. As long as scientific knowledge was defined – despite contradictory evidence – as public knowledge, the social and political authority of science could become an invaluable consensus-inducing political resource.

This power gradually extended beyond science to encompass diverse groups of experts, and paradoxically, even journalists grew skilled in publicly deploying the authority of expertise without being experts. But this decentralization, and the eventual repoliticization of expert authority, actually reempowered self-selected agents, trusted as a vehicle for the public voice, as participants in evaluating and sometimes challenging professional representations of the world. Under late- and postmodern conditions, the lay public, influenced by the destabilizing effects of a long exposure to shifting and ambiguous, mostly commercialized mass media descriptions of reality, lost much of its own confidence as well as its trust in experts' ability to clearly draw the boundaries between facts and fictions. As we shall see later in this book, this development has inevitably transformed the epistemological, moral, and practical parameters of contemporary politics.

Still within the frame of modernity at least until recently, the free press, building on the culture of commonsense realism, has played a major role in establishing politics as a factual reportable process. The conventions of separating news from entertainment, front-page news from opinions on the op-ed page, editorials from field reports, photojournalism from artistic photography, witnesses' reports from news analyses, and so forth, promoted the establishment of politics as an object of neutral-seeming description, a world of facts that must be presented prior to the work of analysis and interpretation.

One of the important consequences of these processes and of the modernization of common sense, or the rise of commonsense realism, was the option of the modern liberal democratic state to present itself as neutral. As I indicated earlier, the idea of the neutrality of the state was supported by the imagery of the state as a machine and the view of the constitution as a kind of neutral mechanism.[80] In contradistinction to the monarchic welding of the principles

---

[80] See Yaron Ezrahi's "The Theatrics and Mechanics of Action: The Theater and the Machine as Political Metaphors," *Social Research* vol. 62, no. 2 (Summer 1995): 299–322.

of personalism and transcendental divine grace, the mechanist metaphor fuses the artificial, the instrumental, the earthly, the objective, the impersonal, the observable, and the neutral or indifferent.

Contrary to the republican ideal, the aspiration of the liberal democratic state to the status of neutrality relates to the laissez-faire claim – though scarcely to the practice – of the state to refrain from any involvement in political and economic competition. By implication, the claim to state neutrality, the positioning of the state above the political contests over values, ideologies, and priorities, becomes a part of the liberal imaginary of the state as a mere instrument for the implementation of independent voluntary social choices produced by participatory politics. The assumed neutrality of the state is, therefore, a very significant component of the imaginary of a universal election day as the generator of the mandate for public policies.

The neutrality of the state ostensibly combines two different senses of the term *neutrality*. One relates to the political process, which establishes priorities and distributes power among competing political views and agents; the other refers to a sense of professional neutrality in handling and relating facts and means to ends determined by the political process.

In order to buttress such claims of neutrality, the modern state has resorted to a host of measures such as the professionalization of the civil service, the formalization of bureaucratic decisions, and the massive application of technical, legal, statistical, and economic vocabularies in both the contexts of state actions and their public justifications. This liberal democratic cluster is also part of the liberal image of the polity as an association of individuals protected by inalienable rights.

It is noteworthy that there is another, republican kind of state neutrality, also based on a familiar image of an objective "scientistically" certified reality that must be respected by the state and its branches. But it differs from liberal neutrality in that it rests on faith in the possibility of a general commitment to a set of agreed upon collective goals. If liberal neutrality is understood to refrain from taking sides in the free competition among values and interests, a republican state's neutrality can be imagined only by those who take for granted the particular hegemonic republican view of a consensus on goals and collective good and, therefore, can accept in theory the selection and employment of instrumentally effective means to promoting this collective good as apolitical.

By contrast, in a liberal democracy, any citizen, or any particular group of citizens, can imagine the state as neutral only by assuming that their own particular goals must compete on an equal basis with other goals, and that those state actions that are not consistent with their particular goals and interests *can* nevertheless be both neutral and legitimate. In the communitarian setting of republican democracy in which the majority is more unambiguously privileged over the individual as the source of political authority, claims to neutrality can only rest on the assumption that the goals endorsed by a majority and promoted by the state are both coherent and collective.

9

Animated Fictions: Self (as) Fulfilling Prophecy and the Performative Imaginaries of Democratic Political Agencies

[O]nly animals who are below civilization and the angels who are beyond it can be sincere. Human beings are necessarily actors who cannot become something before they have first pretended to be it; and they can be divided, not into the hypocritical and the sincere but into the sane who know they are acting and the mad who do not.

– W. H. Auden, *The Age of Anxiety: A Baroque Eclogue*

INTRODUCTION

Democratic political causalities – the conceptions of cause and effect in terms of which democratic citizens imagine their political world's creation, structure, and functioning – presuppose an imagining of democratic agents that can act as political causes. The central, most important democratic agent (underlying the manifold composite democratic agents such as citizens, the people, voluntary organizations, or public opinion) is, of course, the individual.

It is difficult to conceive the extent to which individualism, the interiority we experience in ourselves and in others, is a complex cultural-historical creation, an animated imaginary. To apprehend the fabric of the democratic political universe in which we live, we must realize that individualism, in the sense we now acknowledge it, did not always exist. The notion of the individual as a paramount cause of the political and moral order in which we are embedded tends to conceal its historicity. This is, no doubt, partly the result of a process of naturalization. The reification of the individual as essentially real and, in important respects, a natural given, has enabled modern individualism to become the basis of democratic political imaginaries and practices.

Democratic political universes depend not only on the willingness to regard and relate to the individual as a primary agent, but also on the degree of reality granted the individual in relation to the reality granted to other, potentially competing imagined agents such as God, nature, society, nation, and state. Consistent with the drift of democratic moral epistemology to materialize causality, it is possible to trace the shift toward privileging the physically embodied individual as the ultimate source of political values and actions, the culmination of the process of materializing the liberal democratic political agency.[1]

From a phenomenological viewpoint, the physically observable individual has, within the parameters of democratic materialist epistemology, a superior claim to exist than more abstract illiberal agents such as God, community, or nation.[2] In this limited respect, there is a break in the continuity between the unobservable spiritual religious agents that are the sources of authority in medieval theocracies and the physically observable and perishable citizen that is the primary modern political agent.

But, ironically, there is also a degree of continuity between the physical liberal individual citizen and the physically embodied king of early modern monarchies. Thomas Hobbes was keenly aware of the dilemma inherent in transforming the abstraction of the state into an agency. He observed that the state has no capacity "to do any thing" because it is "but a word, without substance, and cannot stand."[3] The drawing of the sovereign on the frontispiece of Hobbes's *Leviathan*, one of the early sources of modern individualism, ingeniously exploits the corporeity of the individual subject in order to compose a material image of the sovereign as a giant "artificial person" consisting of a multitude of what Hobbes called "natural persons."

This was only one of a range of strategies employed to hypostatize abstract agents such as the nation and the state. Nevertheless, the more abstract such agents have been, the less amenable they have been to practicing democratic standards of transparency, accountability, and responsibility. When the reality granted to the individual decreases in relation to that ascribed to an abstract collective entity, the political universe that emerges is not liberal democratic, but rather communitarian or republican. When the collective or the group becomes even more ontologically and normatively superior to the individual (who is downgraded to the status of a mere derivative of the group), we are on the verge of confronting nationalist and, in more extreme versions, fascist political imaginaries.

The history of western individualism is richly diverse and not all forms of individualism are democratic. "Democratic individualism" is a particular imaginary of individualism that combines elements that have evolved in variegated contexts over a period of many centuries. My purpose here is not to provide a systematic comprehensive account of the evolution of a western democratic imaginary of individualism or the degrees of its performance in different societies, but to explore briefly some of its key components and the circumstances

---

[1] See also Mark B. Brown, *Science in Democracy: Expertise, Institutions, and Representation* (Cambridge, MA: MIT Press, 2009).

[2] This observation does not apply, of course, to women and minorities who were not recognized as real political agents until relatively recently, at least in the West, not because of their material but moral invisibility. See for instance Seyla Benhabib, *Situating the Self: Gender, Community, and Postmodernism in Contemporary Ethics* (New York: Routledge, 1992).

[3] Cited and interpreted in Quentin Skinner, "Hobbes and the Purely Artificial Person of the State," *The Journal of Political Philosophy*, vol. 7, no. 1 (1999): 2.

of their emergence in order to illuminate the abundance and complexity of democratic individualism as a political configuration.

Obviously, some of the elements of democratic individualism may be discernable in other types of modern individualism such as Romantic, fascist, economic, and Protestant. But they configure very differently. In nondemocratic political universes such as fascism, communism, and economic neoliberalism, the balance among the diverse components of the individual, and, consequently, the relations of individual to group, differ radically. Democratic individualism is a form of individualism related to the moral principles, procedures, and structure of democratic politics. The "democratic individual" cannot assume the form of an inaccessible subjective self, nor of a self which can easily disappear in or be swallowed by a group. As an ideal, a fiction that can be performed, democratic individualism presupposes, therefore, very specific forms of societies or groups that can accommodate, preserve, and cultivate this type of individual.

The rise of modern individualism is associated with the evolution of the most fundamental democratic political imaginaries and with the state structured as a voluntary association of free persons. Imagining the individual as a separate, detribalized entity, as a moral agent endowed with freedom and reason, has opened the imagination to a nonhierarchical political order erected not from top to bottom but rather from the bottom up. George Kateb, a prominent contemporary thinker of democratic individualism, insists that "[d]emocracy and individualism are inseparable phenomena," that "democratic individualism is a full code of life, the life that should grow and flower when rights are genuinely recognized" and, in a thought he attributes to Plato, that the individual subject "is not the *demos* as an undifferentiated mass, but as an aggregation of souls, each trying to be itself."[4]

The view of the individual as a source of values, authority, and political judgment has provided the most significant modern ethical and cultural resources for criticizing earlier regimes and for imagining and justifying participatory politics and the decentralization of political power. The perception of the individual as a person whose life has intrinsic value led to considering the body of the individual and his or her soul as beyond the legitimate limits of the invasive power of the state – a protected sanctuary constraining both state and society. At the same time, these very imaginaries required that in order to develop the political order from the bottom up by means of a real or a tacit social contract, individuals should be protected from other individuals and, at the same time, be able to cooperate and generate concerted collective actions independent of external agents such as God or another superior third party. The paradoxes and contradictions of the concurrent liberal democratic commitments to individual autonomy, individual safety, and nonhierarchical

---

[4] George Kateb, "Democratic Individualism and its Critics," *Annual Review of Political Science*, vol. 6 (2003): 275–6, 281. See also by George Kateb, *The Inner Ocean: Individualism and Democratic Culture* (Ithaca: Cornell University Press, 1992).

and nonviolent interaction among individuals have nourished a good part of modern political and legal theory.

As a historico-political configuration, democratic individualism has constantly faced the problem of achieving a viable balance between individual freedom, the imperatives of individual autonomy, liberty of self-experimentation, and the logic of collective action, while aiming to preserve the individual's integrity within the larger society. These tensions, and the struggle to balance such opposites, have been central to the politico-historical genealogy of democratic individualism and the constant rearrangement of its diverse elements. I shall, therefore, relate to approximations of the ideal of democratic individualism as historically precarious and dynamic configurations whose transformations are linked to changes in available culturally developing elements and "technologies of selfhood" that depend on shifts in the forms and requirements of democratic society and politics.

Critics of liberal and democratic individualism conveniently ignore the multiple cultural layers that have given rise to the idea of the individual as a meaning-seeking, free agent capable of self-rule. Reimagining democracy in the twenty-first century requires a massive act of retrieval of the often overlooked richness of the sources of modern individualism.

Democratic individuals are conscious of their separateness and vulnerability as perishable organisms that exist as discrete physical entities. Especially since the latter seventeenth century, following the discourse on the individual body and property framed largely by John Locke, the increasing focus on the individual's body has become a very significant aspect of the drive toward materialization and demystification of democratic agency. Movement has been toward rendering democratic agency physical and visible in contrast to the otherworldly and supernatural agents that have populated religious and monarchic political universes.[5]

The emphasis on the physicality of the democratic individual is inexorably related also to the keen awareness of imminent death, to inescapable mortality in contrast with the immortality of enduring collective or transhuman entities. Whereas in the Catholic mind *memento mori* has been associated with privileging the afterlife, in the democratic mind awareness of human transience has resolved into a normative privileging of the present and the concomitant value accorded politics as the enterprise of the living.

In various authoritarian regimes, adoption of a perspective that privileges the distant future over the present has often been associated with denigration of the democratic conception of politics as a sphere of living voluntary human discourse and action. The democratic individual's keen sense of his or her own mortality and vulnerability to physical destruction has played a major role in shaping democratic attitudes toward political time and power. Above all, the

---

[5] For a radical interpretation of the materialization of the body politic and its political implications in the postmonarchic state, see Eric L. Santner's *The Royal Remains: The People's Two Bodies and the Endgames of Sovereignty* (Chicago: University of Chicago Press, 2011).

short life expectancy of the individual conditions democratic constitutional and political constraints imposed on the domestic and external uses of the power to take life or expose a citizen to mortal danger.[6]

This attitude is associated with the conception of each individual as possessing interiority, a unique inner life, and a capacity for freedom and moral choices. It underlies the value that democratic theory confers upon each individual life alongside the ascription of human dignity. The freedom and dignity universally ascribed to all human beings entail also the equality of all individuals, first and foremost, as moral agents capable of morally significant political acts. Granting freedom and dignity to all individuals alike, regardless of their respective actual, physical, or social inequalities, is also the foundation of the status of the individual as a subject of the law and his or her equality before the law. In the liberal democratic political imaginary, the individual emerges as a participant in making and navigating the political order. In other words, in this political tradition, the self-performance of individuals as free autonomous agents is a condition for the possibility of a collective performance of democracy as a participatory political enterprise.

Democratic individuals, more than merely strictly liberal ones, trust themselves and others in negotiating the relations between their inner selves and their social conduct as autonomous and partly interdependent citizens. Imagining themselves as possessing moral consciousness and conscience, as continuously engaging in an internal dialogue between their aspirations, motives, experience, and conduct, contributes to their self-conception as moral and political agents capable of voluntary association to further the achievement of personal and shared goals. The democratic individual imagines himself or herself as a voluntary social being who does not depend solely on hierarchy or external regulatory mechanisms for coordination with others.

I suggest, then, that we consider *physicality, interiority, capacity for freedom, intrinsic value and dignity, agency, and associability* as pivotal elements of political democratic imaginaries of the individual. Although combined and dynamically balanced within the complex sociohistorical embodiment of the democratic individual, the origins of these elements vary. Our main concern here is not with the relations between concepts or ideas of democratic individualism as a category of philosophical discourse, but with the relations between its active presence in the popular imagination and aspects of its sociopolitical (and psychological) practices in concrete historical contexts. We will therefore direct our attention to some of the cultural contexts endowed with the capacity to generate and widely diffuse these key elements of democratic individualism.

These contexts include religion, art, economy (markets), the legal system, popular culture (including scientism), philosophy, and the educational system. Each of these contexts is comprised of a combination of a particular repertoire

---

[6] For a further discussion of this point see Ezrahi, *Rubber Bullets: Power and Conscience in Modern Israel* (Berkeley: Berkeley University Press, 1998), chapter 5.

of imaginaries and practices that have generated and naturalized facets of the fabric of modern democratic individualism.

I have already alluded to the fact that science usually enters the mundane universe as scientism, that is, as the residue that remains following a process of selection by common sense. This kind of selective editing and adaptation also determines the impact of philosophical ideas. From our perspective, interest in a reconstruction of the original ideas of influential thinkers, scientists, or writers is guided less by a focus on logical coherence, systematicity, intellectual innovation, or tradition than by interest in the selections and frequent politically consequential distortions involved in their adaptations to and uses by the democratic political imagination. Moreover, the broad influence of the ideas or practices of exceptionally prominent figures such as St. Paul, St. Augustine, Dürer, Copernicus, Shakespeare, Hobbes, Locke, Rousseau, Smith, Pestalozzi, and Marx is inevitably mitigated by the historic discursive and institutional contexts of religion, economy, the court, popular culture, and the educational systems that largely select, edit, and diffuse them. In the following discussion, I outline my interpretive approach by focusing on a few such components of the modern democratic political imaginary of the individual and on their dynamic interrelations.

I confine myself to a thematic examination of those elements of democratic individualism that have proved most pertinent to the political imaginary of the modern individual as a citizen, an active participant in the making and unmaking of modern governments, indeed the very source of the state. Since I have based the following discussion on a body of valuable but sometimes inevitably contested studies of the history of western societies, cultures, and politics, a significant part of the following discussion is openly speculative.

I shall refer freely to all seven features of democratic individualism mentioned previously but will concentrate particularly on the fabrics of human interiority, human worth, human agency and associability, and on their interrelations. I have a special interest in exploring the relationships between diverse imaginaries of human interiority and agency, relations with far-reaching implications for the relative and changing roles of religion, economy, science, law, and the arts in fashioning modern imaginaries of democratic individualism and their decline since late modernity.

IMAGINARIES OF THE INDIVIDUAL IN ANTIQUITY AND EARLY MODERNITY

Perhaps the earliest imaginary of the individual (and the paradigm of western individualism as well as its non-western transmutations) is to be found in the book of Genesis: "And God created man in his own image, in the image of God he created him, male and female he created them" (1: 27). This single sentence, the idea that man was created in the image of God, has spawned countless interpretations and references in western religious and secular popular imagination, as well as in the more specialized elite discourses in theology, law, ideology, politics, poetry, and the arts. Of particular importance here are the relations between this imaginary and almost all the elements of democratic individualism – the consecration of the human form; the human body as the incarnation of the form of divinity; the value accorded human interiority, freedom, and dignity, and the establishment of human agency.

Each of these aspects has been extensively discussed and developed in classical Hebrew texts since the first century B.C.E. and has played a central role in the entire corpus of Jewish theology, law, Aggadah, Kabbalah, poetry, and literature. In modern Israel, this theme has become the crux of fierce ideological and political debates between those who interpret "man in the image of God" as sanctioning an inclusive humanistic image of the element of divinity in all men and women, including the enemies of Israel, and those who opt for a narrower ethnocentric interpretation.[7] In a comprehensive study of the extensive presence of the biblical idea of man's creation in the image of God in Jewish theological, legal, and cultural traditions, Yair Lorberbaum traces key themes later developed and reinterpreted within the various strains of Christianity and humanism.[8]

The Jewish idea of an abstract divinity beyond any visually representable shape or form has, of course, militated against notions of earthly embodiments of the divine. This attitude is manifest in the critique of pagan worship of gods made of stone or wood dramatized in the story of the Golden Calf (Exodus 32). It is powerfully articulated in the denunciation of material pagan gods by prophets such as Jeremiah, and reiterated in the manifold diatribes against the idea of human divinity, such as the apotheosis of Jesus as a human being (Hebrews 2) or the attribution of divine status to kings.

The paucity and elusiveness of particular figurative descriptions of God in the Bible has provided a powerful basis for the critique of pagan material embodiments of divinity. It has also left a wide margin for imagining and interpreting the biblical allusion to man's creation in the image of God. Despite this powerful tradition, the biblical imaginary of man as a universal category bearing an iconic relation to God has been continually present in Hebrew-Jewish discussions on the sacredness of the human body, in the value ascribed to man's responsibility to tend to his body and keep it clean, in the early Jewish objections to the death penalty, and in the objection to mutilating the human body even in the course of legally sanctioned executions, as Lorberbaum, among others, records. Hence even within Hebrew-Jewish tradition, the dichotomy between an invisible and a physically present divinity is often ambiguous and loaded with tensions.

---

[7] A central voluntary Israeli organization that records violations of human rights in the occupied territories, mostly (but not only) for the sake of Israelis, chose the name "B'tzelem," meaning literally "in the image" thus alluding to the image of God idea in Genesis 1.

[8] Yair Lorberbaum, *Image of God: Halacha and Agada*, in Hebrew (Tel-Aviv: Schocken, 2004); Charles Edward Trinkaus, *In Our Image and Likeness: Humanity and Divinity in Italian Humanist Thought* (Chicago: University of Chicago Press, 1970).

As Lorberbaum stresses, at least part of the tension between the imaginaries of God as an abstract concept and as an embodied entity are smoothed over when the iconic relation between divinity and man is not interpreted in anthropomorphic terms, as man imagining God in man's own image, but in theosophical terms as God's presence in man – the making of man in the image of God as a way to enhance God's presence in the world. On such basis, human dignity could be interpreted as related to the grandeur of the divine within man and to man's responsibility to cultivate the divine in himself. In the Midrash, and later in Jewish philosophy, the notion of God's presence or representation was extended beyond the human body to the human soul, to human inner and moral qualities.

The *mitzvoth* – the Jewish religious commandments – have provided the observant Jew with tools and guidelines for the practice of expanding God's presence within the self and in the world at large. This tendency was apparently increased with the destruction of the Second Temple, which encouraged a further shift of the locus of divine presence from the Temple to the individual person and the community of the faithful. These early imaginaries of human physical and spiritual dignity and worth have had deep impact on the genealogy of imaginaries of human physicality and interiority in the West.

These early imaginaries of the individual as a locus for the presence of divinity possess an additional dimension particularly relevant to the evolution of the imaginary of the individual as an agent. A number of scholars have stressed the possibility that early imaginaries of man as created in the image of God also bore a theurgist significance for establishing man as an agent whose actions are necessary components of divine creation, whose agency acts upon the world to support, reinforce, or complement divine actions, which in themselves are considered insufficient.[9]

There is a chasm, of course, between a world in which a subject imagines that his prayers, his conduct as an individual, or his manipulation of names or words can function as causes affecting the course of human and cosmic events, and a world in which a democratic citizen can imagine himself or herself as part of the causal chain that makes or unmakes governments. Still, from our perspective, these two ostensibly distant imaginings of individual power can be regarded as related phases in a complex history of the evolution of the modern imaginaries of human agency and democratic individualism.

Of particular interest to this discussion is the kabbalistic performative conception of language and its Renaissance reverberations and parallels – the view that language can function as a means to produce or affect actions and bring about events in the world. This power, however, was not believed to

---

[9] See ibid., especially pp. 83–104, 146–56, and 436–75. Jonathan Garb, *Manifestations of Power in Jewish Mysticism from Rabbinic Literature to Safedian Kabbalah*, in Hebrew (Jerusalem: Hebrew University Magnes Press, 2005), p. 264; Moshe Idel, *Golem: Jewish Magical and Mystical Traditions on the Artificial Anthropoid* (Albany: State University of New York Press, 1990).

be universally available, but only accessible to extraordinary individuals with privileged esoteric capacity such as the magician, the alchemist, or, in the East-European Hassidic tradition, the Jewish *Tzaddik*.[10] Such imaginaries of the individual Jew as agent were bound to be problematized, however, by the more dominant imaginary of the individual's subordination to the commands of divine law.

Kabbalistic imaginaries and techniques that cultivated individual agency were therefore long suppressed, censured, or practiced in secrecy in some elite circles. Rabbi Moshe Chaim Luzzatto (1707–46) traced a connection between the language of Kabbalah and the fashioning of the illusion that power and governance exist anywhere other than divine kingship.[11] But even these elitist imaginings of human agency could join diverse non-Jewish traditions of magic, alchemy, and active astrology in generating resources from which later imaginaries of the individual's participation in creating the political order could have drawn. While such affirmations of human agency may have inspired the emergence of individual agency in the modern political imagination, it must be stressed that their characteristic association with vertical rather than horizontal accountability, with self-mystification, religious enthusiasm, and radical violence, more often contributed to the integration of individual agency within thoroughly nondemocratic political cultures and practices.

There is a vast distance between the centuries-old Jewish legend of the Golem, an artificial man created by a righteous rabbi (a *Tzaddik*) who knows the secret of how to manipulate Hebrew characters and names in order to create and destroy the Golem, and the role played by language in the enactment of the social contract which, in Hobbes's political imaginary *Leviathan*, produces the sovereign as an artificial man created by an aggregate of individual verbal or oral acts. In principle, artificial entities – the Golem and the Sovereign – were similarly prone to disintegration through the use of words, the very means whereby they were created.[12]

The futility of confining the imagination to the sphere of fantasy and magic is evident in the different contemporary views of the Golem and the sovereign. The idea of the sovereign, born of the concept of a tacit social contract, seems to us to be less dependent on magic than the creation of the Golem. Centuries of systematic legal and political discourse have rationalized, naturalized, legalized, and instrumentalized the necessary political fiction of the sovereign.

Although scholars have apparently not found solid documentary evidence that would prove that the legend of the Golem constitutes one of several traditions that inspired the political imagination of Hobbes and his idea of the

---

[10] Idel stresses the role of Christian kabbalists such as Henry Cornelius Agrippa and Johannes Reuchlin in exposing Christians to Jewish magical and occult ideas and practices. See in this connection also Frances A. Yates, *The Occult Philosophy in the Elizabethan Age* (London: Routledge and Kegan Paul, 1979).

[11] Jonathan Garb, *The Chosen will Become Herds: Studies in Twentieth-Century Kabbalah*, Yaffah Berkovits-Murciano (trans.) (Jerusalem: Shalom Hartman Institute and Carmel, 2005), p. 75.

[12] Idel, *Golem.*

sovereign as an artificial man, it is, I believe, quite plausible to speculate on a link between the two. The similarities between the creation of artificial men by the manipulation of words in these two contexts suggest an association between the urgent search for a new political imaginary that would link human agency to the creation of the state and the legend of the Golem (in its many versions), which was apparently well known at the time.[13]

Following the destruction of the Second Temple and up to the second half of the twentieth century, differences between Jewish and Christian contexts undoubtedly issued, very significantly, from the chasm between a powerless, stateless minority and a powerful, hegemonic majority. The Jewish context was not very amenable to evolving political imaginaries that could be tested and amended in light of an ongoing responsibility for governance and the experience of wielding power. This might have contributed to a lack of restraint in rabbinic, particularly kabbalistic, fantasies of power.

The contemporary role of the Jewish religious imagination in Israeli politics may illuminate the dangers deriving from this historic segregation of Jewish religious imaginaries of agency and power from the lessons and constraints of political experience. Modern democratic politics and constitutions are inconceivable without constant arduous encounters and adjustments between religious ideals and the actual experience of governing and maintaining order. It is significant that, following the destruction of the Second Temple, a kind of "Protestant" transformation took place in Judaism, transposing the locus or space of the holy from the Temple onto man, a shift whose religious context implied the empowerment of the individual with a consequent increase in individual responsibility, albeit within the context of the tight Jewish community.[14]

In the particular Jewish context, the imperative of unmediated reading and study of the Hebrew Bible, the Mishna and Talmud, has been a source of individual empowerment that can check the power and influence of rabbinic and scholarly elites. The traditional Jewish community, however, usually did privilege outstanding scholarly rabbis, whose election was largely based on merit. In the final analysis, also beyond the Jewish context, such early religious imaginings of individual agency could not have sufficed for the emergence of the individual as an active political agent unless accompanied by massive sociopsychological processes of individual emancipation and disengagement from hegemonic, holistically encompassing imaginaries and entrenched practices that chained the subject within interlocking cosmic and social hierarchies.

In pre-Christian sources such as Greek tragedy, the disharmony between individual intentions or aspirations and fate may be indicative of a family of early imaginings of such a potential split of the individual from the cosmos, an

---

[13] See, for instance, Emily D. Bilski, *Golem! Danger, Deliverance and Art* (New York: The Jewish Museum, 1988); Also Idel, *Golem*.

[14] On the shift from shrine to man see Lorberbaum, *Image of God*, pp. 443–54; see also Ezrahi, *Rubber Bullets*, pp. 87–90; and Taylor, *Sources of the* Self, p. 131.

incongruity issuing from the irresoluble conflict between inexorable external forces and the wishes, intentions, and actions of the individual. Man's tragic predicament and ultimate loneliness would still be framed in the modern era as due to the inherent limitations of individual knowledge and control of the circumstances of one's life in this world, a condition in which the subject is often the unwitting cause of her or his own demise. Bernard Williams notes the liberal sensibility implicit in the Greek tragedian's unwillingness to accept harmony between the individual and the world as a given or even as an achievable goal.[15] I have suggested elsewhere that:

> Once one substitutes social reality for supernatural necessity as the inexorable constraint on the ability of the individual to control his own fate, the tragic hero represents the vulnerability of the individual to the overwhelming and often incomprehensible social forces which threaten to crush him from the outside, to the sense that there is no inherent purpose or good in terms of which the lives of all individuals can necessarily or voluntarily be harmonized, that society and politics may doom the individual to an unjust fate.[16]

Still, it is precisely the Greek *polis* that gave rise to crucial early components of modern democratic individual agency. Jean-Pierre Vernant traces such indicators of the emergent Greek individual in Athens in the development of funeral practices and individual wills, in forms of religious individualism expressed, for instance, through the individual choice of god and religious practice, in the legal definition of the private individual as both "the subject of the offense and the object of judgment," and in the emergence of the individual as equal participant in the political sphere.[17]

Nevertheless, this Greek appreciation for the singularity of the individual, which postulated the existence of a private sphere, and the emergence of the individual as an agent in the institutional context, were not accompanied, as Vernant points out, by a corresponding apprehension or appreciation of the individual's unique interiority. The Greek individual lacked a sense of bounded internal unity and was largely extroverted and externally oriented.[18] Lacking reflexivity and introspection in the modern sense, the individual tended to experience himself or herself as "a 'he' and not yet an 'I.'"[19]

Historians locate the emergence of early premodern imaginings of the inner self in late antiquity – between the third and fourth centuries of our era – often regarding Saint Augustine's *Confessions* as a paradigmatic text reflecting the ontologization of the individual's innermost feelings, anxieties, thoughts, and

---

[15] Bernard Williams, *Shame and Necessity* (Berkeley: University of California Press, 1993), pp. 64–5.

[16] Ezrahi, *Rubber Bullets*, p. 92.

[17] Jean-Pierre Vernant, "The Individual Within the City State" in Froma I. Zeitlin (ed.), *Mortals and Immortals, Collected Essays* (Princeton: Princeton University Press, 1991), pp. 318–33.

[18] Ibid., pp. 327–8.

[19] Bernard Groethuysen, *Anthropologie Philosophique*, 2nd ed. (Paris: Gallimard, 1980), p. 61. Cited ibid., p. 329.

imaginings that anticipates the fashioning of modern individual interiority. St. Augustine's personal dialogue with God, in which he refers to himself as "I,"[20] is particularly significant. There are, of course, many biblical antecedents to the use of the first-person singular pronoun. In Genesis (22:1), Abraham responds to God's call "Abraham" by saying "Here I am" ("*Hineni*" in Hebrew). The book of Ecclesiastes renders Kohelet's memorable words: "I have seen all the works that are done under the sun; and behold, all is vanity and a striving after wind." In this chapter, Kohelet says: "I spoke ... I gave my heart ... I perceived ... I said in my heart ... I will try thee (1). In many sections of Psalms, one hears the reflective voice of the agonizing, praying individual: "My tears have been my bread.... When I remember these things, I pour out my soul in me" (42).[21] But St. Augustine's *Confessions* (written in the fourth century), undoubtedly inspired by these and other earlier sources, a most dramatic, lengthy, and continual articulation of the narrative of a single and singularly rich, restless, tense, conflicted, internal self, is a milestone in the development of Christian, humanistic, and modern individualisms, feeding both religious and secular traditions.

As the particular case of St. Augustine indicates, acknowledging the reality of a vibrant and profound individual interiority and its capacity for choice includes the possibility of voluntary submission. While St. Augustine presents a revolutionarily multifaceted and dynamic imaginary of the individual's inner self in his *Confessions*, he normatively disparages active mundane individualism as a low form of human existence, idealizing subordination of individual interiority to a transcendental God. While St. Augustine, as Charles Taylor puts it, "introduced the inwardness of radical reflexivity and bequeathed it to the western tradition of thought,"[22] he concomitantly weakened it at least partially as an engine fueling a life of individual civic choices and actions.

The humbleness of the spiritualized Augustinian self before God and his association of the internal struggles of the soul with a contemplative rather than an active individual life opened the path for many versions of the clustering of a complex and sophisticated radical subjectivity with constrained individual agency. At the same time, of course, the Augustinian breakthrough inaugurated an unprecedented, abundant vocabulary for the internal reflective discourse of the self. The individual's own motivations, desires, emotions, memory, will, dreams, body, temptations, temporality, and moral conduct, as articulated in St. Augustine's *Confessions*, have inspired centuries of religious, literary, cultural, and political imaginaries of selfhood, including those that link robust and resilient selfhood to strong worldly political agency.

---

[20] Peter Brown, *Augustine of Hippo: A Biography* (Berkeley: University of California Press, 1969); and *The Making of Late Antiquity* (Cambridge, MA: Harvard University Press, 1982).

[21] Ruth HaCohen, "The Dramaturgy of Religious Emotions in Bach's Cantatas: Aristotelian Processes in Neoplatonic Frames," *Understanding Bach* 4 (2009).

[22] Charles Taylor, *Sources of the Self*, p. 131.

In the course of time, the rich internal world of the self conferred value and dignity upon the life of the individual, empowering him or her as a source of authority and judgment as well as independent agency, and positing the private domain of the individual as a barrier against the invasiveness of society and the jurisdiction of state power. The links between the internal self and the democratic citizen as a political agent have remained central to centuries of debate concerning relations between religion, culture, and politics, as well as the conditions of associability. While processes of ontologizing the individual's interiority could be enlisted to set limits to state intervention in human lives, as the historical record shows, highly dynamic and multifarious individual inner lives could also seriously constrain horizontal cooperation among individuals, that is to say, their associability.

PRELIMINARY REFLECTIONS ON MODERN VERSIONS
OF EARLY INDIVIDUALISMS AND HOLISMS

The particular configuration of the imaginary of democratic individualism is compatible with several versions of the balance between the individual's interior self and the individual's external life as a political agent. Conservative critics of the core of democratic individualism characteristically question the very possibility of maintaining such a balance when unaided by the fundamental bonds of the self to family, religion, and ethnos, or other modern versions of Augustinian holism.[23] Charles Taylor, one of the most influential political philosophers of communitarianism in our time, is deeply dubious about the modern individual's capacity to transcend unaided subjectivity, instrumental egotism, materialism, and "the murkier depths of [his] motivations."[24] He is certainly skeptical about the potential of the modern individual to move beyond the private self and perform, as an agent, civic tasks toward goals promoting the public good.

While neo-Stoic criticism of democratic individualism tends to negate or radically weaken the dimension of political agency in order to protect the individual's rich inner life, undisturbed by the vicissitudes of the world of action, interests, or violence, Taylor and other communitarians invoke temperate modern versions of old imaginaries that disparage the individual. In isolation from family, Church, or nation, the individual is often viewed as but a loose, purposeless, unconstrained entity, spiritually flat or lost.[25] Their insistence on

---

[23] Alasdair MacIntyre, *After Virtue* (Notre Dame: University of Notre Dame Press, 1984); Michael J. Sandel, *Democracy's Discontent: America in Search of a Public Philosophy* (Cambridge, MA: The Belknap Press of Harvard University Press, 1996).

[24] Taylor, *Sources of the Self*, p. 517.

[25] This struggle between individualism and communitarianism is poignantly enacted in Joyce's *A Portrait of the Artist as a Young Man*, the paradigmatic modern *Bildungsroman*, in which the antithesis to the nets of Ireland, home, and religion is embodied in the motif of flight as both escape and artistic soaring: "When the soul of a man is born in this country there are nets flung at it to hold it back from flight. You talk to me of nationality, language, religion. I shall try to fly by those nets" (*Portrait*, p. 184).

the moral, spiritual, or cultural poverty of individualism leads communitarian thinkers and ideologues to invoke modern versions of holism, a kind of self-imagining or self-understanding that makes the individual always consider himself or herself a mere part of a larger binding, bounding, bonding, and worthier whole within which he or she must find an appropriate place and sense of a meaningful life. Taylor criticizes both what he defines as "disengaged reason," which he attributes to the modern individual and "expressive individualism" or "disengaged subjectivity." The Cartesian individual is, in his reading, an "unsituated" subject, a kind of "disembodied soul," the Lockean individual is but "a punctual power of self-remaking," and the Kantian individual is a "pure rational being."[26]

All such definitions seem to him too narrow, partial, and therefore unsatisfactory. In the religious imagination of Augustine, and generally of Christianity, Taylor finds a more hopeful resource for the contemporary political individual and his role in political world making than in the imagination generated by the influential creed of Enlightenment naturalism, which so successfully opposed the explicit religious imagination in the modern period. He finds hope "implicit in Judeo-Christian theism (however terrible the record of its adherents in history), and in its central promise of a divine affirmation of the human, more total than humans can ever attain unaided."[27]

But Taylor's version of Augustine takes into account a limited aspect of what Augustine and especially his *Confessions* entailed as a source of imaginings of the individual in the western tradition. Augustine's wider impact on western literary and poetical traditions cannot be overestimated. John Freccero rightly observes that, especially in light of his contribution to the literary imagination of the individual as a subject, Augustine's work belongs as much to the twentieth century as to the fifth: "His *Confessions*," argues Freccero, "present for the first time the literary self-creation of an individual seen both as object and subject, with all of the contradictions that those aspects imply."[28]

In contrast to Taylor's attempts to enlist Augustine's Christian holism for the sake of communitarianism, centuries of humanistic, poetical, literary, and psychological readings of the *Confessions* found in it a treasury of resources and strategies of individuation. These include Augustine's early reflection on adolescence and separation from parents as a stage in the disengagement of the self from its originary attachments; self-narration as a way of construing an individual identity; sin as an aspect of individuation; conversion as a paradigm of both religious and secular rebirth; and autobiography as a literary and imaginary genre in which the self examines and inscribes itself as object.[29]

---

[26] Ibid., p. 514.

[27] Ibid., p. 121.

[28] John Freccero, "Autobiography and Narrative" in T. C. Heller, Morton Sosna, and David E. Wellbery (eds.), *Reconstructing Individualism: Autonomy, Individuality, and the Self in Western Thought* (Stanford: Stanford University Press, 1988), p. 16.

[29] See ibid., pp. 16–29; for a particular contemporary cultural version of self-narration see Ezrahi, *Rubber Bullets*, p. 77ff.

When the missionary Christian didacticism of Augustine is granted the power and the breadth that would overshadow the great innovations of the *Confessions* and subordinate them to the theological Christian purpose of constraining individual agency, it can be used as a model or a frame for diverse attacks on liberal individualism. A critique of democratic liberal individualism from a perspective that combines holism, secularism, and antihumanism, such as that of Carl Schmitt, for instance, reveals significant traces of Christian holism and concepts of evil.

Like Taylor and other communitarians, Schmitt is critical of the fragmentation of holistic political imaginaries, the weakening of common group identities by narrower, mostly economic interests, the flattening of modern individual life as well as the depletion of political energies by a benevolent image of man cultivated by what he regarded as unrealistic universalism and global humanism. The evil, dark side of the individual weighs heavily in Schmitt's scheme of things, as it does in the views of some Christian political theologians. But, unlike Taylor's Christian humanism, Schmitt's skeptical outlook follows Hobbes's in relating to the evil in man as a usable resource: "All genuine political theories," he argues, "presuppose man to be evil."[30] He considers group antagonism the principal glue of association, the bond welding vital political collectives out of isolated individuals. Elements of a non-universalist Augustinian image of a sinful man, then, reemerge in Schmitt's influential theory in different garments.

Whereas for Taylor, the Judeo-Christian image of the individual provides a humanistic bridge from the potentially sinful and selfish individual to a subject engaged in the larger promoting of the collective good, for Schmitt, it is paradoxically man's sinful, evil predisposition for enmity, conflict, and struggle, his capacity to imagine an enemy worthy of his willingness to sacrifice his life, that connects the self to the political collective. Whereas religious imagination infuses Taylor with the hope that the "society of self-fulfillers"[31] can be transcended, it is another dimension of the religious imagination that, according to Schmitt, can extricate human beings from the depoliticizing anomies of liberal humanism, ethics, economy, and what he regards as the liberal negation of the very hostilities that energize political life.

Both Taylor and Schmitt seem more concerned about losing the whole in its parts, in the individuals, than about losing the individual within the whole. For them, the depth and the worthiness of individual life are not sustainable without some form of subordination to the group. This may largely account for their respective ambivalence, and often antagonism, toward modern scientistic disenchantment of the world and the consequent waning of the transcendental and the metaphysical sources of authority and meaning, a rift Tocqueville associated with the rise of democratic individualism.

[30] Carl Schmitt, *The Concept of the Political*, George Schwab (trans.) (first pub. Germany 1932; Chicago: University of Chicago Press, 1996), p. 61.
[31] Taylor, *Sources of the Self*, p. 508.

I argue later that, in both cases, a commitment to a collective system of meaning capable of rendering birth and death profoundly significant underlies such approaches. It is this commitment that allows both political worldviews to generate configurations of power less amenable to decentralization by means of democratic individualism, whether explicitly, as in the case of Schmitt, or more obliquely, as in the case of Taylor and other communitarians. Configurations such as these, insofar as they are less constrained by individual creativity and by the diversity, uniqueness, and intrinsic value of each individual, are more threatening to the well-being and lives of individuals and of the democratic order than the liberal individualism that they challenge.

My concern here is that when we move from the plain of philosophical arguments to the sphere controlled by the dynamics of collective political behavior, even moderate communitarian holism can easily lapse into coercive groupism. The notion entertained by some political theorists, who claim to be both communitarian and liberal, that communitarism can be endorsed as a benign corrective to self-centered liberal individualism, may be a misleading and even dangerous illusion.

Undeniably, however, critics of liberal democratic individualism have a point, in light of the devaluation of rich metaphysical collective systems of meaning in the political life of modern liberal democracy. This fact, or trend, has multiple causes. It nevertheless relates also to the very essence of democratic individualism, to the fundamental democratic intuition about the association between the role of rich systems of meaning in cementing individuals within thick solidarity groups and the propensity of such groups to be exclusive and coercive toward domestic minorities and violent toward external enemies. It involves the profound difference between two valuations of life. On one hand is the willingness to take another's life and die in order to protect what the individual often unreflexively and unreflectively imagines as the only system of meaning, the fountainhead of converging dominant narratives of self, family, and community. On the other hand is the far more minimalist willingness to undertake ultimate sacrifices solely in strict self-defense in order to protect lives regardless of their meaning, that is, to defend the conditions of free, meaning-building, heterogeneous individualism and avoid death.

In certain respects, of course, these two rationales echo Émile Durkheim, who belongs more in the camp of the advocates of collective systems of meaning than the defenders of bare lives, when he highlights the connection between the erosion of social norms, or "anomy," and suicide, which he attributes to the loss of meaningfulness in a normless society and the consequent decline of the will to live. Against the minimalist liberal position, one can further invoke a moderate modern version of Hobbes's belief that discrete individuals are ultimately more prone to extinction than individuals who are freely organized and disciplined in groups. This argument would go beyond Hobbes's in maintaining that such groups and their armies can neither be formed nor sustained in the absence of the glue that binds thick systems of meaning. Similar reasoning grounds the almost five-hundred-year-old argument made by Machiavelli to justify his preference for a national over a mercenary army.

Contrary to critical opinion, the imaginary of democratic individualism does not necessarily require or encourage impoverished individual meaning systems, nor must it necessarily invoke a thick communal meaning system as the only way to overcome the aridity of economic and other flat individualisms. The problem with contemporary liberal democratic individualism lies elsewhere, in the neglect of the wealthy treasure of cultures of individualism developed over centuries and marginalized or abused by the practices of ruthless capitalistic individualism and its neoliberal advocates. Democratic individualism gravitates naturally toward resisting privileged selective institutionalization of any particular comprehensive system of meaning precisely in order to protect and facilitate individuals' freedom to explore and choose their own frame of meaning from an infinite store of possibilities, changing or switching such frames at will.

In the early modern period, toleration of alternative religious convictions and ways of life was justified on the grounds that questions of individual faith and the belief in the right way to salvation were considered too important to be relegated by the individual to the jurisdiction of collective or hierarchical authorities. Similarly, in the context of contemporary liberal democracy, the meaning of individual life and the practices surrounding it, including religious beliefs and sermons, as well as lifestyles and sexual practices, are regarded as too essential to be handed over to the jurisdiction of the state or a political majority. It is here that human rights shield the freedom and dignity of the individual, insulating him or her from direct state intervention in private life.

It is evident that, under conditions of freedom, systems of meaning and lifestyles tend to proliferate in abundant and diverse configurations. This means that some options of individual choice of largely coherent or homogenous collective forms of life, which depend on a multiplicity of converging or similar choices as well as on the cooperation of many individuals, may diminish. This can and has certainly been experienced as a loss by a large number of people who seem to seek, or depend on, community-embedded identities.

On what basis can one defend the elimination of such choices and the ensuing pluralism for the sake of a particular meaning system? I argue that even a qualified normative and ontological privileging of the collective over the individual suffices to unleash a political dynamics that ultimately undermines the option of self-creating individualism or, more precisely, the very conditions of individual freedom as understood in our time.

Democracy is a system in which every individual has the freedom to dream, hope, and peacefully promote his or her vision of the good society, but in which no one is likely to have enough power to fully realize that dream collectively. Not surprisingly, this implies that conditions of individual freedom not only enlarge but also impose significant constraints upon the options and choices available to the democratic individual as a political agent. Many coherent ideological visions of a fully realized and institutionalized conception of the macro-political order appear politically unfeasible. Under these conditions, the balance between individual interiority and agency rests on the imperative of maintaining the possibility for each individual (and each voluntary association) to explore almost any system of meaning while practicing only those visions that, without being imposed upon society at large, elicit the voluntary participation of a sufficient number of individuals to enable a local version.

The only generalized aspect of such a pluralistic system is that it depends on the readiness of the democratic individual to make sacrifices, including risking the loss of the individual's life, to protect this freedom of choice. The charge that the struggle for such freedom is futile overlooks the premise that this freedom is a necessary precondition for the ability of the modern subject to live freely and meaningfully as a democratic citizen. To be sure, not all individuals are inclined or able to exploit their freedom to create meaningful lives. This should not be used as a rationale to substitute such freedom with an institutionalized, and therefore potentially coercive, collective system of meaning, or to accept involuntary structures of association and meaning as ineluctable givens.[32]

It is useful to fashion (with Claude Lefort) the core of the democratic system as an empty space, a space uninhabited by a specific body, power, individual, religion, ideology, or doctrine. Within the democratic system, this empty space possesses the potential of both freeing and constraining democratic individuals. On one hand, it drastically reduces the danger that a privileged agent, committed to a particular doctrine, could legitimize the employment of collective power in order to mold society in its own image. It releases the individual citizen from the threat of the lethal alliance of collective idealism and brute force. On the other hand, it reduces his/her prospects of participating as an agent in the realization of a coherent, inclusive, collective vision of communal life.

If in the Christian version of communitarianism it is the fullness of divine holism and the imperative and reward of integration that constrains the inherently sinful individual, in democracy it is this empty core that constrains the individual by controlling the urge to shape and integrate the collective. Claude Lefort has given eloquent expression to an important aspect of this idea, which he characterizes as the "disincorporation of power in a society which can no longer be represented by the model of the body, and which accepts division and the effects of division in every domain." He observes that in a democracy, a public space is

a space which is so constituted that everyone is encouraged to speak and to listen without being subject to the authority of another, that everyone is encouraged to will the power he was given. This space, which is always indeterminate, has the virtue of

---

[32] In one of his most moderate defenses of his long-standing commitment to the communitarian position, Michael Walzer argues that a liberal system is "a self-subverting doctrine ... [that] require[s] periodic communitarian correction." See Michael Walzer, *Politics and Passion: Toward a More Egalitarian Liberalism* (New Haven: Yale University Press, 2004), p. 154.

belonging to no one, of being large enough to accommodate only those who recognize one another within it.[33]

While the often centralized, largely privatized power structure underlying the mass media of contemporary democracy would seem to counter Lefort's idea that public space is a no man's land and is thus sheltered from the excessive influence of privileged agents, this idea entails both a normative and a productive strategy of the performative democratic political imagination.[34] The absence of a hegemonic doctrine, the inherent contemporary cultural sense of the indeterminate nature of any general idea or principle of existence, undercuts the rationale behind a massive use of chiseling political power while, at the same time, it accommodates democratic individual agents.

Thus the emptiness of meaning at the core of the democratic state is a condition of voluntary, meaning-building lives. The critique that such a system breeds flat hedonistic individuals is no more valid than the critique of religion for fostering unreflective pedestrian believers. No regime is immune to abuse and deterioration.

Another popular communitarian critique has been that liberal democrats impoverish the politics of principles and the larger vision of the good society by replacing adherence to ideas and contents with commitments to rules. They claim that liberal democratic "proceduralism" is oblivious to, among other things, the crucial difference between a partial privatization of meaning-building lives and meaningless individualism. Buttressing the charge of proceduralism with examples of spiritually flat, ethically irresponsible, and politically indifferent lives is actually a denigration of democratic individualism by way of examples of its alternative or degenerate versions. Such criticism does not differ from disregard of the merits and values of communitarian life while focusing solely upon its coercive and militaristic versions.

In this version of democratic individualism, the balance between the interiority, freedom, and agency of the democratic citizen is achieved at what liberal democrats consider the reasonable expense of radically curtailing the possibility, favored by many, of anchoring and cultivating any inclusive universe of meaning. This loss is preferred by those in democratic societies who resist holism or institutionalized collective systems of meaning as more serious threats to individual freedom. In this connection, one can no longer regard skepticism, irony, and ambivalence as attitudes mostly typical of philosophers or other elites. In response to the diminishing seductive power of political visions of

---

[33] Claude Lefort, *Democracy and Political Theory*, David Macey (trans.), (Cambridge: Polity Press, 1988), pp. 41, 179–80. For further debates on this theme, see Chantal Mouffe, *The Democratic Paradox* (London: Verso, 2000); Ernesto Laclau, *On Populist Reason* (London: Verso, 2005); and the debate between Slavoj Žižek and Ernesto Laclau in *Critical Inquiry*, vol. 32, no. 3 (Spring 2006); vol. 32, no. 4 (Summer 2006); and vol. 33, no. 1 (Autumn 2006).

[34] See for instance, Yaron Ezrahi, Zohar Goshen, and Shmuel Leshem, *Cross Ownership: Control and Competition in the Israeli Media: Economic and Legal Aspects and the Impact on Israeli Democracy*, in Hebrew (Jerusalem: The Israeli Democracy Institute, 2003), pp. 24–7.

macro-integration and homogenization of culture and society, these attitudes are more widely diffused in society and popular culture.[35]

The western political imaginary of the democratic individual as a meaning maker, rather than a mere passive vessel of collective meaning, obedient believer, or economic man and the corresponding imagining of the individual as capable of leading a meaningful personal life and as endowed with moral sensibilities was created over many centuries. It has an uneven history in western countries and a very selective record of dissemination beyond the West. Following its beginnings in antiquity, early Judaism, and Christianity, some salient moments and figures in this very rich history are worthy of particular consideration because of their special significance in the gradual ontologization of the modern self and the configuration of democratic individualism as a particular balance between the individual's physicality, interiority, freedom, agency, dignity, and value.

MODERN IMAGININGS OF INTELLECTUAL, MORAL, AND LEGAL MODES OF HORIZONTAL ASSOCIABILITY

Drawing on the multilayered repositories of earlier imaginings of the individual, the most important development from the perspective of the emergence of the imaginary of democratic individualism was, perhaps, the transformation of the individual as a subject subordinate to a superior authority into an agent capable of independent individual judgment. This agent was an entity that, without losing its integrity, could associate with other equal individuals, forming groups that would generate collective opinions and actions. Obviously, such a radical shift from a view of the individual as a passive subject or as an agent strictly confined within a framework of vertical, hierarchical relationships to an apprehension of the individual as an autonomous mobile moral and political[36] agent within a framework of volitional, equal, or horizontal relations does not take place at once.

The significant role played by the Protestant movement within Christianity in generating key elements of the modern self cannot be overstated. Following Ernst Troeltsch, Louis Dumont describes the change within Christianity as a development from an understanding of the individual as merely, or mostly, an otherworldly entity oriented toward and dependent on a transcendent God to the modern or worldly individual who, in addition to a vertical orientation,

---

[35] On the operation of larger forces against social and cultural homogenization, see Clifford Geertz's *Available Light: Anthropological Reflections on Philosophical Topics* (Princeton: Princeton University Press, 2000), especially pp. 218–63. See on this point also Amartya Sen, *Identity and Violence: The Illusion of Destiny* (London: Allen Lane, 2006).

[36] A particularly rich philosophical development of the idea of the individual as an ethical self whose subjectivity is not insular but a condition and a trigger for relations to other subjects can be found in the works of philosopher Emmanuel Levinas. See for instance his *Totality and Infinity* (Pittsburgh: Duquesne University Press, 1969).

can live and act individually, that is, embodying transcendental values in the fabric of his worldly existence.[37] In Dumont's words:

> Luther and Calvin attack in the first place the Catholic Church as an institute of salvation. In the name of the self-sufficiency of the individual-in-relation-to-God they cancel the division of religious labor instituted by the Church. At the same time they accept, or Calvin most distinctly accepts, the unification obtained by the Church on the political side.[38]

Still deeply within Christian holism, the reformed individual is now liberated from strict dependence on the mediating institutional authority of the Church. But the enormous political potential created by the autonomy of a spiritualized and moralized individual interiority would only be released later in the more (albeit almost never fully) secularized universes of modern politics, imagined or described by Machiavelli, Spinoza, Locke, Vico, Rousseau, Kant, Tocqueville, J. S. Mill, and others.

An especially important consequence stemming from the process of shifting the responsibility for moral development and salvation onto the individual was the fashioning of the subject as an agent that could be constrained, and therefore also trusted, through moral commitments. Imagining God as witness to the moral commitments of the individual (to the correspondence, for instance, between promises and intentions) facilitated continuity between a vertical religious to a horizontal moral discipline. Although rituals of taking an oath on the Bible persisted, with the process of secularization, new bases for horizontal trust and association (such as individual rationality, transparency, compassion, and moral conscience) were explored and developed.

Imaginaries of communities of religious faith were at least partly supplanted or superseded by imaginaries of communities of rational and therefore also often mutually transparent individuals, communities of ideology, communities of shared moral and cultural sensibilities, and communities bound together by human law. All such elements were culturally and socially developed and politically employed to support imaginaries, strategies, and institutions geared to buttress anew a sustainable and justifiable political order built by modern individuals from the bottom up.

The religious bases of human associability, of the evolution of imaginaries of interpersonal social trust, were often accompanied or eclipsed by imaginaries of trust based on rationality and transparency. As I have already indicated, these subsequent imaginaries and their corresponding performative scripts and practices formed part of a larger cultural-political configuration, the centerpiece of which was the modern cluster of science (as a form of public, not

---

[37] Louis Dumont, *Essays on Individualism: Modern Ideology in Anthropological Perspective* (Chicago: University of Chicago Press, 1986), pp. 51–3, 59.

[38] Ibid., p. 59. Lutheran church music is a sonic embodiment of this ideology. Based on vernacular chorales set to relatively simple tunes and sung by the community as a whole, it symbolically and experientially renounced hierarchical mediation. Eventually it also gave rise to the expression of individual personae emerging from the community and further embraced by it.

esoteric knowledge), the individual, market economy, rationality, and commonsense realism. All these imaginaries enabled horizontal coordination or cooperation among free agents potentially independent of supernatural or hierarchical mediation.

From an analytical viewpoint, however, such a separation between the two clusters or contexts of individual agency must be qualified, considering the persistence of residual religious, metaphysical, and hierarchical elements and values in the modern categories of the individual and the community, as well as in the latent normative dimensions of rational, legal, economic, and scientific frames of horizontal human interactions. In the final analysis and in line with the introduction of political individualism by thinkers such as Thomas Hobbes, I argue that (contrary to Hobbes's own final commitment to hierarchy) the horizontal social patterns of individual interactions were greatly reinforced by his and others' concepts of radical individualism and their huge impact on subsequent liberal legal and political theories of legitimation.

This point is most powerfully conveyed by Hobbes's reference to the morality of witnessing. In *Leviathan*, Hobbes is concerned primarily with the institution of civil law as a public standard for mediating and coordinating individual interactions. He realizes, nevertheless, that positive law cannot cover all the spheres of human interaction he seeks to stabilize. He relies, therefore, on complementary modes of binding individuals in common attitudes, such as public knowledge. He observes, for example, that when

two or more men know of one and the same fact, they are said to be conscious of it one to another; which is as much as to know it together. And because such are the fittest witnesses of the facts of one another, or of a third, it was, and ever will be reputed a very evil act, for any man to speak against his conscience; or to corrupt or force another to so do.

Hobbes proceeds to assert in this section, to which I return later, that the individual conscience is like "a thousand witnesses."[39] His commitment to radical materialist individualism compelled him to explore different ways of overcoming its potential anarchic implications. Whereas in the final analysis, Hobbes trusted witnessing less than mathematical or logical reasoning as a means of binding individual into group knowledge, his contemporary adversary Robert Boyle perfected the system of group witnessing, of trust building by means of "face-to-face interaction," and credible reporting of experiments as a key mode to achieving trustworthy valid truths about the world.[40]

Steven Shapin and Simon Schaffer indicate the close relation between intersubjective credibility in matters of fact and seventeenth-century genteel English

[39] Thomas Hobbes, *Leviathan*, Michael Oakeshott (ed.) (New York: Collier, 1962), p. 131. Hobbes was also concerned that by producing a sense of individual certainty, conscience can disrupt social bonding.

[40] Steven Shapin and Simon Schaffer, *Leviathan and the Air-Pump: Hobbes, Boyle, and the Experimental Life* (Princeton: Princeton University Press, 1985). See also Steven Shapin, *A Social History of Truth: Civility and Science in Seventeenth-Century England* (Chicago: University of Chicago Press, 1994).

culture and its norms of morality and civility, the milieu of Hobbes and Boyle.[41] While genteel society and social class were restrictive, the culture of experimental science was far more open. Its social network and its standards of witnessing, of testifying, and of rendering reliable knowledge claims, as they evolved in the seventeenth century, eventually expanded to wider social circles, promoted by democratic spokesmen such as Jefferson, Paine, Condorcet, Priestly, and Franklin as norms of democratic politics. In Tocqueville's *Democracy in America*, some of the primary characteristics ascribed to the orientations and interactions of democratic citizens, such as trusting visually observable evidence and distrusting metaphysical arguments, correspond to key virtues and techniques of trustworthy scientists.[42]

The presence of a connection – influenced primarily by the diffusion of Protestantism – between the moralized self and the possibility of generating intersubjective trust and works is discernable also in the context of the law. Yves Charles Zarka argues that "the modern promotion of man as subject of the law, and the necessary reciprocity that must obtain between this and other subjects ... is linked to an initial formulation of juridical intersubjectivity."[43] Zarka attributes to Grotius and Leibniz the innovation of linking the modern school of natural law to the moral capacity of the individual, a quality that can uphold the notion of the law as a framework for attaining a horizontally interactive individualism. According to Zarka, Grotius produced "a schematization of juridical theory which bases natural law on the definition of law as moral quality, in order to deduce the principles of a theory of civil and political law."[44] Attributing natural morality and reason to the subject of the law, Grotius introduced into modern legal culture the crucial connection that rendered the individual capable of voluntary horizontal associability.

The moral core of the individual personality underlined such crucial closely related expectations as consistency in one's actions, correspondence between a person's words and conduct, and transparency of one's intentions. Devoid of such a moral center, often imagined as located in the subject's conscience, the individual could not imagine certain actions and utterances as delivered by his or her own agency, and therefore as his or her responsibility. Obviously, *in order for an individual to be a subject of the law and an associable agent, he or she must dwell in a world in which words and actions are attributable to individual agents and regarded sufficiently frequently as his or her voluntary "externalizations."*

The imaginary clusters that enabled the production of such trustworthy externalizations have, of course, varied in different contexts. In seventeenth-

---

[41] Shapin and Schaffer, ibid. See also Michael Polanyi, "The Republic of Science" in *Minerva* vol. 1 (Autumn 1962): 54–73.

[42] Tocqueville, *Democracy in America*, p. 404.

[43] Yves Charles Zarka, "The Invention of the Subject of the Law," *British Journal for the History of Philosophy*, vol. 7, no. 2 (1999): 246.

[44] Ibid., p. 249.

century Europe, a widespread moral, legal, and political frame of horizontal interaction was anchored in imaginaries of divinely ordained natural law rendered accessible to mankind through the light of individual reason. As a guiding mental faculty, reason has emerged as capable of controlling the individual body and action. Zarka stresses the link between this development and the consolidation of the individual as "a moral being irreducible to any physicalistic or naturalistic perspective."[45]

The link between the individual as a moral being and as a subject of the law defines his or her freedom and responsibility as an agent in the context of intersubjective, horizontal orientation, thus integrating physicality, interiority, agency, freedom, dignity, and associability. Within this cluster of imaginaries, man's interiority, his conscience, radiates his moral self onto his presence as a materially embodied agent and, at the same time, his materialized self-expression – primarily in actions and sounds (words) – provides physical external articulation of his interiority. In this way, the individual brings to his associability, to his social and political life as an agent, his "divine" attributes as a moral and conscious being as well as his attributes as a perceptible, observable, *meaningful* bodily presence. John Locke, who elaborated and conceptualized the relations among these diverse elements, underscored the role of private property as an externalized embodiment of the individual capacity to alter and imprint elements of his interior upon the material world. I argue that these "physicalizations" of individual personality were part and parcel of a wider process of repositioning politics from a heavenly onto an earthly plane through the materialization of liberal democratic political agents and democratic causalities, relocating both as inhabitants in the sphere of commonsense realism – the intersubjective epistemological and ontological realm of participatory politics. This shift responded to the general cultural trend to link visible materiality with horizontal interhuman trust. It was reflected also in Locke's objection to conventional or abstract notions of money and his insistence that trust between transacting individuals would be better protected if coins would embody the "intrinsick value" of the silver of which they are made.[46]

This shift toward the epistemological materialization of voluntary politics reflects the intuition that physical embodiment constitutes a vital condition for the ontologization of the new political agents and their actions at the level of lay commonsense perception. Even though this was a liberal democratic insight embedded in a modern epistemological frame, it was certainly inspired by earlier religious and mystical monarchic strategies of incarnating and embodying the divine and the dead, as in the Corpus Christi rituals, and the monarchy in the body of the king.

---

[45] Zarka, "The Invention of the Subject of the Law," p. 262.
[46] Douglas John Casson, *Liberating Judgment: Fanatics, Skeptics, and John Locke's Politics of Probability* (Princeton: Princeton University Press, 2011), pp. 235–7, 253.

The legalization of the status of the individual, the translation of individual political status concomitantly into the respective categories of subject and agent of the law, was indeed a modern development of the fifth-century B.C.E. Athenian concept of the free citizen as both ruler and ruled. But here too the individual's externalization as a voluntary agent was bound to face enormous constraints. The principal difficulty has been to preserve the distinct autonomy of the individual as a legal subject-agent and resist the powerful pull toward its obliteration by incorporation, by subordination as a mere part in corporative political-legal entities such as the state, the city, the community, and the party, as well as in nonpolitical entities such as the Church, the university, the business corporation, and the trade union.

BALANCING SUBJECTS AND OBJECTS IN THE SHAPING
OF DEMOCRATIC INDIVIDUALISM

My purpose in framing democratic individualism as a composite of often disparate elements is to resist a reductionist and, therefore, ahistorical discourse on democratic individualism, so common among philosophers, legal theorists, and ideologues, as well as to highlight the importance of certain kinds of tensions or frictions between attributes such as physicality and interiority, or agency and associability, in the shaping of democratic individualism. Perhaps more than any other contexts and institutional mechanisms for the generation and diffusion of imaginaries and practices of democratic individualism, the educational system has tended to adopt a more synoptic and integrative, though by no means necessarily coherent, approach.

The main preoccupation of liberal democratic education seems to have been the search for ways of cultivating individuality without jeopardizing associability. The liberal democratic commitment to individual freedom and autonomy has accentuated the problem of behavioral constraints. Rejecting traditional principles of order and obedience (such as hierarchy, paternalism, and fear), liberal democratic sources of discipline and restraint require compatibility with individual agency, freedom, autonomy, and dignity.

Standard approaches to liberal democratic resources of individual restraint have tended to overemphasize the role of reason, rationality, nature, and reality, often mediated by science and self-regulating mechanisms such as the market and the constitution. A clear conception of the elements entailed in a liberal democratic emotional education is generally lacking. What is needed is an approach that aims at linking restraint and toleration with the capacity for emotional empathy or at least ambivalence toward the other and respect for diversity and ambiguity.[47] On the other hand, emphasis on the cultivation of interiority, usually outside the context of citizenship, has characteristically invoked the creative or expressive practices of poetry, literature, and the arts, as

---

[47] Dana Blander, *Ambivalence as a Challenge to the Political Order,* unpublished doctoral thesis (Jerusalem: The Hebrew University, 2007).

well as the contributions of clinical psychology and psychoanalysis in private and social domains, removed from the civic sphere of politics.

The particular appeal of the belief in reason, then, lies in imagining its special dualistic feature as both an individual capacity that can voluntarize the subject's assent and discipline and, at the same time, have a public dimension that can uphold associability, consensus, and cooperation. Hobbes, Locke, Rousseau, Kant, Pestalozzi, and Dewey were among the most prominent thinkers who enlisted this dualism, in various ways and degrees, to shape their respective solutions to the tensions between individual freedom and individual restraint and associability.

An important element of this strategy of the liberal theory of restraint, particularly in the cases of Locke, Rousseau, and Pestalozzi, was their emphasis on the role of the *external* world as a publicly accessible sphere populated by objects. Due to their inestimable influence on the formation of modern liberal and democratic imaginaries of the child, the individual, the citizen, the polity, as well as their supportive educational practices, Locke, Rousseau, Pestalozzi, and to some extent Dewey, warrant special attention.

In Locke's theory of personality, the balance between agency and associability is advanced by the double motion toward an objectification of the self, or an embodiment of personality in property through labor. This requires the exercise of individual freedom and faculties on one hand, and on the other, the application of human senses and reason to nature, the external world, in order to formulate probable and therefore sharable judgments of reality. Concerning private property, Locke observes that, with respect to the individual person

[T]he labor of his body, the work of his own hands, we may say, are properly his. Whatsoever then he removes out of the state that nature has provided and left it in, *he has mixed his labor with, and joined to it something that is his own*, and thereby makes it his own property. (my emphasis)[48]

The very idea that property is created by persons, rather than granted by God, luck, nature, or manufactured by a government, has allowed, in the Lockean scheme, extension of the individual's rights to his body to the objects created by his own body and person. Against the background of classical and modern distinctions between slaves and free persons, the idea that freedom is expressed, among other ways, in the individual's unconstrained employment of body and personality for the sake of labor was widely acknowledged. Locke's contribution may be interpreted as supplementing another dimension of freedom – the projection of personality (including talent, judgment, and energy) onto the world of material objects.

In the most general terms, one may argue that a person's private property, to the extent that it is the product of his or her labor, is, like a self-portrait, a projection of his or her own self or image, an autobiographical expression. This creative dimension of labor-produced property and its contribution to the

---

[48] John Locke, *The Second Treatise*, ch. V, § 27.

epistemology of the internal individual was, to be sure, partly obliterated by the depersonalizing effects of the market and its currency.

This material externalization of personality has been the subject of powerful criticism on behalf of humanists, Romantic individualists, Marxists, and other ideological opponents to private property. However, when considered from a perspective of placing the political onto an epistemic frame of democratic politics, the material externalization of individual personality seemed to have had the advantage of concretizing the presence of invisible human interiority in the public sphere of common perception and the domain of law, thus empowering the individual as a bearer of rights and as an agent in relation to the social collective and the state. In other words, in the competition between the individual and the state over the rhetorical political resources of self-concretization in the common material sphere of sense perception, Locke has imaginatively and conceptually endowed the individual with the capacity, and ensuing power, of persuasively projecting himself or herself onto the sphere of created material objects.

I think that Locke, a believing Christian, could have been impressed by the efficacy of the embodiment of divinity in Christianity as the hypostatic union of human and divine in the figure of Christ and by its many sculptural and visual reproductions. Locke must have appreciated the magnetic power of materialization to enhance the presence of the spiritual and invisible subject, be it God or man's personality. His concept of private property as the manifestation or embodiment of the individual inner person in the material public world of commonsense realism may be regarded as an attempt to encourage the individual citizen to deploy his or her own material projections, his or her own corpus and property, against the powerful self-projections of the Church and the state in *Corpus Christi*, *Corpus Mysticum*, and *Corpus Politicum* – the *persona ficta* of the *body politic*.

Against these overwhelming entities, Locke, the philosopher of modern individualism, posits the corpus of the citizen, as a material projection of the presence and claims of the individual in the political arena. Locke is fairly explicit on this point in his classification of types of power. "Paternal power," he maintains, "is only where minority makes the child incapable to manage his property; political, where men have property in their own disposal; and despotical, over such as have no property at all."[49] In the introduction to his critical edition of Locke's *Two Treatises of Government*, Peter Laslett observes:

[T]he fact that he was prepared to allow material property, labour-mixed-with-natural-objects property, to stand for many or all the abstract rights of the individual, does help us to understand why the concept as a whole enters into his account of the foundations of civil society. For property, to Locke, seems to symbolize rights in their concrete form, or perhaps rather to provide the tangible subject of an individual's powers and attitudes.[50]

---

[49] Ibid., Second Treatise, ch. XV, § 174.

[50] See Laslett's introduction to John Locke in *Two Treatises of Government*, Peter Laslett (ed.), second edition (Cambridge: Cambridge University Press, 1967), p. 102.

Eventually, one of the clearest extensions of this imaginary would comprise the rights of intellectual property granted to literary as well as other creators.

With this move, Locke advances the role of objects as epistemologically accessible referents for the relations between subjects, thus facilitating horizontal associability. Here Locke develops another key dimension of liberal democratic culture and politics – the attenuation of the exclusive dependence of politics on the relations among subjects. The strategy of partially mediating the relations between individuals by relations between individuals and things – the use of objects as indirect projections of persons, desires, and interests – generated at that time politically precious resources for framing political actions partly as instrumental, impersonal, visually transparent, and therefore also as binding public facts.[51] Unfortunately, the gains of partially depersonalizing and facilitating horizontal interactions have also increased the exposure of the individual to the kind of economic reductionism I criticized previously, a material objectification that marginalizes the inward dimensions of the individual citizen.

But a stance that merely criticizes the degenerative aspects of the materialization of democratic politics and culture and the role played by the market and technology, its negative potential to deplete life, enhance domination over others, and therefore to curtail freedom (often adopted, for instance, by the "sages" of the Frankfurt School), tends to overlook the powerful impulse of the Enlightenment as a democratic epistemological revolution, and its enormous educational implications. Such a perspective misses the powerful endeavor to bring politics from heaven to earth, to materialize political power in the epistemological *Agora* of commonsense realism, to render it perceptually accessible as real and malleable, harboring the possibility of participatory politics and governmental accountability. Louis Dumont has pointed out that German and Italian fascists posited their concepts of personality and inward individualism precisely against the liberal democratic materialization of the political, as illustrated, for instance, by Thomas Mann's rejection of politics in his notorious *Reflections of a Nonpolitical Man* (1922).

Realizing the political implications of such attitudes, Dumont argues that "this purely internal individualism leaves the surrounding holism standing."[52] He observes that "Hitler rejects the modern primacy of the man-nature relation and reasserts the primacy of the relation between men."[53] In his treatise *The Concept of the Political*, published in German in 1932, German political theorist Carl Schmitt focused his critique of liberalism on what he regarded as the negative role of technology and economics as instruments of the materialization and depoliticization of the political. He held that this liberal tendency

---

[51] Ezrahi, *Descent of Icarus: Science and the Transformation of Contemporary Democracy* (Cambridge MA: Harvard University Press, 1990).

[52] Dumont, *Essays on Individualism*, p. 138. See also Gordon S. Wood, "Conspiracy and the Paranoid Style: Causality and Deceit in the Eighteenth Century" in *The William and Mary Quarterly*, series III, 39 (July 1982): 401–41.

[53] Ibid. *Essays on Individualism*, p. 166.

saps the energies of politics, which stems from the antagonism between subjects who imagine themselves as belonging to adverse groups of friends and
enemies.[54]

This attitude has enabled fascists to criticize the centrality of the economy
and of economic ideas in liberal and socialist thought and practice as signifying degenerative shifts in *Kultur*, a decadence of the human spirit. Against
these strains of twentieth-century culture and politics, early liberal preoccupations with the uses of nature or objective reality to constrain the degeneration
of individualism into a culture of solipsism, or group emotional and spiritual
unities, assume a special meaning. In this context, democratic individualism
has required a balance between overspiritualizing and overmaterializing the
citizen – an endeavor to which theories of personality and education associated with Locke, Rousseau, Pestalozzi, and Dewey have been particularly
pertinent.

Locke greatly influenced the very significant shift in the appraisal of physical
reality as both an arena of individual freedom and a constraint on the unruly
imagination. In his *An Essay Concerning Human Understanding*, he insists on
the importance of direct sense experience of the physical world as a more reliable source of knowledge than people's subjective opinions:

The floating of other men's opinions in our brains makes us not one jot the more knowing, though they happened to be true. What in them was science is in us but opiniatrety
(opinion); whilst we give up our assent only to reverend names, and do not, as they did,
employ our own reason to understand those truths which gave them reputation.[55]

His theory of the mind as a *tabula rasa* imprinted by the outer world implied
that knowledge acquired at present is more reliable than knowledge mediated
from the past and that, in light of the presumed sameness of the world outside us, a corresponding theory of truth enhances the possibility of sharing
judgments and knowledge and, therefore, associability. Confidence in the ideas
a person has formed of the world derives, according to Locke, from sensations that the rational faculty in our mind has processed by reflection and
association.

Locke's empiricism and reasonableness were both reflective of, and influential in determining, the coordinates of modern commonsense realism as
the sphere of liberal democratic politics. Like others, he was concerned about
protecting commonsense realism from the fictions and fantasies of individuals
who are melancholic or possess "a warmed or overweening brain" which can
sweep men "when got above common sense."[56] For Locke, "wrong assent"
lacks a basis in the experiments and observations that convince rational men
to concur. This point is central to his contention that individuals will tend, in

[54] See Carl Schmitt, *The Concept of the Political*, G. Schwab (trans.) (Chicago: University of
Chicago Press, 1996).
[55] John Locke, *An Essay Concerning Human Understanding*, First Treatise, chapter III, § 24.
[56] Ibid., book II, chapter XIX, § 4–7.

the final analysis, to prefer more probable propositions to less probable ones and that there are therefore "not so many men in errors and wrong opinions, as is commonly supposed."[57]

This cautious optimism, the idea that the majority might be right, later developed mathematically by French thinkers like Condorcet, linked insistence on the integrity of such discrete individual judgments, reflecting the individual's propensity to prefer more probable propositions, to the weight ascribed to opinions formed by majority groups.[58] According to the liberal democratic theory of political knowledge, it is the autonomy of each individual's judgment that grants the aggregate of individuals the potential sanction of the ruling majority, the authority of the greater number. It is particularly relevant to this discussion that Locke's theory of knowledge is based on deep skepticism regarding the human capacity to achieve certain knowledge and therefore on his insistence on the need to trust well-constructed probable judgments as alternatives to dogmatism and radical skepticism.

Because knowledge is probable rather than absolute it remains infinitely open to examination and reconsideration. In the sociopolitical context, a not-wholly-knowable objective world can leave individuals a wide margin of freedom to sense, experience, reflect, learn, relearn, and debate reality, while conversely, the considerable powers of individual observation and reflection can protect commonsense realism from the disruptive effects of the fictions, fantasies, and religious enthusiasm generated by melancholy and other triggers of the unruly fantastic imagination. This Lockean synthesis supports the delicate balance between the ontological status of the subject and the ontology of the object, preventing either from swallowing the other while, at the same time, enlisting both to create a middle ground in which individual agency, freedom, autonomy, and interiority are balanced and checked by shared probable individual judgments of experiences of the external world.

For Rousseau too, the great virtue of the objective world, of nature, for the new political society is its power as an impersonal and therefore amoral constraint on human conduct. Perhaps more than other influential political thinkers, Rousseau has made powerful moves in both directions. On one hand, he exemplified, triggered, and externalized the individual's subjective interiority by means of such writings as his *Confessions* and his works in fiction and music;[59] on the other, he attempted to internalize external nature as an amoral constraint on individual ambition, as expressed, for instance, in *Émile*,

---

[57] Ibid., chapter XX, p. 18.

[58] On mathematical and experimental models of certifying collective decisions, see Yaron Ezrahi, "Science and the Problem of Authority in Democracy" in Thomas F. Gieryn (ed.), *Science and Social Structure: A Festschrift for Robert Merton* Transactions of the New York Academy of Sciences, series II, vol. 39 (New York, NY: New York Academy of Sciences, 1980), pp. 43–60. See also Keith M. Baker; *Condorcet from Natural Philosophy to Social Mathematics* (Chicago: University of Chicago Press, 1976).

[59] See Jean-Jacques Rousseau, *On the Origin of Language*, J. H Moran and A. Gode (eds.) (first pub. 1753; New York: Fredrick Ungar, 1966), pp. 3–83.

his book on education. The tensions so sharply manifest in his writings – tensions that remain largely unresolved – between the emotional and the rational self, individual freedom and the general will, the invisible interior and the artificial exterior, or between individual and society, have become an integral part of the permanent agenda of democratic individualism and the fragile political imaginaries of modern democracy.

Like Locke, who was a physician, Rousseau, who had botanical knowledge, felt respect for the external physical world and strove to "appropriate" it for a democratic political world making. In *Émile*, Rousseau urges his reader to

> keep the child dependent on things only. By this course of education you will have followed the order of nature. Let his unreasonable wishes meet with physical obstacles only, or the punishment which results from his own actions, lessons which will be recalled when the same circumstances occur again. It is enough to prevent him from wrong doing without forbidding him to do wrong. Experience or lack of power should take the place of law.[60]

Resembling Locke in some respects, Rousseau here enlists the physical world for the sake of an amoral theory of constraints based upon, in his words, "dependence on things" rather than "dependence on men."[61] He actually thought it would be ideal "[i]f the laws of nations, like the laws of nature, could never be broken by any human power." Under such conditions, "dependence on men will become dependence on things."[62] For Rousseau, in the "school" of nature the child is trained to respect limits imposed by things on his autonomy as a free individual, learning thus to protect his integrity against the corruptive effects of the unnatural constraints imposed by society and public opinion. For Locke, the sooner the child learns to labor and use nature to create his or her own property, the sooner he or she learns to be independent of parental authority and stronger vis-à-vis other external authorities.

Locke and Rousseau differ, therefore, in the schemas they adopt for reaching equilibrium between individuation and the world of material objects on both the individual and social levels. Locke develops a theory of appropriation and a theory of external constraints, a theory of private property that stresses the creative potential of the individual to externalize the self in the phenomenal world of common sense, as well as a theory of knowledge and learning from experience that would check individual tendencies to be moved by improbable fictions and fantasies. Rousseau, who no less than Locke is concerned about the disruptive power of unrestrained human desires and fantasies, nevertheless relates to interiority and externality within a different framework.

He stresses the aforementioned importance of educating the child to internalize the world of physical objects as a way to achieve restraint without resorting

---

[60] Jean-Jacques Rousseau, *Émile*, B. Foxley (trans.) (first pub. 1762; Dutton, New York: Everyman's Library, 1977), p. 49.
[61] Ibid.
[62] Ibid.

to humiliating dependence on other individuals or being driven by fear. But at the same time, in his essay *On the Origins of Inequality*, he strongly objects to the idea and practices that enable private property. To use our own vocabulary, the performance of the imaginary of private property leads, according to Rousseau, to the performance of intolerable inequalities and degenerate forms of social interaction. Unlike Locke and in anticipation of Marx, whom he greatly influenced, Rousseau does not assert private property as a way to empower individuals in civil society, as affirmed by liberal democratic principles, but as a condition or force that undermines freedom.

To reiterate, both Locke and Rousseau maintain that the world of objective reality plays an important role in shaping the imaginaries of freedom. For Locke, appropriation through labor empowers the individual as citizen, while for Rousseau the cultivation of private property unleashes destructive psychological, social, and political forces that actually threaten the civic order. If Rousseau appreciates labor, it is primarily as a way of training in the logic of natural necessity and love of one's country. He imagines the ideal citizen as a peasant-soldier living close to nature, willing to defend his own, as well as his country's, freedom, remaining uncontaminated by the hypocrisy of city life, under whose sway the individual can easily be tempted by "a deceitful and frivolous exterior, honor without virtue, reason without wisdom, and pleasure without happiness."[63]

In contradistinction to the classical modern liberal democratic model, which combines the cultural fostering of individual inwardness with its rational economic and political externalizations in the space of public affairs, Rousseau regards the effects of the arts and the sciences as a largely corruptive influence on his democratic individual, the peasant who lives close to, and therefore respects, the necessities of nature. According to Rousseau, the conditions of a free, innocent, individual existence in a society that tends to metamorphose every individual into an actor on the public stage cannot be attained or improved by private property, science, or art.

For Rousseau, the only safe realization of human faculties compatible with moral-political autonomy takes the shape of a participatory republican democracy in which the people make the laws and are ready to defend their country as citizen-soldiers. Whereas Locke focuses on the *epistemological* conditions of liberal individual freedom and on the possibilities of toleration, agreement, and the rights of revolution, Rousseau concentrates on the *moral-legal* imaginaries and practices of freedom and the prospect of communal civic solidarities.

In the course of the nineteenth century, Heinrich Pestalozzi's reforms in western educational systems in Europe and America in fact combined elements of Rousseau and Locke's uses of nature to educate the young to sharpen their faculties of observation, judgment, and the responsible use of language. A new emphasis on vision and observation in the teaching process of elementary schools encouraged instruction in fields like geography, geology, zoology,

---

[63] Rousseau, *The Second Discourse*, p. 180.

botany, and physics, turning teachers, who had formerly functioned as the sole authoritative mediators and interpreters of texts, into lay "experimental scientists" whose authority depended on the success with which their students' experience with the external world corroborated their claims to knowledge.[64]

Liberal ideas on the ways in which the worlds of natural phenomena and man-made artifacts could be employed to enhance individual autonomy, presence, discipline, and power have always had to compete with religious, Romantic, poetical, and philosophical imaginaries that have often been enlisted to promote competing values. In the early twentieth century, the American pragmatists presented a particularly enduring challenge to the dichotomy of subject and object and the implicit liberal "spectator theory of knowledge." Their criticism reflects the cumulative power of diverse cultural strains that have undermined the credibility of classical modern liberal democratic imaginaries of the natural individual as an isolated entity capable of acquiring – as a detached witness – objective knowledge of the world. "If we see that knowing is not the act of [an] outside spectator but of a participator inside the natural and social scene," maintains John Dewey, "then the true object of knowledge resides in the consequences of directed action."[65] Here Dewey anticipates the postmodern shift, which seeks a new synthesis of individual and reality, of subject and object, based on radically more plastic, dynamic, and underdetermined imaginaries of agency and facts.

---

[64] For a further discussion of this issue see Ezrahi, *Descent of Icarus*, chapters 3 and 4.

[65] John Dewey, *The Quest for Certainty: A Study in the Relation of Knowledge and Action* (New York: Capricorn Books, 1960), p. 23. For a comprehensive discussion see Yaron Ezrahi, "Dewey's Critique of Democratic Visual Culture" in David Michael Levin (ed.), *Sites of Vision: The Discursive Construction of Sight in the History of Philosophy* (Cambridge: MIT Press, 1997), pp. 315–36.

10

Individuals between Liberal and Illiberal Corporations

The issue of the status of the individual as a subject-agent within the group or the corporate body is, undoubtedly, intimately related to genres of the modern political imagination such as nationalism, communitarianism, and liberalism, and is a continual subject of contention in modern political and legal theory. This, in fact, is an area in which one may observe a rich interaction and a mutual borrowing of imaginaries of the individual and the group, which have evolved concomitantly in jurisprudence, political theory, and the popular political imagination. In each of these fields, indeed, fictions and metaphors were often devised as a means of coping with different practical problems and producing specific effects. Once they migrated from one area to the other, their receptions and deployments were subject to different criteria, including considerations of expected but unintended effects.

A field of research that we may tentatively label "comparative politico-legal imaginology" could fruitfully help trace the cultural, political, and legal trajectories of competing imaginary clusters of the individual and the group from their origins through their selections and rejections as terms of political and legal conduct and institutions. The range of such imaginaries, which have emerged in western politico-legal traditions, is extremely wide. It includes diverse imaginaries of the state (or the leader, the government, and so forth) as a guardian, a shepherd, a partnership, a fellowship, a trust, an organism, a machine (or a machine-like whole), an artificial person, a fictive person (*persona ficta*), an organization, an association by contract, a real individual (who can decide, will, and act as an agency independent of its parts), or some combination of these.

Depending very much on the particular context, obviously, each of these imaginaries would tend to have different effects and implications for the status of the individual and the balance between his or her physicality, interiority, freedom, dignity, value, agency, and associability. Hence the political history and theory of democratic individualism as part of the history of the democratic political imagination would entail the examination of the selective processes whereby such competing imaginaries that define the place of the individual in relation to the collective have reinforced or weakened liberal democratic political configurations. It is from this perspective that I criticize the tendency of communitarian political imaginaries to exclude outsiders and to encourage oppressive political practices in both democratic and undemocratic regimes.

I turn now to examine only one pair, apparently the most persistently important one, of such competing political imaginaries (or rather families of imaginaries). One has characterized the state as some kind of partnership that is, in many important respects, no more than the sum of its parts, including their voluntary transactions, and the other typecasts the state as an entity distinct from and in many respects independent of the individuals who comprise it.

Following continental theorists, English legal theorist-historian F. W. Maitland introduced, in his discussion of this issue, a distinction between "corporation sole" (the corporation itself) and "corporation aggregate."[1] "Corporation aggregate" draws on an imagining of the group as a partnership of individual agents. This view recognizes as real only natural, not legal, persons. Maitland stresses the prevalence of this notion of corporation aggregate in the English political and legal traditions. By contrast, he discerns a marked tendency toward an alternative imaginary of the group as a "corporation sole" mostly in the German, French, and Italian continental legal and political traditions.

There are several versions of this imaginary of the state as a corporation, as well as of nonpolitical corporations (such as the Church, the local club, or the business firm). The weak version would simply refer to the corporation as a "person," consciously adapting the language of legal fictions with the intention of achieving practical benefits such as a simplification of the attachment and the uses of property in legal proceedings involving associations of individuals or groups beyond the limited time span of the lives of the individuals comprising the association or the corporation at any given moment. The strong version, which has attracted most of the attention of legal and political theorists, refers to the corporation not as an association of individuals treated conveniently as a "*persona ficta*," but as a real person, an autonomous individual agent that can subordinate its parts.

Analyzing this imaginary of the corporation as an artificial person from the perspective of an English legal and political theorist, Maitland critically asks: "Can we allow the group – gild, town, village, nation – to stand over against each and all its members as a distinct person?"[2] In another publication, Maitland argues: "Also we may observe, and in history it is important, that this theory might play into the hands of a Prince or a princeling inclined to paternal despotism."[3] No wonder modern democratic political imaginaries tended

---

[1] See F. W. Maitland's introduction to *Political Theories of the Middle Ages* by Otto Gierke, F. W. Maitland (trans.), (Cambridge: Cambridge University Press, 1927); Maitland, *Selected Essays*. H. D. Hazeltine, G. Lapsley, and P. H. Winfield (eds.) (Cambridge: Cambridge University Press, 1936).

[2] Maitland, *Selected Essays*, p. 227.

[3] Maitland, "Introduction" to Gierke (1927), p. xxi.

to draw more upon the legal construct of the contract to bind individuals to the state than upon that of the corporation. Maitland discerns the origins of the metaphysical rendering of the group as an individual person in certain strains of Roman law and medieval Christianity that he considers particularly influential in continental Europe. He refers especially to the German effort to develop an alternative to the contract theory of association, designating it as a theory that would facilitate and simplify the legal handling of "the persistence in Germany of agrarian communities with world-old histories, [and] the intricate problems that their dissolution presented." In this text, published in 1927, he significantly adds: "Nor should the triumphs of biological science be forgotten."[4]

According to this imaginary, the corporation, the collective, is a kind of organic whole referred to as *Genossenschaft*. This theory, developed by Gierke, was considered genuinely German. "German Fellowship," writes Maitland, insisting on distinguishing it from the English imaginary of partnership,

is no fiction, no symbol, no piece of state's machinery, no collective name for individuals, but a living organism and a real person, with body and members and a will of its own. Itself can will, itself can act; it wills and acts by the men who are its organs as a man wills and acts by brain, mouth and hand. It is not a fictitious person; it is a Gesammtperson, and its will is a Gesammtwille; it is a group-person, and its will is a group will.[5]

To the *Weltanschauung* embodied in the *Genossenschaft*, the proud English jurist juxtaposes the tendency in his own legal-political tradition to reject concepts that grew in the traditions of "sacred texts" and "unassociative people."[6] Maitland introduces the alternative serviceable concepts of trust and trustees that evolved in the context of English private law. It was, he asserts, much more English to imagine the king as a trustee of his people. In the course of the eighteenth century, he argues, it became a parliamentary commonplace that "all political power is a trust."[7] Rather than proceeding from the medieval whole to its parts, it shifted from discrete individuals to the whole.

This approach was obviously more receptive to both mechanistic (which admittedly also has a coercive potential) and voluntaristic rather than to organic imaginaries of the whole; more responsive to metaphors originating in modern physics and mechanics and, in some respects, also ethics, than to those borrowed from biology.[8] This more atomistic approach has obviously been politically attractive to liberal democratic thinkers and ideologues, just as the more holistic organic version of the imaginary of the state as a "corporate

---

[4] Ibid., p. xxv.
[5] Ibid., p. xxvi.
[6] Ibid., p. xxviii.
[7] Ibid., p. xxxvi.
[8] On the compatibility of individual voluntarism and mechanical metaphors of social causality, see Ezrahi's *The Descent of Icarus*, p. 173 and Theodore M. Porter, *The Rise of Statistical Thinking, 1820–1900* (Princeton: Princeton University Press, 1986).

sole," as an autonomous entity politically, legally, and morally superior to the individual, has appealed to nationalist ideologues and authoritarian leaders.

For centuries, the answer to the question of the balance between the status of the individual and the group has depended on which of these two kinds of legal-political imaginaries of the group was taken for granted. While the atomistic imaginary of political groups as aggregates has gathered special strength, even predominance, in the western, especially Anglo-Saxon, political imagination, the presence of the holistic view has prevailed with sufficient resilience to actually survive as an important component of what would emerge as the modern mixed democratic nation-states like Israel, Germany, and France. Moreover, the idea of a corporate person, largely rejected by liberal democratic political imaginaries, has continued to be particularly useful and persistent in the legal context of private economic associations and business firms.

In modern legal organizational and political discourses on private as well as public organizations, both personification and aggregation persist as ways of framing issues.[9] Most pertinent to our discussion are the apparent affinities between the imaginaries regulating relations of individuals and groups in the legal-economic sphere of the private sector and in the public-political context. Katsuhito Iwai has traced a relation between American liberal democratic political culture and the predilection in American law for the term "corporation aggregate" over "corporation sole," to which he refers respectively as "corporate nominalism" (acknowledging only the reality of individuals), and "corporate realism" (regarding the corporation as a real and distinct entity). By comparison, he notices a strong connection between Japanese history and culture and the tendency in the Japanese legal context to opt for German-style corporate realism, and thus regard shareholders as subsidiary to the corporate personality.[10] It is noteworthy that in the American case, resistance to hypostatizing nonhuman entities, to sometimes attributing personhood to corporations while denying it to natural individuals, echoes the fierce historical controversies surrounding the depersonalization of slaves and the criminalization of abortion.

In 1973, *Roe v. Wade*'s famous assertion that fetuses are not constitutional persons has further problematized the move to extend personhood to corporations.[11] This is largely due to the fact that "when the law manipulates status distinctions through the use of the metaphor 'person,' it necessarily expresses a conception of the relative worth of the objects included and excluded by the scope of the metaphor."[12] Against this background, as well as the record of regarding, by law, human entities such as slaves "as less than human, or at

---

[9] See, for instance, Meir Dan-Cohen, *Rights, Persons, and Organizations: A Legal Theory for Bureaucratic Society* (Berkeley: University of California Press, 1986).

[10] Katsuhito Iwai, "Persons, Things and Corporations: The Corporate Personality Controversy and Comparative Corporate Governance," *The American Journal of Comparative Law*, vol. 47 (1999): 583–632.

[11] *Roe v. Wade*, 410 U. S. 113, 158, 162 (1973).

[12] Notes, "What We Talk About When We Talk About Persons: The Language of a Legal Fiction." *Harvard Law Review* vol. 114, no. 6 (April 2001): 1760.

least, as less than full legal persons," one can understand Justice Eugene Black's concern that the granting of "legal personality to corporations may cheapen the social meaning of humans' legal personality."[13]

These sensitivities and concerns, so specific to the context of the American as compared to the Japanese or the continental experience, suggest the subtle factors involved in the fashioning of corporate bodies in diverse cultural and political contexts. Professor Iwai notes, however, that despite such sharp differences, in the final analysis, neither the American nor the Japanese system can give up the benefits that accrue from the flexibility generated by occasionally stressing the reality of the corporation as a legal device

which simplifies and stabilizes the complicated web of contractual relationships that an association of shareholders has to have with a multitude of outside parties ... [and] encourages shareholders to make long-term commitments to it by reducing the risks of sudden dissolution ... [as well as] increasing the efficiency of the use of its assets.[14]

Iwai also notices the importance of sometimes invoking a nominalist "corporation aggregate" imaginary, which would highlight the responsibilities of managers to attend to the returns of the shareholders rather than merely care about the survival and the growth of the corporation itself.[15] He suggests, therefore, that trends in continental Europe and, to a lesser extent, even in the United States and Japan, exhibit an inclination to maintain a degree of dualism by integrating elements of the two models.

The analogy to the imaginaries of the state as a corporation is obvious. Here too a more flexible pluralistic approach entertaining elements of both "essentialist corporate realism," which requires that a body of persons be regarded as a real person, and elements of "corporate nominalism," which regards the corporation merely as a legal fiction signifying an aggregate or an association of real natural persons, opens the mind to an appreciation of the virtues of indeterminism and toward a richer vocabulary of imaginaries whose coexistence would not be tolerated by traditional metaphysics and the philosophical criterion of coherence.

This is precisely the point at which one may observe how the philosophical and legal incompatibilities between a group persona and an association of individuals imagined as an aggregate could most fruitfully be overcome by a functional eclecticism, which could succeed in combining a richer sociopolitical repertoire of diverse strategies for relating individuals to a group in varying contexts such as the market, election day, and the battlefield. The balance between these largely distinctive strategies changes, of course, according to time and place. An emphasis on the reality of individuals is, as I noted earlier, fundamental to weakening hierarchical authority and diminishing the individual's

---

[13] Ibid., 1762, 1764.

[14] Ibid., 590.

[15] Ibid., 606. The ripple effects of the collapse of banks and other financial institutions as a result of the financial crisis that broke out in September 2008 has accentuated pressures to hold managers individually and collectively responsible for bankruptcy.

willingness to put his life on the line in the battlefield, while supporting a more instrumental conception of politics.[16] I discuss its implications for the availability and the uses of military force in democracies in the following section.

This view of the private individual as the ultimate political unit is also consistent with the deployment of the imaginaries of the market economy and its agents in politics, and with the minimalist conception of state powers and authority. An emphasis on the superior reality of the group, the collective, or the people that implies an imaginary of the individual as a secondary, often merely derivative entity or an epiphenomenon, is more compatible with a normative, spiritual, legal, and military sanctioning of individual sacrifices for the group and to granting the state vast power and authority to educate, regulate, act on behalf, and direct its citizens.[17]

Paradoxically, the modern individualism fundamental to liberal democratic revolutions also provided the powerful metaphor of the nation as a person, as a collective individual that can will and act. This was the very stuff of a romantic mystical nationalist politics that also generated the imaginary of discrete and isolated individuals fundamental to totalitarian political unities.[18] Dumont observes that "totalitarianism is a disease of modern society that results from the attempt, in a society where individualism is deeply rooted and predominant, to subordinate it to the primacy of the society as a whole.... The violence of the movement is rooted in this contradiction."[19] These political variations on the imaginary of the modern individual emphasize the precariousness and the specificity of democratic individualism as a balance between the individual's physicality, interiority, freedom, value, dignity, agency, and associability. Such variations reflect the combined effects of cultural and political differences as conditions of democratic individualism and democratic political practice.

There is a broad consensus that the United States exemplifies the most extreme version of strong individualism and weak holism. In a celebratory essay on American poet Walt Whitman, Gilles Deleuze observes that what defines America as an experience is its polyphony of fragments:

Europeans have an innate sense of organic totality, or composition, but they have to acquire the sense of the fragment, and can do so only through a tragic reflection or an experience of disaster. Americans, on the contrary, have a natural sense of the fragment, and what they have to conquer is the feel for the totality, for beautiful composition. The fragment already exists in a non-reflective manner, preceding any effort ... what is characteristic of America is not the fragmentary, but the spontaneity of the fragmentary.[20]

[16] Ezrahi, *The Descent of Icarus*.
[17] This collective persona has cultural roots in medieval theology like the allegorical reading of the beloved woman in the Song of Songs as the Catholic Church. See E. Ann Matter, *The Voice of My Beloved: The Song of Songs in Western Medieval Christianity* (Philadelphia: University of Pennsylvania Press, 1990).
[18] Louis Dumont, *Essays on Individualism: Modern Ideology in Anthropological Perspective* (Chicago: University of Chicago Press, 1992), pp. 113–79.
[19] Ibid., p. 158.
[20] Gilles Deleuze, *Essays Critical and Clinical*, D. W. Smith and M. A. Greco (trans.) (Minneapolis: University of Minnesota Press, 1993), p. 56.

According to Deleuze, the conception of whole in America differs from that on the European continent, for instance, in that it is "a whole that is all the more paradoxical in that it comes after the fragments and leaves them intact, making no attempt to totalize them." It is a whole that is not "a totality but an assembly."[21] This, of course, cannot be an all-inclusive, static state of affairs. While America exemplifies this vision more than any other society, even in America holism has moments of resurgence.[22]

If the American liberal democracy can be regarded as a radical version of the democratic individual as a fragment unconstrained by the reality of a particular whole, Italian fascism may be considered an example of its polar opposite, a political system regulated by an imaginary of the primacy of a whole unconstrained by the reality of individuals. "The fascist regime," argues Mabel Berezin, "sought to penetrate the principal sources of the Italian self, religion, and family and to replace them with a fascist self based on a new conception of citizenship that fused the public and the private self in the state."[23] Influenced by the visions of Giuseppe Mazzini and Giovanni Gentile, fascists imagined that "true liberty is located not in the individual but is collectively represented by the state or the nation."[24]

In his famous "The Doctrine of Fascism," Benito Mussolini was very explicit about downgrading the individual in favor of the group. He sought to spiritualize and collectivize the consciousness of the individual by divesting him or her of the distinct material reality of the body and by rejecting what I have defined as a democratic political epistemology – the sphere of commonsense realism within the frame of which, as a democratic agent, the existence of the individual and his or her actions are rendered observable and relatable as physical, material, and moral objects/subjects of lay perception. Mussolini argued:

Fascism is opposed to all the abstractions of an individualistic character based upon materialism.... Fascism reaffirms the state as the only expression of the individual.... The nation is created by the state, which gives the people consciousness of their own moral unity, the will, and thereby an effective existence.[25]

As expounded by Mussolini, the fascist political imaginary ontologizes the corporate state while deontologizing and dematerializing the individual. Hence his insistence that the fascist state could not defer to (or even consider) majorities based on counting and aggregating individuals. The individual, the group, and the people are realized "in the consciousness and the will of the few or even one only ... the higher personality is truly the nation, inasmuch as it is the state....

[21] Ibid. pp. 18–59.
[22] Michael J. Sandel, *Democracy's Discontent: America in Search of a Public Philosophy* (Cambridge, MA: The Belknap Press of Harvard University Press, 1996).
[23] Mabel Berezin, *Making The Fascist Self: The Political Culture of Interwar Italy* (Ithaca: Cornell University Press, 1997), p. 41.
[24] Ibid., p. 57.
[25] Benito Mussolini, "The Doctrine of Fascism," from the English translation of the text in *Encyclopedia Italiana*, vol. XIV, in *Fascism and World-Power* (London: Alexander Maclehose & Co., 1933).

In the conception of Fascism, the state is an absolute before which individuals and groups are relative."[26]

From the perspective of our discussion, the radical versions of the individual as an isolated fragment or a mere derivative part of the corporate state represents gross deviations from the balance between individual interiority, agency, and associability essential to democratic individualism. Democratic individualism does not, as some of its critics insist, deplete the association or associability of free individuals of all meaning. It envisions individuals who can voluntarily associate for the purpose of building the political order from the bottom up and a political culture that facilitates such associations.

Similarly, the democratic individualism that encourages the search for meaningful communities and is committed to the ethics of public life does not endorse the kind of institutionalization of collective norms or meaning systems that constrain individual interiority, freedom (including creativity in cultural, social, and political life), dignity, physicality, and agency. So, beyond the democratic individual, democratic agents would characteristically consist of a range of voluntary associations of democratic individuals. If we can imagine a spectrum between corporate holism and atomistic individualism, between unified corporate bodies and discrete and insulated individuals, democratic agents would be located between the center of the line and the pole of atomistic individualism, neither close enough to that pole to risk anarchy nor far enough beyond that center in the direction of the opposite pole to risk despotism or authoritarianism.

Liberal democracies can, nevertheless, tolerate nondemocratic nongovernmental collective agents such as centralized business corporations, authoritarian religious parties, or hierarchical trade unions, provided they accept the rules of free competition in the democratic social and political system and do not venture to conquer or monopolize the system. Characteristic nongovernmental democratic agents would normally include voluntary associations and organizations in the economic, social, cultural, and political spheres in which the whole is imagined as an aggregate, or a free partnership, rather than as a unified entity that strictly subordinates all its parts.

PUBLIC OPINION AND THE MARKET AS LIBERAL
DEMOCRATIC AGENTS

I have suggested that in the democratic state, the imaginary of the whole is openly underdetermined and unfixable. That fact and its underlying concomitants raise the problem of how, in such a system, a legitimate and binding collective that produces group decisions can be imagined and performed at all. The answer to this question is extremely complex and a large part of the following discussion addresses it directly and indirectly.

[26] Ibid.

Perhaps the most crucial modern political imaginary that has contributed to the making and legitimating of collective group decisions in modern democracies has been public opinion, which, I will argue, is the elusive, indeed invisible, surrogate sovereign in the modern democratic state. From a mere rhetorical category and a visionary, almost utopian, imagining evolving during the late eighteenth century in European countries such as England and France, public opinion, imagined as a dynamic aggregate of individual attitudes or beliefs, developed (by the late twentieth century) into a suasive imaginary of a full-fledged embodied democratic political agency capable of making and unmaking political leaders, of toppling authoritarian as well as unpopular democratic governments even between elections, and of setting up new ones in their place.

The significance of public opinion as a modern democratic political imaginary, which the performative political imagination has transformed into a resilient democratic political agent, cannot be overestimated. In his *Democracy in America*, Tocqueville was one of the first theorists-observers to recognize the pivotal significance of public opinion as a novel political agent. He observed:

The King of France is absolute master in the field of executive power. The President of the United States is responsible for his actions. French law says that the person of the king of France is inviolable. Nevertheless above the one as above the other stands a directing power, that of public opinion. This power is less defined in France than in the United States; less recognized, less formulated in the laws; but it does in fact exist there. France and the United States, despite the diversity of their constitutions, thus have this point in common, that public opinion is, as a result, the dominant power.[27]

Perhaps one of the most instructive moments in the early dawning of public opinion has been its emergence during the French Revolution as a new fiction of a noncorporate political whole beyond the declining corporate body politic and power structure of the old regime. Perhaps no one at the time characterized this new development better than Jacques Necker, the Geneva-born French financier and statesman who served as Louis XVI's minister of state, when he described public opinion as

an invisible power that, without treasury, guard, or army, gives its laws to the city, the court, and even the palaces of kings … a tribunal before which all men who attract attention are obliged to appear: There public opinion, as if from the heights of the throne, awards prizes and honors, makes and unmakes reputations.[28]

A reform-minded minister, dramatically supported by the public in his conflict with enemies who forced his resignation from his position at the royal court, Necker was especially qualified by experience to discern the new emerging force of public opinion. I would suggest that much of the success of public

---

[27] Alexis de Tocqueville, *Democracy in America*, Harvey C. Mansfield and Delba Winthrop (trans. and ed.) (first pub. 1835; Chicago: University of Chicago Press, 2002), p. 117.
[28] Cited in Keith Michael Baker, *Inventing the French Revolution: Essays on French Political Culture in the Eighteenth Century* (Cambridge: Cambridge University Press, 1990), p. 193.

opinion in becoming a self-realizing democratic political fiction can be attributed to its ability to combine the spirit of the corporate whole without actually being a corporate whole and without becoming sufficiently reified, specific, and therefore predictable to obliterate the freedom and integrity of the discrete individuals of which it is ostensibly composed.

It was precisely because in the course of the eighteenth century the public could increasingly be imagined as an aggregate of individuals that a shared imaginary of public opinion could exercise such power and authority in democratic societies. Furthermore, the autonomy of public opinion as an animated democratic agent has been protected by its elusiveness and, with some important exceptions, by the difficulties entailed in the attempt to effectively control it from above. In those societies in which public opinion has become incorporated into one naturalized, mystical, or legal whole, often embodied in a single person or in a cluster of individuals, it has, at least temporarily, disappeared as a credible democratic agent and has shrunk to a mere rhetorical category of authoritarian political speech.

Without entering into the interesting scholarly debate on the history and nature of public opinion, I shall briefly examine a few aspects of this imaginary particularly pertinent to its role as a democratic agent in the modern democratic political imagination. Keith Baker observes that the concept (in his terms) or the imaginary (in mine) of public opinion emerged in late eighteenth-century France in response to a crisis in the legitimacy of the absolute monarchy. Since this crisis took the form of a contest between the monarchy and its rivals, the monarch who took sides lost the privileged status of impartial tribunal or arbitrator.

Within the framework of this new "politics of contestation," Baker argues, both parties were driven to appeal to the "court" of public opinion, identified with an increasingly public debate beyond official circles, a debate the monarchic government failed to prevent, to which it therefore had no choice but to acquiesce.[29] Baker argues further that, while during the 1750s and 1760s the public opinion to which the contesting sides appealed was no more than an "ideological construct" lacking institutional expression, its presence was reinforced by the circulation of French newspapers and pamphlets that peaked toward the French Revolution.[30]

As a democratic agent, public opinion had to be imagined as a profoundly different entity than that identified by Jean-Jacques Rousseau as a form of group despotism. Rousseau insisted that when exposed to the public gaze, individual behavior tends to become theatrical and inauthentic. This view presented serious obstacles as to the very possibility of imagining the aggregation of individual attitudes and judgments qua "public opinion" that is not a "group mind" or a posturing particular opinion, rather – as Condorcet attempted to

---

[29] Ibid., pp. 168–72.
[30] See Robert Darnton, *The Literary Underground of the Old Regime* (Cambridge, MA: Harvard University Press, 1982).

demonstrate and Locke before him had tried to conceptualize – public opinion as the collective outcome of a multitude of discrete individual opinions.

This dilemma was also reflected in Rousseau's struggle to conceive a general will that would be neither the mere sum of all wills nor a group will.[31] It was along the lines of the Marquis de Condorcet's thinking that the imaginary of the majority was at times interchangeable with public opinion or the public will. However, in order for the political imaginary of public opinion to evolve into a working democratic agent compatible with the imaginary of the democratic individual as the primary political agent, public opinion had to stand for something superior to mere opinion in the sense of the Greek *doxa* (or *fama*, distinguished from *episteme* in antiquity as denoting mere opinion as opposed to knowledge) without acquiring a status equivalent to knowledge.

It was here, of course, that the modern scientistic frame of commonsense realism and the rise of the modern imaginary of the social world (like the physical world) as consisting of public facts that can be the object of shared popular perceptions became so crucial. Especially in France, the prestige of the sciences of mathematics and logic was enlisted by revolutionary pamphleteers to replace the historical genealogies of the traditionalists by the "self-evident," rational principles of the new constitution.[32] Baker locates the trend toward such an enlightened imaginary of public opinion in the 1770s.

The diverse cultural technologies of the Enlightenment – encyclopedias, dictionaries, accurate drawings and their mass dissemination through printing – language reforms, the advancement and promulgation of natural science, and the rise of the mass press, especially in the following century, carried the promise of strengthening voluntary individualism, constraining the theatricalization of public behavior, anchoring safe factual referents for public discourse, and enhancing the rationalization of public opinion, and, therefore, also the ostensible preservation of the balance between individual autonomy, agency, and associability.

This imagery, linked for a long time to the illusions of a sociocultural progressive process of harmonization between freedom and a universal consensus, was premised on the belief in the power of universally accessible rational truths and public knowledge to combine discrete individuals into a public whole without generating an artificial corporate person.[33] The advocates of the liberal democratic reconfiguration of the state had to uphold the notion that the emergence of a multitude of individuals into the political sphere would yield an ordered whole rather than a formless, haphazard assemblage, as their critics predicted, or, even worse, a mob. They had to present the feasibility and prospect of a new kind of whole, better or more legitimate than the corporate one,

---

[31] See the references of Rousseau to the "War of the Buffoons" around the operatic style that preserves the authentic voice of the individual in his *Confessions*, chapter 8.

[32] Paul Friedland, *Political Actors: Representative Bodies and Theatricality in the Age of the French Revolution* (Ithaca: Cornell University Press, 2003), pp. 105–6.

[33] For an extensive discussion of this theme, see my *Descent of Icarus*.

that consisted, in their opinion, of parasitic classes, such as the aristocracy, to which they had characteristically referred to as "fungus."[34] They had to show how democratic individuals could be both independent and associable, how they could come together to produce a collective voice and, at the same time, maintain their discrete independent individual integrity.

The idealized imaginary of an enlightened, dynamic public opinion, which is both a whole and an aggregate, was crucial for such a welding of the individual and the group. Democratic individualism as a balance between individual autonomy, agency, and associability was vital for enabling public opinion as an unincorporated whole. No wonder critics of the corporate organic political imaginaries of the old regime endorsed cultural and educational forms – which Michael Foucault would later term "technologies of the self" – such as "dispassionate and thoughtful reading" by lone individuals, which contributed to the rise of the autonomous individual as the authentic elementary unit of the sociopolitical whole.[35] Such technologies of selfhood appeared to strengthen the individual as a source of independent judgment and reduce the threat of the subject's disappearance by incorporation into the collective abstractions of the group.

The emergence of the market as another version of an unincorporated whole upheld by voluntary interactive individuals was inspired by the developing commercial culture. It was most compellingly "poeticized" by Bernard Mandeville and conceptualized by Adam Smith. This led to the development of a tradition of economic thinking that cultivated imaginaries of unincorporated wholes, conceived as a systemic balance of cumulative effects, achieved unwittingly and unpurposefully by self-seeking individuals engaged in the pursuit of their own interests. This imaginary of self-seeking individuals tended to engage and encourage a unidimensional, materialistic, hedonistic individualism, which enlists or mobilizes the rational faculty toward the fulfillment of passions and desires rather than toward the development of higher moral, aesthetic, and spiritual aspects of the individual's interiority.

This model of a democratic whole, composed of self-seeking discrete economic individuals, is undoubtedly no less of an imaginary abstraction than the imaginary of enlightened public opinion. There are some suggestive parallelisms between constructs that aggregate real persons into market forces, abstractions that aggregate real individuals into a whole-like public opinion and abstractions that accumulate commodities and convert labor into paper money. Marc Shell has shed light on the process whereby faith becomes a substitute for material realities through materialized abstractions: "During its historical metamorphosis from commodity (a lump of gold) to coin (a commodity impressed with the stamp of the state) to paper money (a mere impression), a solid metal undergoes and participates in culturally and philosophically

---

[34] Friedland, *Political Actors*, pp. 65, 76.
[35] Yaron Ezrahi, "The Theatrics and Mechanics of Action: The Theatre and the Machine as Political Metaphors," *Social Research* vol. 62, no. 2 (Summer 1995): 299–322.

subversive changes."[36] Shell means that objects such as coins are both commodities and symbols, whereas paper money is already primarily a symbol, largely disassociated from commodities.[37] It is precisely this very process of a disassociation of money as a symbol from its base in solid valuable metal that Locke feared would easily undermine public trust. It was, of course, primarily as a symbol that money gained the efficiency that was so congenial for the modernization of the market economy and later for the evolution of the financial market. We may recapitulate in this context what we said earlier: In spite of Locke's scepticism beliefs that select certain abstractions and lend them a tinge of material reality as collective imaginaries may be validated for social currency – also in the wider sense – by mere reference to a small number of "hard facts."

The association with money, exchange, banks, and the mechanisms of the market as an impersonal coordinating device has granted abstractions from the field of economy an additional advantage. The market as a device for enabling individuals to voluntarily produce collective benefits appeared, until effectively questioned by Marxist challenges, a reliable, neutral means of reconciling voluntary individualism and aggregative liberal holism.

At the center of this imaginary stood the machine metaphor, which Hobbes devised in the legal-political context as a kind of "corporation aggregate," a system to weld free action and order. Mandeville and Smith metamorphosed it into an even more impersonal and horizontally interactive mechanism aggregating a multitude of voluntary individual actions into a dynamic whole.[38] Given these idealizing premises, the legitimacy of the market imaginary of a liberal democratic whole was vulnerable to any indication that, for at least some of the actors in the market, action is not voluntary and interaction is based on monopoly over capital, commodities, exclusive forums, and forms of exchange or other kinds of domination rather than universally equal exchange.

The appeal of the imaginary of public opinion in contrast to that of the market bespoke, among other things, resistance to replacing the emerging imaginary of democratic individualism and its corresponding conception of citizenship and civic virtue with the narrower, private-regarding, egotistically oriented economic man. The imaginary of the economic man has nevertheless become central and often dominant in liberal political discourse and practice, advancing a view of the sociopolitical whole in market terms of a dynamic, self-regulating, self-balancing system of aggregates, which has been continually enlisted to empower attempts to limit the authority and power of state bureaucracies.

---

[36] Marc Shell, *Money, Language, and Thought: Literary and Philosophic Economies from the Medieval to the Modern Era* (Berkeley: University of California Press, 1982), p. 105.

[37] Ibid.

[38] Bernard Mandeville, *The Fable of the Bees*, Phillip Harth (ed.) (Harmondsworth: Penguin, 1970); Adam Smith, *An Inquiry into the Nature and Causes of the Wealth of Nations* (London: W. Strahan and T. Cadell, 1776).

These imaginaries of economic individualism have been resilient enough to dominate large parts of private law, noneconomic social interactions, and the policies and actions of the modern liberal democratic state toward its citizens. This process has been reinforced by major modern intellectual schools and movements, especially in the course of the nineteenth century, such as utilitarianism in philosophy. Even more salient are social sciences such as economics, widely regarded as the most quantifiable or mathematifiable and, therefore, scientifically prestigious as well as the most relevant among the social sciences. In late modern times, the diffusion of this version of the individual as a despiritualized, egotistic, rational man aroused the powerful antagonism of Romantic individualists and fundamentalist collectivists.

The whole construed by economists constitutes a system of free voluntary agents with the virtues of an unincorporated whole with dynamic boundaries. However, as compared to the individual citizens imagined as the constituents of public opinion, the imaginaries of economic individualism benefit from the considerable advantage of association with a cluster of more specific visible and concrete rules and instruments of horizontal interaction and transaction such as money, banks, specialized self-regulated markets, well-defined roles, and, most significantly, part of the financial system's impersonal quantitative procedures for assessing and fixing values.

As a dynamic cluster of rules, calculative techniques, institutions, and voluntary agents, the market could appear a less elusive and more constant operating means for the articulation of the will of shifting aggregates than public opinion. By transferring the moral burden of conceiving and creating a whole from the shoulders of discrete public-regarding citizens to a self-regulating mechanism, by delegating questions of aggregate and individual interests and values to an ostensibly neutral institutional mechanism, the market's foundations in economic individualism and its supporting cluster of imaginaries and practices could often be presented as apolitical or even natural.

As a configuration at the very heart of the modern liberal democratic state, economic individualism, like the more civic individualism underlying the imaginaries of public opinion, was supported by important traditions of Enlightenment rationalism. Civic individualism tended to draw on an image of individual choices in matters of public, social, and political concern. In contrast, Adam Smith's imaginary of economic individualism as it was later interpreted by economists appeared compatible with forms of egotistic individualism whose effects were imagined to transmute into public goods by the invisible hand of an impersonal mechanism without the support of public-regarding orientations.

As Albert Hirschman has persuasively argued, the market, despite its individual self-centeredness and rational economic individualism, appeared to carry the promise of mitigating human conflicts by translating loaded, often violent individual passions into the rational language of calculable and negotiable interests. The latent political function of commerce and market exchange seemed able to increase social harmony.[39] This liberal imaginary was, of course, seriously challenged by Marxist criticism and the power with which it sought to denaturalize and repoliticize the imaginary of the market and its distributive effects by reframing it as a hidden form of class war.

The liberal democratic attraction of a mechanistic rather than a purposely moral-rational integration of parts into wholes went far beyond liberal economic imaginaries, as evinced by the deployment of machine metaphors in the legal-political discourse on modern constitutions.[40] Moreover, much of the strength and resilience of economic individualism in liberal democratic societies seems to have stemmed from the ostensible fact that the conception of the individual as a self-seeking egotist seemed to laymen more credible and more familiar than the idea of the public-regarding citizen.[41] Thus, while the imaginary of economic individualism could be successfully integrated into the sphere of commonsense realism, much of the strength of the imaginary of the public-oriented individual citizen, as well as its weakness, has come to increasingly derive from the sphere of commonsense idealism.

As a cardinal imaginary in the modern liberal democratic state, economic individualism was also greatly empowered by its extraordinary instrumentality for the state as an actor in the economic sphere. At the horizontal level of individual interactions, the presumed rationality of economic individuals could enhance mutual transparencies of transacting parties and increase their reciprocal predictability and trust in relations between citizens and the state, and possibly also between citizens and other nongovernmental hierarchical organizations. The assumed transparency of individual actors in the market was transformed into the state's presumption of the legibility of the values and preferences of the mass of its citizens.

The modern democratic state has developed extensive practices of employing experts, especially economists and pollsters, for the production of data that avowedly allow the government to discern and aggregate the "value preferences" of their citizens in order to buttress the rhetorical claim that its policies serve the public interest, understood in aggregate terms. While economic individualism could engage imaginaries of voluntary horizontal individual interactions that imply a mechanistic self-regulation and the minimalization of the intervention of the liberal state in socioeconomic contexts, it could, as the record shows, easily support an interventionist mode as well by exploiting the presumed transparency of the multitude of rational self-interested individuals

[39] Albert O. Hirschman, *The Passions and the Interests: Political Arguments for Capitalism Before its Triumph* (Princeton: Princeton University Press, 1997).

[40] See on this aspect Ezrahi's *Descent of Icarus*, pp. 128–66; 227–9 (on the shift to an interventionist liberal state). On the machine as a constitutional metaphor, see Michael Kammen, *A Machine that Would Go of Itself: The Constitution in American Culture* (New York: Alfred A. Knopf, 1986).

[41] Edward C. Banfield and Laura F. Banfield, *The Moral Basis of a Backward Society* (New York: The Free Press, 1967).

in a way that actually limits horizontal interaction while claiming to act on behalf of the public.

The imaginaries and practices of the market economy and its experts have fostered a viable political fiction of the democratic state as a neutral organization, an instrument directed by elected and appointed rulers ostensibly to serve an aggregate whole conjured by experts and politicians. While periodic elections, a free press, and frequent polls have invigorated the imaginary of such a democratic polity as consisting of a voluntary aggregate of free individuals, the modern democratic state could, under the cover of this fiction, simultaneously develop powerful hierarchical bureaucracies and engage in distributive and redistributive policies that resemble the conduct of nonaggregate corporate structures in some respects.[42]

From the viewpoint of democratic individualism, such developments could be attributed to the conversion of the discrete horizontal transparencies of voluntary, rational, and instrumentally oriented economic individuals into the presumed transparencies of their aggregates as patterned collective behavior rendered manifest to a government that is observing, acting, and presiding from above.

Since the flaws of this cluster of market macroeconomic imaginaries have been the subject of vast research and criticism from the perspective of liberal democratic theory, we need not enter this very rich discourse except to briefly note a few points of particular significance to our discussion. Obviously one such point is the association between the presumption that the value preferences of the mass of men are discernible to the government and the tendency to flatten individual interiority and thereby also to weaken the normative rationale of individual agency and autonomy.

In the modern liberal market state, impoverishment of the standard imaginary of the individual was facilitated by at least a partial segregation of the direct links of art, religion, morality, and more generally of culture to politics, and by a certain compartmentalization of the contexts and codes applicable to the links between democratic individuals' interiority and agency. Boosted by the market economy, the separation of the domain of politics from the domain of the cultural cultivation of the modern secular individual is particularly instructive in light of its contribution to the emergence of the unidimensional economic individual as a dominant category in neoliberal political discourse.

Antiliberal Marxist and communitarian critics have characteristically targeted this alienation from rich cultural individual inwardness as an expression of the aridity of liberalism, often dismissed as the political façade of crass, egotistic, bourgeois materialism. They never fail to highlight the often hidden relations between political power, the economy, and materialist bourgeois

---

[42] The dramatic fall of the financial markets in September 2008 was one of those rare moments when the fiction of a pure, unregulated market as the optimal condition for promoting the public welfare was sufficiently exposed to, at least temporarily, lose much of its power to guide behavior.

culture.[43] Those critics have in mind very different notions of possible and desirable convergences or compartmentalizations of individual and community, far removed from the liberal democratic empowerment of the individual as a civic agent. On the whole, then, the advantages associated with economic individualism with respect to aggregate groupings have appeared to exact a high price in terms of the ontology of individual interiority and the vigor of individual agency in the political sphere. Ironically, democratic norms of transparency have combined with the use of an economic framing of individual behavior to render citizens intelligible to each other as well as to the state, often without rendering the state more intelligible to its own citizens.

FICTIONS OF REPRESENTATION

Alongside dependence on democratic wholes such as public opinion and the voluntary interactive market system, the liberal democratic state has relied on the political imaginary of the parliament as representative of the citizens as a whole. The democratic political and constitutional tradition evolved the political imaginaries and institutional practices of representative bodies as an intermediate configuration between the individual agent and the whole, regarded as the inclusive incorporation or aggregate of all citizens. Elected representative bodies have depended on a complex cluster of fictions naturalized by means of the performative political imagination over many centuries. As a working democratic political fiction, representation has nevertheless been constantly disrupted by its own ambiguities and internal contradictions.[44]

Like other aspects of the formal or informal constitution, the origins of particular structures and mechanisms of representation set up during the formative postrevolutionary phase of the state could often be traced back to an amalgamation of prerevolutionary traditions, power configurations, contingent events, and arbitrary choices. The constitutionalization of a democratic regime aims at repressing or retrospectively legalizing the violence of its birth. New constitutions tend to mythologize the revolutionary violence against the old regime and redefine postrevolutionary uses of force by the state as constitutional.

This process is always facilitated by a functional collective amnesia and elaborate supportive mixtures of fictive and historical facts. On one hand, residues of violence and arbitrariness dormant in the foundations of a constitutional democracy endure like a frozen political volcano that threatens to erupt at any time. On the other hand, as I intimated earlier, unlike the other building

---

[43] See, for instance, Max Horkheimer and Theodor W. Adorno, *Dialectics of Enlightenment: Philosophical Fragments*, Gunzelin Schmid Noerr (ed.), Edmund Jephcott (trans.) (Stanford: Stanford University Press, 2002); see also sections in Michael Lowy, *Redemption and Utopia* (Stanford: Stanford University Press, 1992).

[44] See for instance Hanna Fenichel Pitkin's *The Concept of Representation* (Berkeley: University of California, 1967); Joseph Schumpeter's *Capitalism, Socialism and Democracy* (London: Allen & Unwin, 1976); Ruth W. Grant and Robert O. Keohane, "Accountability and Abuses of Power in World Politics" in *American Political Science Review*, vol. 99, no. 1 (Feb. 2005): 29–43.

blocks of the institutional structure erected by the constitution, the adequacy of representation remains a particularly contestable aspect of government.

The fragility of representative structures relates to four inherently underdetermined sociohistorical elements of representative systems: the elusive boundaries of the collective, or of the people, represented; the complexity and fluidity of the modern subject; the ambiguity of the identity of legitimate representatives; and the uncertainty about what constitutes representative actions.

I discussed the particular role played by social and natural sciences in generating the necessary facts that would render the fiction of representation credible enough to become workable. More specifically, social sciences such as statistics, anthropology, sociology, and political science have played a pivotal role first in rendering the people (that need to be represented) perceptible to governments by concretizing the imaginary of the people and providing scientifically and intellectually or ideologically authoritative definitions of its properties and boundaries. Political scientists and legal experts are employed in validating the neutrality and fairness of the procedures whereby representatives are elected, selected, and authorized, and expert authority is deployed in judging the performance of representatives qua representatives, distinguishing actions that appear merely empty theatrical gestures from those that are instrumentally appropriate to promote public goals.[45]

The persistent aura of an ideal of direct democracy has continually forced representatives to be on the defensive, especially against charges of acting in their own self-interest in defiance of public opinion. Political theorists and ideologues often sought to shield representative governments by defining the imagined alternative of a direct democracy as mob rule, evoking the destabilizing effects of volatile mass passions and potential popular violence. Madison and John Adams frequently referred to direct Athenian democracy as "turbulent democracy." Nevertheless, the persistence of public ambivalence toward representatives, often accentuated by corruption scandals, has reinforced the claims of public opinion to superior legitimacy as a semi-direct democratic practice. The technological option presented by the modern mass media of direct appeals by political candidates to mass audiences, skirting the traditional channels of political parties and legislatures, and new technologies that have facilitated extraparty and extraparliamentary horizontal citizens' communications and actions, have further diminished the status of representatives in many parliamentary democracies. The civic, although usually amorphous, whole of public opinion and the economic whole (composed of producers, consumers, and other players in the market system) could therefore often appear to complement or to weaken representative political bodies.

---

[45] For an illuminating discussion on the role of experts in rendering the population legible to the government, see James Scott, *Seeing Like a State: How Certain Schemes to Improve the Human Condition Have Failed* (New Haven, CT: Yale University Press, 1998); Ezrahi's *Descent of Icarus*; and Theodore M. Porter, *Trust in Numbers: The Pursuit of Objectivity in Science and Public Life* (Princeton: Princeton University Press, 1995).

Precisely because representativeness is a form of mediation that inevitably seems less authentic than direct participation, and because any given structure of representation can be disparaged in relation to the classical instance of direct democracy, some democracies, like the United States or Switzerland, enhance their resources of legitimation by combining several methods and units of election and representation such as the proportional, majoritarian, federal, regional, directly participatory, and others. In this context, public opinion, often supported by strikes, demonstrations, polls, the press, and the Internet, has functioned as a kind of weather vane, encouraging representatives to adjust their political course during the sometimes long periods between elections.

While the invisibility of public opinion has often encouraged skepticism regarding its very existence, the public could and did come into sight with sufficient frequency in crucial historical moments to sustain the imaginary of its constant presence. The revolutions in Eastern Europe during the closing decades of the twentieth century are a case in point. The 1989 Romanian revolution provides a particularly salient illustration, as do the Arab revolts of 2011. Barely a few days after national television aired pictures of President Nicolae Ceauşescu in full control, welcomed with applause by his supporters in the parliament, the cameras were redirected to the masses of protesting citizens in the streets who momentarily took over the government. Like an elusive sovereign, the public could function as a kind of elastic signifier, displaying great functional flexibility in acquiring and switching contents and references according to circumstances. In contrast to the public, representatives could not have shown such flexibility in radically switching positions without facing charges of opportunism, bribery, hypocrisy, and theatricality.

This brings us back to the problem of authenticity and theatricality in politics. When representatives attempt to simultaneously satisfy conflicting demands within their own constituency, they become vulnerable to charges of hypocrisy and theatricality. The elusiveness of public opinion as an agent, particularly when it is produced by polls, may sometimes prompt charges of manipulation and deception against pollsters, but not against the public. It does not make sense to attribute theatricality or hypocrisy to masses of protesting citizens, whereas theatricality has always appeared inherent in the very function of representation. Thomas Hobbes explicitly included the representative and the stage actor in the same general category. In *Leviathan* he distinguishes "natural persons" from "artificial persons." In the latter category he casts deputies, as well as actors in the theater.[46] Here the role of the representative can be continually evaluated in terms of often contradictory criteria or expectations, depending on the relative success whereby he or she appear to represent the public that authorized it.

But since the identity and the boundaries of represented individuals or groups are often contested and inherently underdetermined, the problem of an accurate, legitimate, or fully authorized representation remains unsolvable.

---

[46] Thomas Hobbes, *Leviathan*, Michael Oakeshott (ed.), (New York: Collier, 1962), pp. 217–19.

Thus the advantages of the physical embodiment and specificity of representatives as individuals and groups whose utterances and actions can be recorded and evaluated are often eclipsed by the disadvantages entailed in their vulnerability. Facing the dilemma of having to address conflicting groups of supporters, some political candidates or elected representatives have discovered the political efficacy of combining the rhetoric of emotional and moral appeal with programmatically ambiguous political speech that lends itself to conflicting interpretations. Again, the invisibility and indeterminacy of public opinion in modern democracies have often tended to enhance its flexibility and power in comparison with visible government.

Rulers can never be sure when the public is gazing at them because the referent of the public eye metaphor remains largely elusive. The possibility that the public eye might be open and watching at any moment, like the eye in Bentham's *Panopticon*, has been disturbing enough to induce continual anxiety and alertness on of the part of rulers and representatives. This may largely account for the preoccupation of democratic governments with attempts to project actual and virtual accountability through gestures of transparency, and for the fact that many of the tensions between the state and its citizens focus on issues of secrecy and publicity, concealment and disclosure.

A large part of the political game between governments and citizens in the modern democratic state could be described as the attempt of each party to pin down and decipher the other, to render it intelligible, transparent, and, therefore, more controllable, while concealing itself or remaining as elusive as possible.[47] In this struggle, each party has obvious advantages and weaknesses. Governments could typically employ a range of procedures from secret services, through censorship, to the more benign measures of laws, administrative classifications, collection of information about citizens by means such as the national census and similar procedures established by state health and tax authorities.

The public has the advantage of its own inherent elusiveness and unruliness, evinced in the inability of the government to predict which individuals or groups could suddenly assume the power of effective spokespersons on behalf of the public and under what circumstances they might do so. The public has also discovered the power of rumor to circumvent censorship, and the often devastating sway of muckraking pamphlets, underground and public mass media, Internet campaigns and influential bloggers.[48] As I indicated, the wave of antigovernment mass demonstrations that took global dimensions in 2011 has been a dramatic reminder of the potential of public opinion to unexpectedly materialize itself in the political arena and force governments to either adjust to public demands or collapse. But perhaps more significant, especially after the French Revolution, was the usually unmentioned but ubiquitous and occasionally demonstrated deterrent potential of popular mass violence and nonviolent resistance.

---

[47] See James Scott, *Seeing Like a State*.
[48] Darnton, *The Literary Underground of the Old Regime*.

A particularly revealing historical moment in the emergence of noncorporate, numerically perceived political agents such as public opinion and its potential to reconfigure itself as a nation, as a new powerful political agent, took place around the convocation of the Estates-General during the French revolution in 1787. That memorable event was associated with the readiness of the king to acknowledge that not all elements of sovereignty reside in the body of the monarch.[49] The king was compelled to respond to the increasing European trend of the eighteenth century to reframe political power in terms of public trust, viewing the monarch as a trustee of the people. This shift to the people as a source of authority continually forced the question of what constitutes the people, or how to imagine the people. In the French case, it was in the course of the deliberations of the Estates-General that the national body was "reconceptualized," to borrow Friedland's terms, or reimagined as consisting of individuals rather than orders (or Estates). Friedland adds:

For in a national body which has been broken down into individual wills, where each individual is the exact equivalent of another, regardless of what social class or geographical region the individual might belong to, the only corporate entity that has the right to exist is the political body that represents these individual wills.... Whereas under the old system constituencies were themselves regarded as corporate entities with a right to will, under the new system constituencies are individuals whose wills are inevitably regarded as inferior to the will of the whole.[50]

The political history of France, England, Germany, the United States of America, as well as of other modern democracies, has to a large extent revolved around politically shaping this new whole and its relations to the multitude of individuals who compose it or are represented by it. This process can also be described as a movement on our spectrum between the pole of strong corporate unity and the pole of atomistic (close to anarchic) individualism, an oscillation subject, in each state, to different tendencies and circumstances. The shift of political orders from corporate models to the irreducible primacy of natural individuals actually opened the way to the identification of the Third Estate with the nation. One of the clearest expressions of this shift in political imaginary is illustrated in the pamphlet of Rabaud Saint-Etienne, in which he insists:

[C]ut off, by supposition, the two hundred thousand people of the Church that might be in France, and you will have a nation. Cut off even the whole nobility, again by supposition, you still have the nation; because a thousand nobles can be created by tomorrow, as was done on the return from the crusades. But if you cut off the twenty-four million Frenchmen known by the name of the Third Estate, what would you have left? Some nobles and some people of the Church? But there wouldn't be any nation anymore. Therefore, it is evident that the Third Estate is ... the nation minus the nobility and the clergy.[51]

---

[49] Friedland, *Political Actors*, p. 91.
[50] Ibid., p. 123.
[51] Cited ibid., pp. 113–14.

This reimagining of the whole as a nation in the sense of numerical majority was gradually translated into a set of actions and rituals based on the principle of one vote per individual citizen, which facilitated the reframing of the Estates-General as the National Assembly and its reconstitution according to a new concept of representation.[52]

Once legitimation and authority were linked to numbers rather than social positions and qualities, it became possible to provide scientific verification of the reality of new noncorporate democratic agents. Because majorities rise and fall by counting votes, voting has become a dynamic device for begetting and switching to ever-new aggregates of the multitude, ever-new democratic agents, even when procedures of voting and counting votes have been flawed. Such changes have ensured the limited and often short-term life expectancy of any collective configuration, thus preserving the privileged reality of the natural individuals who periodically rearrange themselves as new political wholes and new representations.

It is significant that such ceaseless shifts have ensured that the majority, which at any given time has stood for one kind of a whole or for its representation, could generate legitimacy only for a limited period of time, following which another kind of majority and representation could balance it, thus creating a more dynamic, temporally responsive and open-ended imaginary of the political whole. In parliamentary democracies, the provisional status of any majority and therefore also of the elected representatives plays an important role in mitigating the legitimacy deficit of representation by the prospect of replacement and renewal.

The vision of participatory democratic politics, in which free individuals voluntarily associate for the promotion of both private and public goals, was largely inconsistent with an imagining of the individual as a mere egotistic hedonist or as a self-pursuing, unidimensional rationalist. Interactive economic individualism could function well with fairly impoverished notions of individual interiority. The presumed transparency of economic individuals facilitated the coordination of the voluntary horizontal interactions required by the market economy. But this contrived transparency and the reduction of the individual to an economic man have also enabled governments to assume that they could calculate the value preferences of their citizens. Reinforced by the scientific authority and the vocabulary of economics, the powerful ethos of modern capitalism has usurped and distorted the moral and cultural ideals of liberal democracy as a self-governing association of equals that secures freedom as a condition for human growth and self-fulfillment. John Dunn has noted this triumph of what he aptly calls "the order of egoism." He claims that "Democracy has altered its meaning ... because it passed ... to the political leaders of the order of egoism." Dunn observes further that "in embracing the term democracy so steadily and so purposefully, the political leaders of capitalism ... have

---

[52] Ibid., pp. 124–64.

recognized, and done their best to appropriate and tap, a deep reservoir of political power."[53]

From the viewpoint of democratic political theory and its imaginaries of citizenship, economic individualism and its deployment in politics have entailed thoroughly distorted forms of personhood. Economic individualism has marginalized or disregarded the multifariousness of individual inwardness and human dignity as necessary elements of a culture of freedom. Perhaps nothing can convey more clearly the dimension and significance of such loss than the replacement of the imaginaries of democratic individuals as citizens by imaginaries of individuals as consumers. This trend has been reinforced by the growing role of marketing techniques used in the mass media for selling political candidates like commodities, and by scientifically respectable social and political theories of citizens' behavior modeled on consumers' market choices.[54]

That is one of the reasons why the role of the arts – of literature, music, painting, and the theater – in generating and disseminating imaginaries of abundant individual inwardness has been compartmentalized in the private social sphere, thus diminishing the power of liberal democratic citizens to resist the arbitrary quasi-scientific aggregations and classifications imposed by government bureaucracies.[55]

A reconsideration, reconceptualization, and reintroduction of the crucial constitutive role of these cultural fields in the emergence of modern individualism would provide a basis for a critique of the dehumanizing, flattening, reductive effects of market individualism and for alternative revisionist theories that substantiate the practices of democratic individualism. Such a perspective could explicitly reconnect postmodern democratic individualism with the neglected cultural sources and resources of the democratization of individual uniqueness and its role in constraining standardized and mechanically aggregated holisms.

---

[53] John Dunn, *Democracy: A History* (New York: Atlantic Monthly Press, 2005), pp. 134, 160.

[54] For an early influential attempt to use economic models in explaining political behavior, see Anthony Downs, *An Economic Theory of Democracy* (New York: Harper, 1957).

[55] Don Handelman, *Nationalism and the Israeli State: Bureaucratic Logic in Public Events* (Oxford: Berg, 2004).

The Impact of Culture: The Cultivation of the Individual Interior in Literature, Painting, and Music

The assumption underlying this chapter is that there is a strong connection between the inner cultural development of the liberal democratic individual and his or her strength as a civic agent. The cultural cultivation of the internal self does not only contribute to the self-ontologization and the social ontologization of the individual's interior as a source of authority and judgment, but also enhances the individual's capacity to resist external social and political powers that relentlessly attempt to colonize his or her body and soul. Deeply individuated reflective individuals can better protect themselves against the restrictive bureaucratic logic of state and social classifications and thereby lend greater value to their choices as citizens in a participatory democracy.[1] At the same time, one cannot disregard the fact that some extreme kinds of cultural self-cultivation can actually erode civic individual agency and undermine horizontal social accountabilities.

Obviously, the scope and depth of the impact of culture on the evolution of modern individualism, and even on the subcategory of democratic individualism that concerns us here, is beyond the scope of this book. I therefore limit the following discussion to a few very select cultural developments that may illuminate ways whereby poetry, literature, and the arts have influenced such crucial aspects of democratic individualism as the ontologization of the individual's interiority and freedom, and what I refer to as the "democratization of uniqueness."

Since late modernity, the historical impact of culture on the social ontology of the individual's inwardness and its articulation in the civic context have failed to serve as a bulwark against the processes whereby the modern state, aided by the economic and statistical sciences, has been able to impoverish and ignore the modern citizen, rendering the individual an easy target of bureaucratic, ethnic, and legal classifications and their often manipulative enactment. These processes have been supported by a tendency to drain the law of moral content, subordinating legal and judicial decisions to considerations of utility,

---

[1] Don Handelman, *Nationalism and the Israeli State*.

efficiency, and costs and benefits. Roger Berkowitz notes that "with the reduction of the law to a mechanism of legitimate decision making and justice to fairness, we are – to a degree until recently impossible to conceive – in danger of dissolving law's once sacrosanct bond to the ethical activity of life."[2]

Certain strains of psychology, as a science, have evolved vocabularies of self and inwardness that have eclipsed authenticity, moral sensibility, and agency as key elements in balanced democratic individualism. Recovering the human reflexive imagination as a power in the creation of culturally empowered subjects and their moral environment is by no means a panacea to these adverse processes. It may, however, begin to equip the postmodern individual with the resources to resist what he or she increasingly recognizes or intuits as invasive arbitrary political power and overextended scientific or quasi-scientific authorities.

Retrieving the historical and cultural underpinnings of modern robust individualism is, of course, a complex, long, and perhaps not entirely attainable endeavor. Even as a strictly intellectual enterprise, the effects of the cultural forms and strains that have contributed to the evolution of the modern reflexive-reflective individual and his or her presence as an agent are uneven, often paradoxical, and contradictory. The attempt to reconstruct the historical processes that contributed to the formation of modern imaginaries of the individual's body, interior self, freedom, value, dignity, agency, and associability is fraught with great methodological and conceptual difficulties. These difficulties are further intensified by the fact that influential contemporary cultural trends have undermined cultural resources of earlier modern democratic individualism, particularly those relating to the integrity and uniqueness of the individual's inner self and agency. Mindful of these constraints and developments, I restrict myself in the following discussion to reflecting upon a few instructive examples of the early contributions of literature, theater, painting, and music to the fashioning of the modern imaginary of the self.

In many respects, however, the various fashionings of individual interiority in early modern culture already contained the subversive potential that has grown to unprecedented dimensions in the postmodern condition. While Hamlet's complexity, the rich and dynamic *psychomachia* of Doctor Faustus, or the internal dialogues of Don Quixote may have contributed to the psychocultural process of imagining or recognizing the interiority of natural individuals as real and therefore potentially resistant to invasive external wills and powers, these fictional characters represent vastly different models of relations between the reality of the inner self and its expression as an agent in the external domain of social and political action.

Similarly, the artist's projection of the inner self may reflect diverse, often politically contradictory, thematizations of the modern artist and the fictive persona as a paradigm of a creative public actor. Rubens, Rembrandt, Picasso,

---

[2] Roger Berkowitz, *The Gift of Science: Leibnitz and the Modern Legal Tradition* (Cambridge, MA: Harvard University Press, 2005), p. xiii.

Rivera, Marinetti, Beethoven, Brahms, and Richard Wagner all offer very different resources for narratives of the artist, as well as of his fictive persona as an agent, a model for the individual as a cultural-political actor-creator. The difficulty of isolating the links between such influences and the specific features of democratic individualism lies in the multitude of sociopolitical uses actually and potentially made of identical cultural materials, sometimes even within the same society, and in the shifting meanings and effects of cultural creations such as lyric poetry and self-portraiture over time.

Changes in the meaning and in the scope of such effects particularly concern us here, since they have a discernable impact on the popular political imagination when cultural effects are perceived as externalizations of types of individual or group agencies. The cumulative direct and indirect effect of Rembrandt's more than seventy self-portraits was apparently enormous, though perhaps negligible during his lifetime and immediately afterward.

As Vico understood it, the history of the imagination as a force in the shaping of society and politics is largely the history of the developments of, or the multiple variations on, a few basic themes of the imagination created in response to human passions, anxieties, and needs. Our focus on such cultural innovations as the early self-portraits of Albrecht Dürer or the love sonnets of Francesco Petrarch is rooted in the options and processes of individual self-reflection, as well as in the languages of externalizing the individual's interiority they created or developed.

What concerns us in this discussion is the vocabulary of imaginaries of selfhood created by cultural developments and the repertory of Foucault's "technologies of the self" made available by such innovations. While taking into account historical sequences, I do not attempt to advance an historical argument here, but rather to discern a few cultural products made available to the modern democratic political imagination in the course of centuries of cultural creativity.

Among those, one of the most important outcomes has been the ability to imagine the association of a specific individual body with a distinct invisible interiority, sometimes referred to as soul. Despite the well-known early contributions made by Hebrew, Greek, and Christian cultures to the idea of the individual soul, it took many centuries for western culture to evolve images of an earthly individual whose discrete utterances and actions emanate from an inner core.

This development entailed the weakening of imaginaries in which individual conduct and fate were attributed to predetermined destiny, inexplicable divine will, or overwhelming external forces.[3] Although in the poetry and arts of the early modern era the individuation of character as an earthly phenomenon was often linked to the individual's fate in the world to come, the particularization, psychologization, and historicization of fictional characters, particularly in poetry and painting, as well as their integration into the familiar realities of

---

[3] See, for example, Ruth Padel's *In and Out of the Mind: Greek Images of the Tragic Self* (Princeton: Princeton University Press, 1992).

the human body, human behavior, and social interaction, enabled poetry and art to increasingly influence the imaginaries of modern individualism in the sociopolitical context.

Erich Auerbach considers Dante's oeuvre a major turn in this direction. He associates the stress on man's awareness of his inherent sinfulness with an intensified individual sense of his "unique, inescapable personality."[4] The Christian practice of confession and the conception of individual life as a path of moral, spiritual progress or decline were vessels that could be filled by different, even secular, contents. The finite organic human body, its limited lifespan on this earth, alerts the mortal individual to his impending earthly demise and, therefore, to limits in fashioning a unified whole from the internal and often contingent external fabrics of existence.

In the course of time, such diverse materials as Augustine's *Confessions*, the Catholic practices of confession, retreat, and private meditations, as well as the idea of spiritual progress through faith and deeds, have generated secular equivalents that construe individual behavior as the expression of an inner self, with fate no longer considered the offspring of divine judgment but a reflection of the interaction between individual conduct, personality, and circumstances.

An important aspect of the Renaissance invention of imaginaries of human personality was the acknowledgment of the unbridgeable gap between the limits of human knowledge and the necessities of action within the contingent uncertain world in which the individual must live and conduct his or her life. For Augustine, God could grant ultimate coherence to human life. While the individual is unable to transcend the limits of his or her knowledge and perishable body, God knows how the "word" (to use Augustine's own allegory), which stands for each individual's life, fits in with the other words in the "sentence" of being, which stretches between mortal and eternal time. Whereas each word can know the words that preceded it, it cannot foresee the words that would follow. Only God can know the end of the sentence and, therefore, the full meaning of the individual's life.

Subsequent skeptical and secular versions of the self-discovery of the individual's limitations and uncertainties, such as Montaigne's "non-narrative self fashioning,"[5] engage selves unredeemable by an imagined transcendental knower or discernable whole. But even when wholes or unities were imagined outside the Christian religious tradition, they were of a vastly different kind. Auerbach observed that "[n]o poet or artist after Dante required an ultimate, eschatological destiny in order to perceive the unity of the human person: sheer intuitive power seems to have enabled subsequent writers to combine inner and outward observations into a whole."[6]

[4] Erich Auerbach, *Dante: Poet of the Secular World*, Ralph Manheim (trans.) (Chicago: University of Chicago Press, 1961), p. 14.
[5] Stephen Greenblatt, *Renaissance Self-Fashioning: From More to Shakespeare* (Chicago: University of Chicago Press, 1980), p. 252.
[6] Erich Auerbach, *Dante*, p. 177.

Combine they did, but the wholes they fashioned were forever unstable. In many ways, it has been precisely the fragility and perceived arbitrariness of secular imaginaries of the individual as a unity, or a part of a coherent collective or whole, that have later produced contrary results. On one hand is the national state, which strives to fixate and freeze a particular collective identity; on the other is the democratic state, which renders the sociopolitical whole unfixable while developing concepts of freedom that encompass the contingencies and uncertainties inherent in both individual and social existence.

Against the background of Protestant criticism of Catholic methods of self-scrutiny and moral examination, sixteenth-century literary and artistic explorations of individual inwardness acquired novel force. Stephen Greenblatt discerns "a powerful ideology of inwardness but few strained expressions of inwardness that may stand apart from the hated institutional structure. What we find then in the early sixteenth century is a crucial moment of passage from one mode of interiority to another."[7] He suggests that in the course of the century, writers fashioned fictional persons who posit themselves in opposition to hierarchy, Christianity, God, sanctified rites of kingship – persons who embody, in a challenging fashion, the ultimate other.[8] But it was probably in Shakespeare's plays, he suggests, that intricate and dynamic individual inwardness found its most convincing and lasting expression. Shakespeare, observes Greenblatt,

possessed a limitless talent for entering into the consciousness of another, perceiving its deepest structures as a manipulable fiction, reinscribing it into his own narrative form. If in the late plays, he experiments with controlled disruptions of narrative, moments of eddying and ecstasy, these invariably give way to reaffirmations of self-fashioning through story.[9]

Fashioning the self through stories made literature a cardinal means for shaping mass imaginaries that encompass the diversity, complexity, and dramatic temporal flow of the individual's inwardness and its externalizations. The performance of diverse dramatis personæ on the stage, the impersonation or embodiment of fictional characters in the theater, became a major occasion for contemplation of the inner self of others as well as for introspection. Approximately a century and a half later, the power of the theater to influence the moral and political imagination of citizens was sufficiently evident to convince an anxious Rousseau of the need to echo Plato's demand for censorship.

The theater displayed a special capacity for exploring and validating the links between a gamut of possible internal states and their manifestations in words, facial expressions, gestures, garments, or actions. Playwrights and actors were, in fact, perfecting, codifying, and diffusing a partly new vocabulary of externalizations of the individual's inwardness. The theater encouraged audiences to

---

[7] Greenblatt, *Renaissance Self-Fashioning*, p. 85.
[8] Ibid., p. 203.
[9] Ibid., p. 252.

continually entertain hypotheses about the meaning of the protagonists' words and gestures as reflecting their inner motives as well as more constant features of their character. The role of plot in making sense of discrete elements of the individual's phenomenology and conduct was vital also to the sustaining and channeling of human attention and judgments in art and politics.[10]

While theater contributed to the integration of individual utterances and gestures in codes or relatively stable formulas for reading individual internal states, it has also accentuated the dilemma of distinguishing sincere or authentic from hypocritical and theatrical behavior. Actors on the stage have demonstrated that such codes can be learned and used to project convincing images of character and personality detached from the individual's inner self.

For Rousseau, the greatest threat to the self lies in the individual's potential for witting or unwitting attachment to an alien social image of the self, which could lead to the loss of a sense of the genuine inner self in a maze of external reflections in the mirror of others' opinions. He was concerned about the powers of art to induce the individual to pursue dangerous and unrealizable fantasies, to evoke emotional and aesthetic identification with immoral characters, and to encourage the individual to adopt false self-images. He warned against the power of the theater to instruct citizens to engage in the kind of self-theatricalization that would obstruct the honest externalization of self in the social context.[11] Rousseau's concerns reflect, of course, his idealization of the civic virtues of the farmer in his conception of the ideal republican order, which he clearly preferred over the cultivated individual he associated with the political culture of Athens.

With the Renaissance's emphasis on human interiority, the search for ways to assess the reality of other persons, as well as of oneself, became a constant preoccupation in art and politics. Shakespearean characters, such as Hamlet and Othello, may be regarded as two studies in diametrically opposed models of the relations between interiority and action. Among the many interpretations of these characters, it is not implausible to choose, for our purposes, the not uncommon one that links Othello's reliance on external signs, on "ocular proof" as revealing the inner state of other characters (Desdemona's handkerchief as a sign of her betrayal), with his propensity to act rashly. Hamlet's deep recognition of the uncertainties inherent in extrapolating inner motives from external behavior or devising narratives of causality in human affairs (the inconclusive imputation of Claudius's guilt on the basis of his response to the dumb show of Hamlet's father's murder) is linked to his propensity to indecisiveness in action. By focusing on the limits of our ability to know other

---

[10] I discuss modern and postmodern theories of attention, its time frames, and political implications in Part Four.

[11] In "The Letter to M. d'Alembert on the Theatre" (1758), Rousseau expresses his concern that the citizen would learn from the actor "the art of counterfeiting himself, of putting on another character than his own, of appearing different than he is ... [a]nd of forgetting his own place by dint of taking another's." Cited in *Politics and the Arts*, Allan Bloom (trans.) (Ithaca: Cornell University Press, 1968), p. 79.

persons, these two tragedies problematized one of the principal requirements of democratic social epistemology, that is, horizontal interpersonal transparency and its role in relating conduct to interiority.[12]

Juxtaposed to the late modern imaginaries of economic man, imaginaries of individuals or persons created and diffused by the arts usually seem resistant to standardized transparency of the kind assumed by the former. The transparency of actors in the market, pursuing their self-interest, initially tended to appear attractive by virtue of seeming more objective and reliable in the context of social interaction. It certainly facilitated attempts to plan and coordinate agents to aggregate individual actions and choices into "market trends." But this has been achieved by a tacit commitment to a basically unidimensional theory of motives and action that omits the intricate web of desires, emotions, and relations so richly embodied, for instance, in the persona of Montaigne's essays, the characters of the plays of Marlowe and Shakespeare, and the protagonists of modern novels such as Dostoyevsky's Raskolnikov or Joyce's Stephen Dedalus. Surely a wider recognition of such profound and variegated individual interiorities could subvert the authority of any reductionist theory of motives and action and challenge any unidimensional bureaucratic classifications and aggregation of individuals into wholes.

The inner logic of artistic and literary works, the resistance to the kind of standardizations, repetitions, and predictability that result in aesthetic fatigue and boredom, undoubtedly enhance the tendency of the arts to embrace the richness, drama, and surprise inherent in the conduct of diverse and largely unpredictable personae.[13] By comparison to the standardized flatness and personal aridity of individuals imagined as one-dimensional materialistic egotists, generally the uniqueness of literary or theatrical personae projects more humane and culturally robust imaginaries of the individual, more compatible with the dignity, interiority, and freedom we need to attribute to democratic individuals as self-governing sovereigns.

Nevertheless, under conditions that tolerate hierarchies, hermetic, and exclusivist emotional group solidarity, high aristocratic and heroic individualism, such heterogeneous imaginaries of the individual could obviously be congruent with the critique of egalitarianism. No less problematic for voluntary liberal democratic associations and aggregates have been the aforementioned Montaignesque "non-narrative selves" (to use Greenblatt's terms) – skeptical,

---

[12] On issues of sincerity and authenticity in culture and politics, see for instance Lionel Trilling's *Sincerity and Authenticity* (Cambridge, MA: Harvard University Press, 1972); Yaron Ezrahi, "The Theatrics and Mechanics of Action: The Theatre and the Machine as Political Metaphors," *Social Research* vol. 62, no.2 (Summer 1995): 299–322; Geoffrey Hartman, *Scars of the Spirit: The Struggle Against Inauthenticity* (New York: Palgrave Macmillan, 2002); Judith N. Shklar, *Ordinary Vices* (Cambridge, MA: Harvard University Press, 1984). On the inner diversity of the modern subject see for instance Anthony J. Cascardi, *The Subject of Modernity* (Cambridge: Cambridge University Press, 1992).

[13] On the relation between aesthetic fatigue and repetitiousness without variation see George Kubler's *Building the Escorial* (Princeton: Princeton University Press, 1982).

ever-improvising individuals, both horizontally and vertically opaque. Such individuals, while elusive to the bureaucratic schemes of state authorities, are also limited in voluntarily generating and sustaining rules, institutions, and routines of a democratic political order, and may either encourage anarchic tendencies or become fertile ground for the emergence of charismatic illiberal leaders and group despotism.

To reiterate, the imaginary of liberal democratic individualism represents the attempt to imagine a midpoint between the pole of lively imagining and practicing of individual interiority, radically subjectivized beyond the conditions of predictability and associability, and the opposite pole of standardized imaginings of individuals who lend themselves to mechanical aggregation and bureaucratic classification unconstrained by rich and diverse inwardness, the dignity of the individual, and the self's authentic, unpredictable choices as a voluntary agent.

As we shall see in Part Four of this book, if in the modern liberal democratic state the imaginary of the economic-political man has generated an externalized individualism that marginalizes the multifaceted religious, humanistic, and cultural sources of a robust modern self, in the postmodern condition, the imbalance between the individual's inwardness as ground for civic agency and associability has been induced by powerful social and cultural forces that fragment individual interiority and disperse it in a series of discontinuous temporally shifting states.

Whereas in its radical forms the late modern individual has emerged in only limited social circles, the dissemination of its model, often in vulgar versions, clearly erodes the integrity of the modern individual as a transparent, largely predictable, political agent. In order to appreciate that which has apparently been lost to current postmodern liberal politics, we must first consider the benefits of the political imaginaries of early modern democratic individualism.

The rise of the modern individual as an agent necessitated the kinds of imaginaries that would enable the subject to be decipherable to itself and to others as the author of at least part of its own life story. But this required a substantial process of disembedding individuals from the hierarchies and holistic structures long perceived as the principal determinants of their behavior. This process included the dissemination of new imaginaries of the individual that would replace a tradition of imaginaries that anchored the subject as an immutable part in a divine cosmic order, chained to a preordained position by overwhelming external forces, hierarchically imposed duties, and an unchanging soul. It meant also that the individual generally could not extricate himself or herself from such shackles by magic or be delivered from catastrophe by fiat.

The decline of transcendent referents, which has accounted for reversals in the wheel of fortune, has invited novel referents that fashion an imaginary of the individual as an agent capable of psychic and social mobility, unaided by magic and supernatural forces. Ian Watt observes that, whereas early literary myths of the individual stressed its negative features and rendered its presence as a challenge to the established order, individualism, over time, acquired many different positive connotations. Watt adds that while the

> original versions of *Faust* (1587), *Don Quixote* (1605), and *Don Juan* (ca. 1620) presented unflattering portrayals of the three ... the Romantic period two centuries later re-created them as admirable and even heroic. Also *Robinson Crusoe* (1719) is seen as representative of the new religious, economic and social attitudes. All four myths have been transformed, often by major writers (Rousseau, Goethe, Byron, Dostoyevsky), and given a more universal application with a favorable view of individualism.[14]

In Goethe's *Faust*, Watt maintains, we see none of the fascination with magic he finds in Marlowe's *Doctor Faustus*.[15]

The rise of the novel as a major modern literary genre with appeal to a mass readership during the eighteenth century has been particularly significant for the generation and spread of modern imaginaries of individualism. In one of the early studies of the novel, Watt notes the close affinities between the endeavor to "concretize" the fictive characters in the novel as unique individuals and the attempt to place them within realistically familiar settings: "The novel," he argues, "is surely distinguished from other genres and from previous forms of fiction by the amount of attention it habitually accords both to the individualization of its characters and to the detailed presentation of their environment."[16]

These values were upheld by a rich variety of new or renewed literary means such as the use of proper names, the particularization of space and time, a visible "causal connection operating through time" that replaced, according to Watt, "the reliance of earlier narratives on disguises and coincidences," the uses of the literary equivalent of the cinematic close-up in the representation of reality, attention to the detailed features of objects, a far more extensive designative or referential use of language, and the attempt to provide readers with a more intense sense of the physical and emotional immediacy of the characters.[17] Watt correctly assesses these developments as reflecting a larger shift from "the unified world picture of the Middle Ages [to] another very different one which presents us, essentially, with a developing but unplanned aggregate of particular individuals having particular experiences at particular times and at particular places."[18]

---

[14] Ian Watt, *Myths of Modern Individualism: Faust, Don Quixote, Don Juan, Robinson Crusoe* (Cambridge: Cambridge University Press, 1997), p. III.

[15] Ibid., p. 196.

[16] Ian Watt, *The Rise of the Novel: Studies in Defoe, Richardson and Fielding* (Harmondsworth: Penguin, 1957; reprinted by Peregrine, 1981), p. 19; on the development of detailed depiction of domestic environments in painting see the studies of Svetlana Alpers, *The Art of Describing: Dutch Art in the Seventeenth Century* (Chicago: University of Chicago Press, 1983) and Norman Bryson, *Looking at the Overlooked: Four Essays on Still Life Painting* (Cambridge, MA: Harvard University Press, 1990).

[17] Watt, *The Rise of the Novel*, pp. 19, 23–4, 27, 32–4.

[18] Ibid., p. 34.

The novel has generated and disseminated a rich range of personae; such a multiplicity of personal narratives of character in action could serve as a continual object lesson for a curious public. Watt observes that, in contrast to the epic protagonists of earlier literary genres – the type of individuals Vico located in the social phase defined by him as the "age of heroes," in which individual character and fate were an allegory for a life mostly controlled by external forces – the character in the novel has increasingly evolved as an internally robust and partly autonomous agent driven largely by complex interactions between inner motives and external circumstances and operating in convincingly familiar or conceivable settings. Watts considers the works of Defoe as "the supreme illustration in the novel of the connection between the democratic individualism of Puritanism and the objective representation of the world of everyday reality and all those who inhabit it." [19]

A fact of special significance for our discussion is that these developments in literary culture have, by and large, been paralleled by the development of modern journalism. In the case of journalism, the credibility of reports also depends on verisimilitude in the description of characters and settings and in the construction and deployment of narratives about individuals and their interactions. Journalists, like writers of fiction, discovered that realism or *vraisemblance* in the depiction of characters, their interactions, and particularly their conflicts, not only generates credibility but also arrests the attention of the readers.

While the novel enhanced confidence in the potential horizontal transparency of robust individuals, in the existence of clues to the correct reading of characters deduced from their external behavior, journalism has evolved and disseminated similar codes of description within manifestly documentary and often more unidimensional frames. Their combined impact on the rise of democratic individualism as a political imaginary cannot be overestimated.

While generally perceived as belonging to the opposed realms of fiction and reality, literature and journalism have actually complemented each other in integrating imaginaries of individuals as agents and their interactions – as causally or virtually observable facts – within modern commonsense realism, the perceptual-interpretive field of democratic politics. While fiction resorts to a wide range of strategies to create reality effects that lead to a suspension of disbelief and to an experience of illusory characters as real, journalism cannot rest its credibility on a mere claim that reporters are impartial observers describing agents and events. Also journalism as mediating between reality and the public has to employ rhetorical and literary techniques of inducing reality effects.

Not surprising, the effective employment of the documentary genre in modern novels and the appropriation of such literary techniques in journalistic writing – most instructively illustrated in Daniel Defoe's (1660–1731) double career and experience as journalist and author – reveal the extent to which methods of rendering the description of characters and events credible to mod-

---

[19] Watt, *The Rise of the Novel*, pp. 88–9.

ern publics could migrate between literature and journalism, despite attempts to confine them within opposed frames of fiction and fact.

In modern societies, then, linguistic, rhetorical, aesthetic, and epistemological realism converged at least partly in the fields of literature, painting, theater, cinema, journalism, and politics.[20] Drawing on traditions of Christian imaginaries of human inwardness as an unfolding narrative of a continual internal dialogue and moral struggle, literature and journalism discovered the spell they could exercise on their readers when they succeeded in persuasively relating accounts of their fictive or real characters' inner motives and external behavior.

Literature and journalism democratized the drama of human interaction, of conflicts of conscience, honor, self-interest, and power well beyond the narrow circles of the royal courts dramatized by Marlowe and Shakespeare. This fact constituted a very significant contribution to the rise of democratic politics as an ongoing, discernable public spectacle. No less than monarchic politics, modern mass democratic politics has also displayed, from its early days, many features in common with the performing arts. But if Inigo Jones could produce and largely control the circumscribed spectacles of the monarchic state for the Stuart kings, democratic political spectacles, as ongoing dramas, have usually involved too many agents, actors, producers, supporting casts, image makers, and mass media to be effectively centralized.

The point I wish to emphasize here is that the leveling of politics in democratic societies required the development of reasonable public confidence in the capacity of democratic citizens and governors to publicly project themselves as agents, as well as to interpret and partly, at least, anticipate each other's conduct. It called for a culture of *presumed* horizontal transparency that could achieve a reasonable balance between individual freedom, interiority, agency, accountability, and associability-related transparency.

In journalism and literature, and, for that matter, in art in general, realism has often manifested its power to instigate readers to take matters seriously enough to form an emotional or a moral stance. Rousseau discerned in his time the power of the illusion of reality in the theater both to exhaust the moral energies of an audience driven toward moral and emotional responses to fictive personae and situations on the stage, and to encourage the public's empathy for immoral characters whom they have temporarily experienced as real. He definitely anticipated the experience of contemporary spectators of virtual reality on television who often respond to the fictive as if it were real. Precisely because readers and spectators' disbelief has always, albeit in different ways, threatened to unmask the workings of literature, journalism, and politics, all three have taken great pains to generate trust in their projections or representations of reality.

---

[20] See for instance Linda Nochlin, *Realism: Style and Civilization* (New York: Penguin, 1976); Carl Dahlhaus, *Realism in Nineteenth-Century Music*, Mary Whittall (trans.) (Cambridge: Cambridge University Press, 1985); Pam Morris, *Realism: The New Critical Idiom* (London: Routledge, 2003).

The achievements and innovations developed by each for the sake of reality effects have become readily available for use and adaptation by the others. All this has aided the culture of democratic individualism in relating the reality and discernability of the individual to his or her ordinary life settings, thus welding interiority, agency, and associability. The integrity of the individual as the elementary democratic agent can thus be upheld, though not always successfully, in the context of multiple interpersonal and institutional interactions and political causalities.

If influence is a criterion for choosing where to look, it is hard to conceive of an author who could equal Jean-Jacques Rousseau in the scope, diversity, and persistence of his impact on modern imaginaries of the individual and on framing the dilemma of the individual in relation to society. In a series of texts, including his *First Discourse (On the Arts and Sciences)* and his *Second Discourse (On the Origin of Inequality)*; his main political theoretical treatise, *The Social Contract*; his book on education, *Émile*; his literary works, *Julie* and *the New Heloise* and his many other compositions, Rousseau articulated and contextualized some of the central themes of modern cultural, literary, educational, and political discourses on, and practices of, individualism.

Rousseau's impact on the development of the western democratic political imagination stems also from the mass circulation of his literary and political oeuvre and his influence on the thought and rhetoric of cultural and political revolutionary and, at times, also conservative movements. Rousseau had a particular appreciation for the role of reading in the development of the imaginary of one's self as well as that of other individuals. In his *Confessions*, he attributes to his early devotion to reading a crucial influence on the evolution of his self-consciousness. Aware of the sway of literature and the arts, particularly the theater, in shaping the individual imagination, Rousseau, like Hobbes and Plato, thought that persons, especially when young, should not be exposed to cultural experiences of the kind that would encourage them to pursue fantastic passions and visions, but only to those that would enhance their capacity to function as citizens.

However, unlike Plato or Hobbes, Rousseau's concept of the individual, as it emerges in his essays on culture, education, and politics, engages and ontologizes a deeper sense of individual emotions, self-reflection, and, therefore, freedom. In order to encourage introspection, Rousseau often devised ways to allow the individual to imagine himself or herself outside the social context. No wonder that in *Emile*, for instance, he recommends *Robinson Crusoe* as particularly appropriate reading for the cultivation of self-reliance in the young.

Although I shall not attempt now to assess the entire range of Rousseau's contributions to modern imaginaries of democratic individualism, I would like to briefly dwell on his arguably most important and most problematic one – the emotional self. In the opening sentences of the *Confessions*, Rousseau famously writes:

I have resolved on an enterprise which has no precedent, and which, once complete, will have no imitator. My purpose is to display to my kind a portrait in every way true to nature, and the man I shall portray will be I. Simply I. I know my own heart and understand my fellow man. But I am made unlike any one I have ever met; I will even venture to say that I am like no one in the whole world. I may be no better, but at least I am different.[21]

By insisting that autobiography, the history of the self, is first and foremost the history of an individual's "heart," of the self's inner emotional life, Rousseau made a powerful attempt to ontologize each individual as distinct from all others and from society, and to problematize individual associability as a partner in political or, for that matter, any human, association. This move toward the authentication of subjectivity has been associated with a number of crucial wider cultural shifts. These include the dawning appeal of new literary and poetical genres consisting of journeys into the depth of the self (in contradistinction to epic genres, which center on heroes and communities); the related fascination with details of family, intimate, and private worlds; the associated cultural expressions of the erotic imagination; the preoccupation with the struggles between the emotional and the rational self; and the representations of the individual's psychological and relational mobility within the diverse contexts of romantic relations, family, work, public spaces, and politics. In other words, Rousseau was both a major trigger and an exemplification of a broadly based sociocultural process whose most radical effect was probably the democratization of individual uniqueness – the dissemination of an imaginary of every common individual as a unique configuration of life history, body, emotions, thoughts, dreams, and relations later developed by Freud.

Rousseau's focus on the emotional inwardness of the individual, while reinforcing the self's ontological status in relation to society, is associated with other often illiberal trends that reflect a waning of trust in the sufficiency of the Enlightenment notion of reason as a means to secure voluntary political association. While reason, in both its utilitarian-economic and competing Kantian moral versions, seemed a relatively safe bond of individuals capable of voluntary rational compliance, emotional solidarity seemed less suitable for keeping the balance between individual integrity and associability. More volatile and, therefore, politically unstable – less instrumental than reason in cultivating and protecting a moderate, irenic and controlled political temper in public affairs – emotions and emotional solidarity implied another kind of democratic polity incompatible with the delicate balance of liberal democratic individualism.[22]

---

[21] Jean-Jacques Rousseau, *The Confessions*, J. M. Cohen (trans.) (Harmondsworth: Penguin 1975), p. 17. For an extensive discussion of Rousseau's individualism, see Jean Starobinsky, *Jean-Jacques Rousseau: Transparency and Obstruction*, Arthur Goldhammer (trans.) (Chicago: University of Chicago Press, 1971).

[22] On interests and economic rationality as a means of constraining passions, see Albert O. Hirschman, *The Passions and the Interests: Political Arguments for Capitalism before its Triumph* (Princeton: Princeton University Press, 1997).

By universalizing the emotive dimension as a key to the personal (beyond its narrow stereotypical attribution to the female gender that, as such, was long excluded from politics), Rousseau endorsed an opening of the political realm to the engagement of emotions. Not surprisingly, in addition to the enhancement of the wealth and authenticity of the self's inwardness, Rousseau's powerful imaginary of the individual as an emotional entity has paradoxically facilitated the emergence of political forms based on convergence of democratization with national-emotional solidarities, democratic freedoms attached to collectives rather than to individuals, and the development of political configurations based on forms of affective group attachments that potentially and actually swallow individual uniqueness.

As the high priest of the modern emotional self, Rousseau is rightly regarded as pivotal to democratic and nondemocratic, often nationalistic, movements. His greatness as a political thinker resided in his ability to encompass the irresolvable conflict between a radical sense of selfhood and democratic individualism, between the emotional self and the public-regarding citizen. Rousseau's own resistance to glossing over the tensions between individual integrity and social solidarity or between individual freedom and the reality of the nation as a whole are revealed in his attempt to harness reason to the powers of the general will. His struggle with this dilemma memorably unfolded in his critique of the theatricality of the social self and his preoccupation with the problem of individual sincerity.

This tension between the integrity of the emotional self and the associability of the more transparent rational self was bound to persistently problematize liberal and democratic critiques of modern nationalism and socialism.[23] Liberal democratic suspicions of the introduction of emotional solidarities into politics were also bound to seriously weaken the power of liberal democratic political imaginaries of the individual and of the polity as an aggregate of individuals to compete with the effective appeal of these and other modern collectivist movements.[24]

While the externalization of subjectivities persisted and developed as a major preoccupation in literature and the arts, its performance and manifestation in politics has been far more ambiguous, since it has often encouraged political actors to engage in the theatrical projections of their inwardness and private lives as a major political strategy of self-legitimation. I shall later address aspects of this development and its implications for the mass media environment of contemporary democracies.

---

[23] During the French Revolution, Abbé Sièyes, inspired by Rousseau's concept of the general will, projected an imaginary of the nation, defined by Keith Baker as "a unitary body of citizens exercising an inalienable common will." In this discourse, "the nation was the ultimate political reality upon whose identity and will all else depended" (Baker, *Inventing the French Revolution*, pp. 246–7).

[24] Nietzsche and Foucault have elaborated further on this theme, expressing a basic skepticism as to the possibility of achieving a balance between authentic individuals and a democratic regime.

Rousseau's claim (at the beginning of the *Confessions*) that in writing his own story he is unfolding the narrative of a unique individual, unlike anyone else in the world, has become paradigmatic of modern autobiographies. Eventually, this postulation was universalized as a drift toward what I have called the democratization of uniqueness. I return to this development to advance the point that whereas on one hand the democratization of uniqueness could be costly to the practice of the liberal democratic value of horizontal communications or coordination, on the other it could support the liberal commitment to the sacredness of individual life and the critique of any unnecessary domestic and external use of life-threatening force.

It is hard, of course, to exaggerate the symbolic import of the genre of (especially confessional) autobiography in advancing the values and practices of reflexivity, self-examination, and self-knowledge in the evolution of the modern liberal democratic culture of individualism. At the same time, of course, autobiographies were often abused by apologetics and deliberate misrepresentations. Nevertheless, probing critical eyes could sometimes obtain insights into an author's interior behind such screens. The important thing is that both literary professionals and laymen became increasingly fascinated with and engaged by the possibility of making human interiors transparent.

In the plastic arts, self-portraiture constitutes a correspondingly significant enterprise. Like the autobiographer, the self-portraitist has privileged access to the interiority of his object, although the language and techniques of self-description are clearly different. The creation of the painter's self-image may not involve a conscious endeavor to represent inwardness. But when it does, the painter may be regarded as akin or analogous to any human actor in the search for true or verisimilar visual, facial, and gestural externalizations of his inner state. An actor usually impersonates a real or fictive persona, external to his or her own. But in order to be persuasive, the actor needs to use or invent a gestural language of externalization that can convey inner states of a character situated in a particular cultural context of conventions, practices, and expectations.

Without entering the debate of how, if at all, authentic self-representations can be distinguished from inauthentic ones, for Hobbes every "natural person" actually "acts" himself, not another, through his words and actions.[25] In the political universe constructed by Hobbes, writers, artists, and laymen, although they "act themselves" in different ways, substantiate the ontology and epistemology of democratic individualism. The ability of the autobiographer and the self-portraitist to link an insider's and an outsider's internal and external perspective on the self is one of the main keys to the invention and social diffusion of visual and lingual vocabularies of individual interiority.

Supported by the development of the experiences and vocabularies of introspection and compassion, this convergence of the outsider (social) with the interior (subjective) gaze has created the possibility of social

[25] Hobbes, *Leviathan*, chapter XVI.

phenomenological materialization of subjectivities and their role in the generation and degeneration of interpersonal trust. The modern preoccupation with the problems of hypocrisy, sincerity, and authenticity relates, indeed, to this development.[26]

Rendering internal states visible is a further paradox of self-portraiture. This paradox entails the regression *ad infinitum* of a subject entangled in the process of depicting himself as a subject depicting himself as a subject.[27] Acts of self-imaging, of artists painting or sculpting their own image and signing their works, are undoubtedly as old as art itself. It is said that Phidias, the Greek sculptor, created a small self-portrait, signed in 438 B.C.E. More important to our concern is, of course, the emergence of a tradition of self-portraiture, which could be considered a significant factor in the rise of modern individualism. Despite reservations, many cultural and art historians regard Albrecht Dürer's sketch of 1491 as a particularly significant "moment of self portraiture." It is described by Joseph Leo Koerner as

the first modern self-portrait, because for the first time the artist seems to depict not only his physical appearance, but his unique inner self.... This artist not only dated and monogrammed this work but also included a lengthy inscription that cites his own age and full name and attests unequivocally to the panel's status as self-portrait.[28]

The repeated attempts to interpret the details of the face and the gesture depicted in this image – the eyes, the hair, and the hand held against the head – as signs of inner states such as melancholy reflect Dürer's contribution to a culturally and politically profoundly consequential discourse on the reading of human images. About a century later, Rembrandt's creation of over seventy self-portraits, spanning most of his life history, constituted another important phase in this tradition. As Victor Stoichita observes,

[T]he self-portrait recounts nothing; it only describes the state of the authorial self. But it can a-posteriori become a person's "history." This is in fact what Rembrandt did ... the corpus of his self-portraits becomes, in the last instance, an autobiographical account. The programmatic apprehension inherent in the series of self-portraits he painted allows us to reconstruct the artist's life.[29]

The discourse on Rembrandt's self-portraits provides further illustration of the relentless attempts made to fixate, even codify, external pictorial details as signs of inner states. Here the signs of melancholy have become more specific and are richly contextualized. The device of shading the eyes is associated with extreme introspection, meditation on death, self-absorption, and projections

---

[26] Shklar, *Ordinary Vices*; Trilling, *Sincerity and Authenticity*; Hartman, *Scars of the Spirit*.
[27] For an illuminating discussion on the double purpose of self-projection and the mirroring of the act of self-painting, see Victor Stoichita, *The Self-Aware Image: An Insight into Early Modern Meta-Painting* (Cambridge: Cambridge University Press, 1997).
[28] Joseph Leo Koerner, *The Moment of Self-Portraiture in German Renaissance Art* (Chicago: University of Chicago Press, 1993), p. 37.
[29] Stoichita, *The Self-Aware Image*, p. 227.

of the artist's temper.[30] Modern painters such as Picasso, Chagall, Cézanne, Van Gogh, Frida Kahlo, and Jackson Pollock continued to expand the plastic languages of self-externalization and self-expression to cover a huge spectrum of genres, including realism, abstract expressionism, and postmodern realism, often challenging conventions of stylization and juxtaposing the realism of disordered and fragmented lives with the aesthetics of harmony, coherence, and the beautiful.

In retrospect, it becomes evident that self-referential works of art or literature such as autobiography and self-portraiture are only the most obvious genres of reflexive self-projection. Far more pervasive, often deeper and subtler, expressions of human inwardness are actually discernable in all works of art and literature, not excluding those genres of literature, painting, and documentary film that explicitly deny and attempt to obliterate the creator's presence. In this sense, Albrecht Dürer's signature on his work, the AD monogram, even more than the depiction of his own image, represents an important moment in the personalization of the relation of any work of art to the artist. As art historians have repeatedly argued, the signature pointed to the work of art as in itself embodying a particular artist by means of his act of artistic creation, as the reification of an object whose main value lies in the creative imagination and skills of an individual artist rather than in the value of the person or the object depicted or of the materials used for the work. Referring to Dürer's famous self-portrait, dated 1500, in which Dürer fashioned his image after the iconography of Christ, Joseph Koerner argues the painting

is a statement less about Dürer's person than about his art. It proclaims that art and artist are consubstantial; that the value and the meaning of an image derives from its being by someone; that the artist paints, as Dürer himself writes to 'make himself seen in his works"; and that every signed picture is in some sense a self-portrait.[31]

In the evolution of self-realizing imaginaries of the individual, music, like literature and painting, has played an important role. In our western culture, the fact that the individual voice bursts out from within the body endows it with a special power to authenticate the voice as the expression of interiority.[32] As a mark of individual identity and presence, the human voice is often more reliably representative against the silent background of the night than the individual's

[30] H. Perry Chapman, *Rembrandt's Self-Portraits: A Study in Seventeenth-Century Identity* (Princeton: Princeton University Press, 1990), pp. 25–31.

[31] Koerner, *The Moment of Self-Portraiture in German Renaissance Art*, p. XVIII.

[32] In writing this section on the music of individualism I greatly benefited from my collaboration with Ruth HaCohen, which includes our joint book *The Voices of the Individual and the Voice of the Many: Interactions between Music and Politics in Western Culture* (in Hebrew: forthcoming). See also HaCohen's discussion of *The Merchant of Venice* in her "Between Noise and Harmony: The Oratorical Moment in the Musical Entanglements of Jews and Christians," *Critical Inquiry* vol. 32, no. 2 (Winter 2006): 251–6; and her "The Music of Sympathy in the Arts of the Baroque Or the Use of Difference to Overcome Indifference," *Poetics Today* vol. 22, no. 3 (Fall 2001): 607–50.

physical figure or visual image.[33] As a vehicle for expression, its pitch, intensity, timbre, duration, movement, texture, and gestural articulation were gradually orchestrated to convey feelings, passions, and moods with immediacy usually beyond the power of words or static sculptures and paintings.

Perhaps more than any other externalization of the individual, the human voice is a continuous performative of the individual's identity, presence, and message. In both modern Hebrew and German, to cast a vote is "to give one's voice" to a party or a candidate.[34] Such usage reflects a commonsense association of voice and the state of individual inwardness. Composers and musicians have explored this link, especially since the discovery of the unique powers of music to convey the temporal flow, movements, and fluctuations of emotions and moods at the turn of the seventeenth century.

Reinhard Strohm observes that, whereas "in the philosophy of Renaissance humanism, poetic and musical inspiration in song and dance could be a physical or metaphysical process of divine origin … [it] could become an individual performative act with its own solidity."[35] Subsequently the aria, for instance, as an elaborate musical monologue in dramatic musical works, was appropriated as a vehicle for the personalized expressions of emotions, reflections, and personae. Strohm explains:

On a simple theatrical level … we perceive the feelings or thoughts expressed in the aria as belonging to the singing character, in that dramatic context…. As the use of arias in opera became ubiquitous, singing came to be accepted as a natural form of self-expression in the theater … the passions, and to a lesser extent the reasons, expressed by the characters became the legitimation of the arias and the building-blocks of drama.[36]

Following and parallel to the development of the aria as self-expression in the opera, popular singers are marked and personalized by their association with particular songs serving as their vocal signature, a particularized embodiment of personality in music. Most significantly, in both the cultural contexts of the opera and the theater, and later also of popular music, songs emerged as a principal vehicle for the vocalization and representation of the woman as an individual in modern culture.

The genealogy of the emergence of the individual is also illuminating in the realm of music. The history of music and music theory provide particularly important insights into the modern shift toward the ontologization and "animation" of the individual in art and politics and, therefore, also into the exacerbation of the perennial dilemma concerning the relation between the

---

[33] Figaro, in an evening scene with many in disguise, discerns his new wife Susanna's real voice and identity in Mozart's *The Marriage of Figaro*, which she had tried in vain to hide through vocal masking.

[34] In Hebrew, the translation of the expression "the individual gives his or her voice" is "*habocher noten et kolo*," and in German, "*eine Stimme abgeben*."

[35] Reinhard Strohm, "Aria and Recitative from the Beginnings to the Nineteenth Century," in J. J. Nattiez (ed.), *Enciclopedia della Musica*, vol. 4 (Turin: Einaudi, 2004), pp. 416–29.

[36] Ibid.

individual's inwardness to his or her associability. To frame this in musical terms, the issue was how to relate the different voices of individuals to the voice of the group.

The modern emancipation of the voice of the individual in music has been associated with the transformation of music, imagined earlier as an artistic embodiment of the cosmic divine order, into an art of expressive composition, especially since the late sixteenth century. Katz and HaCohen observe: "As a representation or exemplification, music before 1600, philosophically speaking, related primarily to ideal structures – 'numerical proportions' – rather than to expressive and dramatic contents."[37] In order to appreciate the dimensions of this shift and its wider implications, it is useful to recall the meanings and uses of probably the most ancient and persistent aesthetic principle in western music and culture – the principle of harmony. Leo Spitzer notes:

[I]n spite of the fact that the simile world harmony-musical harmony was derived (historically speaking) from a human instrument, the Pythagoreans inverted the order by admitting that the human lute (as imagined in the hands of the god Apollo) was an imitation of the music of the stars; human activities had to be patterned on godly activities, i.e., on processes in nature.[38]

Musical harmony was conceived by the ancients as a profound expression of the principles of the cosmic order, as well as the objective structure of the human soul. As such, the imaginary of harmony became an appealing religious and political resource deployed in medieval and, in modified forms, in modern religious and political rituals, rhetoric, and practices. The medieval Milan community sang Ambrosian hymns as a way, in Spitzer's words, to "perform" world harmony, signifying the unity of man and nature. "Music in the Middle Ages," he observes, "was intended not as an appeal to man's subjective irrationality but as an objective reminder of laws ultimately inaccessible to the human mind."[39]

Once this imaginary of a cosmic musical system and its association with the given divine order had been established, it could lend the aesthetics of harmony, as a principle in western art and particularly music, the powers of a constitutive metaphor in the spheres of society and politics as well. As an explicit model of inclusion and unification, as well as an instrument of tacit exclusion, harmony had special potential for drawing cultural-political boundaries. When the pre-Socratic Pythagorean imaginary of harmony as an immanent cosmic principle migrated into the human context, this ancient frame encouraged the naturalization of imagined social and political wholes into which only some individuals or groups coherently fit as parts. Whereas such harmonizations

---

[37] Ruth Katz and Ruth HaCohen, *Tuning The Mind: Connecting Aesthetics to Cognitive Science* (New Brunswick, NJ: Transaction Publishers, 2003), p. 86.

[38] Leo Spitzer, *Classical and Christian Ideas of World Harmony: Prolegomena to the Interpretation of the Word "Stimmung,"*, A. G. Hatcher (ed.), (Baltimore: The Johns Hopkins Press, 1963), pp. 8–9.

[39] Ibid., pp. 24–5, 36.

could function coercively as a means of selective integration and rejection of human beings, modern culture generated powerful formulas for evolving musical forms and sociopolitical imaginaries of harmony that drew on a greater balance between the integrity of individual interiority and associability, diversity and inclusiveness, the singular voices of individuals and the collective voice of the group.[40]

Still, once deployed in the contexts of society and politics, the imaginary of harmony functioned primarily as a means to aestheticize and sacralize order and obedience rather than promote uniqueness and autonomy. Spitzer sees this "union of hearts and minds reflected in the Middle Ages as relatively non-individualistic attitudes which reveal only one direction of thought, a subordination to the meaning of the Whole." In his discussion of Shakespeare, he reiterates the view that music was seen as "a union, a family of sounds: 'each in each,' 'all in one,' 'many seeming one,' and *a single note is no music, a single man no man*" (my emphasis).[41]

Clearly, in order for the individual voice to be emancipated, it had to be disembedded from the music of the spheres and from a conception of harmony as *mimetic* of the cosmic order. The new understanding of music as a human composition, no longer a natural given to be discovered but a human artifact, facilitated such a process of disembedding.[42] This apprehension originated, by and large, with the music of composers such as Monteverdi at the beginning of the seventeenth century. "The purpose of music," argue Katz and HaCohen, "was now to move human affections, and composers everywhere enlisted their creative powers towards the realization of this professed purpose."[43] Once music was liberated from the chains of the cosmological order when the physicalization of astronomy undermined the grip of the ancient myth of the harmony of the spheres, it began to be understood as an art of human expression and communication. It could then join the other arts in shaping modern individualism and societies.

As a uniquely nonverbal and nonfigurative language, music had an important advantage over all other artistic media in its power to convey the nontextual and abstract. Paradoxically, music – the most abstract and spiritual of arts – both hypostatizes and sensualizes. Precisely because music has the power to ontologize the individual's inwardness without verbal or visual externalization, it could integrate selfhood within the real without conceding its immateriality. Rousseau, who (probably more than any other modern thinker) was preoccupied with the desire to protect the integrity of sincere communication of the interior self, apprehended this unique power of music when he

---

[40] Ruth HaCohen, "Between Noise and Harmony," pp. 250–77.

[41] Spitzer, *Classical and Christian Ideas of World Harmony*, p. 102.

[42] Katz and HaCohen, *Tuning the Mind*; on early cultural moves of disembedding in Renaissance England see Stephen L. Collins, *From Divine Cosmos to Sovereign State: An Intellectual History of Consciousness and the Idea of Order in Renaissance England* (Oxford: Oxford University Press, 1989).

[43] Ibid., p. 85.

observed that "the musician's art consists of substituting for an imperceptible image of the object the movements which its presence excites in the heart of the contemplator."[44]

It is impossible to exaggerate, then, the significance of the metamorphosis that took place almost simultaneously in both music and politics, mostly since the seventeenth century, with the shift from imagining harmony as a cosmological or a celestial given to construing it as man-made by combining multiple voices into a unified whole, a human composition.[45] Harmony was no longer conceived as Pythagoras's music of the spheres or Kepler's "everlasting polyphony," or the inherent God-given, natural, mechanical, or organic structures of society. It was now imagined as a composition, a human artifice associated with the attempt to voluntarize the integration of individuals as parts in a whole in a process of shaping noncoercive wholes from the bottom up.

As demonstrated by the legal and political ideas of the social contract, the revival of classical theories of citizenship, and the rise of modern commonsense realism, this step represented an integral part of a wider change from a hierarchical to an egalitarian order, from an order secured from above to one fashioned and upheld by the voluntary horizontal, reciprocal acts of individuals no longer conceived as precast or prearranged "parts."[46]

The humanization of music as a means to communicate emotions and thoughts empowered it to play an important role in the rise of the culture of modern individualism and in the emergence of modern forms of liberal democratic aesthetics. Additionally, this development was linked to a growing awareness of the role played by music in integrating or subsuming the voices of the individual within the voice of the collective, often imagined as a nation. In the collectivization or later secular nationalization of the powers of music, this illiberal course has to some extent been analogous to the medieval uses of music to consolidate the identity and solidarity within communities of Christian believers.

Modern forms of national or communal music have spontaneously or deliberately been enlisted to animate and ontologize abstract collective entities such as society, state, and nation as unified singular agencies.[47] In some respects, the composition and performance of music has become a site of contest between

---

[44] Jean-Jacques Rousseau, *Oeuvres Completes*, vol. XV (Paris: 1966), p. 64. See the discussion of this point also in ibid., pp. 249–52.

[45] Spitzer, *Classical and Christian Ideas of Harmony*; HaCohen and Ezrahi, *The Voices of the Individual*.

[46] Dumont, *Essays on Individualism*.

[47] It is the unifying power of music as a form of collective, shared duration, overcoming difference on one hand and its capacity to stand for individual interior experience on the other that enabled it to evolve a rich vocabulary of relating individual and collective voices. On the symbolic dimension of music see, for example, Victor Zuckerkandl, *Sound and Symbol: Music and the External World*, Willard R. Trask (trans.), (Princeton: Princeton University Press, 1956). On nationalism and music see Carl Dahlhaus' *Between Romanticism and Modernism*, Mary Whittall (trans.) (Berkeley: University of California Press, 1989).

that perceived as liberal against illiberal, totalizing musical genres, embodying different, often conflicting, moral, political, and aesthetic values.

Careful scrutiny of the cultivation of modern artistic and social cultures of individualism, the realization in music and politics that structures and configurations are humanly composed, and the understanding that musical and political wholes are performed rather than heavenly ordained or natural givens, was congenial for the search and development of a host of strategies of horizontal and reciprocal communication and coordination. Such strategies could guarantee an apparently voluntary integration of freely interactive fragments into internally dynamic yet stable wholes.

The configurations and demeanor of audiences in modern opera or concert halls since the early eighteenth century offers a powerful example of the emergence of restrained liberal audiences, familiar to us in our day. This audience is a public that keeps silent during the performance, thus enabling each person to maintain his or her relative separateness and integrity as an individual spectator or listener while seated in the midst of a group. Cultural historians and analysts have suggested that this development relates to the rearrangement of seating space in concert, opera, and theater halls that distanced the audience from the stage or placed the erstwhile informal and mobile audience in the parterre in a formally fixed seating arrangement. The change to a stationary, seated audience in Paris's theaters was associated with the idea that

[T]o seat the audience would have the effect of minimizing spectator interaction. Separation from one another in their seats prevented spectators or listeners from forming into groups and made them less prone to spontaneous outbursts and the tumult of the *parterre* which used to disturb the actors. Moreover, spectators for their part were freed to form their own individual opinions.[48]

In the opera, the transformation of the public's configuration and of musical experience took a similar course. Here too, the noisy, tumultuous groups in the Paris Opera House around 1700 had been transformed, by the end of the eighteenth century, into the silent audience of our day.[49] Nevertheless, changes in the inner structure and seating arrangements of the audience were probably less an attempt to maintain a silent public than an expression of the sociocultural impulse to shape a tempered public that could accommodate individualism.

I agree with Paul Friedland's observation that this trend toward rendering the audience passive in the theater, opera, and concert halls of Europe during and since the eighteenth century anticipated the rise of the new, relatively

[48] Paul Friedland, *Political Actors: Representative Bodies and Theatricality in the Age of the French Revolution* (Ithaca: Cornell University Press, 2003), pp. 86–9.
[49] James H. Johnson, *Listening in Paris: A Cultural History* (Berkeley: University of California Press, 1995); For a rich account of the contradictory trends in the relations between audience in the theater and political culture in France during the eighteenth century see Jeffrey S. Ravel, *The Contested Parterre: Public Theater and French Political Culture 1680–1791* (Ithaca: Cornell University Press, 1999).

passive political audience in subsequent democracies and the partial transformation of politics into a spectacle.[50]

This development is compatible with my contention that, despite some striking parallels and affinities with monarchic displays of power and authority, modern democratic politics constitutes a novel genre of politics as a performing art. However, in relation to the emergence of democratic individualism, the most significant aspect of these configurations of audiences and spectators in the halls of Europe is perhaps the realization of a new balance between individual interiority and associability. The transposed audience offered the exhilarating opportunity for a meaningful individual experience in the midst of the social group. Furthermore, this transposition demonstrated the possibility of the existence of a liberal public that is neither a mob nor a crowd easily inflamed by passions or provoked by a charismatic orator, both of which can lead to violence, nor is it an anomalous aggregate of withdrawn or alienated individuals. (Very pertinent to this discussion are the famous fireside radio talks of President Franklin D. Roosevelt who, using the then novel potential of radio, demonstrated the capacity of a democratic leader to temper the hierarchical connotations of his status as the chief executive by adopting a uniquely liberal democratic rhetorical style and aesthetics of a single person simultaneously addressing each and all listeners.)

It is both intriguing and instructive that this trend coincides with the increasing awareness of the power of music to engage the individual's deepest emotions and inarticulate thoughts and with the individuation of the musical experience at concert halls. It is precisely the freedom of music from referentiality that has enabled each listener to experience it partly within an unconscious frame of reference.[51] This abstract dimension further enhanced the unique capacity of the musical imagination to ontologize the individual person and indirectly affect him or her while remaining elusive. As such, music has probably provided the clearest record of the special efficacy of the performative imagination to hide its operations and erase its traces, as Richard Wagner and, subsequently, movie directors were quick to understand and exploit.

Even more than a theatrical event, the musical experience of a concert or opera requires the silence of the audience as a precondition for the possibility of subjective individual experience. This implies that the disciplined silence of the audience reflects the respect of the group for the individual, and of a large number of individuals for each other.

Moreover, the subjectivization of musical, or, for that matter, other artistic experiences of liberal democratic audiences, amounted to the *diversification* and *decentralization* of emotional and cognitive responses to a *shared performance*, thus diminishing the dangers of "group-mind," collective ecstasy, and violence. The ability to imagine and experience the relative passivity of a public consisting of free individuals was particularly valuable, considering the

[50] Friedland, *Political Actors*; Guy Debord, *The Society of the Spectacle*, Donald Nicholson-Smith (trans.) (New York: Zone Books, 1995).
[51] See the film *The Sacrifice*, directed by Andrei Tarkovsky, Sweden, 1986.

popular violence of the English, American, and French revolutions. It strengthened the credibility of liberal democratic political imaginaries, disentangling
freedom from popular violence, and fostered the fashioning of the individual
citizen and the public as potentially compatible democratic agents.

This analysis does not intend to underestimate the variegated cultural forms
of music, theater, painting, and literature that have cultivated sensibilities and
orientations inimical to, or only partially compatible with, democratic individualism. Nor is it my intention to ignore the corrosive effects of mass commercial culture on the qualities and balances of democratic individualism. Our
discussion has been circumscribed to a particular focus and, as such, it has
inevitably overlooked or distorted important aspects of the relations between
culture, individualism, and politics. However, within the scope of my argument, I would like now to briefly conclude this section by returning to our
earlier discussion of the liberal democratic move to separate the realms of art
and politics.

Liberal democratic culture has developed structural conditions and practices that have enabled the individual to live, cultivate the self, and thrive in the
relatively compartmentalized spheres of art, literature, and private life along an
equivalent yet more simplified, transparent, accessible, typological, legally, and
bureaucratically regulated version of the same individual self as a citizen, as an
agent in the public sphere. The modern democratic state has introduced a host
of legal, bureaucratic, and economic definitions of the individual that bypass
or circumvent the inwardness that the subject might have developed within the
cultural and private spheres. This structural possibility derives mainly from the
earlier separation of church and state and the attempt to protect the inner freedom of the individual believer from the intervention of political power.

That kind of socio-structural dichotomy between art and politics, private
and public, has facilitated the compartmentalization of individual and group
emotional and aesthetic experiences within the relatively safe, apolitical sites
of culture. At the same time, it can hardly resist occasional breaks through the
demarcation lines between art and politics, either by the individual seeking to
defy state power and authority by projecting a thicker, more substantial interiority onto the public realm, or by a group seeking to politically distinguish
itself by claiming to possess and ostensibly projecting an idiosyncratic sensibility, a distinctive cultural configuration and particular emotions unaddressed
by the majority or by other groups. The role of artists, playwrights, poets,
intellectuals, and musicians in the history of democratic resistance and revolutions – their triumphs and mostly their failures – is well documented.

Undoubtedly, the state has also almost routinely broken through these
demarcation boundaries between the private voluntary spheres of art and culture and the publicly regulated sphere of politics in attempting to enlarge its
own presence and control through music, literature, the performing and the
plastic arts. Obviously, the liberal democratic compartmentalization of politics has never been more than an illusion, a fiction useful enough to delegitimize the unauthorized manipulation of the arts to influence politics by means

of emotions, passions, and aesthetic experience, while professing to contain it within the boundaries of reason, transparency, rational deliberation, and moderation.

This attitude has overlooked the emotional and aesthetic dimensions and expressions of reason and moderation in politics. It has also disregarded the role of the compartmentalization of the arts in indirectly supporting such important cultural conditions and constitutive imaginaries of the liberal democratic state as commonsense realism, the epistemological sphere of liberal democratic politics, the neutrality of the state, deliberative government, and enlightened public opinion. By manipulating the explicit self-definition of the arts as the sphere of fictions and illusions, this version of liberal democratic world making has obliquely reinforced the perceived attachment of politics to the realm of facts and rational arguments. To recapitulate, the liberal compartmentalization and depolitization of the arts as well as the "deculturation" of civic politics have had far-reaching consequences for the potential position of the individual in relation to the state. With the occasional exception of the eruption of radical lifestyles, especially in youth cultures, or momentary lapses into fascist conflation of art and politics, the ideological liberal democratic decoupling of politics and culture has inevitably discouraged the deployment and employment of the treasures of selfhood, cultivated for centuries since Renaissance humanism, as a potent resource for evolving or projecting in civic space new subjectivities resistant to the coercive processes of normalization, standardization, and gender discrimination imposed by the classifications of state bureaucracies and the hegemony of flattening materialist economic and statistical definitions of the public will as the aggregate of the desires of consumers.

Presently, perhaps the most consequential cracks in the foundations of recently flattened and materialistically reductionist democratic individualism are caused by an internal crisis in the Enlightenment synthesis of science and democracy, of public and individual rationality, a crisis in what formerly enabled an imaginary of reality to bridge between individual and society. Moreover, the more arid late twentieth-century versions of the partnership between science and democratic politics animated by the vision of deliberative or rational collective choices are gradually disappearing from the politics of public affairs. It is difficult to anticipate what will frame the space of the relations between culture and democratic politics in the future and how it will affect future versions of democratic individualism. Present trends suggest, however, that the radical horizontality and simultaneity enabled by new technologies of individual and mass expression and communication combined with globalization are already reducing the power of the state to influence the political imagination of its own citizens and thereby secure it as a reliable, reasonably coherent, and stable source of legitimacy for major government decisions.

PART FOUR

THE POSTMODERN TURN AND THE RETURN OF POLITICAL THEATRICALITY

12

Mass Media and the Refictionalization of Agency and Reality

The principal impact of the postmodern turn on contemporary democratic political culture can be described as the end of the imaginary of the world as a sphere of decidable external facts. An "external objective reality" often referred to as nature has replaced the will of God as a constraint on human desires and actions in modern secular society. The erosion of the sharp division between the internal and the external, the interiority of the human subject and the external world as an object, or, to put it more generally, the end of the external as a safe boundary of the internal, signifies the decline of the Enlightenment's democratic moral epistemology, which, inspired by the scientific revolution, has rested on sharp distinctions between categories such as objective and subjective, natural and artificial, necessity and freedom.

The end of the external has been associated with a further shift in the historical development of common sense in western societies, a shift away from modern commonsense realism which, for several centuries, was influenced by scientism. In the cultural milieu of contemporary western societies (in particular the modern electronic mass media), common sense has become more reflexively elastic, shifty, and ambiguous in regard to the demarcation lines between facts and fictions. I argue that this development has far-reaching implications for the foundations of democratic politics. It was this dualism between an external physical world of natural facts and the inner world of the human soul that hitherto served as a normative and intellectual model for the move to externalize social, economic, and political facts and thus to deploy and replicate that dualism as a separation between an objective social and political reality and the individual's inwardness.

A weakening of trust in the compelling authority of reality as a domain of publicly evident and certifiable facts has, in my opinion, diminished the power of a host of strategies of horizontal intersubjective communication, cooperation, and coordination necessary for imagining and practicing a political order built from the bottom up. Devoid of firm, reliable referents of universally accessible physical and social facts, deprived of that which is celebrated in modern thought as the basis for the emancipation from mythological and magical modes of consciousness, the balance between interiority and associability required by democratic individualism is barely achievable or sustainable. Moreover, what I have defined as the moral principle of rhetorical induction – the willingness to accept the authority of each individual citizen to generalize from individually experienced or witnessed facts to wider judgments on matters of public concern – is now less sustainable alongside other discredited assumptions crucial for the performance of a liberal democratic political system, such as the materiality and subsequent transparency of the relations of cause and effect in politics and, consequently, the public accountability of democratic governments.[1]

I argue that the weakening of belief in the objective, independent existence of the external has been marked by the emergence of a cluster of mutually reinforcing intellectual, cultural, and political changes in the hegemonic imaginaries of self and world, as well as of their interrelations. I briefly discuss what in my view constitutes the three principal reasons for the erosion of the foundations of the external, the dichotomy between the objective and the subjective, and their political implications: 1) the failure of philosophy to separate from and overcome or deny its links to rhetoric and literature; 2) the constraints imposed by contemporary society on the capacity of scientific knowledge to decisively differentiate itself from opinion and persist in effectively exiling the imagination – construed most often as a category opposed to reason – from the domain of rational discourse to the spheres of religion and art (a move criticized in Vico's *New Science*; and 3) most recent and significant to our discussion, the failure of photography, especially its documentary genres, to overcome theatricality.

PHILOSOPHY, SCIENCE, AND THE FALLACY OF MISPLACED RATIONALITY

The emergence or the invention of the physical world as an external object, like the antithetical postmodern erosion of the external, was an extremely

---

[1] Émile Durkheim criticized American pragmatic philosophers such as William James for challenging this dichotomy between external facts and observing subject. He held that by replacing an objective concept of reality that supports a "spectator" theory of truth as the viable mode in human practice, we lose a concept of truth as "something that in certain respects imposes itself on us." See his *Pragmatism and Sociology*, J. B. Allcock (ed.), J. C. Whitehouse (trans.) (Cambridge: Cambridge University Press, 1983), p. 68. Following Rousseau, Durkheim held that a collective belief in objective reality as an undisputable given is indispensable for a progressive political order based on science rather than myth. Very much in response to the political mythologies of fascism, Albert Einstein made a similar juxtaposition between reality and myth in his foreword to Galileo Galilei's *Dialogue*. There he praises Galileo for overcoming "the anthropocentric and mythical thinking of his contemporaries and [leading] them back to an objective and causal attitude toward the cosmos, an attitude which had become lost to humanity with the decline of Greek culture." See David E. Rowe and Robert Schulman, *Einstein on Politics: His Private Thoughts and Public Stands on Nationalism, Zionism, War, Peace, and the Bomb* (Princeton: Princeton University Press, 2007), p. 132.

complex gradual process. For the purpose of our discussion, I devote my attention to one central aspect inherent in the development of the relation between the physicalization of the external and the rise of early science in ancient Greece. Many classical Greek thinkers were preoccupied with a search for ways to achieve peace of mind (*amerimnia*), to emancipate humanity from fears and anxieties produced by natural disasters commonly interpreted as divine retributions for human flaws (*hamartia*). Historians of antiquity indicate that this quest contributed to the birth of physics as a means to demystify such events, to render phenomena formerly considered divine reprisal mere physical occurrences, thus allaying human worries and sense of guilt and increasing serenity.[2]

Epicurus thought that the goal of philosophy was to emancipate humanity from the terror of nature. In the *Letter to Pythocles,* he wrote: "There is no profit to be derived from the knowledge of celestial phenomena other than peace of mind and firm assurance, just as this is the goal of all research."[3] The invention of the objectively external, the physicalization of nature as a nonagent, an entity indifferent to mankind, opened space for later developments of science as an objective, amoral knowledge of reality and, in many modern western societies, a source of widely implemented apolitical authority in public affairs.

The physicalization of nature could not escape the objectification of the human body. But early Jewish, classical, and Christian imaginaries of the human soul facilitated the crystallization of the body-soul dualism as a constitutive imaginary of western culture and politics. In other words, the invention of the external was the other side of the discovery and the gradual ontologizing, of human inwardness, including those faculties that substantiate the individual's capacity for freedom and judgment.[4] The belief that disasters are mere physical events implicitly created a divide between nature as a sphere of external necessity independent of human aspirations and conduct and politics as the domain of voluntary human action, a field in which human beings may act as agents, as causes of social and political events and institutions.

In the modern era, these early complementary moves to physicalize the natural and voluntarize the political have opened up a domain of historical, as distinguished from natural, events. Nature, imagined as purged of religion and myth, could eventually emerge as an object of scientific rather than theological or moral knowledge, as a sphere that lends itself only partially to human intervention, such as digging tunnels or building bridges within strict physical limitations. Imagined as a force external to human agency rather than driven by the intention or will of inferior or superior agents, the natural and the physical

---

[2] Pierre Hadot, *What is Ancient Philosophy?* (Cambridge, MA: Harvard University Press, 1990).

[3] Cited and discussed ibid., p. 118.

[4] In our times, this ancient dualism of soul and body has triggered repeated efforts to redraw their boundaries by elevating mind and soul to a position of hegemony over the body or, conversely, by subordinating human mental and spiritual faculties under material physiological causes.

could constitute an amoral and therefore legitimate constraint on voluntary human action and, consequently, on politics as well.

The other side of the physicalization of nature in ancient Greece entailed the Greek invention of politics, the emergence in fifth-century B.C.E. Athens of the nucleus of democracy – a system of direct political participation linking individual freedom with self-government as its realization in the political sphere. The co-emergence of a given, objective, and necessary nature and of politics as the enterprise of free agents founded two distinct and often competing sources of authority in public affairs: knowledge and participation, frequently associated respectively with truth and opinion. The former was formulated by some of Athens' leading contemporary philosophers and critics of democracy such as Plato and Aristotle, whereas the latter was memorably displayed in the practice of the assemblies in the *Agora* and in other forms of direct participatory democracy in Athens.

In Athens, when politics was the sphere of freedom, political participation was the factor that distinguished citizens from slaves and, therefore, legitimated obedience as expressing voluntary rather than coercive conduct. However, as Greek dramatists such as Sophocles and Euripides repeatedly thematized, the choices and actions undertaken by voluntary individuals, including the people's political participation, did not guarantee that the consequences of their decisions would necessarily be less disastrous than those made by tyrants, or that a democratic regime would prove more stable than a despotic one. The sole reward that decisions made by means of popular opinion as the expression of freedom could provide was not happier results but dignity to politically engaged citizens and legitimacy for the consequences of their actions as free agents.

This was precisely the problem Plato sought to address in his critique of democracy and to which he responded by advancing his Republic as a regime in which power legitimated by inclusive voluntary participation was to be replaced by power legitimated by superior knowledge. Plato laid the foundations of the influential western philosophical and scientific traditions that privileged knowledge over participation as a source of social and sociopolitical authority and power. Whereas the ultimate principle of democratic participation promised to overcome subordination and legitimize the results of decisions driven by popular opinion even when tragic, knowledge presented as a source of legitimate power held the promise of evading tragic results. But this supposed achievement was to be purchased by the willingness to live with hierarchy, under the privileged reign of the knowledgeable. In other words, human dignity, acquired by free political participation, was substituted in Plato's Republic by the dignity achieved through conduct corresponding to the ideas and rational principles of the ideal state.[5]

---

[5] According to Josiah Ober's *Democracy and Knowledge: Innovation and Learning in Classical Athens* (Princeton: Princeton University Press, 2010). Contrary to Plato's insistence on the superiority of government by elite experts, ancient democratic Athens actually exemplified the capacity

In the *Republic* of Plato and its many followers in the western tradition, the inferred equation of hierarchy with tyranny and dominion was to be mitigated by the assumption that political power, guided by knowledge rather than caprice, depersonalizes agency and depoliticizes its employment. A philosopher-king who rules in accordance with the truth and the public interest rather than whim is purportedly not a tyrant. Much of the force of this western vision of the mission of philosophy and science in politics derives from this redemptive concept of knowledge and the ethos of a politics tamed by reason.

In many respects, the history of western democratic politics has been a story of competition and occasional convergence between participation and knowledge as distinct principles of legitimate political power. The chapter of this history most relevant to our concerns is associated with the central role of science in imaginaries of modern democracy and the decline of the imagined partnership of science (including technology) and democracy since the mid-twentieth century.

The Enlightenment may be interpreted as a massive attempt to fuse knowledge and participation, rendering an enlightened public the ultimate agent of power grounded in public participation and informed and rational decision making that can avoid tragic results. This attempt to turn every citizen into a miniature philosopher-king, to cultivate the aspiration for a government guided by rational public knowledge, this faith in the possibility of consensus on self-evident truths and, therefore, on voluntary rational obedience, was built up slowly in the West by a cumulative repository of sociocultural processes that had lasted for centuries. Such seeming convergence of political democratization with the advancement and diffusion of knowledge constituted the foundation of the western ethos of progress.

I have already discussed key aspects of these processes in Parts Two and Three, including the combined democratization and modernization of the political imagination since the seventeenth century, as well as the impact of scientism on the materialization of modern perceptions of political agents and causalities. I now turn briefly to the role of the external – the world as an entity accessible to the perception and knowledge of the individual subject – in the development of realism, or rather the rhetoric of realism, as a component of modern democratic cultures of discourse, knowledge, painting, and photography and its decline in our postmodern universe.

I would like to suggest that the process I have defined as the postmodern decline of the external – increasing apprehension of the impossibility to totally separate assertions about the properties of the world from particular worldviews – has exposed the fragility of the philosophical endeavor to sharply distinguish philosophy from rhetoric and advocacy, and the weakness of the

to merge participatory democracy with a decentralized process whereby useful knowledge is gained by lay citizens in the process of self-government. This practical knowledge, according to Ober, had been widely shared and served for administrative and political innovations thus posing a challenge to the Platonic dichotomy between *doxa* and *episteme*.

commitment, embedded in the ethos and practice of science, to enhance the dichotomy between knowledge and opinion. My purpose here is not to raise this claim as a problem in the philosophy of language or in epistemology, but as an instructive marker of an emerging politically consequential shift in the boundaries and relations between imaginaries of reality and agency.

The observation that acts of discarding established modern imaginaries of reality and agency are related to postmodern shifts in the deep structure of Western culture and politics does not imply that the antecedents of these shifts are necessarily recent. On the contrary, particularly in the political context, the frailty and vulnerability of the dichotomy between philosophy, or science and rhetoric, or between knowledge and opinion was already exposed in the early endeavors of influential political thinkers such as Thomas Hobbes, who explored the uses of scientific language as a particular means of persuading his audience to acknowledge the objective realities and logic of the political world as he saw it. Quentin Skinner observes:

Hobbes's conception of civil science in *The Elements of Law* and *De Cive* is founded on the belief that scientific reasoning possesses an inherent power to persuade us of the truths it finds out. By contrast, *Leviathan* declares that the sciences are a small power, and reverts to the typically humanist assumption that, if we are to succeed in persuading others to accept our arguments, we shall have to supplement the findings of reason with the moving force of eloquence.[6]

Whereas for the purposes of his analysis Skinner juxtaposes "scientific reasoning" and "eloquence," it is more fruitful for our analysis to redescribe them in Hobbes's writings as distinct yet complementary rhetorical strategies. For instance, Hobbes certainly examined the language of reasoning, modeled on geometry, in comparison with the techniques of classical rhetorical persuasion to evaluate their relative political efficacy, concluding that he must use both. Skinner attributes Hobbes's resort to "rhetoric" in the classical sense of the word to his belief that the English Revolution was "a victory for the irrational but overwhelming power of neo-classical and antinomian rhetoric over the small power of science and rationality."[7] This dichotomy between the rational and the irrational is, I think, beside the point. Hobbes might have merely realized that he could not afford to overlook the rhetorical value of these distinct canons of persuasion.

While "the small power" of science encouraged Hobbes to supplement "the methods of science [with] the techniques of Renaissance humanism,"[8] in the course of subsequent centuries, the rhetorical powers of modern science have grown sufficiently to render scientism – as a synthesis of elements belonging in lay versions of the rhetoric of knowledge and in political participation – a significant component of popular culture and modernized common sense.

[6] Quentin Skinner, *Reason and Rhetoric in the Philosophy of Hobbes* (Cambridge: Cambridge University Press, 1996), p. 426.
[7] Ibid., p. 435.
[8] Ibid., p. 437.

In contradistinction to the position held by Hobbes, whose desire to present the truths of politics in the language of science led him to appeal to conceptions of indisputable knowledge modeled on geometry, mathematics, and logic, the rhetorical power of modern science has drawn far more from the tradition of experimental science, pioneered by early scientists such as Robert Boyle. Its strength derives largely from relating to the world as an object, interrogating external nature through experiments performed in the presence of reliable witnesses, and distributing the meticulously recorded protocols of these experiments, rendered in referential-descriptive language, to other scientists and learned people.[9]

As indicated by the historical record of the relations between science and democratic politics, the aforementioned experimental scientific tradition, of which Boyle was one of the leading pioneers, has had far greater impact on political culture than geometry, mathematics, or the other "deductive sciences."[10] This influence can be attributed, by and large, to the fact that experimental science has stressed the status of nature as an external object subject to both sensory perception and intellectual understanding; experiments could be perceived as a way of interrogating nature through human operations and artificial instruments. Moreover, as Ian Hacking, among others, has shown, experimental science engaged modes of observing and judging sensory experience that, unlike earlier, more elitist, esoteric ones, *appeared* to substantiate a concept of knowledge closer to commonsense experience and public opinion.[11]

The view of the world as a picture, an object of sensory perception, was associated with the emancipation of the human eye as an instrument of the scientific advancement of knowledge and, therefore, with the promise of a new, more democratic form of knowledge that could substantiate the fusion of science, lay sensory perception and political participation as complementary sources of legitimate political power.[12]

In contrast to the language of deductive reasoning, the language of experimental science appeared materialistically representational rather than formal or logical, a referential or designative language reflecting the external objects of nature rather than the abstract operations of the mind. As such, the language of experimental science – later modified to accommodate the aims of the social

---

[9] Yaron Ezrahi, "Science and the Problem of Authority in Democracy" in Thomas F. Gieryn (ed.), *Science and Social Structure: A Festschrift for Robert K. Merton: Transactions of the New York Academy of Sciences*, series II, vol. 39 (New York: New York Academy of Sciences 1980); Steven Shapin and Simon Schaffer, *Leviathan and the Air-Pump: Hobbes, Boyle, and the Experimental Life* (Princeton: Princeton University Press, 1985).

[10] In contradistinction to their limited impact on political culture, the deductive sciences have continued to exert, however, great influence on legal culture.

[11] Ian Hacking, *The Emergence of Probability: A Philosophical Study of Early Ideas About Probability, Induction and Statistical Inference* (Cambridge: Cambridge University Press, 1975).

[12] Martin Heidegger, "The Age of the World Picture" in *The Question Concerning Technology and other Essays*, William Lovitt (ed.) (New York: Harper Torchbooks, 1977), § 115–54.

sciences to perceptually materialize and represent social and political entities, actions, and events – has become a crucial tool for the performance of democratic political orders in which power, presumed to derive from the people as an aggregate of observing and knowing individuals, is held accountable in a universe of commonsense knowledge of publicly observable facts.

Obviously, after modernity, the subsequent subversive realization that, in both science and politics, the language of representation is largely constitutive of the world it represents, that it participates in inventing and consolidating its very referents, or that the respective boundaries and identities of physical and political objects are made or construed rather than found or given, was not yet widely shared. Although Nietzsche posed a powerful challenge to the entrenched modern conventions of linguistic representation in the late 1880s,[13] the development and spread of popular distrust of the proliferating languages of representation, including the language of photography, would become far more pronounced only in the next century.

The association of experimental science with artificial instruments and operations aimed at interrogating the objective world, or rather the world as an object, has made an additional substantive contribution to the rhetorical power of experimental science in modern democratic societies. These instruments and operations projected the persuasive power of works over words to a wider public, facilitating the shift from a culture of authoritative texts to a culture that authorizes observable objects and operations as sources of knowledge that often derive not only from the powers of observation but also from the confirming sense of touch.[14]

The experimental scientific orientation seemed to support the commonsense belief that truths are inscribed on surfaces, on universally accessible experiences, and that when properly ordered and rationally disciplined, they can direct human discourse and action. The fact that the ways in which scientists observe nature and manipulate it to generate knowledge have always been profoundly different from the ways laymen experience the material world has rarely disturbed the general illusion that scientists and laymen encounter the same external world within a shared epistemological frame. Laymen widely imagine that the objects referred to by scientists are the same as those they usually encounter in their ordinary lives and that the instruments employed by scientists in their research objectify their judgments by controlling their subjective inclinations and protecting their theories from the contaminating effects of undisciplined perceptions.

Especially since the mid-nineteenth century, the tangible presence of science in the domain of ordinary human perception has been dramatically broadcast to society by the translation of theories in physics into powerful instruments

---

[13] See for instance Friedrich Nietzsche's *The Will to Power*, Walter Kaufmann (ed.), Walter Kaufmann and R. J. Hollingdale (trans.) (New York: Vintage Books, 1968), pp. 472, 477, 479.

[14] Yaron Ezrahi, *Words and Works in the Social Iconography of Scientific Knowledge: A Study in Science as a Cultural System* (Jerusalem: unpublished manuscript, 1976).

of communication, electrical energy, and transportation. The modern culture of science and technology, in contradistinction to its later advanced versions, appeared to confirm a simple notion of material causality whose metaphorical deployment in social and political discourse is well recorded in the mass press of the period.[15] Given the medieval traditions of faith in the existence of invisible entities and the influence of Platonism, logic, geometry, and mathematics on the belief in unobservable truths, early signs of the process of materializing objects of experimental scientific knowledge were bound to encounter some resistance. Critics from the Royal Society of London questioned the seriousness of fellows such as Robert Hooke, the author of the famous *Micrographia* (1665), who preferred, in their opinion, to focus on lower natural objects such as flies while ignoring the lofty discourse on angels. The willingness to study such insignificant lower creatures and upgrade the status of ordinary experience indeed constituted a challenge to conventional cosmology and the established hierarchical chain of being.

As a powerful exemplification of the thesis of the coproduction of knowledge and the social order, the effects of the new experimental science, narrowing the perceived gap between knowledge and opinion, were no less consequential for the legitimation of lay participation in the production and possession of knowledge, as well as for the performance of democracy. Let us dwell briefly on the argument made by Ian Hacking that the medieval notion of demonstrable knowledge implied a sharp distinction between knowledge and opinion.[16] This attitude was widely shared by Renaissance scientists committed to the possibility of undeniable truths. In his famous *Letter to the Grand Duchess* (1615), Galileo actually unfolded the argument concerning the "difference between demonstrative knowledge and knowledge where opinion is possible" to defend himself against the pressures exerted on him by the Church to change his assumptions: "The demonstrated conclusions touching the things of nature and of the heavens cannot be changed with the same facility as opinions about what is legal or not in a contract."[17]

Once this distinction between demonstrable and probable truths (in the earlier sense of truths held by opinion) had blurred and the boundaries of the discourses of opinion and science had become more mutually porous, scientists were less protected from opinions; but opinions on matters "touching the things of nature," when informed by less ostensibly esoteric science, could also become more respectable. Dating this change around 1660, Hacking aligns it with both the legacy of low sciences such as medicine, which had to assess regularities on the basis of practice and experience, and with the emergence of experimental scientific methodologies. Locke, a philosopher and a physician,

[15] See for instance David Layton, *Science for the People: The Origins of the School Science Curriculum in England* (London: Allen & Unwin, 1973).

[16] Ian Hacking, *The Emergence of Probability* (Cambridge: Cambridge University Press, 1985).

[17] Cited in A. C. Crombie, *Medieval And Early Modern Science*, vol. II, second edition (Garden City, NY: Doubleday Anchor Books, 1959), p. 203.

served as a major bridge between the emerging culture of experimental science and commonsense realism as the epistemological frame of public opinion and politics. Casson calls attention to the lifelong friendship between Locke and Robert Boyle, a leading member of the Royal Society of London. He notes the "new mode of discourse that Locke encountered when he entered into the circle of theologians, experimentalists and medical men surrounding Robert Boyle."[18] Obviously the very kind of accessible discourse in the public meetings of the Royal Society and its inclusion of lay participants encouraged such symbiosis between science and opinion.

The crux of our discussion is the role played by these developments in facilitating the penetration of modes of scientific rhetoric into commonsense discourse, and even more by their contribution to the flexibility such changes introduced later into social science and commonsense imaginaries of causality. Inasmuch as the evidence endorsed by the new experimental science appeared to derive from the functioning of things rather than from personal testimonies or subjective opinion, even relatively loose notions of probability lent additional respectability to claims (formerly considered merely opinion) now appearing in the garments of the impersonal language of science disciplined by the minute observation of events, motions of objects, and human actions in public space.

Hobbes memorably deployed the metaphors of motion and mechanics to fashion his influential behavioral imaginary of the citizens and the state, although in the *Leviathan*, he preferred to express it in mathematical geometrical and legal terms rather than the experimental imagery of scientific knowledge. The newly apprehended elasticity of scientific and scientistic imaginaries of truths and the corresponding loosening of imaginaries of causality continued to expand in the eighteenth century.

Hacking finds the intellectual expression of a growing modern merger of probability and opinion in David Hume's discourse on causality. Noting Hume's attempts to refute the idea that it is possible to demonstrate a necessary causal connection between successive events from first principles, Hacking argues that Hume could imagine probability as an attribute of natural events, thus facilitating the transference of causality from knowledge to opinion. He sums up Hume's argument as follows: "Reasoning concerning cause and effect is not knowledge. Therefore it must be opinion or probability."[19] Probable notions of causality could thus be more amenable to the role of opinion in discourses on causality, wresting causality from the guarded sphere of professional knowledge.

Since the discourse on causality and the notion of probable causes were detached from the strictures of demonstrations from first principles, it could more easily expand to include, beyond the causes and effects in nature, the

[18] Douglas John Casson, *Liberating Judgment: Fanatics, Skeptics, and John Locke's Politics of Probability* (Princeton: Princeton University Press, 2011), p. 116.
[19] Hacking, *The Emergence of Probability*, pp. 179–81.

causes and effects in social and political events. The borrowed elements of the rhetoric of experimental science could be more easily deployed in social and political discourses, thus facilitating the integration of the quasi-objective languages that relate to nature and society as external facts within the moral-ideological discourses of politics.

In earlier chapters I aimed to show that the scientific and quasi-scientific languages of the external had an important function in democratic political discourse, facilitating a desirable balance between the subjective and the objective, the causal and the ethical, between visible or transparent actions and hidden inner individual motives. To reiterate, in the democratic political context, linguistic and rhetorical practices of relating to ostensibly public material facts were part and parcel of the vital need to – at least partially – depersonalize and depoliticize claims made by horizontally situated social and political actors, as well as claims made reciprocally by state and citizens. As such, the external together with human inwardness could function as vital components of the integrated moral and causal orders.

Liberal democratic cultures have been driven by the impulse to balance the objective and the subjective in order to avoid the pitfall of shifting toward radical exteriority or radical interiority, neither of which can uphold a democratic political order. An analysis of the changing links between causal, moral, and political components of public discourse and the relative weight assigned to instrumental and symbolic public actions over time would probably yield further significant insights into fluctuations in the performance of democratic regimes. Studies of the responses of western democracies to the threats and challenges posed by World War II, for instance, indicate a marked increase in the significance granted to the instrumental rhetoric and languages of science and technology as opposed to the rhetoric and languages of legal-political procedures of legitimation.

In the years following that war, many American scientists referred with nostalgia to the war years, "when the goals of the government were clear" and their influence on its actions, or, in our own terms, their power to impose considerations of the physical or objective external on government decisions, was far greater. In turn, the terms of integrating science, politics, and social values changed markedly ten or fifteen years after the war, reflecting the increasing importance of domestic moral and political concerns.

In each context, the significance of balancing the considerations of science, politics, and the moral order is often dramatized in controversies triggered by scientists who, consciously or unwittingly, eschew the moral and political effects of scientific and technological approaches to social problems and public policy choices. When scientists buttress themselves on the assumption that the internal validity of science constitutes sufficient grounds for decisions and actions in areas of public concern, they tend to elicit a host of socially, politically, and morally corrective responses. Very often in such instances we can perceive the triumph of the complex and integrating wisdom of opinion over the more narrowly cast scientific knowledge of the mandarins.

Such cases illustrate the impracticality of the inclination of many contemporary scientists to ignore the extrinsic imports of scientifically certified descriptions of the world, or scientific recommendations for how to act in it when they are deployed in the sociopolitical context. Obviously, in such cases, the conditional defense of the authority of science in the name of rationality or professional autonomy is a weak defense. Within the context of public affairs, such scientific assertions may become – as illustrated in the course of the twentieth century in a series of repeated IQ controversies – a contested political resource manipulated, in the name of science, to privilege particular moral and political positions while discrediting others.[20] In other words, once elements of scientific discourse are deployed in the context of public affairs, they become a political resource whose rhetorical and behavioral import may, in effect, latently redistribute political costs and assets among adversaries. When scientific arguments enter public discourse, they almost automatically metamorphose into political rhetoric. Scientists oblivious to the possibility that, in the context of public affairs, scientific authority and bodies of scientific knowledge can be converted into political resources are sometimes baffled by the intensity of their rejection or adoption by policy makers and political groups.

The IQ controversy that ignited again in the 1970s following the publication of an article by Arthur Jensen in the *Harvard Educational Review* 39 (Winter 1969) revolved around Jensen's claim that analysis of testing data warrants the assertion that there are differences in the average IQ scores of black and white populations and that these differences may be traced to hereditary factors. In light of these data, Jensen questioned the wisdom of investing in educational efforts to boost the IQ of blacks. In the face of the public storm provoked by the article, Jensen observed:

> Unnecessary difficulties arise when we allow the scientific question to become mixed up with the social-political aspects of the problem, for when it does we are less able to think clearly about either set of questions. The question of whether or not there are genetical racial differences in intelligence is independent of any questions of its implications, whatever they may be.[21]

This statement can serve as a paradigmatic illustration of an appeal to the claim of unyielding external reality against moral and political definitions of reality as a normative, constitutive category of the sociopolitical. I have termed this the "fallacy of misplaced rationality," for this particular transgression is commonly committed by scientists who fail to recognize the logic whereby a scientific authority, deployed in relation to a publicly controversial problem, can be transformed into a partisan political resource. According to Lee Cronbach, to "make a statement about race differences even at the level of hypothesis was

[20] Lee J. Cronbach, "Five Decades of Public Controversy Over Mental Testing" and Yaron Ezrahi, "The Jensen Controversy: A Study in the Ethics and Politics of Knowledge in Democracy" in Charles Frankel (ed.), *Controversies and Decisions* (New York: Russell Sage Foundation, 1976), pp. 123–70.
[21] Cited in Cronbach, ibid., pp. 133–4.

to offend blacks and threaten their political interests in America of 1969."[22] Such scientific statements could have power by virtue of an entrenched belief that external reality can coerce moral and political attitudes to either adjust to the facts or be discarded as irrational.

Arthur Jensen insists that it is necessary to separate scientific from social and political aspects of a problem in order "to think clearly" about it. However, clear thinking within the confines of the scientific community qualitatively differs from thinking clearly and constructively in the sociopolitical contexts of public policy making. Likewise, the logic of the practices of philosophers or scientists is very different from the logic of the practices of government and citizens engaged in performing democratic politics. The political culture of liberal democracy certainly requires that ethical and political considerations take objective external facts into consideration. But as Tocqueville and Dewey realized and as democratic practices indicate, liberal democratic cultures also set up moral and political conditions before granting scientific assertions the status of binding external reality in the sociopolitical context.

The weight of extra-scientific tests that would certify the authority of scientific ascriptions of causality in the sociopolitical context has increased in our time due to a wider realization that they are both theory-dependent and, at best, shaped by judgments of probabilities. Another aspect of the choice to apply a particular concept or imaginary of causality in a given context concerns the normative and political acceptability of the consequences, including the attributions of responsibility that follow. Upon considering the place of causation in the law, jurists Hart and Honoré observed that

[T]he cause of a great famine in India may be identified by the Indian peasant as the draught, but the World Food authority may identify the Indian's government failure to build up reserves as the cause and the draught as a mere condition.... It is cases of this sort that have led writers, notably Collingwood, to insist that the identification of a cause among other "mere" conditions is always dictated by practical interest.[23]

Considering the limitations imposed on the application of philosophical and scientific knowledge in social and political contexts, it is particularly instructive that, as Hart and Honoré observe,

[T]he courts ... often insist that the causal questions which they have to face must be determined on common-sense principles.... Common sense is not a matter of inexplicable or arbitrary assertions, and the causal notions which it employs, though flexible and complex and subtly influenced by context, can be shown to rest, at least in part, on stateable principles; though the ordinary man who uses them may not, without assistance, be able to make them explicit.[24]

[22] Ibid., p. 133.
[23] H. L. A. Hart and A. M. Honoré, *Causation and the Law* (Oxford: Clarendon Press, 1973), p. 33.
[24] Ibid., p. 24.

In the political context, the choice to stress one particular causal connection over other possible ones is politically loaded, especially when the claim of multiple causations is warrantable. In other words, in the context of politics, causality is a matter of both fact and policy, of commonsense evidence and tacit value and practical commitments.

In modern societies, scientists trained to disparage the importance of opinion as opposed to knowledge have often learned the hard way to recognize the complexity of the task of injecting warrantable, and sometimes unwarrantable, claims of scientific knowledge into the complex, highly charged fabrics of society and politics. Despite the well-known case of Arthur Jensen and his advocate, Nobel laureate physicist William Shockley, this lesson apparently and surprisingly escaped Larry Summers, the former president of Harvard University, whose role and past experience as an academic economist and a cabinet secretary made him an unlikely candidate for publicly exemplifying the *fallacy of misplaced rationality*. This occurred in 2005, provoking a scandal that led to his forced resignation. To reiterate, such cases highlight the fact that in society at large, conceptions of causality that either confirm or subvert the hegemonic normative and causal views of the social order are politically loaded, regardless of the extent of their validity by scientific standards. Obviously, even an outstanding scholar or efficient executive who is blind to this fact cannot preside over such a scientifically powerful and socially prominent institution as Harvard University.

In a culture keenly aware of the tensions and contradictions among the true, the good, and the politically legitimate, in a democracy in which power can be legitimized only by knowledge that has passed the test of popular opinion, the fusion of knowledge and participation must depend no less on the ability of scientists to contextualize their knowledge while taking into account the fabric of the political order than on the ability of the public to relate knowledge to its concerns.

On a deeper level, the post-Enlightenment triumph of rhetoric and opinion over attempts to privilege philosophy and scientific knowledge as autonomous grounds for decisions in the context of public affairs relates to the slow yet ceaseless spread of awareness of the rhetorical dimension inherent in all specialized discourses (natural, literary, political, philosophical, and scientific) as discrete enterprises of persuasion. Scientific claims that must earn their validity within the scientific community by satisfying internal – often highly technical – standards of scientific persuasion must satisfy other standards as well, including the absence of visible signs of internal dissent, in order to have authority in the lay community.

The long historical rivalry between philosophy and science on one hand and rhetoric on the other is misleading. The self-denying rhetoric of philosophy and science is obviously in itself a powerful rhetorical strategy. Alan Gross made the apt observation that "the sciences create bodies of knowledge so persuasive as to seem unrhetorical – to seem, simply the way the world is."[25] He notes further the

---

[25] Alan G. Gross, *The Rhetoric of Science* (Cambridge, MA: Harvard University Press, 1990), p. 207.

reversal of the subordinate status of rhetoric from mere servant of science and philosophy to subsuming science and philosophy into particular instances of rhetoric as the art of persuasion. Science and logic are defined now in terms of "their specialized rhetoric [deriving from] their common heritage of persuasion."[26]

The efficacy with which science and philosophy were able to deny their rhetorical dimension was long an important source of their respective social authority. Particularly in the case of science, extensive use of the mirror metaphor to describe scientific knowledge as a reflection of external nature rendered scientific authority a powerful political resource for depersonalizing and depoliticizing political decisions and actions.[27] In other words, science's efficiency in repressing its own rhetorical foundations as a specialized enterprise of persuasion and its claim to fix external facts as safe referents for guiding human behavior rendered science an invaluable resource for denying, concealing, and repressing the rhetorical and gestural nature of political utterances and actions. Nietzsche famously insisted that "truth" is but a

mobile army of metaphors, metonymies, and anthropomorphisms, in short a sum of human relationships which have been enhanced, transposed and embellished poetically and rhetorically and which after long use seem firm, canonical and obligatory to a people. Truths are illusions about which one has forgotten that this is what they are; metaphors that are worn out without sensuous power; coins which have lost their pictures and now matter only as metal, no longer as coins.[28]

The forgetfulness that turns former illusions into truths is, of course, only a fragment of the complex, often hidden process whereby the imagination turns particular mixtures of experience and illusions into realities. Again, this is only a part of the process whereby the performative imagination creates the realities or the objects the reflective imagination then claims to represent, thus constituting the duality of reality and representation. In each epistemological-political regime, the "selection" or "allocation" of issues on behalf of the performative imagination for forgetfulness or for representation as facts is related to the social values that have the power to orient these selective processes.

It is precisely this connection that raises the question of the extent of the voluntary element in the process of collective selection and elevation of hegemonic political imaginaries, and the question as to whether there is a basis for an ethics of political imagining discussed in the conclusion of this book. In the final analysis, the realization that, as human enterprises of persuasion, philosophy and science are inescapably specialized branches of rhetoric as the general art of persuasion negates the endeavors of philosophy and science to downgrade rhetoric and opinion. As distinct configurations of imaginaries and rhetorical strategies, science, philosophy, politics, and literature are important

[26] Ibid., p. 206.
[27] See Richard Rorty, *Philosophy and the Mirror of Nature* (Princeton: Princeton University Press, 1979).
[28] Friedrich Nietzsche, "On Truth and Lies in an Extra-Moral Sense" (1873) in Walter Kaufmann (ed. and trans.) *The Portable Nietzsche* (New York: Penguin, 1976), pp. 46–7.

sociocultural enterprises for advancing certain values and opening different possibilities of experience. The problem we have discussed, then, does not center on the relative validities of the authorities generated by these respective configurations, but rather on the sociopolitical implications of their partial convergences and contradictions.

THE IDEAL OF REALISM IN PHOTOGRAPHY AND
CINEMATOGRAPHY AND THE IRREPRESSIBILITY OF STAGING

A considerable analogy may be found between the increasing failure of philosophy and science to persuasively deny the fundamental rhetorical layer inherent in their discursive practices or to effectively distance themselves from opinion, and the failure of (documentary) photography to sustain its promise of objective representation that could overcome subjectivity, staging, or theatricality. The recalcitrance of both theatricality and rhetoric stems from the unavoidably elusive, fictive, and often arbitrary foundations of reality as a referent of philosophy, science, and politics. In all three domains, albeit in different ways, the powerful impulse to ground claims in safe and stable anchorage has lost much of its earlier sway. The process whereby this drive has usually been pursued entails the conversion of imaginaries temporarily hegemonic in each field into "given foundations," into kinds of naturalized entities or procedures taken for granted.

Postmodern consciousness reflects, in part, the spread of the intuition that below the hard crest on which philosophers, scientists, and political leaders stand, there lies a liquid volcanic core threatening to erupt at any moment. Awareness of the fragile foundations of claims to knowledge, truth, and facts, especially, but not only, in the social sciences, has undoubtedly weakened the force with which such claims can be advanced in the public sphere.[29] In the instance of philosophy and science, critical scholarly analysis of the fragility of entrenched dogmas of nature, objectivity, coherence, rational explanation, and universalism has roused the wrath of practicing scientists and ideologues of the external against a host of philosophers, historians, and sociologists such as Michel Foucault, Richard Rorty, Jacques Derrida, Paul Feyerabend, Bruno Latour, Steven Shapin, and David Bloor, whom they regard as subversive relativists, slayers of cherished certitudes.

In the case of politics, fear of the failure to conceal the rhetorical and theatrical components of power and authority has been attenuated by almost two centuries of entrenched faith in the power of the camera as a scientific instrument to penetrate the fictional and imaginary foundations of the real and disclose to viewers an unstaged reality. The history of photography, the production of still and moving images, can be construed in part as a narrative

---

[29] See the Sokal controversy in Paul R. Gross and Norman Levitt, *Higher Superstition: The Academic Left and its Quarrels with Science* (Baltimore, MD: John Hopkins University Press, 1994), pp. 70–3.

of an invention that, for a long time, raised hopes in the power of the camera to register accurate, objective images of physical objects, persons, and social events. Support for the existence of accessible, incontestable factual reality has been reinforced by the metamorphosis of imaginings of the real into photographically "certified" facts. These hopes have clearly faded. In his influential exploration of "the society of the spectacle," Guy Debord made the apt observation that the

spectacle cannot be understood either as a deliberate distortion of the visual world or as a product of the technology of the mass dissemination of images. It is far better viewed as a *Weltanschauung* (worldview) that has been actualized, translated into the material realm – a world view transformed into an objective force.[30]

On one hand, the act of viewing as a form of contact with the external world was influenced by a tradition that associated the experience of vision with the sense of touch, a visual translation of tangibility, the bodily experience of the individual observer.[31] On the other hand, however, recognition of the complex physiological aspect of perception, especially its roots in the brain, opened the way not only for further objective materialization but also for the individualization and cultural particularization of visual experience.[32] Indeed, the early history of photography reveals the emergence of two distinct traditions of photography as art and science, as creator and recorder:[33] realistic photography seeking to produce objective pictures of the external world, and artistic or experimental photography seeking to externalize the artist's inwardness and project a subjective vision.

It is, however, precisely the distinct paths of artistic and documentary photography and their many intended and unintended convergences that point to the inexorable coexistence of the respective rhetoric of art and science, of the staged and the unstageable. This dualism of the creative-expressive and the documentary has persistently problematized the massive attempts to harness photography to the "attestive visual culture" of modern democracy. The aesthetics and the pleasures of viewing could lend political objects mediated by the camera elements of persuasiveness borrowed from photography. But, like all artistic works, the visual aesthetization of political objects and events could also alert viewers to their contrived nature.

It is because of this constant fear of exposure of the creative behind the documentary, the staged and the theatrical or, more fundamentally, the hidden work of a composing imagination posturing as pure representation, that photography and cinematography constitute such instructive sites for examining the resources used to repress awareness of the rhetorical and the theatrical and

---

[30] Guy Debord, *The Society of the Spectacle*, section 5.
[31] Jonathan Crary, *Techniques of the Observer: On Vision and Modernity in the Nineteenth Century* (Cambridge: MIT Press, 1990), pp. 59, 69.
[32] Ibid., p. 81.
[33] See, for instance, Alan Trachtenberg (ed.), *Classic Essays on Photography* (New Haven: Leete's Island Books, 1980).

to transform imaginaries into factual realities. These resources have included the mechanical and automatic dimensions of the production of photographic images, the development of genres of documentary photography and cinematography (comparable to realism in painting), and a preoccupation with themes particularly resistant to theatricality and staging, such as death, nature, and disaster. I argue that each of these means, instrumental in framing representation as accurate visual possession of the objective external world and for enacting the liberal democratic regime, has been seriously weakened by the erosion of commonsense realism and key norms of democratic political epistemology.

In predemocratic political cultures, the external was guaranteed by God, by a transcendental all-encompassing divine vision or by the synoptic vision of the monarch at the top of the pyramid. In the liberal democratic state, in the absence of either a superhuman or a human outsider, and given the rejection of all claims to a privileged vision, the external – an objective world of facts – could arise only *among* the citizens, not above them. In other words, among democratic individuals, the external, so vital for horizontal persuasion and cooperation, was bound to depend on a new rhetoric that could certify the facticity of the external worlds of nature and society without violating the norms of freedom and egalitarian individualism.

To reiterate the most potent rhetoric employed to validate the structure, regularities, and independence of the external world in the modern democratic state, science and technology are invoked. Combining both, the camera has been a key and perhaps the main popular rhetorical instrument for the performance of external reality in modern democratic societies. Nevertheless, the power of photography to confirm the objective facts of an external world has been limited to a particular historical period whose end seems to have come.

The power to objectify the experience of vision as vision of external objects was achieved in the seventeenth and eighteenth centuries by the *camera obscura* (a darkened box or chamber with an aperture for projecting an image of external objects on a screen placed at the focus of the lens). As Jonathan Crary observes, the *camera obscura* created the possibility of separating natural objects and their representations, thus emulating an outsider's eye gazing from "a vantage point onto the world analogous to the eye of God."[34] The properties of the *camera obscura* as a fixed optical system that conceals the role of the observer seemed to encourage the sense of a distinct separation between interior and exterior, "the corporal subjectivity of the observer" and the object.[35]

The later invention of the daguerreotype as a mechanical device seemed but another stage in the same process, reinforcing dichotomies and expectations generated by the *camera obscura*. As such, the rhetorical powers of the camera in the performance of the world as object were part of the wider rhetorical force of modern technology as a material embodiment of the laws of external nature harnessed to human purposes. This power of technology to objectify

[34] Crary, *Techniques of the Observer*, p. 48.
[35] Ibid., pp. 68–9.

scientific claims about the structure of external reality and its implications for the representation of technologically framed choices and behaviors as rational and apolitical made technology an appealing means of legitimation in the modern state.[36]

The ontological position of the machine between objective nature and human creativity has produced mechanisms such as the clock and the flying machine, which seemed to project, respectively, the poles of necessity and freedom. But the machine metaphor usually chosen as a rhetorical means to anchor and objectify political imaginaries of democratic societies and constitutions was the clock and other self-regulating machines, rather than the airplane, which embodied the human fantasy of transcending the limits of nature and became the favorite metaphor of the fascist regimes of Mussolini and Hitler.[37] Despite occasional fluctuations, the camera, like other machines, had the great rhetorical virtue of at least partially concealing from the lay public the interests and value choices reflected in hardware, modes of operation, and products. In other words, the camera came to be a most powerful socially available tool for performing the Enlightenment democratic imaginary of reality as a visually and publicly accessible domain of facts.

Unlike painting, mechanically mediated photography appeared to produce pictures of the external unmediated by the subjective sensations and choices of the photographer. André Bazin thought that the invention of photography enabled the automatic production of an image of the world for the first time, without the creative intervention of man.[38] Until the late twentieth century, the camera, as a branch of physical technology, could conceal the ethical aspects of this technology. The perceived power of automatic photography to represent unmediated truth was illustrated in the famous case of a photographer, fallen in a Vietnam battlefield, whose camera continued for a few seconds to take pictures of the scene, including the body of the dead subject who could no longer direct his camera.

The camera's credibility as a neutral mediator of the external derived not only from the elements of automation, incorporated into the material hardware of the camera as a machine, but also from the imagined materialism of the chemical process of picture production. Roland Barthes observed: "Painting can feign reality without having seen it. Discourse combines signs which have referents, of course, but these referents can be and are most often 'chimeras.' Contrary to these imitations, in photography I can never deny that the thing has been there."[39] Barthes stressed the power of the photograph to certify that

---

[36] Yaron Ezrahi, *The Descent of Icarus: Science and the Transformation of Contemporary Democracy* (Cambridge, MA: Harvard University Press, 1990); James C. Scott, *Seeing Like a State: How Certain Schemes to Improve the Human Condition Have Failed* (New Haven: Yale University Press, 1998).

[37] Ezrahi, *Descent of Icarus*, pp. 128–66.

[38] André Bazin, "The Ontology of the Photographic Image" in Trachtenberg (1980), p. 241.

[39] Roland Barthes, *Camera Lucida: Reflections on Photography*, Richard Howard (trans.) (New York: Hill and Wang, 1981), p. 76.

an external referent really existed and had been positioned in front of the camera. In *Camera Lucida*, he invokes a version of a materialistic ancient Greek theory of vision according to which the "photograph is literally an emanation of the referent. From the real body, which was there, proceed radiations which ultimately touch me … as Susan Sontag says … like the delayed rays of a star."[40] In the popular mind, such literal and metaphoric materialistic images of photography as mediating material objects and material visual perceptions were instrumental in enabling and supporting a host of cultural-political techniques of presenting power as technical, transparent, accountable and, apolitical.

Eventually, authoritarian as well as democratic governments found in photography a powerful means to monitor and control their citizens, for example, through hidden cameras used to record antigovernment demonstrators. In the hands of citizens and photojournalists, the camera has concomitantly constituted a vital instrument for empowering criticism of the government from below. Assumptions about the unity, givenness, and perceptual accessibility of the external have allowed an imaginary of a common objective reality as a fixed yet rich referent to serve diverse purposes, including communication and coordination between the state and its citizens, or among the citizens themselves.[41] As long as such a system of assumptions and practices was sustainable, photography could appear a powerful means to procure accurate representations of real facts. As such, it was instrumental in the repression of the merely rhetorical and exposure of the inauthentic and the theatrical in social and political interactions.

The reality effect of photography, supported by its mechanical and chemical aspects, was greatly enhanced by the emergence and proliferation of documentary genres in film and newsreels. The popularity of the documentary movie was associated with the rise of modern realism as a grand strategy for enlisting public participation and trust, encompassing the various fields of art and literature as well. Predictably the deployment of the documentary style in art, literature, and politics was bound to strain the dichotomy between facts and fictions in culture and public affairs.

Documentary film became one of the most powerful and influential means for enacting physical and social realities as aspects of the objective external and therefore for a considerable time a reliable resource of apolitical referents of social and political discourse. Besides the selection of themes, the rhetorical techniques of the realistic trend in documentary film have concentrated on concealing the photographer and creating an illusion of a godlike view or omniscient gaze of a human observer who does not interfere with the representation of the objects – and the subjects – as they really are in themselves. Especially since the early twentieth-century social documentary, the illusion of photography without the photographer was crucial for imparting to "social facts" the

---

[40] Ibid. pp. 80–1.
[41] In the production of *Othello* by the Khan Theater in Jerusalem in 2008–9, Iago uses a camera to provide Othello with the "ocular evidence" of Desdemona's betrayal.

nontheatrical or unstageable properties of natural objects and events. László Moholy-Nagy (1895–1945) expressed this ideal of suppressing the influence of the subjective human imagination on vision when he observed that

in the photographic camera we have the most reliable aid to a beginning of objective vision. Everyone will be compelled to see that which is optically true, is explicable in its own terms, and is objective, before he can arrive at any possible subjective position. This will abolish that pictorial and imaginative association pattern which has remained unsuperseded for centuries and which has been stamped upon our vision by great individual painters.[42]

Moholy-Nagy formulates here the optical code of the attestive visual orientation, which, splitting objective from subjective vision, has supported the democratic citizen's belief that he or she can distinguish fact from opinion, external from subjective response.

One of the most effective strategies of documentary certification of social agents and events as external observable facts has been, according to Nichols,

the presentation of things as they appear to the eye in everyday life. The camera and sound recorder are well suited to such a task since – with proper lighting, distance, angle, lens, and placement – an image (or recorded sound) can be made to appear highly similar to the way in which a typical observer might have noted the same occurrence. Realism presents life, life as lived and observed.[43]

But ordinary life experience or the sense of the real is not confined to the familiar, normal, and predictable. It also includes unpredictable and uncontrollable events that disrupt the expected flow of life. Considering this aspect of experienced reality, documentary film discovered the powerful reality effects of unexpected and, therefore, unstageable and unstylizable occurrences. The witnessing of such events through photography has enhanced the experience of reality as autonomous and resistant to human wishes and manipulations.

Musicologist Carl Dahlhaus must have taken note of this particular relation between the experience of the unexpected and the sense of reality when he observed that in music "what is decisive for the concept of realism ... is also the form which shatters an aesthetic form for the sake of reality."[44] Reality effects are produced by breaking conventional rules of stylization, including the stylization of ordinary life. Dahlhaus links the intention to produce reality effects with the introduction of new subjects and new artistic forms previously considered unsuitable or aesthetically taboo. In addition to the effects of the mechanical and chemical materiality of photographic representations and the strategies of effacing or concealing the photographer, documentary filmmakers enhanced persuasiveness and resisted suspicions of staging and posturing by their choice of themes, that is, by juxtaposing expected and unexpected events

---

[42] Laszlo Moholy-Nagy, "Photography" in Trachtenberg (1980), p. 166.
[43] Bill Nichols, *Representing Reality: Issues and Concepts in Documentary* (Bloomington, IN: Indiana University Press, 1991), pp. 165–6.
[44] Carl Dahlhaus, *Realism in Nineteenth-Century Music*, p. 53.

to further reinforce the experience of reality as that which escapes and resists human control. It is more effective to represent or render the external world as a reality, resistant to staging and inauthentic representations, when the themes of documentary films are death, nature, and disaster.

Lacking the advantages of photography in generating reality effects, painting, even more than photography, has opted for the maximization of reality effects through the selection of themes or objects painted. Michael Fried has observed that, in paintings belonging to the realist tradition, antitheatrical effects were achieved by depicting persons in a state of sleep, absorption or blindness, hence unaware of being observed.[45] Whether authentic or staged, such themes and situations have tended to be associated with documentary films or with documentary-style fiction. André Bazin famously argued that the "practice of embalming the dead might turn out to be a fundamental factor" in the creation of the plastic arts: "[B]y providing a defense against the passage of time it satisfied a basic psychological need in man, for death is but a victory of time. To preserve, artificially, his bodily appearance is to snatch it from the flow of time, to stow it away neatly, so to speak, in the hold of life."[46] Bazin argued that photography and cinema satisfied the impulse of immortalizing the likeness of the dead more successfully than portraiture, thus emancipating the creative potential of painting from the yoke of realism to fully exploit its freedom to "recover its aesthetic autonomy."[47]

Given the need of an established democratic political power to project its reality as stable, structured, and controlled while objectifying political agents and events as observable referents of political discourse and action, the power of photography to immortalize has, in my opinion, been less significant than the apparent power of the theme of death to, at least temporarily, emancipate politics and photography from suspicions of staging. Even more than a blind man, a corpse cannot adjust to the presence of the camera or spectators and, perhaps more than any other situation, dying or being dead is the ultimate antitheatrical state. While acts of killing or committing suicide can be theatrical, when the reality of death sets in, the show seems to suddenly evaporate. As I indicated earlier, death caused by political power renders the perception of political power more resistant to the "unreality effects" of theatricality than the decisions or policies proclaimed by the rulers. The intuition or recognition of the inherent imaginary foundations of political power that has driven the obsessive preoccupation with antitheatrical modes of its self-representation has characteristically made photographic representations of executions and other acts of official killing into a powerful means for objectifying the presence of political power. Obviously, when politically induced death is delegitimized by

---

[45] Michael Fried, *Absorption and Theatricality: Painting and Beholder in the Age of Diderot* (Berkeley: University of California Press, 1980).

[46] Bazin, "The Ontology of the Photographic Image" in Alan Trachtenberg (ed.), *Classic Essays on Photography* (New Haven: Leete's Island Books, 1980), pp. 237–8.

[47] Ibid., p. 243.

public opinion, the same objectification of political power can have negative effects. In both cases, though, the antitheatrical effect of the association with death establishes political power as a serious cause. This has often been manifest in cases in which power significantly grows or shrinks following decisions to wage a war supported or condemned by public opinion.

Even beyond the context of politics, I believe that the antitheatrical uses of the theme of death, rather than the desire for commemoration, could account for the fact that, as Nichols has observed, "[death] may ... be the underlying theme of the great majority of documentaries" and the reason it has been important "to a category of filmmaking that lacks the appeal to fantasy and imagination possessed by fiction."[48] I would only add to Nichols' observation that the theme of death does not appeal only to a kind of filmmaking that "lacks the appeal to fantasy and imagination" but also to fiction, in which the latent function of the theme of death is transformed. In addition to reinforcing the documentary claim of such a fiction to represent reality, the theme or the scene of death employs elements of documentary to buttress the temporary suspension of disbelief.[49]

Barthes concludes his last book by observing that photography can be either realistic or fantastic, "mad or tame ... the choice is mine: to subject its spectacle to the civilized code of perfect illusions or to confront in it the wakening of intractable reality."[50] Although it is not possible to consistently attribute to Barthes such a clear choice in his reflections on photography, his preoccupation with the theme of death in photography seems indeed to give special weight to the anti-illusionary or antitheatrical and, therefore, realistic bent of this choice. Sontag aptly characterized Barthes' treatment of photographs "as found objects ... as *memento mori*."[51] For Barthes, photographs are a series of records of the death of "past-presents" of people, events, and moments that have expired.[52] What he finds "in any photograph" is the "return of the dead."[53] The photographic fixation of any person as an image in a particular moment turns person into object, a sort of "Death in person."[54] The arrest of "past-presents" triggers in Barthes the sense that "this has been" and is no longer. He adds: "I can never

---

[48] Nichols, *Representing Reality*, pp. 110–11.

[49] Documentary insertions in the fictional movie on the Kennedy assassination could serve as an illustration of a spreading cinematic practice that aims at subverting an official or common perception of reality. See also Nicolas Poussin's painting *Landscape with a Man Killed by a Snake* and T. J. Clark's meditations on this painting in his *The Sight of Death: An Experiment in Art Writing* (New Haven: Yale University Press, 2006).

[50] Barthes, *Camera Lucida*, p. 119.

[51] See Susan Sontag's introduction to *A Roland Barthes Reader*, Susan Sontag (ed.) (London: Vintage, 1993), p. xxix.

[52] On "past-presents" see Ruth HaCohen, "Intricate Temporalities: The Transfiguration of Proper and 'Improper' Sounds from Christian to Jewish Environments" in Tyrus Miller (ed.), *Given World and Time: Temporalities in Context* (Budapest: Central European University Press, 2008).

[53] Barthes, *Camera Lucida*, p. 9.

[54] Ibid., p. 14.

see or see again in a film certain actors whom I know to be dead without a kind of melancholy: the melancholy of photography itself."[55]

Looking at Alexander Gardner's *Portrait of Lewis Payne* (1865), viewing the young, handsome man waiting in his cell to be hanged for the attempted murder of the secretary of state, Barthes can only think: "He is dead and he is going to die."[56] "Photography," Barthes thinks, "may correspond to the intrusion, in our society, of an asymbolic Death, outside of religion, outside of ritual, a kind of abrupt dive into literal death."[57] I think that one can interpret Barthes' association of photography with asymbolic Death outside religion and outside ritual as also outside the theatrical. If Barthes is right, if photography as such is inexorably associated with a melancholy triggered by the underlying theme of death, mourning, and a lost past, then photography has enormous rhetorical powers to conceal its own theatrical, imaginary, deep structure. Photography has rhetorical powers to divert attention from its deliberate attempt to show (inherent in any photograph), and therefore possesses the paradoxical power to create the illusion of a theatricality-resistant reality.

The historic role played by photography in temporarily concealing the gestural, theatrical, and rhetorical dimensions of images of social and political realities can be more fully appreciated by listing the sources of its reality effects. These reality effects are produced by the material, mechanical, automatic, and chemical components inherent in the production of photographs; elicited by the use of documentary genres of photography; generated by the associations between photography and science; and yielded by the limited control that every photographer has over all the details (including the objects, persons, and contingent events that erupt into the photographed scene). Michael Fried has observed that, as such, *Camera Lucida* can be situated "in relation to the all-important current of *antitheatrical* critical thought and pictorial practice."[58] Fried aims at showing that, in painting, this trend runs from Diderot and Greuze through David and Courbet to Manet.[59] Whereas the history of painting reveals the means used by painters to maximize the reality effects of representations, photography, as André Bazin pointed out, appeared at first far superior to painting in embodying the ideal of perfect realistic representation. I shall argue that it is precisely in light of these pivotal modern expectations regarding the role of photography in the externalization of social and political behaviors and events as photographed objects that the decline of the camera as a key device for upholding the imaginary of the external world as a picture assumes its full potential dramatic significance in contemporary democracy.

[55] Ibid., p. 79.
[56] Ibid., pp. 95–6.
[57] Ibid. p. 92
[58] Michael Fried, "Barthes's Punctum" in *Critical Inquiry* (Spring 2005): 545.
[59] See Michael Fried's *Absorption and Theatricality*; *Courbet's Realism* (Chicago: University of Chicago Press, 1990); and *Manet's Modernism or the Face of Painting in the 1860s* (Chicago: University of Chicago Press, 1998).

If the theme of death has proved to be a particularly forceful means of repressing or marginalizing the awareness of theatricality, the themes of innocence and nature have displayed similar power, as revealed in ethnographic documentaries of native peoples and landscape documentaries. In ethnographic scientific documentaries, the claims of unstageable truths, of pure observation of untrained and undirected people whose innocent natural authenticity obviates any possible theatricality in front of the camera, could be particularly persuasive.

The record of scientific or journalistic ethnographic documentaries shows, moreover, that the rhetorical force of the theme of innocence could be augmented by photographing naked dancing natives in states of trance.[60] If nakedness could project "primitive" unawareness, trance could represent ultimate "absorption," in Michael Fried's sense, as a state of inattention to the presence of the photographer, the camera, or their meaning. Other aspects of these documentaries, such as thin or absent narrative, as well as the otherness of natives, have clearly rendered the sense of observing peoples as natural objects almost as unproblematic as documentaries of natural landscapes.

In documentaries on primitive societies, nature, and natural disasters, the verisimilitude of untheatrical representations of reality could also be, and has been, geared to advance a host of other goals. Documentaries of authentically naked natives could respond to the demand for a voyeuristic erotic pleasure legitimized by indirection. Documentaries of nature could implicitly reinforce, especially among children, a Darwinian image of the organic world as a merciless, competitive struggle for existence that could lay the foundations for later receptivity to neoliberal justifications of a market society, whereas photographs of the epic beauty of inspiring natural landscapes and ruins could be enlisted to promote theological imaginaries of the grandeur of divine creation and the glory of God, illustrating themes of curse or redemption in the Holy Land, or boosting suasive secular imaginaries of homeland to promote patriotism.[61]

THE DECLINE OF THE EXTERNAL WORLD AS A PICTURE
AND THE END OF THE LIBERAL BALANCE BETWEEN CAUSALITY
AND AGENCY

Since the mid-twentieth century, the political practices of liberal democracy have become increasingly incongruent with long-standing democratic norms and political epistemology. Based on a dichotomy between the subject and the world supported by modern science and visual culture, these norms and

---

[60] This claim could, indeed, not be made regarding naked individuals who feature in pornographic movies.

[61] See Nichols' *Representing Reality*, pp. 201–28; Robert Hughes, *American Visions: The Epic History of Art in America* (New York: Alfred A. Knopf, 1997); Yeshayahu Nir, *History of Photography in the Holy Land between 1839 and 1899* (Philadelphia: University of Pennsylvania Press, 1986).

practices promoted the balance between the ontological status of the subject and external society. The latter had been influenced by the metaphorical applications of the dichotomy between the subject and the world, cultivated by modern science and visual culture.

Heidegger regards it as the mark of modernity that the world is conceived as a picture, and that, correspondingly, the individual rises in status as a subject that observes and generates representations of the world. "Humanism," he suggests, "first arises where the world becomes picture."[62] He adds that "whatever is, is considered to be in being only to the degree and to the extent that it is taken into and referred back to this life, i.e., is lived out and becomes life-experience."[63] My point is that from the perspective of political anthropology, the decline of science, photography, and other cultural and socio-psychological reinforcements of the world as an external object in relation to the individual as subject encourages the disruption of entrenched Enlightenment dichotomies between matter and mind. It also redefines the interplay between objectivism and subjectivism so that the conception of the external world, including the partly metaphorical projection of society as an object, becomes more consciously subordinate to a subjective human perspective. When this postmodern metaphysical insight is strengthened and is in turn reinforced by practices of science, technology, and especially photography that subjectivize the experience of the world and problematize its status as an external object, its implications permeate the common political experience.

In the field of human political action, the classical modern democratic conception of the balance between subjectivity and objectivity previously rested, among other factors, on the belief that the physical and, analogously, the socio-political worlds, are visually accessible to citizens as public facts and can function as constraints on individual or group agents' claims and actions. In other words, as indicated in former chapters, the external world as a picture was invoked to restrain the chaotic and anarchistic potential of a voluntary subjectivism unchecked by social reality.

Historically influential Enlightenment scientists, statesmen, and thinkers such as John Locke, Joseph Priestly, Thomas Paine, Thomas Jefferson, Jeremy Bentham, and to a somewhat lesser extent, John Stuart Mill and John Dewey have presented science as instrumental for the emergence of a democratic order based on free individuals guided by empirical observation of public facts, rational assessments of their implications, and a moral commitment to the norm of objectivity. All these commitments have become at least partially anachronistic. The gaps that have visibly developed between these political imaginary and contemporary political practices indicate a process of inevitable transformation.

Jonathan Crary has pointed out that trends corresponding to what I have characterized as the decline of the external world as an objective, intersubjective,

---

[62] Martin Heidegger, *The Question Concerning Technology and other Essays*, William Lovitt (trans.) (New York: Harper Torchbooks, 1977), § 132.
[63] Ibid., § 133.

visual representation are already manifest in nineteenth-century shifts from mechanical to physiological conceptions of human vision, anticipated even earlier by Goethe and Schopenhauer. In place of the individual observer of the classical model of vision, according to which he was conceived as a mere passive recipient of impressions (sometimes transmitted by means of a neutral device) coming from the outside, the body of the physiologized observer (especially his brain) has emerged as an active participant in both the acts and experiences of viewing.

Crary argues that the very subjective vision affirmed by Goethe and Schopenhauer that "endowed the observer with a new perceptual autonomy, also coincided with the making of the observer into a subject of new knowledge and new techniques of power."[64] This shift toward a physiological understanding of the sensory experience of viewing – the new focus on the role of nerves, chemical agents, and other material (and internal psychological) influences on acts of seeing and perceiving – cast into doubt the reliability of denotative-referential relations between our visual representations of the world and the real world outside us. He indicates that in the early 1830s an important landmark in the development of "physiological optics" was Johannes Müller's "potentially nihilistic" theory of vision according to which, contrary to classical theories of vision, "vision is redefined as a capacity for being affected by sensations [like blood or mechanical pressure] that have no necessary link to a referent."[65]

The aforementioned vulnerability of the assumed dichotomy between viewer and visible object has encouraged the resort to several technical, organizational, and rhetorical means for saving the objective world and its knowledge from the impact of radical subjective conceptions of vision. These means were necessary in order to secure trust in such crucial democratic political institutions and norms as the public realm, the visibility and accountability of power, and the public press. Among such measures, education and standardization have featured very prominently.

Faith in the possibility of making exactly identical reproductions of pictorial and standard images of things and persons, in the enhanced reliability of visual representations of reality, prevailed long before the invention of the camera, stemming from the invention of the printing press.[66] As William Ivins argues, the tendency to concentrate on the importance of mechanical reproduction and standardization of texts has often eclipsed the impact of the Gutenberg revolution in the mass reproduction and dissemination of illustrations and prints.

Following this tradition, photographs, like words and metaphors, once integrated into working currencies of social discourse, by their standardization and repetition induce a heightened sense of trust in their fidelity to reality. Standardization and repetition encourage in each individual observer the sense

---

[64] Crary, *Techniques of the Observer*, p. 79.
[65] Ibid., pp. 88–92.
[66] William M. Ivins, Jr., *Prints and Visual Communications* (Cambridge, MA: MIT Press, 1953).

that other persons observe or use the same object, that that object is therefore public and resistant to distortion by an idiosyncratic subjective vision. In other words, by means of standardization, repetition, and social diffusion, society can construe and build on pictorial representations as objective reality even when unsupported by references to visible material referents.

Education has obviously been another means of objectifying social artifacts and standardizing images of nature, thus overcoming the anarchic potential of subjective vision. As I have shown, Pestalozzi's "object method" of showing, naming, and classifying objects of nature before a class of students is a way of normalizing or standardizing the meanings and experiences of things among individuals, thus facilitating the enactment of the external.[67] The more the social order operates according to modern liberal democratic principles of equality, the more important such techniques for enacting the external become in sustaining the imaginary of a commonly experienced world.

Toward the end of the nineteenth century, undercurrents of processes of individualizing and subjectivizing visual perception continued to erode these foundations of democratic political epistemology and commonsense realism. In a later book focusing on issues of attention, spectacle, and modern culture, Jonathan Crary points out that toward the end of the nineteenth century, many theorists of perception, painters, and thinkers had a growing sense of the important role of the indeterminacy and instability of attention patterns in the subjectivization of visual experience.[68] He argues that "in the second part of the 19th century attention becomes a fundamentally new object within the 'modernization of subjectivity,'" and that development has been associated with "the collapse of models of vision and of the stable, punctual subject those models presupposed."[69] Apprehension of the dynamic and individual character of patterns of attention has gradually led to the realization that even the positioning of the same pictures or objects before a multitude of observing subjects does not ensure a common visual experience. Psychological, physiological, and cultural factors diversify what subjects focus on and, therefore, what each sees and interprets as its viewing experience.

The destabilization of the perceiving subject has been inextricably linked to the destabilization of the object. As indicated in Part Three, democratic political agency and causality presupposed one another. They could either be fixed or dissolve together, although not necessarily symmetrically. The latent function of liberal democratic political imaginaries has been to both stabilize the

---

[67] Pestalozzi's object method echoes the seventeenth-century practice of the Royal Society of London to collectively observe samples of nature and then place them under the emerging scientific classification of the objects of nature. We have discussed how, from their very different perspectives, for Albert Einstein and Benedict Anderson the experience of simultaneous cross individual response to an event creates or reinforces the imaginary of external reality, physical or social reality.

[68] Jonathan Crary, *Suspensions of Perception: Attention, Spectacle, and Modern Culture* (Cambridge, MA: MIT Press, 2001).

[69] Ibid., p. 20.

individual observer and fix the objects selected for this observer to focus on. These converging processes of selection isolate the parts of the reigning imaginary promoted to the status of the politically real; and it is by stabilizing these segments of the imaginary as political reality that they are accorded additional protection against the corrosive effects of theatricality and rhetoric.

When shifts between imaginaries of reality become transparent to the lay public, they promote an awareness of the usually concealed means whereby imaginaries of reality have been produced and naturalized. Knowledge, or even intuition regarding the complexity, multiple causality, and undecidability involved in the process of ordinary visual perception have – according to critics defending the declining modern synthesis – weakened trust in its capacity to deliver the objective world as a constraint on an arbitrary political power, thus dangerously flying on the wings of metaphysical fantasies.

This break with the classical modern model of vision and the world as its visible object have drastically diminished the powers of photography, cinema, science, technology, liberal scientific education, and the schools of realism in art and philosophy to enact external objective reality as one of the foundations of the modern Enlightenment imaginary of democratic politics. This is also the reason why in the postmodern condition, realism in painting, for example, as in many other fields, could be experienced as just a genre or another mode of fantasy.

Throughout the twentieth century, particularly illuminating indicators of the cultural ramifications of this change are discernable in tendencies to subvert classical realism in the fields of documentary movies and avant-garde film. The genre of documentary realism characteristically aimed at first to conceal the presence of the camera in support of the pretense to show "the world as it is," to present, without any mediation or intervention, the persons and objects that populate the commonsense world of everyday life and pretend that, as a structure of viewing and representing the world, photography is not inherently interpretive. One can apply Jenny Slatman's argument about television to the camera used in realistic documentaries: "As a visual medium, television asks us to believe in something that we have not seen with our own eyes. Thus, it obscures the apparently clear-cut distinction between faith and seeing, a distinction that has thoroughly dominated our tradition."[70]

It is precisely this gap between faith and seeing or between seeing and knowing that avant-garde film and postrealist reflexive documentary movies have sought to exploit. As Nichols points out, reflexive documentaries do not claim so much to represent the world as to interrogate the very process of representation.[71] Such interrogation has been directed at the technical, epistemological, and ethical dimensions of photographic representation, thus disrupting the

---

[70] Jenny Slatman, "Tele-Vision: Between Blind Trust and Perceptual Faith" in Hent De Vries and Samuel Weber (eds.), *Religion and Media* (Stanford, CA: Stanford University Press, 2001), p. 216.

[71] Nichols, *Representing Reality*, p. 56.

whole complex of realism and its enactment in "observational documentaries." Nichols further argues that "reflexive documentaries" gained a degree of prominence in the 1970s and 1980s, when the genre was reinforced by a critique of the view of language as a medium and by political criticism of the affinities between the epistemology of representation and bourgeois values.[72]

Nevertheless, the introduction of reflexivity into acts of photographic and cinematic representation can also be regarded as having advanced realism in the deeper sense of explicating the realities of perceptual indeterminism, exposing the selective values embedded in the technological hardware and its alternative uses, and questioning the beliefs that make us interpret certain visual experiences as real. Gilles Deleuze observed that in the cinema "making false becomes the sign of a new realism in opposition to making true," a deeper realism which he regards as attempting to overcome the dualism of idealism and materialism, of consciousness and things.[73]

Such reflexive self-interrogating cinema has disrupted key conventions and habits of seeing and representing reality that have long served as a vital resource of the democratic fashioning and uses of the public realm and its furnishings. This disruption has been greatly augmented by continual mass exposure to distant suffering through television. Luc Boltanski observed that

[I]n fact, when the spectacle of the unfortunate and his suffering is conveyed to a distant and sheltered spectator there is a greater likelihood of this spectacle being apprehended in a fictional mode the more the horizon of action recedes into the distance. The distinction between reality and fiction loses its relevance for the utterly powerless spectator for ever separated from what he views.[74]

Aiming at presenting the fantastic as real, commercials have further enhanced the growing public sense of undecidability regarding the dividing line between facts and fictions. It is no wonder that this postmodern new realism has been relentlessly criticized by conventional realists and moralists accustomed to utilize earlier modern realism in support of their moral and political arguments.

Erosion of the habits, expectations, and epistemology of the attestive visual culture of realism in modern democracy has, no doubt, also been influenced by avant-garde film. Here too there was a passion for shocking audiences by undermining their trust in earlier modern genres of realistic fiction and codes of common visual realism. William Wees has shown in some detail how irregular, often experimental uses of the cinematic apparatus have enabled avant-garde film to disrupt standardized modes of viewing previously cultivated by the movie industry.[75] By exploring diverse forms of subjective vision, avant-

[72] Ibid., p. 63.
[73] Gilles Deleuze, *Cinema 1: Movement-Image*, Hugh Tomlinson and Barbara Habberjam (trans.) (Minneapolis: University of Minnesota Press, 1986), p. 218.
[74] Luc Boltanski, *Distant Suffering, Morality, Media and Politics*, Graham Burchell (trans.) (Cambridge: Cambridge University Press, 1999), p. 23.
[75] William C. Wees, *Light Moving in Time: Studies in the Visual Aesthetics of Avant-Garde Film* (Berkeley: University of California Press, 1992).

garde film has helped to explicate and socially project the visual expressions of twentieth-century trends to empower subjective over socially shared modes of experiencing the world.

The earlier mechanical conception of the human eye and of the camera as its extension was far more congruent with the claim that standardized visual reproductions of the world as a picture correspond to reality than the physiological conception of the eye as an organic biological device. The mechanical image was far more conducive to the balance between the ontology of the individual's unique interiority and the existence of an intersubjective perceptual domain of associability sought by democratic individualism.

Avant-garde film joined other cultural trends in posing a powerful challenge to the belief in the possibility of innocent or natural vision, of an untutored human eye safe from the influences of its cultural and political milieu. Moreover, together with self-interrogating documentaries, it has exposed the futility of conceiving a primordial human vision capable of capturing the world as it is, outside the imaginaries and the expectations that guide the eye to select and integrate certain parts of visual experience into distinguishable objects while marginalizing others. Obviously, once the fixed perspective of the observer was destabilized and no spatial or temporal position could be convincingly privileged, the perceived fixity of the object was doomed to vanish as well.

Through the employment and manipulation of multiple perspectives, through the simultaneous projection of diverse time frames, and through manipulating the pace and direction of movement, avant-garde film and the mass movie industry, which borrowed some of its techniques, engaged the popular imagination with a host of believable worlds outside the common experience. Writing about one of the most influential experimental twentieth-century filmmakers, Wees observes that "the lens of [Stan] Brakhage's camera is also a 'glass trap'.... But the trap is sprung by the superimpositions, the overexposure, the cuts, fades, and dissolves with which Brakhage undercuts the single and immobile, precise, and authoritarian point of view built into the camera's lens."[76]

The emancipation of the camera from the strictures of conventional codes of representation, the ability to break down the elements of visual experience in the cinema and recompose them, has led to a recognition of the diversity of cultural and national movie-making traditions. An understanding of the creative compositional aspects of filmmaking, of its complex physiological, technological, cultural, and, therefore, its latent or explicit ideological components, enabled a fresh comparative look at the various national traditions of filmmaking in countries such as Italy, Germany, Russia, France, and America, as Gilles Deleuze demonstrates.[77] This perspective clearly reveals specific local modes of cinematographic handling of the relations between reality and fantasy,

[76] Ibid., p. 50.
[77] Deleuze, *Cinema 1*.

interiority and exteriority, as well as different modes of manipulating time and movement.

The consequences of the erosion of the particular modern visual culture that upheld the subject-object dichotomy and the view of the world as a publicly accessible picture were compounded, in the course of the twentieth century, by occasionally dramatic scientific conflicts of opinion, such as the IQ controversy, the question of the safety of nuclear energy, threats of pollution to the environment, scientific disagreements about the space program, or the debate about the risks and opportunities of stem cell research. The cumulative effects of the inability of scientists to project consensus on crucial issues of public concern have weakened the social authority of science and its capacity to produce authoritative pictures of reality.

Even where they have agreed on the science, scientists have often found themselves entangled in controversies over the ethical and political criteria of the application of their knowledge in the social context. It is ironic that vast areas of scientific agreement have been eclipsed by the media and public focus on a few major controversies. In the course of the twentieth century, socially relevant scientific knowledge in democratic states has, therefore, increasingly appeared to laypersons too underdetermined and esoteric to effectively check arbitrary political power. Political power, in turn, has become too fragmented, diffuse, unstable, and elusive to guide the production and application of socially relevant knowledge.[78]

Under current conditions, the difficulty of the encounter between science and politics derives only partly from the tendency of politicians and clerks to convert the authority of science into a political resource while neglecting the potential of scientific knowledge to improve policies and programs. This was also the case in the recent past. The current quandary is how to integrate knowledge and decisions in a climate devoid of earlier political expectations that the authority of science could depoliticize uses of political power and be effectively enlisted in the legitimation of – particularly costly (in a political sense) – public policy decisions.

Paradoxically, while scientific knowledge has continued to advance rapidly, the scientific community has increasingly projected a more elastic, negotiable, and pluralistic image of knowledge less congenial to the deployment of scientific authority as an effective resource of depoliticization.

Similar trends are discernable in the art world. Whereas abstract art – like avant-garde film and reflexive documentary movies – has reflected the breakdown of conventional realism in visual culture and has relocated much of contemporary painting in elite culture, the fragmentation of the authority of curators in public art and science museums has been a consequence of the emancipation of the subjective vision and the weakened ability to clearly

---

[78] Charles E. Lindblom, *Inquiry and Change: The Troubled Attempt to Understand and Shape Society* (New Haven: Yale University Press and New York: Russell Sage Foundation, 1990).

distinguish expertise from opinion in art criticism.[79] Since the late decades of the twentieth century, curators of art and science exhibitions have experienced a decline in their autonomy to select objects for their exhibitions and freely frame them within an interpretive narrative. The subjectivization, and often also the politicization, of vision has weakened the authority of curators to tell us what we see, how to look at what we see, and which interpretation of what we see can be privileged.

The massive exposure of contemporary publics to television programs including staged news and "reality" shows has accelerated the spread of this lay sense of undecidability between facts and fictions, between objective (in the sense of intersubjective) and subjective visual experience, because of the tendency to blur boundaries separating fictional movies from news and news from commercial advertisement. The need to increase ratings of television programs due to powerful economic interests has augmented the trends enlisting documentary genres as an aesthetic device in feature films, employing techniques of fictional narrative in order to enhance the entertaining and aesthetic appeal of news and documentary programs, mixing aesthetic, documentary, and news reporting styles in order to boost the efficacy of commercial advertising.

FROM THE EXTERNAL BACK TO THE TRANSCENDENTAL?

Quite a few thinkers and cultural analysts who have discerned the erosion of the Enlightenment ideal of a synthesis between knowledge and participation and the decline in the social and political authority of science have associated these developments with signs of what they have defined as "the return of religion." This view, no doubt, relates to the breakdown of the trust, formerly induced by democratic epistemology and commonsense realism, in the intelligibility of a world experienced by our senses as a constraining external object. Samuel Weber made the apt observation that, in "the age of rapidly expanding media, the world of 'sense-perception' is experienced as increasingly 'uncanny.'"[80]

In the domain of the uncanny, of unexpected and untraceable fluctuations between familiar facts and weird virtual realities, religion was obviously bound to gain significant ascendancy in its competition with science. The blurring of boundaries between the kinds of worlds imagined respectively by science and religion has been enhanced by the psycho-cultural effects of the increasing popularity of literary and cinematic genres of science fiction, many of which have appealed directly to the religious imagination.[81] Historically, the rise of

---

[79] See, for instance, Hans Belting's *The End of the History of Art?* Christopher S. Wood (trans.), (Chicago: University of Chicago Press, 1987). On the plight of contemporary curators I have learned from private conversations with Ms. Emily Bilski Motzkin.

[80] See Laurence A. Rickels' interview by Samuel Weber in "Theory on TV: 'After Thoughts,'" in Hent De Vries and Samuel Weber (eds.), *Religion and Media* (Stanford, CA: Stanford University Press, 2001), p. 95.

[81] Stanley Kubrick's film: *2001: A Space Odyssey* (1968) may be one example.

science and its enormous influence on western culture has weakened, albeit never overshadowed, the ability of Christianity, as the dominant western religion, to enlist lay sensory experience of the material world in support of the rhetoric of divine design and the glorification of God.

Whereas early scientists such as Boyle, Newton, and Priestly provided powerful theological rationales for scientific research and theories, the process, accelerating especially since the eighteenth-century European Enlightenment, of harnessing science and the scientific world picture to the program of secularization has become pervasive. Many of the contemporary cultural wars in the West may be viewed as another chapter in the competition between religious and secular cosmologies and their respective implicit imaginaries of the sociopolitical order, competition over the appropriation of the lay sense experience of the external world as a rhetorical and political resource.

The question I raise in the next and final chapter of this book is whether the decline of the partnership between the respective imaginaries of participatory democracy and objective public external reality simply leaves postmodern democracy defenseless in the face of the return of a re-empowered religious imagination that signifies a shift back from the external to the transcendental. Can the vitality of contemporary and future democracies be saved – given the currently decaying program of the Enlightenment – by rebuilding it on new cultural foundations?

Presently, signs of a new assertiveness of the religious imagination in the public sphere are mounting. The acrimonious conflict in North America between advocates of creationism or Intelligent Design and the scientific community is a case in point. While the "evolution wars" started during Darwin's lifetime, the impact of deep cultural undercurrents such as the growing legitimation of new individual subjectivities, including the subjectivization of visual experience, has, over the last century or so, weakened the authority of scientists to tell us what we see, especially when it contradicts widely shared narratives of our naïve commonsense experience or our trusted imaginaries.

The fact that contemporary theories in physics seem to have withdrawn from the domain of commonsense visual experiences of the world, that the referent of such theories is a world outside lay visual metaphors, has dramatically weakened the power of science to defend itself against such attacks. In addition, obviously the rise of powerful religious fundamentalism in North America and other parts of the West, as well as the impact of mass communication, have given the diatribes on the authority of the scientific worldview a new edge. Under these conditions, relations between major scientific institutions and the lay public are beset by new tensions.

The Intelligent Design movement has become part of the creationist attempt to advance the view that God is the designer of the universe and that, in contrast to the cold mechanistic image of the world constructed by modern science, the divinely created world has purpose and meaning. The creationist image of the world has enormous emotional appeal as a resource for coping with the angst triggered by existential human solitude in a world indifferent to man.

Ironically, the very physicalization of nature, which was introduced by ancient Greek philosophers to cope with human anxiety, is now discarded by those who, fearful of a meaningless existence, seek to recover a belief in a supreme intelligent and benevolent deity long marginalized by secular science.

Recognizing the vulnerability of the social authority of science, advocates of Intelligent Design have been using quasi-scientific terms such as *theistic realism* in order to present their argument of design as a legitimate heir to science and commonsense realism. As a rhetorical device against scientific materialism, theistic realism can actually be regarded as an endeavor to usurp reality from modern science and philosophy. Gianni Vattimo notes that the return of religious orientations "coincides with the dissolution of the great systems that accompanied the development of science, technology and the modern social organization." He pertinently observes that the

return of the religious experience in popular consciousness and, in a different sense, in philosophical discourse (where the metaphysical, scientistic or historicist prohibitions of religion break down), presents itself as a discovery of positivity that appears identical in its meaning to the thought of the event-like character of Being taken up in philosophy on the basis of Heidegger.[82]

The anti-evolution campaign waged in many school districts and state legislatures in the United States has not passed over such major scientific institutions as the National Academy of Science and the Smithsonian Institute. A particularly "high profile controversy" was reported by *Physics Today* in "the halls of the bastion of science, the Smithsonian Institution, with the planned showing ... of the movie *The privileged planet: The search for purpose in the Universe*." Despite the Smithsonian's declared pluralistic approach to programs, its readiness to host this movie provoked a wave of protest from all sides of the scientific community. The American Physical Society and the American Institute of Physics sent a letter to the Smithsonian board of directors, from which I quote an excerpt:

We urge you to preserve the Smithsonian Institutions' prestigious scientific reputation by not allowing the film to be shown.... The Discovery Institute [which sponsored the movie, is] a religiously based advocacy organization attempting to persuade the public that Intelligent Design is a legitimate scientific theory. It is not. Intelligent Design is a variation of the religious belief of creationism.... [The film] ... blurs the distinction between well-accepted, peer-reviewed, testable and ideologically-based, untestable assertions.[83]

This emphasis on testable assertions does not always support the claims of science. In a review in *Nature*[84] of Lee Smolin's book *The Trouble with Physics: The Rise of String Theory, the Fall of a Science and What Comes Next*,[85] the

---

[82] See Gianni Vattimo's essay "The Trace of the Trace" in Jacques Derrida and Gianni Vattimo (eds.), *Religion* David Webb (trans.) (Cambridge: Polity Press, 1988), p. 89.

[83] Jim Dawson, *Physics Today* (August 2004): 25.

[84] Vol. 443/5 (October 2006), p. 508.

[85] (New York: Houghton Mifflin, 2006).

reviewer states that "scientific opposition to 'Intelligent Design' centers on the insistence that for a theory to be scientific it must be testable observationally or experimentally. Proponents of 'Intelligent Design' must surely welcome the freedom from evidential constraints that some string theorists are proposing."

I do not share the view that the coming apart of the Enlightenment project necessarily means the return of religion. The dematerialization of the resources and referents of politics in contemporary democracies may reflect a turn in the genres of the contemporary political imagination rather than the return of heaven-based politics. José Casanova, who discerned signs of the penetration of religion into the public sphere in the 1980s, noting a significant shift in the European Zeitgeist, nevertheless suggests that it may be premature to speak of a post-secular Europe.[86] While concurring with this observation, Shmuel Eisenstadt adds that what has permeated the contemporary public sphere are religious sensibilities rather than formal religious rituals or institutions. By contrast to the earlier western tradition of sharply separating the secular public sphere and the state from the private domain of religious faith (*laïcité*), Eisenstadt discerns the emergence of novel, partly deterritorialized forms of religion, which inform the shaping of new modernities.[87]

As invisible universes summoned into existence by strategies of self-reification, politics and religion have always been more analogous than politics and science. In a sense, considering the deep religious layers of the foundations of modern science[88] – strata effectively masked by Enlightenment philosophy and culture – nothing should be surprising in the surfacing of explicit religious imagery and in its not wholly unsuccessful capacity to challenge the physicalist scientific worldview in the popular mind. Jacques Derrida observed that, in some sense, the opposition between reason and religion, or between science (and "technoscientific" modernity) and religion, may not be warranted, considering the possibility that "religion and reason have the same source."[89] He also connects this "return of the religious" with the tendency to ignore the relevance of psychoanalysis to political, scientific, and other discourses, losing psychoanalytic insight into the human reaction to radical evil (central to Freudian thought) as well as the logic of the unconscious.[90]

"The return of religion," in the narrow sense of the partial permeation especially of Christian religious imaginaries into the domains of science and politics,

---

[86] José Casanova's observations on the rise of public religion in *Religion and Democracy in Contemporary Europe*, Gabriel Motzkin and Yochi Fischer (eds.) (Jerusalem: Van Leer/Alliance Publishing Trust, 2007).
[87] Shmuel Eisenstadt, ibid.
[88] Edwin Arthur Burtt, *The Metaphysical Foundations of Modern Physical Science* (Garden City, NY: Doubleday, 1954); Frank E. Manuel, *The Religion of Isaac Newton* (Oxford: Clarendon Press, 1974).
[89] See Jacques Derrida's essay "Faith and Knowledge: The Two Sources of 'Religion' at the Limits of Reason Alone," in Jacques Derrida and Gianni Vattimo (eds.), *Religion* (Cambridge: Polity Press, 1998), p. 28.
[90] Ibid., p. 54.

has apparently been further enhanced by the special historical relations between Christianity and visual techniques of concretizing divine presence for layper-sons. Derrida finds a link between the special efficacy with which Christianity uses the mass media in order to engage or command the faith of laymen and the crucial theological and ritualistic role of the incarnation of the divine in Jesus as well as the Eucharist. He asserts a close connection between the power of the media and the Christian theology of mediation. "Why," asks Derrida,

is this mediation fundamentally Christian and not Jewish, Islamic, Buddhist, etc.? There are of course phenomena of mediatization in all religions, but there is a trait that is absolutely singular in the power and structure of Christian mediatization, in what I have been calling 'globlatinization.' There, the religious phenomenon media-tizes itself not only in the form of information, pedagogy, prediction or discourse. If you go to the United States (the reference to America here is fundamental) and if you watch religious programs on television, you will of course remark that there are also Jewish, Moslem and other programs. In France there are now also Buddhist programs. However the non-Christian programs consist of filming a speech, pedagogy, or dis-cussions, but never events. During a Christian mass, by contrast, the thing itself, the event takes place in front of the camera: Communion, the coming of real presence, the Eucharist, in a certain sense even the miracle (miracles are produced on American television) the thing actually takes place "live" *as* a religious event, *as* a sacred event ... God becomes visible.[91]

The special sway of the religious image in the mass media, its direct or indi-rect denunciation of a hegemonic scientific image of the world is undoubtedly another sign of the triumph of an increasingly prescientistic or postscientistic common sense over modern commonsense realism, the periodic contemporary version of the victory of opinion. We may very well be witnessing an emer-ging postmodern common sense dominating philosophy and science in public affairs.

The deterioration of the object of mutually supportive illusions that scien-tists the world over observe and conceptualize and laypersons experience and the alienation of contemporary politics from the frames of a modern demo-cratic citizens-spectators' visual culture do not necessarily represent a regres-sive shift. What we are experiencing is a current version of *doxa*, of what Vico called *sensus communis*, understood as a public sense of the actual versus the idealized state of public affairs, a sense concocted in our time by the mass media from a variety of ingredients, including current influential images of power, authority and legitimacy, collective anxieties and hopes, social experi-ence with current technologies, scientific claims, general, usually vague, notions of ethics, linguistic habits, social values, shifting public moods, emotions, and the impact of major events.

The failure or diminishing normative power and authority of knowledge to replace opinion and conceal the rhetorical techniques inherent in scientific

[91] Jacques Derrida, "Above All No Journalists," in Hent De Vries and Samuel Weber (eds.), *Religion and Media* (Stanford, CA: Stanford University Press, 2001), p. 58.

persuasion renders deeply misguided the attempts – on the part of many scientists – to resist this trend by debunking postmodernism and reinstating the
Enlightenment paradigm of politics by campaigns designed to boost "public understanding of science."[92] As Sheila Jasanoff indicates, these scientists
are oblivious to the enormously complex processes whereby legitimizing and
delegitimizing government policies and actions are effected in contemporary
democracies, the ways whereby the principle of popular sovereignty is contextualized in contemporary societies, and the limited role that even the most
cogent of scientific and philosophical arguments can actually play in these
processes.

Some (mostly physical) scientists, threatened by these developments and
inattentive to the profound undercurrents that have brought them about, have
tried to arrest the erosion of the social authority of science by attacking those
they often label "relativists" or "nihilists," that is, contemporary philosophers,
historians, and sociologists of science, as well as media scholars and cultural
anthropologists. These scholars have often irreverently explicated the presuppositions and practices of the scientific community and the production of
knowledge, analyzing the declining social authority of science in public affairs.
This controversy, which has spilled over to the mass media, has often been
framed as a conflict between "realists" and "postmodernists."[93] Regardless of
the intellectual merits of the arguments exchanged between these adversaries,
it is interesting to note that perhaps the most salient theme of the debate has
been the question of the existence of objective scientific criteria for evaluating
scientific claims. To one party, the very expectation that there are objective
unambiguous criteria for scientific judgment seems an unwarranted dog-
matic reliance on the availability of incontestable factual reality as arbitrator
between competing scientific claims, whereas to the other, asserting precisely
such an unambiguous, accessible external world, separable from the theoretical perspective of the scientist and the apparatus that can record or measure
it, constitutes a bulwark against a subversive relativism that endangers the
scientific enterprise.

This state of affairs clearly reflects the clash between alternative metaphysics and imaginaries of knowledge and the world, as well as the wide gray

---

[92] Sheila Jasanoff, *Designs on Nature: Science and Democracy in Europe and the United States* (Princeton: Princeton University Press, 2005).

[93] In 1994 Gross and Levitt, a biologist and a mathematician, jointly published a book entitled *Higher Superstition: the Academic Left and its Quarrels with Science*, in which they indict "postmodernists" for misunderstanding science. Following their footsteps, Alan Sokal, a profes-sor of physics at New York University, stirred up a large controversy in 1996 by trying to expose the inability of the editorial staff of a leading journal of cultural studies, suspected of postmod-ern relativism, to distinguish between scholarly articles and nonsense. The faults of this editorial staff notwithstanding, it was later further clarified that, for Professor Sokal, nonsense includes postmodernism as well as social constructionism in the sociology of scientific knowledge. See for instance Mara Beller, "The Sokal Hoax: At Whom are We Laughing?" in *Physics Today*, vol. 51, no. 9 (September 1998).

area of uncertainties which it has exposed.[94] Those scholars attacked by the "realists" have undoubtedly contributed to our contemporary understanding of science as an intellectual and institutional enterprise. They have also provided valuable insights into long-concealed gaps between the social ethos of science (which for many generations nourished commonsense scientism) and the process of science. This controversy, however, has been marginal to the major cultural, technological, and psychological forces that have ignited the contemporary struggle between religious and scientific imaginaries of the world, as well as between the various political groups attempting to advance them.

Serious detailed scholarly study of the interrelated intellectual and social practices of science was bound to record the fragile epistemological, empirical, and sociological foundations of the production of scientific knowledge and authority, already intuited by the lay public and manifest in the declining authority of science in guiding political choices and decisions in society at large. Ironically, this decline in the cultural and social status of science coincides with the extraordinary intellectual progress and growing social relevance of contemporary scientific knowledge.

Despite their largely (but not wholly) misguided criticisms, some "realists" have been right to anxiously detect a link between changing imaginaries of science and technology and the future of the liberal democratic order. They have recognized that for a democracy, there are enormous political consequences in the emergence of a society of free individuals whose cultural repertory does not include "external factual reality" as a "control" or stable reliable referents of objective assertions. Such a society will not sustain the democratic order with which we are familiar. Science, technology, and society studies constitute the most serious contemporary effort to explore, understand, and bridge the gaps between the production of scientific knowledge and the democratic order.

The erosion of the object-subject dichotomy and of the view of the world as a picture and of politics as a reliably legible and universally accessible spectacle and the glaring irrepressibility of the theatrical and rhetorical fabrics of politics are not the consequences of a sophisticated "postmodernist" program but of epochal shifts in the foundational imaginaries and communication technologies of our age. However, the end of the Enlightenment synthesis signifies neither the end of the role of scientific knowledge in public affairs nor the irrelevance of political participation in the reification of a government by and of the people. Instead, the phenomenon that seems to be emerging in the contemporary mass electronic *Agora* is a novel post-Enlightenment configuration of collective political orientations and practices involving radically transformed

---

[94] See Yehuda Elkana, "A Programmatic Attempt at an Anthropology of Knowledge" in Everett Mendelsohn and Yehuda Elkana (eds.), *Sciences and Cultures: Anthropological and Historical Studies of the Sciences*, Sociology of the Sciences, vol. V (Dordrecht: D. Reidel Publishing Co., 1981).

ways of imagining, performing, and experiencing reality and agency. Against the background of such developments, we may raise a question, too large to be satisfactorily answered yet too important to be neglected: Under present conditions, on what basis may individuals and voluntary associations still choose, evolve, and perform liberal democratic imaginaries of government?

13

The Ethics and Pragmatics of the Democratic Political Imagination: On Choosing the Imaginaries We Want to Live By

The issues raised in this book cannot be resolved but must not be neglected. The questions raised are complex: Can democracy as a form of political order survive recent radical changes in the modes and contents of the democratic political imagination? Can the vision of liberal democracy as a regime constituted from bottom up by free association of autonomous individuals be sustained despite the erosion of its Enlightenment foundations? Can current notions of the individual as a dynamic entity that reflexively and intuitively continually composes, decomposes, and recomposes itself be compatible with working forms of democratic individualism? Can liberal democracy regenerate itself on a new cultural basis in the absence of earlier constitutive beliefs in the certainty and solidity of an external world of accessible facts and the stability of individual and communal identities? Do the changes unfolding today result from inescapable technological, economic, and social processes, or are individuals and collectives left with room for choice?

In the following speculative discussion, I will only tentatively and partially give an affirmative answer to these questions. I think that, to the extent that political history is partly a record of self-fulfilling beliefs, of enacted political imaginaries, individuals and collectives make choices that influence the rise and fall of different systems of government. The ethics and pragmatics of the selection of such performative political imaginaries relates to conditions in history in which societies are presented with possibilities of choice. In such moments, collectives can opt for constituting themselves along certain orbits while rejecting others. Homi Bhabha clearly thinks along this line when he observes "the growing hybridity of imagined communities" in our time and quotes Renan's famous observation that "a nation's existence is a perpetual plebiscite."[1] Despite the difficulties inherent in discerning the links between a multitude

---

[1] Homi K. Bhabha, *The Location of Culture* (London: Routledge, 2006) p. 7; E. Renan "What is a Nation?" in Homi K. Bhabha (ed.), *Nation and Narration* (London: Routledge, 1990), p. 19. Ian Hacking makes some cogent observations on historical opportunities of choice in his *Historical Ontology* (Cambridge, MA: Harvard University Press, 2002), pp. 1–26.

of – conscious or unconscious – individual political choices within the limits of biographical time and the choices made by collectives in social and historical time, political philosophers and historians have provided ample examples of the possibility of subjecting such choices to an ethical assessment.

Recognizing the primary historical role played by popular political imaginaries in the shaping of political history, one can probe which political imaginaries are most likely to generate antagonism and violence and which are most congenial to freedom, equality, toleration, and a peaceful social existence. Whereas the historical record sheds some light on these queries, we must admit that often the picture is ambiguous. The twentieth century, for example, has frustrated the expectation that politics in modern secular states would generate less violence than earlier politics governed by the great religions. Nevertheless, one cannot but be impressed by Vico's insight regarding the political implications of a state under the sway of a religious faith that imagines God as "fierce and terrible ... armed with deadly weapons" and a state "ruled with a mild religion" (*New Science*, 1090).

We have considerable evidence to support the intuition that a worldview that rests on a dichotomy between good and evil, and a society in which these categories are deployed to distinguish between types of individuals and divide groups, is more prone to bloodshed than an order free of such binary oppositions. The history of the resistance to religious enthusiasm and violence reveals ambivalent and antagonistic attitudes toward imaginaries of God, man, prophecy, and redemption that seemed to disrupt the existing order during the seventeenth and eighteenth centuries. One of the aforementioned modern strategies of coping with such violence-prone religious imaginaries entailed criticism of their validity in the name of secular commonsense realism and distinguishing reasonable from unreasonable religious spokesmen.

From this perspective, the partial decline of the external world as a vital cultural and political resource for checking the religious imagination in the domain of public affairs and the disintegration of reality as a safe reservoir of fixed referents for responsible public discourse or action are bound to be perceived as a regressive shift that invites the return of a political imagination undisciplined by legal texts and facts. Nevertheless, as I suggested in the previous chapter, these might actually herald the emergence of a new post-Enlightenment cluster of political imaginaries that relocates reality in a more reflexive causal relation between what people imagine and how they evolve their individual and collective forms of life. Reality in politics would no longer be modeled on physical reality as a primordial external given,[2] but perhaps on theater or cinema, viewed not merely as branches of the arts of illusion or genres of documentation and representation, but as a way to explore and create possible, performable, livable, and viable worlds and produce alternative externals. The postmodern universe instructs contemporary individuals that

---

[2] Richard Rorty, *Philosophy and the Mirror of Nature* (Princeton: Princeton University Press, 1979).

the suspension of disbelief is not only a temporary condition for entering and enjoying a novel, a play, or a movie, but a permanent condition for entering into and living within the culture and politics of any form of life. Perhaps the reflexive suspension of disbelief can be more universally, freely, and usefully employed as a means to consolidate desirable political imaginaries of social life. Obviously, a politically productive suspension of disbelief in foundational fictions of the emerging forms of contemporary democracy cannot rest on anything like the total support system provided by Christianity to the political fiction of the divine right of kings, or by totalitarian modern ideologies to nationalist or communist regimes. Admittedly, under current postmodern conditions, democratic individuals as civic agents have lost much faith in once precious political and rhetorical resources such as the master narrative of progress, the power of science to define reality and induce consensus, and the perception of the subject as a coherent and constant entity. But the fragmentation of mega-narratives, the controversies around science and technology, and postmodern imaginings of hybrid, self-constituting individualism open paths to a more conscious and pressing search for and experimentation with new potential imaginaries of agency and community.[3] In our time, suspension of political disbelief is bound to be more tentative, fluid, and potentially reflexive, and therefore also more democratic.

Contemporary reflective citizens may, to a larger extent than their predecessors, be able to voluntarily and flexibly use the frame of reality to fix and privilege referents that anchor imaginaries conducive to desirable political and social experiences. Curiously enough, this potential may be illustrated by what David Rodowick has called "the virtual life of film" in the digital culture of the contemporary production and consumption of images.[4] As Rodowick indicates, the now pervasive digital techniques of image production are nonindexical, nonmaterial, nonspatial, and unconstrained by the ontology of material objects, and they lend themselves more readily to manipulative compositions. Digitality opens infinite vistas for image making. And yet, despite these revolutionary shifts in the technology of image making and the symbolic meanings of representation, despite the replacement of film by electronically manipulated algorithmic functions, digital image making imitates conventional cinematographic appearance. "Today" writes Rodowick, "the creative language of digital creation is predominantly the language of movies."[5] Of course, digitally produced representations of reality lack the concreteness of indexical images and function more as simulations. But the persistence of photographic perceptual framing indicates, in my opinion, the resilience of the cultural-moral

---

[3] On such contemporary micro-utopias see Yaron Ezrahi: "Science and Utopia in Late 20th Century Pluralist Democracy" in E. Mendelsohn and H. Nowotny (eds.), *Nineteen Eighty Four: Science between Utopia and Dystopia* (Dordrecht, NL: Reidel, 1984); *Sociology of the Sciences Yearbook*, pp. 273–90.

[4] David N. Rodowick, *The Virtual Life of Film* (Cambridge, MA: Harvard University Press, 2007).

[5] Ibid., p. 133.

force of commonsense realism, the democratic civic and cultural commitment to at least a minimal preservation of a common perceptual world as a prerequisite for horizontal human communications and cooperation. The virtual life of commonsense photographic realism in digital culture represents at least partial persistence of what I have called the moral epistemology of democracy. It expresses a partly reflexive normative, cognitive, and pragmatic collective choice to perform an imagined common world, a world without which democratic politics is impossible.

My assumption is that many aspects of contemporary culture and technology can facilitate such processes of moving by means of conscious or unconscious performance from hegemonic imaginaries to the political and institutional realities they prescribe. *This reversal of outlook, from image to reality rather than from presumed reality to representations*, should create new space for the politics and ethics of imaginings that shape our common life. So we may try to answer the question of how we, human beings living in the post-Enlightenment era, should imagine ourselves and the world so that the long-standing democratic values of individual freedom, equality, and nonviolence become the organizing principles of our political order. I believe this query opens several alternative paths but will limit myself to outlining and reflecting upon one or two of them. Before responding to this question, let us first briefly provide some illustrations of the ways in which a few political thinkers have attempted to link the choice of metaphors or imaginaries and their political consequences.

Influential political thinkers such as Machiavelli, Hobbes, Spinoza, Locke, Rousseau, Nietzsche, Marx, and Schmitt paid special attention to the relations between popular political imaginaries and their anticipated behavioral political consequences as performative guides. They were also keenly mindful of the potential of the metaphors they used in their work to influence the conduct of laypeople who internalized them. Not surprisingly, whatever impact these thinkers had on the perception and performance of individualism and collectivism and their interrelations, these have often been driven more by the popular reception of the metaphors these thinkers used and worked with than by their systematically constructed arguments. As a matter of fact, from the interpretive perspective of this book, a considerable part – but only a part – of modern political theory can now be reread as a prescriptive code or map for the performative political imagination or a deliberate combination of such prescriptive political maps for lay consciousness and philosophical as well as legal arguments aimed at intellectual peers. The tensions between the distinct sensibilities and rhetorical genres that inform philosophical and lay discourses were manifest in the conflict between Athenian orators and philosophers. Josiah Ober observed that:

[T]he split between reasoning implicit in democratic rhetoric and philosophical reasoning has as its defining moment the trial of Socrates in 399 B.C. The incompatibility of philosophy and rhetoric is seemingly established by Socrates' inability to persuade a majority of Athenian jurors of his innocence through a discourse that adjured the customary acceptance of contradictions and adherence to popular ideology. The breach was not fully healed by Aristotle's attempt in the *Rhetoric* to explain a form of reasoning that was less rigorous than formal logic yet remained in fair correspondence with observed social facts.[6]

Clearly, from the very beginning of the western democratic political tradition, the capacity of a political order to cultivate measures of freedom, equality, and stability (as well as to weaken them) had much less to do with the philosophical imagination and the formal methods of philosophical persuasion than with popular political imaginaries.

Throughout later centuries, much of this discussion has taken the form of a clash between philosophy and religion. Spinoza held that the difference between philosophy and religion lies precisely in the difference between an intellectual search for the truth and a host of beliefs intended to render human beings socially obedient and peaceful. This attitude has provoked debate among theologians and philosophers on whether figures such as Moses or Christ were philosophers who achieved a true knowledge of God or leaders who discovered and imparted imaginaries to regulate, discipline, and bond human beings in communities.[7] Spinoza held that beliefs that instigate fear of God need not be truthful in order to render human beings obedient, but when people suspect their truthfulness, these beliefs may lose their grip. Such dualism is also present in two conceptions of politics: the intellectual inquiry into the nature of political man on one hand and politics thought to support a just and stable political order on the other. This dualism underlies much of the history of the relations between political philosophy, popular political faith (sometimes referred to in modern times as ideology), and political practice. The political thinkers I have chosen to discuss in this book have either directly or indirectly attempted to come to grips with both aspects of this dualism. They often, not always explicitly, stressed performative political efficacy over knowledge of truth while endeavoring to harness the authority of the intellect in order to render the political imaginaries they sought to advance truthful.

Hobbes's political theory is a case in point. Considering Hobbes's keen awareness of the power of people to "stand in awe of their own imagination,"[8] he must have realized that, when that which people imagine is politically

---

[6] See "The Orators" by Josiah Ober in Christopher Rowe and Malcolm Schofield (eds.), *The Cambridge History of Greek and Roman Political Thought* (New York: Cambridge University Press, 2005), pp. 140–1.

[7] Baruch Spinoza: *Theological-Political Treatise*, Samuel Shirley (trans.), second edition (Indianapolis: Hackett Publishing, 2001), Chapter 14 [176]; Leo Strauss, *Spinoza's Critique of Religion* (Chicago: University of Chicago Press, 1997); Shlomo Pines, *Studies in the History of Jewish Philosophy: The Transmission of Texts and Ideas* (Jerusalem: Bialik Institute, 1977), pp. 306–49. Ruth HaCohen's interpretation of the basic dramatic conflict in Arnold Schoenberg's *Moses und Aron* (fragment, composed between 1930–2) pursues a similar line, arguing that Moses represents the philosopher in the Spinozian configuration, whereas Aron follows the political theologian, sensitive to the psycho-religious needs of the people. See *The Music Libel Against the Jews* (New Haven: Yale University Press, 2012), chapter 6.

[8] Thomas Hobbes, *Leviathan*, Michael Oakeshott (ed.) (New York: Collier, 1962), p. 168.

consequential, the selection of imaginaries should be guided more by their contribution to the stability and legitimacy of the political order than by their literal correspondence to some external truth. Hobbes can be quite explicit in his preference for imaginaries and metaphors whose anticipated behavioral import advances the stability and legitimacy of the political order over those prone to undermine it. He thought, for instance, that people should be imagined as equal even when nature seems to have made them unequal, because otherwise "men that think themselves equal will not enter conditions of peace."[9] Whereas here Hobbes deliberately advances a morally and politically constructive imaginary that may contradict the evidence, or commonsense experience of nature, he clearly opposes other metaphors like the one used to establish individual "conscience," which he thought could undermine public authority. In chapter 7 of the *Leviathan,* Hobbes first uses the term *conscience* in the sense of *con-science,* that is, in the sense of public knowledge, which he regards as the formerly common use of the word:[10]

When two or more men know of one and the same fact, they are said to be *conscious* of it one to another; which is as much as to know it together. And because such are fittest witnesses of the facts of one another, or of a third, it was, and ever will be reputed a very Evill [*sic*] act, for any man to speak against his Conscience.[11]

But later, Hobbes observes, the meaning of con-science as knowing together was corrupted by its metaphorical transformation into conscience in the sense of inner private confirmation of the certainty of individual claims of truth. Then, he writes:

[M]en made use of the same word (conscience) metaphorically, for the knowledge of their own secrets facts and secret thoughts.... [Being] in love with their own opinions ... and obstinately bent to maintain them, [men] gave those their opinions also the reverenced name of *Conscience* ... pretend[ing] to know that they are true, when they know at most, but that they think so.[12]

As Karen Feldman observes, the "metaphorization of conscience allows knowledge to be taken out of a public realm into a secret, private realm, where, without true witnesses, knowledge will be redefined and dissolved as knowledge, and opinion will be portrayed as knowledge."[13] Whereas at a later stage in the development of liberal individualism, conscience, in the sense of inner individual knowledge and its externalization as the individual's inner voice in public, was a crucial element of the ontological and normative emergence of

---

[9] See discussion of this observation by Hobbes in Yaron Ezrahi's "The Authority of Science in Politics" in Arnold Thackeray and Everett Mendelsohn (eds.), *Science and Values: Patterns of Tradition and Change* (New York: Humanities Press, 1974), p. 229.
[10] Hobbes, *Leviathan,* pp. 131–2.
[11] Ibid.
[12] Ibid.
[13] Karen S. Feldman, "Conscience and the Concealments of Metaphor in Hobbes's *Leviathan*" in *Philosophy and Rhetoric,* vol. 34, no. 1 (2001): 27.

modern individualism; for Hobbes such a degree of individual self-confidence and authority, based on subjective certainty, constituted a real danger to public authority. Hobbes foresaw the anarchic potential of radical subjectivism and was critical of the metaphorical extension of public into private knowledge. Despite this and his other explicit criticism of metaphors, Hobbes did not refrain from extensively using and working with political metaphors such as "Leviathan," "body-politic," "artificial man," "blood circulation," and especially the "social contract," when they advanced his preferred imaginary of the public order.

If Hobbes's discourse was initially confined to esoteric intellectual circles, Rousseau's work, whose powerful rhetoric was a major source of the slogans of the French Revolution, makes a more explicit public gesture. Rousseau makes an open plea to advance public acceptance of a host of imaginaries he deems necessary in order to shape the consciousness of democratic citizens, imaginaries he lumps together under the metaphorical category of "civil religion." He held, for instance, that democratic citizens must believe in "positive dogmas" such as the "sanctity of the social contract and the laws," metaphorically applying religious categories in support of a basically secular imaginary of the democratic state.[14] Such a reinforcement of secular political imaginaries with religious rhetoric was later salient, as we saw in Chapter 8, during the French Revolution.

Obviously, the history of the popular political imagination is a record of shifting contests between leading political imaginaries. Even when themes of the political imagination are repeated in the course of history, the ways in which they are framed and configure vary with time and context. As I have indicated, a major such theme concerns the boundaries between voluntary and involuntary causes of events. In our time this theme has often shaped the contest between communitarian and liberal individual political imaginaries of the political order and the contest between nature and society. While the issue of nature and society had its early contested versions in ancient Greece, Rousseau and Marx gave it particularly influential casts. In her book *The Faces of Injustice* (1990), Judith Shklar continues an important strain in the history of modern political philosophy when she urges us to expand our sense of injustice by disavowing the tendency to attribute disasters such as hunger or the effects of earthquakes to nature or misfortune, rather than to "civic failure" and "private or public acts of injustice."[15] Beyond her analytical arguments, she seeks here an act of radical reimagining, a shift in the public imaginary of disaster intended to denaturalize or to politicize domains of the human experience of distress.

Beyond the observation that shifts between imaginaries or politically constitutive metaphors have been an integral part of political philosophy and an

---

[14] Jean-Jacques Rousseau, *The Social Contract and Discourses*, G. D. H. Cole (trans.) (New York: E. P. Dutton and Co., 1950), p. 139.

[15] Judith N. Shklar, *The Faces of Injustice* (New Haven: Yale University Press, 1990), pp. 51–82.

often unconscious element in political practice, it is important to stress that in the contemporary culture of fast-moving images, the focus on the cultural shaping and transforming of paradigmatic political imaginaries has apparently become far more reflexive. Though this recognition can barely be discerned in the recent discourse of mainstream political philosophers, it seems increasingly manifest in contemporary political practice and in fields of knowledge such as communications, film theory, political analysis, political anthropology, marketing, and management.

The ability of the contemporary mass media to enormously magnify local occurrences into powerful, emotionally loaded global events has certainly contributed to the enhancement of the behavioral and institutional impact of images and imagining in contrast to that of words and texts.[16] One can trace significant shifts in public political attitudes to experiences associated with the mass communication of dramatic events. The destruction of the Twin Towers in New York on September 11, 2001 is perhaps the most glaring example. In response to the spectacular images of this monumental act of terror, a Republican president was able, for a few years, to effectively invoke a contemporary version of the old religiously inspired rhetoric of evil in order to enlist public support for the ensuing use of extreme forms of violence against an elusive enemy.

The power of such fear-inducing images of terror and evil to weaken the social hold of classic liberal values has been greater than that of any conservative-philosophical criticism.[17] But what the political rhetoric of evil, disseminated by the mass media in the post-September 11 period, shares with conservative political attitudes, are imaginaries of a colossal war between the evil sons of darkness and the good sons of light. George W. Bush and some of his allies have given currency to such expressions as "the axis of evil," thus casting entire sectors of the globe onto an evil pole. Such violence-promoting imagery has been reinforced since September 11, 2001 by the extensive use and misuse of influential works by distinguished scholars at Harvard and Princeton, encouraging the prediction of an imminent war between Islamic and western civilizations.[18]

This development has led to a new version of eighteenth- and nineteenth-century conservative attacks on liberal democratic imaginaries of state and citizen and their associated values of moderation, reasonableness, tolerance, and legalism. Echoing the wave of McCarthyism in the 1950s, imaginaries employed after September 11, 2001 to demonize particular individuals and groups have nourished a readiness on the part of a large sector of the American

---

[16] Elihu Katz and Daniel Dayan, *Media Events: The Live Broadcasting of History* (Cambridge: Harvard University Press, 1992).

[17] See for instance Richard J. Bernstein, The Abuse of Evil: The Corruption of Politics and Religion Since 9/11 (Cambridge: Polity, 2005).

[18] See for instance Samuel P. Huntington, *The Clash of Civilizations and the Remaking of World Order* (New York: Simon and Schuster, 1998) and Bernard Lewis, *What Went Wrong? Western Impact and Middle Eastern Response* (New York: Oxford University Press, 2002).

public to – at least temporarily – suspend or restrict the very legal rules and practices of trust that had hitherto provided protection to human and civil rights and supported social inclusiveness. These regulations and norms had been painstakingly cultivated in America and Europe since World War II, and even more so following the Cold War.

In all such instances, the political dynamics of constitutive metaphors or imaginaries and their impact on institutions and policies have tended to create an almost permanent gap between what coherent political theories and their "propositional knowledge" propose and what the public disposes. To reiterate, conflicts between competing approaches to the political order are usually carried out by wars of political imaginaries rather than by cogent propositions. If, to a large extent, this has always been the case, what then is new? The novelty lies in that we are living in a period in which relatively fixed conceptions of objective facts and causes in politics such as human nature, rational persuasion, or the desire for political participation have been deeply challenged by far more dynamic post-foundational imaginings of political agents and realities. This may account for the impression that, to a far larger degree than in former times, laypersons and professional politicians, many of whom employ image managers, have become aware that what connects normative political attitudes with political behavior is more the battle of imaginaries and their derivative images and performative scripts than the clash of philosophical or ideological arguments.

The contemporary debate between communitarians and liberal individualists can serve as an illustration. Proponents of the contesting approaches in this debate often raise the question of who comes first – the individual or the community. Are the individual's interiority and identity derivative of the culture and identity of the community or are the culture and traits of the community derived from the individuals who compose it? Are individuals unique, or do at least many of them have shared identities? Is the community a given, or is it the creation of presocial or socially creative individuals?

These partly unanswerable questions imply different ontological starting points that seem to anchor alternative chains of arguments. But these queries, I suggest, can be fruitfully reversed or reframed in such a way that the crux would become the question of which of these alternative imaginaries is likely to be a cause of behaviors and institutions that more closely approximate our view of meaningful freedom and equality.[19] How, for instance, does the individual or collective internalization of each of these two paradigmatic imaginaries of individual and community influence or shape attitudes toward risking individual lives in time of war and in other instances where force is used by the state? Given the available evidence of their respective behavioral effects, which of these two imaginaries should be ontologized (in social discourse) in order to

---

[19] See Nita Schechet, *Disenthralling Ourselves: Rhetoric of Revenge and Reconciliation in Contemporary Israel* (Madison and Teaneck: Fairleigh Dickinson University Press, 2009) on cultures of revenge and reconciliation.

promote a given set of goals and which should be downgraded as derivative? Or, better still, how shall we distribute the privileging status of reality between the two imaginaries, considering the kind of politics we seek to produce?

The respective positions of the principal advocates of the communitarian and liberal approaches to the political order have not been uniform. On the communitarian side are important differences between Michael Sandel, Charles Taylor, Alasdair MacIntyre, and Michael Walzer, as there are on the liberal side between John Rawls, George Kateb, Judith Shklar, Richard Rorty, Steven Holmes, Seyla Benhabib, John Connolly, and Gilles Deleuze. Very often the differences go beyond matters of emphasis or degree. Whereas Charles Taylor, for instance, seems to persistently maintain the genealogical and moral primacy of society over the individual and criticize the modern tendency toward "disembedded" individualism, the ontological grounds of this position seem to have softened in his later work in which he acknowledges the influence of "collective social imaginaries," "the ways people imagine their social existence" impact social and political behavior.[20] On the side of liberal individualism, John Rawls' rational individual is clearly not Gilles Deleuze's individual as "an assortment of infinite singularities and experiences .... The self is not defined by its identity but by a process of becoming."[21] From the perspective of liberal feminist theory, Seyla Benhabib wisely weighs the balance between the need to resist radical postmodernist notions of the "death of the subject" and to protect the emancipatory imaginary of female agency against its impoverishment by simplistic interpretations of Lyotard's assertion about the end of grand narratives or Judith Butler's view that female identity can be constituted by performances without a subject.[22] It is generally agreed that the question is not whether personhood is a natural given but how and with what cultural and moral fabrics it is constituted and reconstituted in time. It is on that basis that I am concerned here with the ethics and pragmatics of individual and collective choices of alternative modes of being. Since the important controversy between communitarians and liberal individual thinkers and its nuances are easily accessible in their writings and in a vast critical literature assessing the various positions, I shall not elaborate it further.[23]

My purpose is to recast the issue in terms of the performative political imagination, as a question regarding the ethics and pragmatics of selectively choosing political imaginaries as candidates for pragmatic reification, an approach that may altogether reframe the debate.

One of the key elements of this line of thought is the recognition that, insofar as it guides and coordinates human behavior and fulfills particular goals,

[20] Charles Taylor, *Modern Social Imaginaries* (Durham: Duke University Press, 2004).
[21] Gilles Deleuze, *Essays Critical and Clinical*, D. W. Smith and M. A. Greco (trans. and eds.), (Minneapolis: University of Minnesota Press, 1997), p. xxix.
[22] Seyla Benhabib, The Situated Self: Gender, Community and Postmodernism in Contemporary Ethics (New York: Routledge, 1992), pp. 2010–19.
[23] See, for instance, Stephen Mulhall and Adam Swift (eds.), *Liberals and Communitarians*, second edition (Oxford: Blackwell, 2000).

any choice of a reality definition from the multiplicity of potential reality definitions is an ethical one. What renders reality an ethical category in the socio-political context is the very possibility of arranging and rearranging the same physical and social facts in a great variety of ways to support multiple alternative reality definitions. The conscious or unconscious welding of slices of experience, bodies of facts, and theoretical concepts in the production of any particular category of reality assumes the choice of a normative perspective, a particular set of value commitments, and an anticipation of specific desired results. What an individual or a community takes for granted as reality must undergo normative and epistemological tests of acceptability before it becomes a powerful regulator of conduct.

Liberal as well as communitarian philosophers tend to advance imaginaries of reality compatible with their normative positions, as if they unambiguously derived their validity from a realm outside the ethico-political discourse on the nature of individuals and community and the shape of the political order. Since philosophers have a deep commitment to logical coherence, they usually tend to privilege – depending on whether they are liberal individualists or communitarians – either the reality of the individual or of the community, as if they were mutually exclusive. In the context of his discussion on liberal and communitarian theories of human tendencies to segregate as individuals or socially connect, Michael Walzer observes at one point that the two critical arguments "are mutually inconsistent; they cannot both be true."[24] But this logical conclusion may be irrelevant if as political imaginaries both can simultaneously or consecutively be behaviorally productive in a desirable complementary way.

The tendency to eschew or conceal the ethical choices behind specific categories of reality presented as singularly corresponding to the facts of the world is liable, therefore, to preclude the reflexive or intuitive social support of a balanced, shared and less categorical ontological status. A more critical issue is that such quasi-scientific reality definitions descending from above sometimes constitute an effective, if usually subconscious, means for usurping the prerogatives of individual and community to decide which imaginaries of themselves and which imaginary of social reality to ontologically privilege.

For instance, the claim advanced by Walzer and Sandel that liberalism denies the truth about the substantive social genealogy and character of individual persons is largely accurate. But this argument is irrelevant to the question that many modern liberal communities raise and answer either deliberately or intuitively: What degree of reality status should be accorded to the imaginary of the autonomous separate individual in order to produce unexclusive, nonviolent politics? This question is raised against a background of evidence that seems to support the belief that a culture of individualism that attaches the highest value to individual life imposes powerful constraints on the kind of violence facilitated by communalizing and, therefore, depersonalizing both the agents

---

[24] Michael Walzer, *Politics and Passion: Toward a More Egalitarian Liberalism* (New Haven: Yale University Press, 2004), p. 148.

and targets of violence. One can hardly avoid the question of the extent to which competing imaginaries of communally shared identities and individual uniqueness should be emphasized or deemphasized in order to pave the way for an ethico-political preference for a particular political order. Communitarian philosophers and ideologues tend to be inconsistent when they ignore the authenticity and constitutive political logic of communal acts of self-imagining whereby a collective perceives itself as an aggregate of individuals rather than as a given primordial organic entity. The point is not what is true but what kind of politics and institutions a community seeks to produce. It is precisely because community may be part of a deep structure that the performative logic of a self-perception of the community as an aggregate of separate individuals becomes important.

Such questions were also faced and answered in different ways by social scientists such as Durkheim and Weber. The tension between a scientific commitment to a causal social account of the production of the individual and a liberal ethical commitment to individualism is especially pronounced in the work of French sociologist Émile Durkheim. Struggling to reconcile sociological determinism and a voluntaristic theory of action, he insisted that "the impersonal truth developed by science can leave room for everyone's individuality."[25] Edward Tiryakian has suggested that, for Durkheim, part of the solution lies in the way that modern worship of the individual becomes a collective social goal, in the same way that the worship of supernatural beings functioned in earlier societies.[26] In no way does the assertion that individualism arises in modern societies as a "collective representation" obviate a process of its self-animation and self-realization as a substantive political agent. Since reality definitions are also collective representations, isn't it ironic that some communitarians, who do not hesitate to regard language, historical memory, and ethics as social products, would decide for the rest of us that when we imagine ourselves as a community this imaginary corresponds with reality, and when we imagine ourselves as an aggregate of autonomous individuals we entertain a mere illusion?

Moral communitarian criticism of the modern individual as an "empty," "materialistic," "storyless," "egotistic," and "uncommitted" citizen has been commonly accompanied by the argument that the liberal individual is a mere artificial being, that human beings are naturally and essentially social fragments, groups of encumbered selves whose identity is actually embedded in their communal membership. One of the implications of this position has been the charge that, as a theory (which they rarely distinguish from ideology), liberal individualism encourages contemporary forms of false consciousness, that

---

[25] Émile Durkheim, *Pragmatism and Sociology*, J. B. Alcock (ed.), C. Whitehouse (trans.) (Cambridge: Cambridge University Press, 1983), pp. 89–91. See also his *Sociology and Philosophy*, D. F. Pocock (trans.) (Glencoe: Free Press, 1953), pp. 96–7.

[26] Edward Tiryakian, *Sociologism and Existentialism: Two Perspectives on the Individual and Society* (Englewood Cliffs, NJ: Prentice-Hall, 1962), pp. 54–60.

it dehumanizes and corrupts natural individuals who are deeply social beings and fuels degenerative processes of social disintegration.

Nevertheless, it must be admitted that, on the other side, liberal thinkers have often insisted that privileging the reality of community over that of the individual masks the goal of centralizing power in the hands of elites who claim to represent the community. The liberal view is that, as a theory (which they too only rarely distinguish from ideology), communitarianism eschews the primacy of the presocial individual in creating the community. They hold that communitarianism often conceals the origins of communities in presocial individuals and that community is potentially a form of coercion that deprives individuals of their natural freedom. They advance, by contrast, the liberal view that individuals are original, discrete, self-creating entities capable of overcoming the involuntary bonds of birth, religion, ethnicity, and culture and voluntarily joining other groups.

Such reciprocal communitarian/liberal denial of the respective originary realities of individual and community should refocus on the political process of selecting and rejecting models and imaginaries of the social order rather than on winning arguments or defending theories of who came first the individual or the community. Yet, as I have indicated, there is a long tradition of political theorists who seek to win arguments with their intellectual peers rather than contribute to the pedagogy of lay deliberation concerning the comparative practical virtues of the core imaginaries of liberal individualism and communitarianism. Not surprisingly, therefore, much of the debate between the two schools often degenerates into assertions about conflicting "truths" and genealogies rather than offering assessments concerning possible causal relations between the imaginaries they respectively seek to advance and their diverse political effects. Political theory can play a more constructive role in guiding public ethical and pragmatic considerations for choosing from among such competing imaginaries of order.

To illustrate, whereas for many communitarians, liberal individualism is a theory or an ideology that promotes the erosion of cultural coherence and social solidarity, liberals tend to find in the desire for the cultural cohesion of the whole and in the cultivation of in-group solidarity the very sources of repressive and exclusionary practices aimed against various groups, categories of human diversity, and individuals. John Connolly, for instance, considers "the pursuit of wholeness ... a fundamental source of evil." The ethical objective of imagining "the ideal of the self as a work of art ... is to overcome the source of evil installed in the imagination of wholeness already circulating within the selves."[27] By contrast, Michael Sandel regards social pluralism as a constraint on identification "with the good of the whole" and believes that "the crisis of self-government and the erosion of community were closely connected." He

---

[27] William E. Connolly, "Evil and the Imagination of Wholeness" in Austin Sarat and Dana R. Villa (eds.), *Liberal Modernism and Democratic Individuality* (Princeton: Princeton University Press, 1996), pp. 123–4.

further associates this process with the corruption of selfhood, with "the drift to formless, protean, storyless selves unable to weave the various strains of their identity into a coherent whole."[28]

Instead of shifting between attributing the status of objective reality to a metaphor or an imaginary of individual or community in the contexts of political theory and practice, it is much more helpful to facilitate citizens' examination and discussion of the often latent functions of such imaginaries as privileged or constitutive political imaginaries within the rhetorical, behavioral, moral and power contexts of political practice.

As thinkers such as Spinoza, Hobbes, and Vico realized, significant political outcomes are more likely to be produced by believable untruths than by refined cogent philosophical arguments. Hence what is important in the *Agora* is to realize which of these metaphors of personhood or social reality breeds which kinds of conduct and politics. This is also why opinion (*doxa*) is more relevant to such decisions than philosophical or scientific knowledge (*episteme*). It is precisely where a communitarian imaginary of the individual as a social being seeks to anchor its validity (in the authority of scientific assertions about objective facts) that it tends to usurp the process whereby an association of human beings evolves its notions of what is real and what is not as a combined ethical, cognitive political choice or intuition. "Realistic sociology" has been a favorite communitarian resource for narrowing rather than expanding the sphere of voluntary individuals, while expanding the domain of involuntary primordial bonds and economics has been almost universally invoked by liberal individualists to reify economic man as a given agency operating voluntarily within the narrow parameters of consumer choices.

Michael Walzer's predilection for realistic sociology is a case in point. Walzer believes that it is "empirically" wrong to assume that we are all born free and to deny that people are born into many "involuntary associations" such as religion, ethnicity, or geography.[29] He proceeds to assert that "[w]e will succeed in challenging the social hierarchy only if we recognize and work on the realities of involuntary associations as a permanent feature of social existence, and the people who fight for equality like those who struggle to be free are inevitably its creatures."[30] Note the conventional association in this last quote between words such as "realities," "involuntary," "permanent," and "inevitably." They all seem to suggest a compelling external given that must be acknowledged and, hence, constrain the range of our moral choices. Walzer, who seems to claim ontological and epistemological grounds for what he believes is the true social reality, overlooks here the possibility that voluntaristic imaginaries of what he regards as the hard facts of "involuntary associations" can actually work as partly self-realizing imaginaries, thus enlarging the range of human

---

[28] Michael J. Sandel, *Democracy's Discontent: America in Search of a Public Philosophy* (Cambridge, MA: The Belknap Press of Harvard University Press, 1996), pp. 202, 205, 350.

[29] Walzer, *Politics and Passion*, pp. 2–3.

[30] Walzer, ibid.

freedom. Instead he insists that "the deep structure even of liberal society is in fact communitarian. Liberal theory distorts this reality and, insofar as we adopt the theory, deprives us of any ready access to our own experience of communal embeddednes."[31] Does Walzer wish to imply here that individualism is not a deep socio-psychological structure but only a thin, fleeting, and superficial phenomenon, and that liberal rhetoric only distorts or obscures our *real* sense of "personhood and bondedness"?[32] I actually do not think so.

In the final analysis, although Walzer's heart clearly beats with the communitarians, he acknowledges the reality of both associative and dissociative human tendencies and regards communitarianism as a corrective to the pervasive ideology and practice of liberal individualism.[33] He at least implicitly admits here the power of liberal individualism as a politically performed imaginary in our time. However, considering the role of political imaginaries in producing the political order and its behavioral-institutional support system, such assertions about real facts and deep structures, in contradistinction to mere ideologies, fictions, beliefs, and rhetoric, divert attention from the behavioral implications of voluntaristic and emancipatory ethics of political imagining, shifting it toward the factual realities that ostensibly limit human choices.

Historically actual freedom has evidently been advanced largely by faith in illusions of liberty, imaginaries of independence, and voluntarism, in false idealizations of past freedoms as well as utopian visions of future freedoms. The historical records of both politics and religion provide ample examples of collective dreams of freedom, equality, nature, and God that produced important behavioral and institutional facts. A collective illusion of idealized freedom can lead to actions that create actual, if limited, freedom and to an individual conviction that freedom, as a gift of God or nature, has generated (and continues to generate) liberal democratic political resistance to group hierarchies and coercions. Political and cultural elites have tended to employ various versions of realism and rationality to undercut precisely those popular fictions necessary to galvanize popular resistance to established hierarchies.

Rather than thinking of individualism and communitarianism as stark ontological alternatives, a more fruitful way of framing the problem would question how imaginaries of voluntary individualism and involuntary communitarian bonds could be simultaneously acknowledged as legitimate foci of lay imagining and emotion, with the aim of balancing the performance of individual freedom and communal identities.

Such an approach would require the philosophical or scientific intellectual to be more humble and qualify in the political context his or her traditional claim to the authority to certify the boundaries of the real on behalf of laymen (according to philosophical or scientific knowledge) and leave it to the lay public to consciously or intuitively choose what is real or not, according

---

[31] Ibid., p. 147.
[32] Ibid.
[33] Ibid., pp. 154–7.

to its own sense of the political imaginaries it wants to live by. To reiterate, what should concern liberal democrats, beyond the desire to know the given sociological realities or the positive facts about voluntary and involuntary associations, is which political imaginaries are more likely to bring into being voluntarism, freedom, and justice and which modes of imagining and classifying humans are more likely to help fashion democratic individuals. When is this cause advanced by way of relating to communities as illiberal exclusive clubs and when by way of imagining them as associations that can generate popular enthusiasm and solidarity in the fight against common enemies of freedom? When should the imaginary of the unencumbered self be celebrated as a means for resisting the powers that seek to crush the soul and the body of the individual? When should one posit the demands and empower the imaginings of good public-regarding citizens in order to resist narcissistic and anti-social individualism?

Such a complex and elastic perspective on the compositional versatility of the performative political imagination would avoid consigning the entire weight of reality to either individual or community. It would be less prone to commit the fallacy of misplaced realism that, in politics, counterproductively freezes those aspects of our imagination and experience we may wish to voluntarize, at least partially, as matters of ethical and pragmatic choice.

Similarly, we should refrain from prematurely designating as voluntary those elements of behavior that we would like to regard as fixed realities, such as the care of infants or the prohibition of incest. The pretense of basing such decisions on philosophical epistemology, positivist sociology, scientific psychology, biology, or any other claim to objective knowledge of what is naturally real about the individual or the community limits our options and misguidedly subordinates ethically and politically constitutive opinion and practice to science or philosophy. Above all, it erodes the structures of human responsibility and accountability that underlie choices between alternative modes of human relations.

I would like to repeat, then, that the a priori dichotomy between encumbered and unencumbered selves, so central to the liberal-communitarian debate, is not only intellectually uncompelling but also profoundly unwise. Deeply affected by mass electronic communications, contemporary individuals should be able to decide or intuit for themselves when to imagine themselves primarily as unattached autonomous choosers and when as attached individuals who conduct themselves as group members; when to imagine their polity as a voluntary association of discrete individuals, when as an ethnic or national entity. In the postmodern condition, individuals normally imagine themselves as voluntary members of many groups. "Many communitarian thinkers," Amartya Sen pertinently observes,

tend to argue that a dominant communal identity is only a matter of self-realization, not of choice. It is, however, hard to believe that a person really has no choice in deciding what relative importance to attach to the various groups to which he or she belongs, and that she must "discover" her identities, as if it were a purely natural phenomenon.[34]

If one wishes to encourage desirable change from the floor of the *Agora*, from the sphere of ordinary popular politics, from the grounds of Plato's cave, one should certainly not aim to concomitantly discourage laymen from imagining voluntary associations and freedoms not yet embedded in given social and political practices into social and political realities.

Perhaps there is no issue that can illuminate the meanings and uses of realism and idealism in the liberal-communitarian debate more instructively than that of violence. The liberal democratic state has quite frequently confronted the dilemma of cherishing and protecting the lives of its citizens while expecting them to risk those same lives as soldiers defending their state in war. This condition has encouraged liberal democrats to simultaneously or alternately cultivate both liberal individualistic and moderate civic-communitarian self-imaginaries. Obviously, in a society in which hegemonic organic or primordial communitarian imaginaries are not checked by powerful imaginaries of liberal individualism, it is far easier for the government to wage war, while a society in which the liberal virtues of moderation, skepticism, irony, and emotional ambivalence are hegemonic may find it more difficult to mobilize its citizens to fight not only a controversial but also an ostensibly just war.

Moreover, in a society endowed with a heterogeneous vocabulary of self-imagining, in which both liberal and communitarian political imaginaries have the power to check one another as circumstances dictate, group enthusiasm for a clash that might have started as a justified war but ended as an indefensible, costly adventure may be superseded by delegitimizing skepticism and resurgent alienated individualism. In such a case, a government, anticipating the possibility of a political backlash and, at times, even public investigation and criminal inquiries, might be more cautious at the outset. I say "might be" because in democracies it is often not the same government that starts and ends a war.

The two wars waged between Israel and Lebanon in 1982 and 2006 are a case in point. Both wars started in an atmosphere of considerable public support. During the first days of both there was perhaps historically unprecedented public support for a vigorous military response to the provocative attacks across the internationally recognized blue-line border between Israel and Lebanon. But in both wars, Israeli public opinion shifted from endorsement to growing skepticism, even anger, which eventually led to mass demonstrations against government policy and conduct and to the appointment of commissions to investigate those respective governments. While in the first phase of these wars patriotic solidarity, most enthusiastically articulated by right-wing advocates, was joined by weaker support on the part of the political left, in the later phase of both wars, public unanimity was replaced by acrimonious factional

---

[34] Amartya Sen, *Identity and Violence: The Illusion of Destiny* (London: Penguin Books, 2006), p. 5.

exchanges of charges by numerous individuals and groups. In both instances, what was initially experienced by many as an exhilarating moment of group solidarity (which obviously did not extend to the Arab minority among Israel's citizens) suddenly deteriorated into public anger and depression.

Despite such occasional eruptions of public protest that disrupt group solidarity during and immediately after times of emergency, broad public support for the use of force has been the more consistent trend. Since the establishment of the state in May 1948, Israel has experienced nine wars of varying scope. This almost constant state of emergency has given the communitarian political imaginary an enormous edge over liberal imaginaries of autonomous individualism and civil rights. Despite periodic fluctuation, Israeli communal solidarity has constituted an invaluable resource for mobilizing the ultimate sacrifice by three generations of Israelis for over sixty years.

Whereas liberal individualism has been and remains an influential ideology and practice among secular Diaspora Jews, in Israel the ideology and political sway of the liberal Zionist movement often later mislabeled as the Israeli left have been increasingly eclipsed by the powerful collectivist parties and ideologies of the Zionist right. Obviously, in conditioning the willingness to risk one's life and make other sacrifices, collective communitarian solidarity has been far more suasive and effective than liberal individualism and far more popular during the first decades of nation building.

The small liberal party that had a modest though significant presence during Israel's first decades has gradually disintegrated, and its fragments have largely been absorbed by collectivist parties on both sides of the political spectrum. Various attempts to revive liberal parties at the Israeli political center have generally been short-lived and have tended to combine free market with moderate ethnic solidarity or radical ethnocentric nationalism. The opposition to the Israeli collectivist right has actually evolved as a fragmented camp of moderate leftist and social democratic parties often united by opposition to the persistent occupation and the settlements in the West Bank rather than by socioeconomic ideology.

In addition to the predominantly collectivist character of Zionism as a movement of national liberation and the attempts of a young nation state to mobilize its citizens for a continual war effort, Israeli collectivist Zionism has drawn much of its power from the collectivist traditions of Judaism, European nationalism, and socialism. Zionism is a federation of ideological movements in which liberal and social democratic Zionists have been constantly marginalized by coalitions of sometimes socialist, religious-nationalist, and secular-nationalist parties. While these political blocs have often been in conflict with each other over their opposing political views and policies, the Israeli collective has generally shared a view of the individual as a mere part within a larger, more meaningful whole.

However, one can easily find signs of the persistence of imaginaries of liberal individualism in the expressions, explorations, and interrogations of the interiority of the Israeli individual in Hebrew literature, lyric poetry, theater, and the plastic arts, as well as in the Israeli academy. Perhaps the most enduring institutional creation of Israeli liberalism has been the judicial system, especially the Israeli Supreme Court, which, together with Israel's free press and the Israeli intellectual elite, has increasingly acted as guardian of individual rights and freedom of expression. However, for many decades the Supreme Court has functioned under enormous pressure to sacrifice or temper commitments to liberal norms and practices, usually for the sake of privileging considerations of security, the preservation of a Jewish majority, and other components of the perceived national interest. This very restricted Israeli liberalism has had important but limited success in resisting the spread of illegal settlements in the occupied territories, the rising political power of ethnic Jewish collectivism at almost all levels, and the constriction of progressive liberal and civic democratic education in broad sectors of the educational system.[35]

Since the late 1970s, however, with the rapid growth of the middle class and the development of domestic industry and commerce, Israeli society has given rise to an expanding liberal economic individualism with its characteristic commitments to the free market and the vocabulary of material individual interests. Such free-market liberalism was bound to weaken some community bonds as well as the role of the state in protecting the Israeli individual. Wage politics and privatization have diminished the sense of mission and public service formerly associated with teachers at all levels, workers in transportation, electricity and other utilities, public servants, and professional soldiers. Israeli mass communication has been somewhat corrupted by cross-ownership of the media and the dominance of private contracts (over union agreements) that has rendered journalists more vulnerable to economic and political pressures that diminish adherence to professional codes and accountability. Lacking the internal spiritual and cultural resources of robust individualism, Israel's external economic individualism has created a spiritual vacuum that has provided fertile ground for the appeal of the spiritual redemptive rhetoric of religion and of ethnocentric nationalism, both of which have increasingly challenged the earlier influence of socialist and liberal democratic Zionism.

During the earlier decades of statehood, economic individualism was almost universally condemned in Israel as a creeping threat to the ideologically glorified enterprises of collectivist socialist Zionism such as the Kibbutz movement and other forms of agricultural cooperative settlements, the IDF as a cohesive "people's army," and, more generally, detrimental to the consolidation of modern Jewish-national identity. Not surprisingly such complaints have increasingly been replaced by claims in favor of "economic realism," globalism, and

---

[35] To illustrate the last point, in the summer of 1995, the Pedagogic Council of the Ministry of Education published a short assortment of commissioned essays that addressed issues of value in education, including my essay on education for ethical individualism and democracy. Although the Pedagogic Council printed thousands of copies for distribution to school teachers and administrators, the Ministry of Education, headed at the time by the right-wing National Religious Party, decided – just a few weeks before the assassination of Israel's Prime Minister Yitzhak Rabin – to dispose of this apparently too "progressive" booklet.

apologetics for hedonistic individualism. Following the Second Lebanon War (summer of 2006), leading public figures characteristically accused the middle-class youth of Tel-Aviv of failing to volunteer for the riskiest combat units. This accusation later developed into a wholesale critique of Israeli youth.

The fact that, in many respects, economic individualism represents a gross distortion of normative liberal and democratic individualism has not prevented communitarian and right-wing ideologues from equating liberal individualism with the pathologies of a flat, value-free egotism. On the other side, utilitarian advocates of the application of the rationales of economic individualism and its vocabulary to politics have effectively eschewed centuries of development of rich modern individual inwardness and its many expressions in literature, poetry, painting, music, education, psychoanalysis, law, and politics, impoverishing the imaginary of liberal individualism so crucial to many leading early Zionists and followers of modern liberal thinkers such as Immanuel Kant, John Stuart Mill, Alexis de Tocqueville, Alexander von Humboldt, Max Weber, Karl Popper, Jürgen Habermas, and Hannah Arendt as well as the principal founding father ideologue of Zionism, Theodor Herzl.

It is probably this failure of the liberal imagination that has encouraged even nonreligious communitarian Israelis to resort to elements of orthodox Judaism as a resource for bonding individuals as members of a shared, meaningful, communal enterprise. This failure must be shared by many liberal theorists who have framed and defended liberal individualism in terms of the narrow legal and economic languages of rights, interests, and entitlements. Communitarian and fundamentalist movements in our time have been able to exploit these weaknesses of economic – now called neoliberal – individualism and its detachment from its rich historical genealogy originating in Renaissance humanism. The historic electoral victory of the Israeli political and economic right in 1977 and the fast-growing Israeli middle class (since the 1980s) have encouraged the development of economic individualism and consumerism over civic political orientations toward the state, viewing it more as a service station than as an enterprise by and of free, self-creating, and self-governing individuals and groups.

The implications of these facts for Israeli attitudes and policies toward the Arab-Israeli conflict have been enormous. Holistic communitarian political imaginaries most prone to legitimizing the use of violence have not, on the whole, been effectively countered by robust imaginaries of democratic individualism that could sufficiently check or restrain discriminatory politics and the resort to force. Moreover, as Don Handelman observes, the coexistence of many Jewish ethnic groups within an all-encompassing category of the Jewish people creates an illusion of pluralism that coexists with discrimination against non-Jews in Israel. Even Jewish ethnic groups that are discriminated against by other Jewish groups are regarded as part of a Jewish majority politically legitimated by the equation of the democratic rule of the majority with the rule of the largest ethnic group. In this context, only a powerful liberal individualism or universalistic socialism could have granted non-Jews the status and feeling of membership in a political (as distinguished from an ethnic) majority.

An advocacy of communitarianism, which may be remedial in capitalist-individualist America, should therefore be a very low priority in contemporary Israel. In such a context, deepening Jewish communitarianism is bound to further nationalize the content of Israeli democratic politics and aggravate the domestic conflict between Arabs and Jews.

At present, a desirable balance between the political imaginaries of liberal individualism and communitarianism is still a distant possibility. Currently in Israel, communitarian imaginaries can still easily "swallow" liberal ones. In a country – and Israel is only one example – in which the principal alternatives are low-grade uninspiring imaginaries of external economic individualism and suasive political imaginaries of emotionally loaded and culturally rich national, religious, redemptive communitarianism, the ethics of democratic political imagining would require giving priority to attempts to revive or introduce an authentic culturally rich liberalism.

As long as Israel must be prepared to fight for its existence, it cannot afford to drastically disempower solidarity-producing communitarianism. Nevertheless, in order to survive and develop as a democracy, it must also cultivate democratic individualism. The powerful outburst, during the summer of 2011, of a mass nonviolent civic protest demanding social justice from a radical right-wing nationalist government committed to the occupation of the West Bank and to extreme free market economic policies may indicate the potential for a future political change. As of this writing, however, an Israel that must end the occupation and reach a compromise with its neighbors should still strengthen its weak liberal imaginaries and practices. The politics of war and the politics of peace require both communitarian and liberal political imaginaries in a dynamic balance. Essential too are democratic individuals who can internally experience such pluralism and engage diverse facets of themselves at the right moment, sensing when to insist on their individual integrity and when to emphasize membership in a group.

The case of Israel exemplifies how both the pragmatics and ethics of the political imagination may work closely in context. A theory of the performative political imagination can free the discourse on postmodern democratic politics from the constraints of narrow logical and philosophical standards of propositional coherence and reductionist empiricism. Rather than having to choose between consistent liberal individualism and consistent communitarianism, between mutually exclusive prioritizing of either the individual or the community, rendering the subordinate element derivative or an epiphenomenon, the pragmatics and the ethics of the political imagination invite us to expand our horizons and search for their appropriate balance in each social context. This kind of flexibility is unattainable when the rationalist culture of philosophy and science determine the normative and cognitive frames of political rhetoric and action.

Although Enlightenment culture never exercised full control over the discursive practices and actions of modern politics, it had sufficient presence to render uncorrupt pragmatic politicians, exercising the democratic art of compromise, vulnerable to misguided charges of inconsistency, vagueness, and opportunism. Less responsive to the appeal of comprehensive ideologies, contemporary public opinion has been slowly recovering the elasticity and subtlety it lost during the historic episode of the Enlightenment and later during the stormy nineteenth- and early twentieth-century age of ideologies.[36] We live in a period marked by frequent radical shifts in the foci of public attention, by the fluidity of public moods, and by the short lifespan of political mandates. Compared to the visions and aspirations of a deliberative democracy, a rational and transparent public policy, and an efficacious voluntary participatory self-government, contemporary politics may appear hopelessly irrational and current democracy may even seem degenerate. This, however, is not the only valid perspective on current trends.

Many of the criticisms and concerns regarding the performance of contemporary democracies are no doubt justified. But in order to properly assess the present and future courses of postmodern democracy, we should recognize that, in some respects, what is unfolding now is just another chapter in a long history of the conflict between philosophical and popular imaginaries of democratic politics begun in the *Agora* of Athens twenty-five centuries ago. This conflict seems to be heading toward another predictable triumph of rhetoric over philosophy, another victory of the people over the academy. The post-Enlightenment impact of television on the evolution of a mass electronic public arena, the shifts from modern to postmodern imaginaries of self, community, and reality, and the contemporary globalized version of capitalism have combined to render modern forms of democracy increasingly anachronistic. Although the future of democracy is unpredictable, the odds are that, although we seem to be departing from familiar forms of democracy, the extraordinarily resilient democratic vision of politics, which has persisted over so many centuries despite few (mostly episodic) successes and numerous failures, is in the process of discovering the new necessary fictions and the culturally and institutionally novel means to regenerate in the postmodern era, as I have aimed to show in this book. The invention of politics as the unique democratic way of organizing and guiding collective life will have to persist in order for democracy to survive all future transformations. After all, politics as the soul of democracy was neither discovered nor often celebrated by philosophers. It was invented from within the practice of laymen seeking ways to live and make decisions together without surrendering their freedom, dignity, and diversity.

Politics was not born as a method to find a truth, to apply a theory or a coherent set of principles, or to embody a unified collective identity. Politics evolved as a way to authorize public decisions and actions in the midst of uncertainties and differences of opinion, while enabling tolerance for the incoherences, ambiguities, and compromises that are inescapable in any government by the people.

---

[36] Stephen Toulmin, *Cosmopolis: The Hidden Agenda of Modernity* (Chicago: University of Chicago Press, 1990).

Index

Agora, 123; epistemological 85, 93, 203; and the statue group of *Harmodius and Aristogeiton*, 142

art: abstract, 290; of acting, 119, 124; in America, 70; criticism of, 291; documentary style in 278; freedom of, 131; historians of, 248; and the individual, 249; performative, 119, 254; and politics, 119; powers of, 237; and principles of harmony, 250; realism in, 120–121; reality effects in, 124; realms of, 255, 260, 278

Anderson, Benedict: on imagined communities, 32–33; on nationalism, 164; and social simultaneity, 57–58

Arrow, Kenneth, 164n59

associability, 195–200

Auerbach, Erich, 235n4

Austin, L.J. 49n20

Bailyn, Bernard, 22, 70n21, 76n38

Barthes, Roland, 277n39, 281n50

Benhabib, Seyla, 146n21, 177n2, 308

Benjamin Walter, 133n24, 156n40

Bhabha, Homi K., 299n1

Boltansky, Luce, 288n74

Bryson, Norman, 240n16

Collinwood, R.G., 75n35

common sense: modern, 84–85, 98, 114; postmodern, 295; and scientism, 85, 106, 110, 132, 259–265

commonsense realism, 39–40, 94–99; and democracy, 84–85, 93, 104; and photography, 174; and political imagination, 39–40; and politics, 40, 84–86; and scientism, 84–86

Connoly William, 311n27

constitution: democratic, 1, 72, 145, 155; Greek conceptions of, 65–66, 145; of modernity, 33; and Moses tablets, 64; theories of, 29, 64–70; and violence, 145–152

corporation: aggregate, 210–213, 221; American, 212; English, 210; German, 210–212; Japanese, 212; as legal fictions, 210, 213; liberal and illiberal 9, 314, 318; organic 75, 173, 211, 214, 220, 252, 310, 315

corpus Christi: and the catholic political imagination, 126–127; and civic rituals, 133, 199–202; and the theater, 113, 126–127

Dahlhaus Carl, 121n2, 242n20, 279n144, 289n77

Deleuse Gilles, 214n70, 288n73, 308n21

democratic: civic culture, 34, 151; historians, 149; imagination, 15, 154; political causality, 138–140, 148; power, 157, 163n56; visual culture, 35, 103

Derrida, Jacques, 274, 293–295; on Christian theology, 293–294; on mediation, 295; on the uses of television by religions, 295

Dewey John, 164n63

divine right of Kings, 40, 124, 132, 160–163, 301

Dostoyevsky, Feodor, 173, 238, 240

Douglas, Mary, 55n35

Dumont, Louis, 72n29, 195–196, 203, 214, 252n46

Durkheim, Emil, 260n1, 310n2

Dürer, Albrecht, 181, 234m, 247–248

For EU product safety concerns, contact us at Calle de José Abascal, 56–1°, 28003 Madrid, Spain or eugpsr@cambridge.org.

www.ingramcontent.com/pod-product-compliance
Ingram Content Group UK Ltd.
Pitfield, Milton Keynes, MK11 3LW, UK
UKHW040620240426
470322UK00010B/228

* 9 7 8 1 1 0 7 5 2 9 9 2 2 *